MEDIA
AND
CRIME

In this book Clifford and White explore, in an accessible manner,
the complexities of the relationship between crime, the media and justice.
It offers a systematic, though by no means simplistic, analysis of this relationship,
insisting that doing this demands both reflexivity and a willingness to expose and
challenge the existing blind spots in media criminology. In so doing, this book
establishes a coherent agenda for this area of analysis which not only fulfils its aims
but also ensures that it will make a major contribution to the field. It is a must-read
for all those making claims on this increasingly important intellectual space.
You will not be disappointed by the challenges you will face in reading it.
For this reason alone I highly recommend it.

Sandra Walklate, Eleanor Rathbone Chair of Sociology, University of
Liverpool, and conjoint Professor of Criminology, Monash University.

Clifford and White's *Media and Crime* is a breakthrough book.
It ranges across the ever-morphing mediascape in which contemporary
crime and justice are embedded, exploring case studies from across the globe,
and mixing theoretical and analytic sophistication with a keen eye for praxis.
Just as importantly, the book moves beyond the disciplinary provincialism
that often entraps analyses of media and crime to achieve an important,
innovative synthesis: sociological and criminological perspectives integrated
with those offered by journalistic and media studies. In this way Clifford and
White's book not only maps the contours of contemporary media and crime;
it writes a new map for their future study.

Jeff Ferrell, Professor of Sociology, Texas Christian University,
and Visiting Professor of Criminology, University of Kent

This is a fascinating book about the 'media–crime nexus'. As such,
this is a greatly informative text that reminds us how much the media frame,
inform and overshadow our everyday lives. But much more than this, the book
illuminates the worlds of meaning that contemporary media present us
with—whether truths or untruths, nuance or diktat. Making sense of media
has never been more important and this book is an invaluable aid.

Nigel South, Professor of Sociology, University of Essex

MEDIA

AND

CRIME

CONTENT, CONTEXT AND CONSEQUENCE

KATRINA **CLIFFORD** AND ROB **WHITE**

OXFORD
UNIVERSITY PRESS
AUSTRALIA & NEW ZEALAND

OXFORD
UNIVERSITY PRESS

Oxford University Press is a department of the University of Oxford.
It furthers the University's objective of excellence in research, scholarship,
and education by publishing worldwide. Oxford is a registered trademark
of Oxford University Press in the UK and in certain other countries.

Published in Australia by
Oxford University Press
253 Normanby Road, South Melbourne, Victoria 3205, Australia

National Library of Australia Cataloguing-in-Publication data

Creator: Clifford, Katrina, author.
Title: Media and crime: content, context and consequence /
Katrina Clifford, Rob White.
ISBN: 9780195598285 (paperback)
Notes: Includes bibliographical references and index.
Subjects: Mass media and crime.
Mass media and criminal justice.
Police and the press.
Crime in popular culture.
Criminal justice, Administration of.
Other Creators/Contributors:
White, R. D. (Robert Douglas), 1956- author.

Edited by Anne Mulvaney
Cover design by Jennai Lee-Fai
Cover images: Shutterstock
Text design by Denise Lane, Sardine Design
Typeset by Newgen KnowledgeWorks Pvt. Ltd., Chennai, India
Proofread by Vanessa Lanaway
Indexed by Karen Gillen
Printed by Sheck Wah Tong Printing Press Ltd.

CONTENTS

ACKNOWLEDGMENTS

We are grateful to a number of people who provided support and assistance in the realisation of this book. Roberta Julian, our colleague and resident expert in forensic studies, alerted us to various materials relating to the CSI effect for which we are thankful. Thanks are also due to Richard Eccleston and the Institute for the Study of Social Change at the University of Tasmania for providing small funding to assist with the completion of the book.

We are especially appreciative of the input of our students in 'media and crime' who, along this journey, have challenged and inspired us in our own thinking about content for the book and the synthesis of journalism and media studies, and criminology. The team at Oxford University Press (OUP) has also been a pleasure to work with. From the exemplary copyediting of Anne Mulvaney to the guidance provided by Michelle Head, Shari Serjeant and Tiffany Bridger, the OUP team has demonstrated great professionalism and encouragement throughout, and we thank them for this. Writing this book has been a wonderful learning experience for both of us as researchers and authors. Underpinning this have been many others who each in their own way have likewise contributed to its production. Thank you one and all.

The authors and the publisher also wish to thank the following copyright holders for reproduction of their material:

ABC Australia for extract from reporter Mike Sexton, 'Snowtown trial reveals degenerate sub-culture' *The 7.30 Report*, ABC TV (2003), reproduced by permission of the Australian Broadcasting Corporation and ABC Online © 2003 ABC, all rights reserved; **Asra Nomani and Hala Arafa** for extract from Nomani, A. & Arafa, H. (2015), 'As Muslim Women, We Actually Ask You Not to Wear the Hijab in the Name of Interfaith Solidarity' *The Washington Post*, 21 December. 2015; **British Broadcasting Corporation** (BBC) for extracts from (2016a) Crime: Guidance in Full—Editorial Guidelines, Oct 2010; **Fairfax Media** for extract from Cowdery, N. (2013), 'Thomas Kelly: This Was Never a Case of Murder', *The Sydney Morning Herald*. This work has been licensed by Copyright Agency Limited (CAL). Except as permitted by the Copyright Act, you must not re-use this work without the permission of the copyright owner or CAL; **Guardian News and Media Limited** for extract from McMullan, T. (2015), 'What Does the Panopticon Mean in the Age of Digital Surveillance?' *The Guardian*, 23 July © 2015 Guardian News and Media Limited or its affiliated companies, all rights reserved; **Hawkins Press Sydney** for extract from White, R. (2008). 'Class Analysis and the Crime Problem', in T. Anthony & C. Cunneen (eds), *The Critical Criminology Companion*, Sydney: Hawkins Press, pp. 30–42, http://federationpress .com.au/bookstore/book.asp?isbn=9781876067236; **John Wiley and Sons Inc** for extract from Cohen, S (1972), *Folk Devils and Moral Panics: The Creation of the Mods and Rockers*, London: MacGibbon and Kee Ltd. Republished with permission of John Wiley and Sons Inc. Permission conveyed through Copyright Clearance Center, Inc.; **News Ltd** for extract from Devine, M (2012), 'Thomas Kelly Is Everyone's Son—Time to Reclaim Our Streets.' *The Daily Telegraph*, 11 July and Speers, J (2015), 'Domestic Violence: Jodie Speers Asks Why She Hasn't Heard about Two Thirds of Victims', *www.news.com.au*. This work has been licensed by Copyright Agency Limited (CAL). Except as permitted by the Copyright Act, you must not re-use this work without the permission of the copyright owner or CAL; **The Atlantic Media Co** for extract from Wolff, J (2016), 'The New Economics of Cybercrime', *The Atlantic*, 7 June, © 2016 The Atlantic Media Co., as first published in The Atlantic Magazine, all rights reserved. Distributed by Tribune Content Agency.

Every effort has been made to trace the original source of copyright material contained in this book. The publisher will be pleased to hear from copyright holders to rectify any errors or omissions.

1

INTRODUCTION

CHAPTER HIGHLIGHTS

Setting the scene

This book

In Season One, Episode 8 ('The Blackout Part 1: Tragedy Porn', 2012) of the HBO television drama series *The Newsroom*, executive producer MacKenzie McHale (played by actress Emily Mortimer) and news anchor Will McEvoy (Jeff Daniels) are faced with the dilemma of an 'unprecedented' drop in audience numbers for their nightly cable news program, *News Night*. In a week, the program has lost half a million viewers to another show's rolling updates on the trial of Casey Anthony—a real-life mother who was accused of murdering her two-year-old daughter in the United States in 2008, and whose murder trial became a tabloid sensation. *TIME* magazine described it as 'the social-media trial of the century' (Cloud 2011). The main threat comes from television host Nancy Grace (another real-world reference), whose show has shamelessly exploited the public's interest in Anthony with relentless and saturated media coverage of the murder trial and the more salacious details of her life. Still unconvinced that the Casey Anthony case is anything more than 'entertainment ... it's just this side of a snuff film', MacKenzie enlists former executive producer and 'master of the dark arts', Don Keefer (Thomas Sadoski), to brief the *News Night* team on how to market tragedy and play to viewers' expectations. To demonstrate his points, Don plays an actual episode of the Nancy Grace show, deconstructing its televisual strategies (such as showing police evidence and emotionally provocative photographs of Anthony's daughter) to hold audience attention and remind them that they're 'watching the real *CSI Miami*'. As Don tells the team: 'You'll notice little of her coverage in this instance is about the law. It's all based on an emotional appeal; the way she would with a jury if there was no judge there to stop her. Watch how she breaks down courtroom footage.' A jump cut to the television screen shows a slow-motion replay of two seconds of real-life news footage of Anthony walking past her lawyer, looking upset, which Don tells the *News Night* team would be enough to prompt media audiences to flood Facebook with speculation on the reasons for the negative interaction. Concluding his briefing, he says to ensure a ratings winner the team will need to secure Dylan Kagan as talent, described in the closing scene as an agent who 'gropes through the trailer park of American jurisprudence for what he calls "oh my god" stories, then he drops in on the victims, the accused, the jurors, the cops; whoever he can sell to the press, the networks, and the studios—he packages the missing white girl'.

This book is about the media–crime nexus. Our intention is to explore the nature of crime, the dynamics of media, and the complicated relationship between the two. It is a conjunction that at many levels and in many different ways is extraordinarily complex and highly contradictory. The scenario above is our way of saying welcome to the to-ing and fro-ing that marks out the doing of '**media criminology**'—that is, the theoretically and experientially informed analysis of the relationship between crime, criminality and criminal justice, on the one hand, and media and media frames or representation on the other. Interestingly, in this instance, the fictional account in our opening scenario is remarkably accurate in its broad sweep.

SETTING THE SCENE

In many respects, the episode from *The Newsroom* could not have been a more ideal starting point from which to illustrate many of the key themes within this book than if scriptwriter Aaron Sorkin had written it explicitly for such purposes. The intersections between Sorkin's dramatic interpretation of American television's real-world portrayals of the Casey Anthony murder trial and the points of argument and intervention that we seek to make in this book are almost too numerous to mention.

To begin with, the episode captures many of the long-standing debates and anxieties about contemporary media practices; most notably, the perpetual tensions that exist between the professional ideals of journalistic integrity and the economic imperatives of news media organisations. The result, as many media commentators see it, has been a push towards the (re)construction of 'serious news' or '**hard news**' as '**infotainment**'—drawing on the 'softer' and more colourful conventions of entertainment media—in the interests of commercial appeal and ratings grabs. Collapsing the boundaries between fact and fiction in the way that he does, Sorkin specifically invites us to see these concerns from the perspective of the professional 'journalists' on screen. This has a double benefit in that we are, in the process, asked to bear witness to the privilege of hearing journalists talk about *what it is that they do* and *why it is that they do it*. This is something that has been starkly absent from much of the criminological theorising on the relationship between media and crime, and we will return to this theme in Chapter 2.

In these moments of **reflexivity** and intertextuality, the scene lays bare the more naturalised aspects and conventions of media practice (that is, those that are generally taken for granted by direct participants). More to the point, it makes a statement about these practices in the context of the socio-cultural and economic structures of news production. Unfortunately, this statement is an all-too-familiar one that reinforces the long-standing recriminations of media power; implying that, by and large, media organisations are monolithic, communications flows are uni-directional, and media audiences are passive recipients of preferred media messages. As we hope to demonstrate throughout this book, while there may, on occasions, be some kernel of truth to such claims, more broadly the dynamics of the contemporary **mediascape** are far more complex and fluid than such characterisations intimate. By 'mediascape' we mean all of the institutionalised forms of media we use and create to communicate; the 'global cultural flows' of information and images that connect us and shape our understandings of the world (Appadurai 1990); and the virtual spaces or environments we inhabit. We'll return to the challenges of trying to define something so pervasive, diffuse and yet all-encompassing in the next chapter. But, for now, keep in mind that when we refer to the 'mediascape', we are talking about everything from traditional newspapers and broadcast media to evolving forms of digital technologies and social media.

On an even more explicit level, *The Newsroom* episode reflects many of the observations made by scholars towards the real-world dynamics of the relationship between media and crime. These include the individualised nature of **mediated** representations of crime and justice; the tendency towards constructions of 'ideal victims' and typified offenders; the frequent decontextualisation of crime news and the privileging of emotion as a news value over matters of law; the increasingly visible intersections between media and the criminal justice system (such as being able to see inside the courtroom); and the growing need for an improved sense of **media literacy** with regards to crime media consumption. Most strikingly, what the episode also illustrates are the voyeuristic and pleasurable aspects of crime media, and therefore its pervasiveness and public appeal.

Fascination with tales of the dark side of human existence is not a new phenomenon (Weinman 2016). People have long been drawn—purposely or otherwise—to places, attractions and events linked in one way or another to death, **deviance**, violence, punishment, suffering and disaster. In Elizabethan England, for instance, many of the merciless punishments and executions for crimes were witnessed by hundreds of people at a time. Even minor crimes, like stealing birds' eggs, attracted a death sentence. For some, fascination with such public spectacles was motivated by curiosity. For others, it was and continues to be connected to more emotive stimuli, such as pleasure, sentimentality, entertainment, risk, memorialisation, spiritualism, and contemplations of morality and mortality.

Entire industries have sprung up in response to people's fascination with the nefarious and macabre. Foley and Lennon (1996) famously coined the term 'dark tourism' to explain the commodification of death and destruction exemplified by tourist visits (sometimes referred to as 'pilgrimages') to death and disaster zones, including notorious crime scenes and former prisons. It is estimated that Dealey Plaza in Dallas, Texas—the scene of President John F. Kennedy's assassination—attracts over a million visitors annually, while Alcatraz Island ('The Rock') in San Francisco, California, typically receives more than 1.3 million tourists through the doors of its museum penitentiary each year. Port Arthur in Tasmania, Australia, combines the past (a brutal convict prison) with the near-present (a site of multiple homicides) and in so doing attracts tourists with diverse motivations and interests.

In London, the number of Jack the Ripper walking tours has multiplied to the extent that disgruntled residents in Spitalfields and surrounds have retaliated, with reports of tour guides being sprayed with water and threatened with on-the-spot fines (Coffey 2014). In response to the reported discovery of the true identity of the serial killer, allegedly matched to one of the original Jack the Ripper suspects—a Polish-born hairdresser named Aaron Kosminski—through DNA analysis (the veracity of which was later contested), Walters (2014) notes that we often 'treat these horrible, true crimes as an extension of the entertainment industry'.

There is no shortage of examples to illustrate Walters's observation. In January 2015, after allegedly being abducted from a popular wine bar in the tourist hub of Waikiki, Hawaii, and assaulted and robbed, Australian professional golfer Robert Allenby likened the ordeal to an experience reminiscent of the Hollywood film *Taken* (cited in Levy 2015). Scholarly analyses and media commentaries post-September 11, 2001 also frequently made reference to the ways in which the visual excesses of the terrorist attacks on the World Trade Center were reminiscent of the big-budget action shots from any number of Hollywood blockbusters (see, for example, Gabler 2001; Lane 2001; Wilson 2001).

Quite separate to this, there exists an expanding academic oeuvre on the rise (and fall and rise again) of the popularity of filmic adaptations chronicling the exploits of some of society's most notorious mobsters, outlaws and criminal kingpins. Notable mentions within this genre include *American Gangster*, *Goodfellas*, *Bonnie and Clyde*, *City of God*, *Donnie Brasco*, *The Untouchables* and *Battles Without Honor and Humanity*. In the world of television, entertainment parallels abound with popular examples, such as the highly acclaimed American crime drama *Boardwalk Empire*, and in Australia, the *Underbelly* series, the first season of which was loosely based on the underworld figures and events associated with the 1995–2004 period of the gangland wars in Melbourne, Victoria.

The conflation of true crime with crime fiction also has historical antecedents in mediated representations associated with the genre of 'news', inclusive of its oft-discussed ideals of 'objectivity' and 'impartiality'. Popular nineteenth-century press publications like *The Illustrated Police News*—one of Britain's first tabloid newspapers and a descendant of the crime **broadsides** and execution broadsheets of the previous century—regularly provided readers with sensationalised and detailed illustrated accounts of the Jack the Ripper crime scenes and the failure of police to catch the killer. According to the British Library's history website, the story was featured on 184 of *The Illustrated Police News*' front-pages in the four years after the last murder (see www.bl.uk/learning/histcitizen/victorians/crime).

Skip forward to the twenty-first century, and crime newshounds have been doing their sleuthing through more experimental entertainment media forms, as evidenced by the global phenomenon of the podcast *Serial*, a spin-off from the creators of popular radio program *This American Life*. As of December 2014, the debut season of the serialised audio narrative—which investigates the murder of high school student Hae Min Lee in Baltimore in 1999, and the conviction of her former boyfriend, Adnan Syed, for the crime—had been downloaded over 40 million times and was the fastest-ever podcast to reach 5 million downloads on the Apple iTunes store (Roberts 2014).

This inventory of examples is by no means exhaustive, and barely scrapes the surface of the intersections between media, crime and justice. Nonetheless, it readily serves to illustrate the multitudinous, complex and *enduring* nature of these intersections. Even as the definitions and contours of the media environment (i.e. the 'mediascape') have become more fluid, multifarious, innovative and diffuse, so too the relationship between media and crime (also referred to as the 'media–crime nexus') has shifted and evolved. In spite of these changes, as Schlesinger and Tumber (1994: 6) observe, the public fascination with criminal activity and law enforcement remains 'at the very heart of popular culture ... stories about crime and crime-fighting—whether factual or fictional—are an integral part of daily media consumption for virtually all of us'.

Some of the popularity and pervasiveness of crime and law enforcement as issues within society has to do with the centrality of media within our everyday lives. As Couldry (2012: 180) observes: 'We live *with* media, *among* media'. Even when we are not actively engaged with it, we may still be surrounded by media and even 'captured' by it, particularly in an increasingly surveillant society (see Chapter 11). Public knowledge of crime, criminality and criminal justice may develop through a variety of sources, including personal experience and academic research. More often, however, it emerges as a result of and through engagement with media (Bloustien & Israel 2006; Surette 2011).

For many people, then, media may be their sole source of information on crime-related issues and events (McNair 1994). Findings from one of the early studies that sought to measure the relationship showed that 95 per cent of respondents cited media as their primary source of information about crime and criminal justice (Graber 1980). Almost three decades later, a study of crime news in the United States found that over three quarters (76 per cent) of the public said they formed their opinions about crime from what they read or saw in the news. This was more than three times the percentage of people (22 per cent) who said they derived their information about crime from personal experience (Marsh & Melville 2009: 1). For these individuals, as it is for many of us today, crime is typically a **mediated experience**— what Surette (2011: 24) defines as the comparative experience that an individual has when they experience an event 'via the media' versus 'actually personally experiencing' it. This being the case, and if statistics such as those derived from the above studies continue to hold true, the role that media play in shaping public perceptions of crime and criminality, and framing debates about criminal justice and responses to crime, is both undeniable and significant. It is little wonder that the relationship between media and crime has been such a long-standing focus of academic and institutional debate and scrutiny, and rightfully so.

THIS BOOK

The importance of media criminology as a disciplinary field and form of analysis is incontrovertible. But how to undertake such analysis is less than straightforward. The purpose of this book is to map out what we see as the constituent elements of such an endeavour. We start by outlining the *theoretical foundations* of the book in Chapters 2 and 3. These chapters provide extended discussions of framing theory, practice and analysis, and lay out the basic conceptual repertoire of media criminology (as we understand the term). The second part explores *framing effects and media practices* by examining issues pertaining to police, courts and the media; victims and offenders; and prisons and innovative justice. Chapters 4, 5 and 6 focus on mediated accounts of criminal justice institutions and stakeholders, and the implications of these for understanding and interpreting what happens within these particular social contexts. Part three examines *the politics of mediated representation* in Chapters 7, 8 and 9, which deal with particular population groups. These include young people (in particular, young people as offenders), groups subjected to racial vilification in and through media, and institutions and people of power who largely seem to escape the hazards of negative media attention. The final part of the book, *audiences, industries and technologies*, comprises Chapters 10 and 11, which consider the status and dynamics of crime as entertainment (specifically, through the lens of the 'CSI effect'), and the complex issues associated with knowledge production and consumption as mediated in and by cyberspace. The book concludes with a few overarching observations and suggestions for future research in Chapter 12.

The chapters have been designed to stand alone as critical interventions and discussions within their respective fields and in terms of their relationship to the media–crime nexus. Despite this, in writing each of the sections, we have been motivated by a core set of concerns and aims; many of which are elaborated in Chapter 2, and which we return to at different moments throughout the book. These concerns and aims principally include the desire to promote a more integrated and interdisciplinary approach towards the practice of media criminology. We wish to express a more nuanced and applied understanding of 'media' and media practices and, in doing so, encourage readers to upturn and expose some of the potentially hidden intricacies and complexities of the relationship between media and crime in the contemporary mediascape. This includes, but by no means is limited to, a broader and potentially more productive conceptualisation of 'media' and 'media effects'; recognition of the fragmentation of the traditional categories of 'producers' and 'audiences' with the emergence of 'media actors'; and an appreciation of the increasing importance and centrality of the 'visual' within media criminology and mediated representations of crime.

We have also kept in mind the ways in which modules and courses related to media criminology—be they run out of sociology, criminology or journalism and media studies programs within universities—could be structured around this content. In fact, our own learning and teaching experiences have helped to shape the content and the pedagogic features throughout the book, including suggestions for workshop activities, discussion questions, recommendations for further reading, and the Glossary.

In writing this book, however, we have conceived it to be more than simply a teaching text or a literature review. Ultimately, we hope that this book inspires students and scholars— from law, criminology, sociology, journalism, media and communications, and other associated fields and disciplines—to deepen their understandings of media and crime by equipping them with the conceptual and methodological tools and knowledge to further independently and reflexively research, analyse, question, unpack and complicate pre-existing assumptions and emergent trends relevant to the media–crime nexus. We very much view this book as a starting point, not a destination. The opportunities to deepen one's thinking, broaden the scope of the study of the relationship between media and crime, and to flourish in one's discoveries as students and scholars lie within these pages, as well as beyond them. For this reason, we have deliberately provided only basic information about some of the case studies and examples cited within the book, in the hope that these references may spark the interest of readers enough to compel them to do their own 'homework' on them.

On this point, we close this introductory chapter with a word of caution: some of the content within this book (and beyond) may prove confronting for some readers, and distressing for others. We cannot always predict how we will respond to our engagement with sensitive issues, such as violence and trauma, especially where we may have lived experiences of such matters. While these experiences can be informative to an individual's research, they also have the potential to bring the research (and the researcher) undone by triggering, for example, memories or emotive responses, which may have negative, biased or harmful outcomes. More broadly, we know that researchers within media criminology and other associated subject areas constantly deal with the evidence and effects of acts of destruction and darkness. The personal impacts can therefore be cumulative, while at other times they may be triggered by a singular event. Either way, it is important that, as reflexive and responsible researchers and scholars (and educators), we not only maintain a sense of our own subject positions (and those of our students) in relation to the study of the media–crime nexus, but also a sense of self-care.

For useful resources and support materials on this, see Dart Center for Journalism & Trauma at: <http://dartcenter.org>.

We now turn to consider the key concepts of media criminology, and the debates that continue to generate ongoing consternation and fascination among those engaging in the study of media and crime.

PART
I

THEORETICAL
FOUNDATIONS

2

DOING MEDIA CRIMINOLOGY

CHAPTER HIGHLIGHTS

Introduction

The ongoing debate about media influence

Debunking the assumptions of the media effects tradition

Towards a new synthesis

Framing theory, practice and analysis: a conceptual approach

Conclusion

INTRODUCTION

This chapter introduces the foundational concepts of media criminology. We explain each concept and its importance to this type of study, and provide a general grounding in the themes and issues that will form the substance of the book as a whole. The chapter necessarily takes a fair amount of space to define terms and concepts, identify certain methods of analysis and investigation, and provide insight into the basic elements of framing theory, practice and analysis.

At the heart of the discussions here and throughout the book is the ongoing and persistent debate over media influence. Basically, this debate centres on the extent to which, if any, media influence how people, including the present writers, think about, understand and interpret crime. As such, it is a good starting point for the discussion of media criminology.

THE ONGOING DEBATE ABOUT MEDIA INFLUENCE

To begin to appreciate why this debate is both important and necessary, it is essential to understand something about *the way in which media operates* and, in terms of mediated representations of crime, criminality and criminal justice, *to what ends*. Within this endeavour, we need to remain reflexive about the potential impacts of our own subjectivities (that is, how we think and feel about and define ourselves) in regard to media and, as well, our positioning in relation to these mediated representations and media forms—as consumers, researchers and potential critics or even news subjects, and as practitioners and producers too.

Within the field of journalism and media studies, this is broadly characterised by the concept of media literacy, which encompasses the development of an understanding of:

- how media is organised
- how meanings are produced (and contested)
- the basic conventions of various media genres, texts and industries
- being responsive to the changing nature of media
- the skills to participate ethically in media cultures and negotiate the networked world
- how to see and embrace opportunities to interrogate and participate in long-standing debates about the relationship between media and audiences
- how to read, analyse, evaluate, create and communicate in and through media (see Hybels & Weaver 2004).

As Couldry (2012: xi) notes, 'a simple boundary between researching media production or researching consumption is now unsustainable', although 'some division of labour between "political economy" and "audience" research remains necessary, given the sheer size of each domain'. Within criminology, and in the context of our current discussion, these considerations resonate strongly with the principles that underscore the practice of media criminology or rather the study of 'the complex and constantly shifting intersections between crime, criminalisation and control, on the one hand, and media, mediatisation and representation on the other' (Greer 2010a: 5). Or, to put it differently, media criminology is concerned with the apparent concrete realities of crime and criminal justice, the representation of these realities, and how 'reality' and 'image' interact and contribute to the formation and reproduction of the '**Other**'.

One of the fundamental tenets of each of these conceptual frameworks (that is, criminology, and journalism and media studies) is the acknowledgment that media do not represent reality, but a *version* of reality (Hall et al. 1978/2013; O'Shaughnessy & Stadler 2006). This underscores the way in which media content is subject to processes of selection and editing, and media texts and media practices are informed by wider contextual factors, including particular professional and institutional pressures, constraints and opportunities (Hall et al. 1978/2013; Cohen & Young 1981; Schudson 2003). While mainstream criminological theorising of the relationship between media and crime has thoroughly addressed the former, it has not always attended to the latter in a cultivated or comprehensive manner—something that Greer (2010a), in his critical discussions of media criminology, has similarly lamented, and which is a key motivation for the development of this book.

Within the shifting boundaries and intersections between media and crime, there are some aspects of the media–crime nexus that remain constant, albeit contested. One of the most persistent of these within criminological theorising and media/cultural studies is the question of how we make sense of what we see and hear in media, and the extent of media's power to influence our perceptions and understandings of, and responses to, events and issues related to crime and justice, particularly in view of concerns over the selective nature of mediated representations and media practices. These are matters that have long divided academics within and across the fields of criminology, and journalism and media studies. Even now, there remains an impasse over a definitive resolution to questions of media influence, as well as whether it is possible to measure—and therefore evidence—such impacts and, if so, how best to conduct an investigation and analysis of what are commonly referred to as '**media effects**'. Should the focus be on the power of media or on the agency of audiences (or both), or are there other mitigating social factors that serve to determine the presence and limits of media influence?

Despite such uncertainties, the foundations of the media effects tradition remain the same. Much of this research primarily approaches the question of media influence through the lens of potentially *harmful* effects. The assumption is that mediated representations of crime and justice can *inspire certain perceptions and preoccupations* among media audiences—about the efficacy of policing, for example, **moral panics** (see Box 2.1), or the manifestation of a **fear of crime**, where the imminent risk of victimisation is perceived by individuals to be more serious than the statistics on victimisation indicate. At this level, public issues are reduced to issues of personal significance with an intense focus on individual vulnerabilities. Yet, these perceived vulnerabilities are generalised across population groups in very particular ways, potentially affecting all within those groups. The elderly, for instance, are often subjected to crime discourses that stress the threats posed to their well-being precisely because of their age status (e.g. news media stories on home invasions of older people). Such discourses are totalising in ways that leave no one feeling safe or untouched (if one believes the claims and claims-makers).

BOX 2.1

FOLK DEVILS AND MORAL PANICS

The term 'moral panic'—most commonly attributed to the pioneering studies of Jock Young (1971) and Stanley Cohen (1972)—refers to the ways in which certain individuals and groups can be labelled as threats or risks to societal values and interests as a result of their behaviours, which are seen to fall outside the boundaries of social and moral conventions. Public fears and anxieties as well as official reactions, such as state interventions (e.g. policing practices), are often disproportionate to the objective threat posed by the individuals or groups involved (Bonn 2010). Mediated representations can exaggerate the sense of alarm and moral outrage by presenting a sensationalised image of crime, further demonising the individuals or groups involved and serving to amplify their deviant behaviours. The label '**folk devils**', therefore, boasts an interactive relationship with the concept of moral panic, because the 'media attention and increased social control prompt a hardening of the original deviance, or even an enhancement of its attraction for potential deviants' (Garland 2008: 14). To the extent that both discuss the politics of risk, there are also overlaps between the concept of moral panic and Beck's (1992) **risk society** thesis, although the latter tends to involve 'fearful uncertainty about material hazards' in comparison to the former's 'anxious disapproval of moral threats'

(Garland 2008: 27). Contemporary folk devils and moral panics include asylum seekers, particular religious and ethnic minorities, motorcycle gangs, 'hoodies', the sexualisation of children (on the internet and in art and advertising), and the exposure of young people to media violence.

So too, within the media effects tradition, exposure to the mediatisation of crime and criminality has been attributed as the cause for *resultant changes in individual behaviours*, mostly of a negative orientation. Such discourse has typically been preoccupied with community concerns about the exposure (particularly of children) to the mediated representation of criminal acts and violence and the possibility of a causal connection between the two—that is, the potential for mediated representations of crime and violence to cause imitative or 'copycat' acts of violence and destruction. We only need think about the public discourse in the aftermath of atrocities such as the Columbine High School (United States) and Port Arthur (Australia) massacres to see such anxieties energised (see Clifford 2014a). This is in spite of the fact that there is little substantive evidence to show that, if a person is exposed to media violence or mediated representations of crime and criminality, this will engender those same behaviours in their real-world environment.

According to Henry and Milovanovic (2000: 51), such anxieties about the relationship between media and crime are the 'co-produced outcome not only of humans and their environment but of human agents and the wider society, through its excessive investment— to the point of obsession—in crime'. But there is also something to be said for the ways in which these anxieties can be stimulated by the more problematic aspects of 'selectivity' within mainstream media practices—namely, the fact that mediated representations of crime, criminality and criminal justice (particularly within news media) rarely reflect the realities of crime data or, for that matter, crime control. As Grabosky and Wilson (1989: 11) point out, while the most common types of crime according to official statistics may be crimes against property, these crimes tend to receive relatively little media attention in comparison to 'crimes of violence, which are very uncommon in actuarial terms', but are often afforded 'much greater coverage'. Such conjectures are immediately borne out by casting an eye over *TIME* magazine's list of the Top 25 crimes of the century, which features a selection of incidents dominated by kidnappings, art heists, sexual violence, murders and massacres—all 'sensational' in the general meaning of the word, and mostly extremely violent.

There are, of course, other contextual factors and reasons that motivate and inform these processes of selection and editing, which stretch beyond accusations of media ineptitude, salaciousness or deception, and are far more nuanced than such indictments. Still, it is irrefutable that within crime media there is too often a disproportionate focus on violent and interpersonal 'street crime' (e.g. homicides) and bizarre events at the expense of some forms of white-collar crime, like occupational health and safety crimes, environmental destruction, and state crimes and corruption (see Graber 1980; Roshier 1981; Iyengar 1991; Marsh 1991; Schlesinger & Tumber 1994; Barak 2011; White & Perrone 2015). So too, 'success stories' associated with innovative justice initiatives rarely receive the same levels of interest or treatment in either factual or fictional media (Graham & White 2015). Arguably, the exception in many of these cases are *documentaries* where the capacity and scope to explore the complexities of these crimes is often broader than other media forms, and more effective in terms of educational imperatives, presenting counter-narratives to 'accepted wisdom' and interrogating issues of '**public interest**' (see, for example, *Enron: The Smartest Guys in the Room*, *An Inconvenient Truth* and *Inside Job*). These are issues that we explore in more detail in subsequent chapters, especially in the second part of the book.

Interestingly, there is evidence to suggest that news media practitioners, in particular, are not often critical in their engagement with crime statistics. Journalists will often misinterpret such data, usually erring on the side of 'oversimplification' or 'overinterpretation' (Greek 1995; Meyer 2002; Cohn & Cope 2012). One of the potential dangers of this is that increased reporting of particular types of crime increases the public awareness of these crimes. This can lead to the impression of a **crime wave** without necessarily a correlative increase in crime statistics (see Box 2.2). False depictions of crime waves can reflect poorly and inaccurately on the operations of police, courts and corrections (Jerin & Fields 2009), and have real consequences, regardless of factual basis (White & Perrone 2015). As we have already ascertained, these selective portrayals of crime in mainstream media play an important role in 'shaping public definitions of the "crime problem" and hence also its "official" definition' (Roshier 1981: 40). For Altheide (1997; 2013), the discourse of fear forms an inherent part of this frame, formulating social complexities as simplistic problems.

BOX 2.2

HOME INVASION AS AN EXAMPLE OF A 'CRIME WAVE'

One reason crime-wave reporting often touches a public nerve is precisely because it 'tends to implicitly be based on specific notions of risk and **vulnerability**' (White & Perrone 2015: 42). Often, the potential crime wave can be 'as frightening as the actual one-off event' (White & Perrone 2015: 43). Fear of crime and perceptions of crime waves can therefore 'shape the way we treat crime' as well as 'those we criminalise' (Lee 2007: 6). Consider the case of 'home invasion', for example. In terms of media parlance, home invasion is most often equated with the assault of elderly people in their own homes—although this is not necessarily a reflection of actual criminal trends. As White and Perrone (2015) explain, elderly people are the least likely to suffer assaults or more serious crimes (i.e. the risk is low). When they do experience such crimes, however, they are most vulnerable to serious physical and psychological consequences (i.e. the harm is immense). In other words, the impact is greater for them than it is for others who may be victimised in a similar way (White & Perrone 2015). Fear of consequences, where the consequences are grave, can outweigh rational consideration of the odds of being harmed in this way. Conversely, some of those most likely to experience victimisation, such as young men being assaulted, are rarely considered victims in the same way within mainstream media, as it is presumed that they are more capable of withstanding such attacks. The risk is higher, but the harms are assumed to be less important than in the case of other groups in society (see Green 2007). There are exceptions to this general rule such as the issue of the 'coward's punch', which is further discussed in Chapter 7.

Perceptions of crime, as mediated through and by the expansive mediascape, have important consequences for how we think about, and respond to, crime at a personal, and indeed a professional level. No one is immune from the influence of the media–crime nexus.

DEBUNKING THE ASSUMPTIONS OF THE MEDIA EFFECTS TRADITION

The fundamental problem with conceptual frameworks such as 'crime waves' and 'fear of crime', and the assumptions of a causal connection between mediated representations of crime and violence and imitative behaviours, is that both arguments endorse the premise that media only ever sensationalises or glamorises crime—that is, that media's engagement with crime and justice is always distorted and self-serving.

From the perspective of journalism and media studies, this is a problematic approach to media criminology for several reasons. First and foremost, it posits media as solely responsible for negative direct effects, on the one hand, and audiences as passive recipients of preferred media messages, on the other—what is otherwise known as the **hypodermic syringe model**. In short, the media effects tradition tends to overstate the power of media, while simultaneously underestimating the agency of media audiences and overlooking the points of convergence between 'production' and 'consumption' in the contemporary and evolving mediascape. Second, it assumes that the preferred meanings of media frames are deliberately and perpetually negative (which returns us to many of the assumptions inferred by *The Newsroom*'s 'Tragedy Porn' episode outlined in Chapter 1).

Within journalism and media studies, these overly simplistic and outmoded paradigms have long been surpassed by the development of conceptual frameworks such as the **uses and gratifications** thesis—which turned traditional ways of thinking about media effects on its head by asking not what *media do to people*, but what *people do to and with media*—and **audience reception analysis**, which most explicitly advocated for the idea of an 'active audience' and media texts as 'polysemic' (i.e. open to more than one reading) (see Hall 1973; Morley 1980; Kitzinger 2004).

As Moore (2014: 86) observes, the prevailing discourse in research resonant with the media effects tradition is one that continues to be 'focused on the media as something that leads public opinion and behaviour'. This is often to the exclusion of any serious consideration as to whether (and how) media may instead function 'as a distillation of public attitudes'

(Moore 2014: 85). A case in point is that research concerned with measuring media effects in its traditional sense often focuses on the *amount* of violence within media, and neglects more qualitative and interpretive influences, such as people's understandings and definitions of what constitutes 'violence'. So too, the magnitude of media influence remains an open question, since research shows that people tend to source their information about crime and the criminal justice system from traditional news media that accords with their pre-existing views (Iyengar & Hahn 2009). (This does not account for the role of social media in reflecting and shaping public opinions about crime and criminal justice.)

Part of the problem also, as many researchers will attest, is that it is extraordinarily difficult to *evidence* a clear-cut causal connection between crime media consumption and correlative attitudes and behaviours. There are, as Moore (2014: 88) points out, 'a dizzying range of moderating factors, that is, variables that compound or lessen our susceptibility to a media message'. Controlling for these variables in any study of media effects is incredibly challenging.

It is important to not misread our argument here: we are not suggesting that media effects do not exist or that mediated representations of crime and justice do not typically 'frame' certain groups and individuals through specific sorts of typification (White & Perrone 2015). We know, for instance, that media (mis)representation of singular events may unintentionally create or fuel racist, sexist and other stereotypes, and thereby promote social divisiveness (see Chan 1995; Poynting et al. 2004; Morgan & Poynting 2012) and that mediated messages can serve to mobilise publics to commit destructive and criminal acts (see Box 2.3 and the England riots of 2011, for example).

BOX 2.3

MEDIA AS A MOBILISER OF MOB VIOLENCE

In 2007, the Australian Communications and Media Authority (ACMA) found that inflammatory media coverage, spearheaded by radio broadcaster Alan Jones, had been partially responsible for igniting the racial tensions that underscored the Cronulla riots two years earlier on Cronulla beach in Sydney's south, in which men of 'Middle Eastern appearance' were targeted. The riots followed ongoing tensions between Cronulla locals and visitors to the beach, and reports of the assault of two volunteer lifesavers on the beach a week earlier. According to ACMA, Jones's program had breached the Commercial Radio Code of Practice by broadcasting material in the days before the riots that was 'likely to encourage violence or brutality' and 'vilify people of Lebanese background and people of Middle-Eastern background on the basis of ethnicity or nationality' (ACMA 2007). In particular, Jones had asked on-air, 'What kind of grubs?' in response to the assault on the lifesavers, commenting on the alleged perpetrators: 'This lot were Middle Eastern, we're not allowed to say it, but I am saying it' (cited in Marr 2011: 61). He also repeated in full the content of a text message, which had been widely circulated to mobilise the rioters, several times throughout the week. Although social and mobile media technologies and platforms may have carried the 'call to arms' for the mob violence, the repetition of the messages by more traditional media outlets, such as Jones's radio program, had ensured the content reached an even wider audience (Clifford 2014a). Jones and his radio station, 2GB, rejected the ACMA findings absolutely (Marr 2011). We return to the Cronulla riots, discussing the incident in the context of racialised violence and **hate crime**, in Chapter 8.

What we seek to address is the way in which many of the traditional debates about media influence have largely been (and remain) uni-directional and top-down both in their orientation and their conceptualisation of 'media' and media practices. This flies in the face of academic research, particularly within media/cultural studies, which has emphasised the increasingly fragmentary and diffusive nature of contemporary media forms and media flows—and, we would add, media effects. While we need to be careful not to assume an unambiguous causal connection between crime media consumption and public attitudes and behaviours (or to underestimate the power structures of media or romanticise the agency of audiences), there is no escaping the fact that media plays a significant role in contributing to public perceptions about, and responses to, crime, criminality and criminal justice.

However, to speak of media effects as only indicative of a fear of crime and victimisation or 'copycat' behaviours can be restrictive. It does not actively encourage us to see and appreciate the moments of pleasure, resistance and creativity associated with 'crime' and 'deviance' (see Katz 1988; Ferrell & Sanders 1995; Ferrell 1999). More to the point, it does not actively encourage us to think beyond the concept of 'media' as a homogeneous and (detrimentally) powerful entity to consider the entire *schema* of mediatisation, including the *ebbs and flows* of particular crime stories through and between media forms and in relation to shifting media frames, media policies, media environments, media technologies and media practices. Nor does it necessarily encourage us to think about the ways in which mediated representations of crime and justice are not static, but can change over time and in different situational and cultural contexts—even sometimes within the one crime news story (as the crime progresses through the courts, for instance, and new information comes to the fore). As Kitzinger (2004: 26) writes, 'the debate becomes unproductive when the argument is reduced to simplistic binaries ... Emphasising competing brands of thought [between media influence and active audiences] also tends to play up the differences rather than areas of convergence'.

The traditional conceptual approach to media effects, therefore, also does not actively encourage us to consider *why media matters*. This, in turn, obscures the fact that mediated representations of crime and justice can, and often do, (re)invigorate critical discussions about broader social issues, and the prospects of problem-solving. As Lumby (2010) points out in relation to the social construction of moral panics as a media effect, too often the focus tends to be on the recrimination of media, rather than the recognition that moral panics are 'sites of meaning-making that are hot and sore to the touch; they also tell us in diagnostic terms about something that is going on under the social and political skin. They are potentially productive, if sticky, sites for real-time intellectual probing and intervention'. A similar line of argument is advocated by Kitzinger (2004: 181), who points out that mainstream media have the potential to expose new problems, redefine the very nature of issues, publicise accounts that support conversations about previously taboo topics, popularise new types of discursive constructions, and provide a forum for the formation of new types of identity and identity performance.

The result is what might best be described as *positive crime media*, which serves to educate, reorient and mobilise publics as well as legislative reformers in socially productive and responsible ways (see, for example, Saunders & Goddard 2002; Jackson & Gray 2010). As Heath and Gilbert (1996: 385) propose:

> The message is clear. Media messages do not affect all of the people all of the time, but some of the messages affect some of the people some of the time. As we move into an age of ever-expanding technological options in the mass media, we need to recognize that the process is as complex on the human side as it is on the technological side.

With these issues in mind, the imperative then becomes—as we see it—to understand not only *how* crime and justice are *framed* within media (*content*), but *why* they are framed in particular ways (*context*) and *what* the potential implications are of these framing practices (as framing effects), including what harms might inadvertently be produced and what opportunities there are to counter conventional media frames (*consequence*)—hence, the subtitle of this book: 'content, context and consequence'.

TOWARDS A NEW SYNTHESIS

What these sorts of questions highlight is the need for improved media literacy within studies of the relationship between media and crime. This includes a recognition of the complexities and nuances of the media–crime nexus—specifically, an informed consideration of media practices and the contextual factors that serve to inform and shape processes of mediatisation—which has, to date, not sufficiently been addressed within criminological theorising. This is an observation shared by others, such as Greer (2010a: 1), who has also noted 'an ongoing sense of concern about the current orthodoxy in crime and media research, and in particular about the types of research that appear increasingly to be defining the field' of media criminology. Particular to Greer's concerns is the way in which media criminology—which 'should by definition be interdisciplinary'—has mostly reflected a 'tendency towards criminological parochialism' (2010a: 2).

For the most part, scholarly research and academic literature on the relationship between media and crime has derived primarily from sociological and criminological perspectives with an underdeveloped regard for a 'working knowledge' of media practices, and the nuances and layers of complexity that these command and from which they derive. This extends to the consideration of media practitioner discourses or rather the ways in which professional and citizen journalists, for example, think and talk about what it is that they do. In short, criminology's work on media studies has not always reflected media studies' work on crime or even necessarily the work of media practitioners *in practice* (see Lashmar 2013).

There are some notable exceptions to this, including the early work of university centres, such as the Glasgow University Media Group and the Birmingham Centre for Contemporary Cultural Studies, which were influential to criminological theorising of media, crime and justice (Greer 2010b) and, more recently, the intellectual contributions from those within the field of cultural criminology. Specific authors such as Chris Greer; Robert Reiner; Richard Ericson, Patricia Baranek and Janet Chan; Stuart Hall; Yvonne Jewkes; Steve Chibnall; Philip Schlesinger and Howard Tumber; Stanley Cohen; and Gregg Barak have also sought to negotiate the interdisciplinary terrain and analytical junctures between criminology and media/cultural studies. But, as Jewkes (2011: 9) herself points out, 'in the main, scholars in media studies have worked entirely independently of those in criminology, and vice versa'. This says nothing of the applied and theoretical interventions that *journalism studies*—as a more recently established disciplinary field of research (see de Burgh 2003; Zelizer 2004; Wahl-Jorgensen & Franklin 2008; Conboy 2011; Harcup 2011; Nash 2013)—is also able to contribute to such critical discussions and analyses.

While the provincialism evident within the practice of media criminology may not be problematic in itself, we argue that there is much to be gained—in terms of richer, deeper, reflexive, nuanced and applied forms of analyses—from a more deliberate coupling and convergence of the empirical knowledge, conceptual approaches and research methodologies specific to each of these disciplinary fields. As Meadows (2011: 10) concedes: 'Most of us [already] work across disciplinary boundaries in our application of theory and method whether we recognise it or not'. This book aims to remedy many of the oversights outlined earlier, particularly with regards to assumptions of media influence, by consciously, actively and quite literally bringing together the best of criminology, and journalism and media studies, in its analyses of the media–crime nexus. In doing so, we seek to not only revisit the well-worn conceptual paths mapped out by previous scholars, but to build upon these with new and innovative ways of thinking about the relationship between media and crime; at the same time, offering suggestions for potential interventions and interdisciplinary intersections between the fields of criminology, and journalism and media studies. This includes the explicit reorientation of existing conceptual approaches towards a more conversant and applied understanding of journalism and media theory and practice (i.e. an improved sense of media literacy).

We see this as a particularly pertinent exercise within the context of the contemporary mediascape, which continues to foster opportunities to review, re-energise and renew existing scholarly debates through innovative and surfacing lines of argument and analysis. As Greer (2010b: 508) explains: 'The classic modernist frameworks for understanding ...

still have much to offer. But they cannot embrace the complexity of contemporary flows of communication power and associated perceptions of public credibility in the 24-7 news mediasphere' without some modification. Our ambition is to redress the imbalance that has, to date, been evident in analyses of the media–crime nexus, which have tended to privilege the criminological 'at the level of theory and method, over serious and informed consideration of the media' (Greer 2010a: 2). Why is this important? Because if, as we have earlier argued, public knowledge about crime and justice often develops through engagement with media—to the extent that, for some people, this may be their only source of information about these events, issues and formal processes—this means media also plays a substantial role in *problem definition* within society. What we know about journalism and other media practices—in both theory *and* practice—therefore raises important questions about how we evaluate what *we think we know* about crime, criminality and criminal justice, and our societal reactions and institutional responses to such matters. It also enables us to forge important conversations about related topics, such as security, risk and vulnerability, as well as privacy, censorship and the ideals of freedom of expression.

Obviously, this is a considerable undertaking, especially if we recognise (as we do) that even within each of the disciplinary fields of criminology and journalism and media studies, there remains a diversity of opinion, and sometimes conflicting or competing conceptual approaches between individual researchers and scholars (see Zelizer 2004). Still, this is not reason enough to abandon the interdisciplinary enterprise. As our experience demonstrates, the benefits can far outweigh the drawbacks. Part of the absolute pleasure for us in writing this book has been the opportunity to bring together the best of both our disciplinary backgrounds, experiences and expertise and, in doing so, to create a space in which to critically discuss, debate and *learn from one another* in creative and productive ways. It has also given us the chance to try to understand, negotiate and realise what it means to 'do' media criminology. This has inherently involved a secondary, albeit no less important, challenge: defining what we mean by the terms 'media' and 'crime'. What is 'crime'? Which crimes? And what constitutes 'media'? How do the answers differ, according to context and/or those doing the defining?

WHAT DO WE MEAN BY 'MEDIA' AND 'CRIME'?

Studying the relationship between media and crime necessarily elicits questions of this type, particularly in the contemporary mediascape where the boundaries between traditional and emerging media practices, platforms, formats and business models are constantly shifting and evolving. However, this does not diminish the fact that 'crime' in itself is not necessarily a static or straightforward concept. We cannot do justice to the contours and complexities of definitional debates within the scope of this chapter. However, it is fair to say—as elaborated elsewhere (White & Perrone 2015)—that the parameters of 'crime' and 'criminality' are often far more intricate than those intimated by their dominant mediated representations. This is especially so, once we address the notion of 'harm' as an inherent part of defining 'crime' (see Box 2.4). There are obviously some cross-cultural or universal norms—murder, for example, tends to be murder wherever you go (if only by act, not necessarily standards of punishment). More broadly, however, definitions of 'crime' and what is considered 'criminal' are subject to the conditions of particular historical moments (albeit, sometimes only retrospectively understood) and their corresponding socio-cultural norms or commonly accepted standards of public and private behaviours.

BOX 2.4

DIFFERENT WAYS OF DEFINING 'CRIME'

Throughout the book, we consider 'crime' and 'criminality' each in their broadest terms, which for the purposes of definition include the following wide-ranging characterisations (see White & Perrone 2015):

- *Formal legal definition:* regards crime as that activity condemned by the state and deemed deserving of punishment and control.
- *Social harm conception:* encompasses criminal (e.g. assault) and civil offences (e.g. negligence) with the perception being that all acts resulting in harm should attract some penalty.
- *Cross-cultural universal norms perspective:* crime is ubiquitous (e.g. murder) and does not tend to vary across cultures.
- *Labelling approach:* crime only exists when there has been a social response to a particular activity that labels that activity as criminal.
- *Human rights approach:* regards a crime to have occurred where a human right has been violated, regardless of the legality or otherwise (includes oppressive practices such as racism, sexism and class-based exploitation).
- *Human diversity approach:* defines crime in terms of the manner in which deviance represents a normal response to oppressive or unequal circumstances, such as the attempts by dominant groups to restrict the diversity of experience, language and culture.

That these diverse approaches exist alerts us to the fact that defining crime is a contested process, even if we start from the proposition that 'crime is what the law says it is'. Differences in how 'crime' and 'criminality' are defined and conceptualised, and who is doing it, are likewise crucial to the **media framing** process.

Homosexuality, for instance, was only decriminalised in Tasmania in 1997. The September 11, 2001 terrorist attacks in the United States, meanwhile, have often been described in public discourse as a 'turning point' in global conceptions of risk and vulnerability, personal safety and national security. So too, crime does not always require official acknowledgment by a criminal justice source for it to be characterised as a 'crime' within media. As Grabosky and Wilson (1989: 1) explain: 'For crime and criminal justice to become a major public issue, it is often sufficient for the media simply to declare it to be one'—that is, to *frame* it as a *social problem*. 'Road rage' is a classic example of this (see Roberts & Indermaur 2005; Surette 2011). In their analysis of the phenomenon of road rage in the United Kingdom and the United States, Best and Furedi (2001) noted that many journalists themselves considered it a media construction or a 'beat up' rather than a serious crime problem. They write: 'One leading transport editor called road rage a "convenient myth" used to describe routine, road-related violence; he noted that, in October 1996, one of Britain's largest insurance brokers had forced 52,000 customers to buy road-rage coverage, yet a year later, there had not been a single related claim' (Best & Furedi 2001: 114).

The intersections between 'media' and 'crime' are therefore both complex and inestimable, and have the potential to further complicate matters of definition. According to Couldry, now more than ever, the limits of what constitutes 'media', in particular, are ambiguous—although his attempts at definition are broadly consistent with our own sense of the breadth and depth that the term encapsulates:

> 'Media' refers to institutions and infrastructures that make and distribute particular contents in forms that are more or less fixed and carry their context with them, but 'media' are also those contents themselves. Either way, the term links fundamentally to the institutional dimensions of communication, whether as infrastructure or content, production or circulation. Digital media merely comprise the latest phase of media's contribution to modernity, but the most complex of all, a complexity illustrated by the nature of the internet as a network of networks that connects all types of communication from one-to-one to many-to-many into a wider 'space' of communication. Media have become interconnected and flexible enough to make our only starting point the 'media environment', not specific media considered in isolation (Couldry 2012: 25–6).

Couldry's definition resonates, because it pinpoints precisely what we see as the diffusive and changeable qualities of the contemporary mediascape. Rather than approach 'media' as simply an object of inquiry—as a series of texts for analysis—we therefore embrace the term in a more holistic sense (as we do the concept of 'crime') by considering the *agency* inherent within media as a *social process* enacted through a *set of everyday practices*. For us, 'media' is as much about socio-political contexts, technologies, professional practices, communications flows, listening strategies, and forms and functions, as it is about texts (see Box 2.5). This is consistent with a more nuanced conceptualisation of 'media' that moves beyond traditional notions of monolithic structures and unquestioned public influence to encapsulate the complexities and productive—even potentially positive—aspects of the contemporary mediascape. This also recognises the collapse of traditional distinctions between *media producers* and *media audiences*:

> As substantial internet use has become routine in many countries, new media actors have emerged: the producers of *jihadist* videos online or indeed any self-produced clips uploaded to YouTube; celebrities tweeting from their phones; demonstrators, camera-phone upheld, in a crowd ... Specialist media producers/distributors invest not just

in their own content but in stimulating and managing 'user-generated content', while media consumers or audience members have endless opportunities to contribute to or comment upon institutional media production, although who exactly takes up these opportunities remains uncertain (Couldry 2012: 14).

What we see and hear in media is therefore as important as asking what discussions, decisions, practices and contextual constraints—from a criminological *as well as* a journalism and media studies perspective—not only preface, but predicate how crime is represented, as well as how it evolves in its representations, is contested (i.e. challenged, disputed, opposed, especially in terms of meaning), appropriated (i.e. adopted, adapted, reinterpreted, used in other contexts) and (re)circulated in the contemporary mediascape. We ask: Have these social processes and sets of practices changed over time and, if so, in what ways, to what extent, and to what ends?

BOX 2.5

DIFFERENT WAYS OF DEFINING 'MEDIA'

Given its ambiguity and ongoing development as a concept and term, a settled and all-encompassing definition of 'media' remains elusive. Different scholars define its boundaries and limits in different ways, according to their specific purposes, including broadly:

- *Forms, platforms and mediums:* refers to the sites of production and methods of circulation of media content. Often used to distinguish between television, radio and newspapers (also known as traditional, legacy or 'old media') and digital technologies and social media (also known as emerging or 'new media'). Documentaries also serve as an important medium in the media–crime nexus.
- *Content, texts and narratives:* includes distinctions between 'news', 'entertainment' and 'online' media and subset divisions between these as factual or fictional (includes the blurring of the two categories—as with the so-called '**CSI effect**' in regards to understandings of forensic investigations; for more on this see Chapter 10).
- *Technologies and infrastructure:* the result of technological transformations, which have allowed ordinary citizens to become media producers and media to become an intrinsic part of the criminal justice process. This has created new opportunities and risks for crime and victimisation, and for surveillance and crime control (e.g. CCTV), as well as the use of media as intermediaries between police, courts and publics (e.g. '**open justice**' and cameras in the courtroom; judges on social media).
- *Institutions and practitioners:* often discussed in terms of the collective identity of media professionals, the news media outlets or **mastheads** for which they work, and their media proprietors (e.g. the head of News Corporation, Rupert Murdoch).

- *Practices and models:* can range from the editorial decisions and representational practices of media professionals through to the production of **user-generated content** and forms of **citizen journalism**. Media practices can therefore include listening strategies, as well as acts of resistance, such as 'speaking back' to media or the (re)appropriation and recycling of media content (e.g. mash-ups and memes).
- *Social process:* inevitably linked to 'practices' in terms of the power dynamics of media and the conceptualisation of media as sites of struggle (for access, voice and the construction of meaning). Media can also mobilise publics (positively and negatively), create opportunities for crime-solving and the discussion of otherwise taboo topics, while also enabling activities and behaviours that are widely perceived or constructed as 'criminal' (e.g. **happy-slapping**, cybercrime, hacktivism; see also Chapter 11).

We hope that by underpinning the theoretical content and empirical case studies within the book with a sense of the inherent strengths, weaknesses, contradictions and constraints of journalism and other media practices, we might help to expose and address conceptual territories and research methods that have been less visible, though no less significant, in more conventional approaches to the research and teaching of the relationship between media and crime. This assumes that, as much as mainstream criminology can learn something from the applied understandings of journalism and media studies, so too the latter can learn something from criminology's understandings of crime, criminality and criminal justice. Just as 'newsmaking criminology' (Barak 1988; 2007), for example, seeks to deconstruct and destabilise the prevailing structures of meaning established by conventional mediated representations of crime and justice, so too in practising 'media criminology' we seek to address some of the prevailing preconceptions (and misconceptions) identified by mainstream criminology in relation to the media–crime nexus by expanding the conceptualisation of 'media' and locating it within its broader socio-political contexts. This kind of approach, we argue, provides permission to see beyond the negative critiques of media and media effects (for instance, the simplistic assumption that media either distorts or unnecessarily glamorises crime, and causes copycat criminal behaviours), which have predominated media and crime research and scholarship to date.

Readers should not be mistaken, however, in thinking that our intentions are wholly virtuous. It is not unusual to find scholarly texts on media and crime, which abound with case studies of questionable media practices and misrepresentations. To some extent, the same is also true of this book. After all, these examples represent the 'low hanging fruit' of media and crime research in that—ironically, like mainstream media representations of crime—they offer simple, uncomplicated and therefore more accessible morsels of evidence to support researcher claims and analyses. They also readily endorse the recrimination to which the press has long been subjected in terms of media influence. As Barak (2007: 194) states, however, 'the time has come' to at least make the attempt to 'develop more culturally and materially nuanced accounts of the representations of law and order, or of crime and justice, if [media] criminologists are to have an effect'. Media portrayals of crime and justice may be dominated by recurrent, sometimes overly simplistic and often stereotypical representations—which we cannot and should not ignore in our research and scholarship. But, as we argue, it is important to recognise that media can *also* operate as *potential sites for struggle over meaning-making*; replete with silences, resistances and opportunities for 'speaking back'.

These are not empty ideals, but critical perspectives that have formed as a consequence of our own professional and learning and teaching experiences as well as our previous research endeavours. Indeed, this book offers more than simply a theoretical exploration of the relationship between media and crime; it reflects the culmination of years of empirical research and institutional engagement in the areas of youth justice, green criminology, policing and mental illness, media violence, and crime news journalism as well as, for one of us, over a decade's experience as a professional journalist. This is not to say that we presume to know all there is to know about the relationship between media and crime or its associated sets of practices. Nor do we presume to be able to cover all aspects of the media–crime nexus within the one book. This is especially so in view of the contemporary mediascape, which continues to shift and evolve at a rapid pace. So too, it is true in terms of other evolutions within the field of media criminology (e.g. the 'visual turn' in criminological studies) and criminal justice systems—to which news media, in particular, has also had to adapt. Nonetheless, we do believe our combined research and applied experiences and expertise allow us to offer some important insights and interventions into the field.

FRAMING THEORY, PRACTICE AND ANALYSIS: A CONCEPTUAL APPROACH

Studying the relationship between media and crime necessitates that appropriate account be taken of the broad spectrum of theoretical frameworks associated with the field. This is because, to *do* media criminology, one needs to have an appreciation of the changing status of criminology, and journalism and media studies as scholarly disciplines and practices, and acknowledge the key tensions and intellectual challenges associated with conducting contemporary research on the media–crime nexus. As Greer (2010b: 502) explains, '[t]heoretical perspectives rise and fall, and drift in and out of academic favour', but there are several that 'continue to shape the research agenda' in media criminology. We have already touched upon a number of these within this chapter (e.g. folk devils and moral panics, fear of crime, crime waves, media effects).

While a comprehensive review of these theoretical perspectives is not possible within the scope of this work, readers will note that we have deliberately revisited, (re)applied and analysed many of these theoretical perspectives throughout subsequent chapters. They flow throughout the book and, in many cases, converge and synthesise with one another as part of our own critical discussions of the media–crime nexus. This is not unusual, since these concepts are not linear—that is, they do not stand or fall independently of one another—nor are they static in their relationship to the academic theorising of mediated representations of crime, criminality and criminal justice. Like the terms 'media' and 'crime', the definitions and parameters of many of these theoretical and methodological frameworks continue to interweave with one another, and to bend and flex, adapt and advance in response to changing conditions and contexts (see, for example, the 'waves' in which Krinsky (2013) proposes that the moral panics thesis has developed since its origins in the work of Jock Young and Stanley Cohen).

In this spirit, readers will note that we have adopted a broadly critical realist and multi-methods approach to the study of media and crime throughout the book, having combined a range of qualitative, quantitative and interpretive data collection and analysis techniques and, therefore, the need to engage with a variety of data sources (from newspaper databases through to statistical information collected by police services, courts, correctional services, and crime prevention units and regulatory agencies). This spectrum of sources and approaches is drawn together and underscored by our adoption of a principal conceptual framework throughout the book—that of media framing analysis.

Within mediated representations of crime and justice, frames serve as the '*organizing principles* that are socially *shared* and *persistent* over time, that work *symbolically* to meaningfully *structure* the social world' (Reese 2001: 11, emphasis in original). This necessitates that some aspects of a crime story will be highlighted and made *salient* by media frames (i.e. signposted as important) while others will be downplayed, often with the effect of supporting a particular 'problem definition, causal interpretation, moral evaluation, and/ or treatment recommendation' (Entman 1993: 25; see also de Vreese 2005). As Altheide (1997: 651) explains:

> It is helpful to think about 'frames' as very broad thematic emphases or definitions of a report, like a border around a picture, that separates it from the wall, and other possibilities ... An example is treating illegal drug use as a 'public health issue' as opposed to a 'criminal justice issue'. These are two different frames that entail a way of discussing the problem, or the kind of discourse that will follow.

This means that, in terms of a framing analysis, what is identifiable and evident within media texts and framing practices is as important as what is excluded or less visible— although this absence, diminished visibility or exclusion is not always inevitably the result of deliberate framing practices. This is where *context* serves as an unequivocal and inevitable element of framing theory, practice and analysis (see Box 2.6).

BOX 2.6

CONTENT *AND* CONTEXT IN FRAMING ANALYSES

One of the fundamental ideals of journalistic practice is that of *fairness and balance*, which too often is simplistically equated to the inclusion of voices from all sides of a news event or issue to ensure that a diversity of perspectives and discourses, often competing, are represented. By this definition, the absence of certain voices within news narratives of crime and justice can sometimes be misconstrued within a framing analysis as a deliberate act on the part of a news journalist and/or their news media outlet to exclude particular news subjects or sources, or as evidence that a news story 'lacks balance'. There are numerous other mitigating factors (some of which are completely out of the control of media professionals) that may prevent a journalist from including the voices of certain sources—for example, the pressure of news deadlines. It is also important to recognise that the pursuit of 'balance' within a news story does not always equate to fairness or accuracy in news media coverage.

These complexities are borne out by the reporting of fatal police-involved shootings of mentally ill individuals in crisis, for example. On these occasions, the journalistic imperative for balance, which is manifest in the inclusion of the invaluable personal trauma narratives of bereaved family members, can leave frontline police officers vulnerable to negative and harmful constructions of risk-based identities (e.g. trigger-happy cops) with real-world implications for policing practices and crisis encounters with vulnerable people in the community (Clifford 2012). This is why it is important to look beyond the media text in framing analyses to also consider and explore the conditions that may have impacted on the media text's construction; to question not only *what* is missing, but *why*, and what the *consequences* of this might be—for public perceptions as well as broader media practices. As Schudson (2003: 37) suggests, to consider framing, 'opens the discussion to examining unintentional and even unconscious, as well as intentional selective presentation. It diminishes the extent to which evidence of selection can be automatically read as evidence of deceit, dissembling, or prejudice of individual journalists' and allows us to 'accept the possibility that news might speak in more than one voice, even in the same news institution at the same time'.

Framing analysis therefore elaborates on these structural and social processes with questions of how media practitioners (both of a professional or amateur orientation) 'package' information for interpretation and how that information is represented and portrayed (Gamson & Modigliani 1989; Blood & Holland 2004). While framing choices do not fully determine audience interpretations, Pirkis and colleagues (2002: 169) note that 'they can have a potentially powerful impact on them' and can 'limit the information available to audiences who are trying to make sense of an event they cannot experience'. Likewise, these framing practices can also have framing effects on those *with* lived experience, at times prompting the construction of counter-frames by these individuals (Pirkis et al. 2008; Clifford 2012) that contest the dominant mediated representations of crime and justice-related events and issues. Although the academic literature remains unresolved in terms of a unified model of framing research (we propose our own approach in Chapter 3), there are several points of agreement among criminology and journalism and media studies scholars on the basic premises and principles inherent to a framing analysis. Among these is the recognition that 'media framing' differs from 'media bias' in that the practice of framing is not something that media practitioners necessarily consciously consider or commit to as part of their everyday media practices; rather these are *internalised* and *routinised* processes. This is not to say that individual and institutional pressures cannot impact on the ways in which media practitioners will 'frame' a crime-related event or issue (Scheufele 1999), although there has been little evidence systematically collected about this.

According to Sasson (1995: 9), framing analysis involves the following basic premises, which we have adapted in keeping with our own conceptual approach to media criminology:

1. That people should be regarded as active assemblers of meaning;
2. The creation of meaning through the work of framing occurs in various forums, including media and everyday conversation; and
3. Conflicts on particular issues can be fought out in the form of contesting frames (and the construction of counter-frames), including through public and media discourses.

Likewise, there remains some contestation among scholars as to the set of frames most commonly identifiable within media, although 'generic' frames such as *conflict, human interest, attribution of responsibility, morality* and *consequences* have often been cited within the literature (see Semetko & Valkenburg 2000), along with a characterisation of media frames as 'episodic' or 'thematic' in temporal progression (Iyengar 1991). In relation to crime media specifically, Sasson (1995) identifies a catalogue of five basic 'crime frames' in his classic study of American street crime (see Table 2.1), all of which broadly adhere to more contemporary conceptualisations of the 'attribution of responsibility' frame or what might be referred to, within criminological theorising, as the 'determinants of crime'.

TABLE 2.1   Dominant media frames in attributing responsibility for crime

Faulty system	*Diagnosis:* Crime stems from criminal justice leniency and inefficiency. *Prognosis:* The criminal justice system needs to 'get tough' (e.g. through increased numbers of police 'on the street').
Blocked opportunities	*Diagnosis:* Crime stems from poverty, inequality and disadvantage. *Prognosis:* The government must address the 'root causes' of crime by creating jobs and reducing poverty.
Social breakdown	*Diagnosis:* Crime stems from family and community breakdown. *Prognosis:* Citizens should band together to recreate traditional communities and social support structures for individuals or groups.
Media violence	*Diagnosis:* Crime stems from violence in the media (i.e. media effects). *Prognosis:* The government should regulate violent and graphic imagery in media (leading to issues of censorship) and vulnerable individuals (e.g. children) should be protected from exposure to such mediated representations.
Racist system	*Diagnosis:* The criminal justice system, including policing, operates in a racist or discriminatory fashion. *Prognosis:* Marginalised and minority groups should band together to demand justice and institutional reform.

Source: Adapted from Sasson 1995.

Indeed, it is often possible to identify multiple frames within a singular media text, although there is usually one central or overarching frame. The subjectivities or identities of certain individuals associated with the crime narrative will also often be framed in particular ways (e.g. as victims or villains, as risk-based or vulnerable identities). Identifying these primary and secondary frames and framing practices therefore requires a level of qualitative and interpretive analysis on the part of the researcher. Such frames are usually constituted (and evidenced) by certain representational, rhetorical and discursive techniques within media texts—otherwise known as '**framing devices**' (Gamson & Modigliani 1989; D'Angelo 2002; de Vreese 2005). Tankard (2001) proposes the following list of 11 framing devices as focal points for media framing analyses:

1. headlines
2. subheads
3. photos
4. photo captions
5. leads
6. source selection
7. quote selection
8. pull quotes
9. logos
10. statistics and charts
11. concluding statements and paragraphs.

Building on Tankard's list, we broadly categorise the following framing devices as some of the most significant to framing analyses of mediated representations of crime and justice: *news angles*; *sources*; *language choice*; *visual images*; and *statistics* or *crime data*.

For our purposes then, the appeal of media framing (or *news framing* as it is also known) as a theory, practice and analytical tool is that it focuses on the *nature* of mediated representations, rather than simply the *amount* of media attention afforded to a particular crime and justice-related event or issue. This enables a critique of not only media texts (content), but also the broader contextual pressures, constraints and opportunities that both inform and are shaped by these media practices (contexts and consequences).

The basic premises of media framing theory, practice and analysis also provide a useful framework in which to address the challenges of the fragmented information environment, complicated patterns of media texts, and emerging network of new media actors, which define the contemporary mediascape. This is primarily because, as Baresch, Hsu and Reese (2012: 640) argue, framing analysis as a research method crosses 'multiple paradigms and perspectives' and 'bridges various interlocking approaches: quantitative and qualitative, empirical and interpretive, psychological and sociological, and academic and professional ... providing identifiable patterns to see the world we live in'. This includes the reflexive opportunity to turn the spotlight back on ourselves, as media criminologists, to identify, critique and rethink how it is that *we* make sense of (i.e. frame) and approach the underlying processes, practices and structures of the media–crime nexus, and the definition of its core elements (i.e. 'media' and 'crime').

CONCLUSION

We have thus come full circle to the observations and core considerations with which we opened this book, and which we hope will serve as a foundation for the remainder of the discussions herein. It is our intent to provide a theoretically informed analysis of 'media and crime' that reflects the specific knowledge, expertise and practitioner *nous* of both criminology and journalism and media studies. This chapter has provided the initial conceptual building blocks for this exercise. It began by describing a central debate in this area—namely, that of media effects—and from there outlined a series of important concept stepping stones, such as moral panics and crime waves, and an overarching theoretical framework—that of framing theory, practice and analysis. The chapter noted the variable definitions of 'crime' and 'media', which likewise adds to the complexity of the 'doing' of media criminology.

The next chapter continues this conceptual journey by considering the specific character of 'crime' as *news*. Specifically, the concern will be to demonstrate that the framing of crime in the news takes place within certain social, institutional and practitioner contexts that shape whether something *becomes* news and how it is presented if it does. While less theoretically dense than this chapter, Chapter 3 is nonetheless essential to understanding the ways in which crime is mediated in the crucible of broad social processes and interactions. Analysis of the world of news production is thus utilised in order to demonstrate the ways in which mediatisation in general takes place, and the specific importance of context as part of this.

ISSUES FOR CONSIDERATION

Doing media criminology involves the intersection of different kinds of knowledge, expertise and methods. Journalism is generally viewed as a specific *discipline* in the sense that there are intrinsic rules and norms that act as guides on how to 'write like a journalist', 'think like a journalist' and 'act like a journalist'. These are underpinned by professional associations, codes of conduct and established routines of journalistic practice. By contrast, criminology is a *field of study*. The objects of criminology are what makes such study criminological—that is, a focus on crime, criminality and the institutions of criminal justice. But criminology itself is comprised of several different disciplines, such as sociology, law, history, psychology and economics, that each in their own way provides specific disciplinary perspectives on the subject matter of criminology. For example, psychology tends to focus on the individual and aspects of motivation and behaviour stemming from the biographical background, genetic make-up and family environment pertaining to the individual. Sociology tends to analyse crime and criminality as a social process that is linked to group circumstance and social structures such as class, gender and ethnicity. Media criminology needs to be sensitive to differences in perspective and language as it attempts to synthesise the insights of disciplinary and broader field knowledge. This includes instances where the same word—for example, 'framing'—can mean different things to different people (a mode of analysis, a method of coercion), sometimes at different points in time, and yet still be used in relation to matters criminological. There is, therefore, no one correct way to do media criminology. But there will often be weighted emphasis on one or two disciplines (e.g. media studies combined with sociology; or journalism and law), which will inevitably shape how specific topics are discussed and interpreted.

DISCUSSION QUESTIONS

1. To what extent do mainstream media influence public opinion about and responses to contemporary crime and justice-related issues and events?
2. Can you identify at least two behaviours or acts that would be considered a crime in one country or by one culture, but not another?
3. Do mediated representations of crime feature mostly 'episodic' or 'thematic' framing?
4. Is the 'fear of crime' a real or socially constructed phenomenon?
5. Name three examples of contemporary folk devils or moral panics. Explain why or how you think they fit this categorisation.

WORKSHOP ACTIVITY: 'MEDIA' AND 'CRIME' IN EVERYDAY CONTEXTS

Think about the different characterisations of 'media' outlined in Box 2.5 in this chapter. How many examples can you list beside each from the context of your everyday life? Repeat the process in relation to the definitions of 'crime' outlined in Box 2.4—how many examples of high-profile crimes can you list against each category?

FURTHER READING

Couldry, N. (2012). *Media, Society, World: Social Theory and Digital Media Practice*. Cambridge: Polity Press.

de Vreese, C. H. (2005). News Framing: Theory and Typology. *Information Design Journal + Document Design*, 13(1), 51–62.

Greer, C. (2010). News Media Criminology. In E. McLaughlin & T. Newburn (eds), *The SAGE Handbook of Criminological Theory*. London: SAGE Publications, pp. 490–513.

Jerin, R. A. & Fields, C. B. (2009). Murder and Mayhem in the Media: Media Misrepresentation of Crime and Criminality. In R. Muraskin & A. R. Roberts (eds), *Visions for Change: Crime and Justice in the Twenty-First Century*. New Jersey: Pearson Prentice Hall, pp. 217–29.

Lee, M. (2007). *Inventing Fear of Crime: Criminology and the Politics of Anxiety*. Cullompton, Devon: Willan Publishing.

3

CRIME IN THE NEWS

CHAPTER HIGHLIGHTS

Introduction
Types of crimes that make it into the news
Crime news and the concept of 'news values'
News journalists and their sources
Conclusion

INTRODUCTION

This chapter provides an overview of the mediated representations of crime and justice most often seen within news media. News media are not the only way in which crime is represented, since books, movies, video games and other popular and cultural media forms also convey particular images and understandings of crime, deviance and law and order. However, the news provides one of the more prevalent and powerful types of mediated representations of crime, especially as constructed in and by mainstream media organisations. We choose to analyse 'crime in the news' in order to demonstrate the contingent nature of meaning-making when it comes to the media–crime nexus more generally.

Accordingly, the chapter begins on the premise of a **social constructivist approach** to news production; namely, the recognition that news does not present reality, but a *version* of reality (see Box 3.1). Within this, crime continues as a persistent and prominent feature of news reporting. But not all crimes make it into the news. Many of us will have committed misdemeanours of our own—for example, speeding, texting while driving, riding a bike on the footpath or without a helmet, illegally downloading movies and music, littering—safe in the knowledge that our indiscretions may never be known about because either we were not caught or assume these wrongdoings will be of little interest to others outside of law enforcement. Some of us may consider such breaches of the law too minor to even care about, as a poll of 5000 Britons found several years ago (Fernandez 2008). Among the multitude of crimes and criminal activities that occur across the globe on any given day, only some will feature as news headlines. Most will feature in local news, while others will reach national and international audiences. This chapter explores why this is the case, and how those crimes that do make it into the news are most commonly constructed and portrayed.

BOX 3.1

REALISM VERSUS CONSTRUCTIVISM

Crime problems are socially constructed. This process always incorporates subjective and objective elements insofar as social problems are constructed through a combination of material and cultural factors.

- *Realism* refers to an analytical stance that sees 'crime' as objectively existing in its own right. Law and order problems are seen to originate in what is actually happening in the 'real' world.
- *Constructivism* refers to an analytical stance that sees 'crime' as a social construct, as something that is always constructed through the lens of a human culture that sifts and selects, names and categorises, the 'real' world. Law and order problems are seen as bounded by what humans determine to be important or significant.

In part, these positions represent differences in analytical emphasis rather than absolutes. For example, actual crimes and actual harms do occur, but these are interpreted through cultural filters. The study of law and order problems is the study of real, existing problems, but these *become* social problems as the products of a dynamic social process of definition, negotiation and legitimation (see Hannigan 2006). The problems may be 'real', but the definition, magnitude, impact, risk and origins of phenomena such as murder, assault, corruption, graffiti, gang violence and fraud are open to interpretation and dispute.

As part of this, we consider the role that the *routine structures and practices* of news production play in the framing of crime news (Tuchman 1972, 1973; Hall et al. 1978/2013; Shoemaker & Reese 2014). We also revisit some of the key concepts and theoretical frameworks introduced in the previous chapter, which continue to underpin critical discussion and analysis of substantive news media portrayals of crime and justice and the social consequences associated with these. In this respect, we take our lead from Schlesinger and Tumber's (1994: 1) central, albeit well-worn, contention that:

> reporting crime is much more than simply crime-reporting: in order to understand the daily diet of news about crime and criminal justice we need to examine not only the practice of specialized journalism but also the media strategies of the news sources that try to influence its production by managing—or attempting to manage—the news.

TYPES OF CRIMES THAT MAKE IT INTO THE NEWS

Casting an eye over the news headlines in today's newspapers, on any number of online news sites, or as part of the regular radio and television news bulletins, soon makes it apparent that news about crime, justice and disorder constitutes a significant portion of the daily news schedule. We decided to test this for ourselves in the process of writing this chapter and, on one highly regarded international news site alone, discovered a number of news headlines with references to police use of deadly force, terrorist attacks, stabbings, gun violence, international conflicts and civil unrest, sexual assault, and suspicious deaths and murders—and that was before we even clicked through from the website's homepage! For authors such as Chibnall (1977) and Katz (1987), the question of why crime continues to attract such considerable news media attention is attributable to the fact that not only is crime news intrinsically interesting, it is also intrinsically instructive of the norms (and boundaries) of shared morality and communal or collective sentiments. Other scholars suggest crime reporting may have a deterrent effect—assuming that is, of course, that criminals pay attention to the news (Chermak 1995).

Besides demonstrating the extent to which stories of crime and justice dominate news headlines, our small experiment reinforced two other more substantial and broadly accepted conclusions to emerge from the analyses of media criminologists. The first was that, while not all crimes will make it into the news, there are certain types of crimes that will, and these will typically be of a violent and/or interpersonal nature. The second conclusion—true of the broader claims about mediated representations of crime, criminality and criminal justice, outlined in the previous chapters—was that crime news reporting often over-emphasises 'street crime' and bizarre events at the expense of property crimes, which feature more prominently within crime data (see Graber 1980; Roshier 1981; Iyengar 1991; Marsh 1991; Schlesinger & Tumber 1994; Barak 2011; Moore 2014; White & Perrone 2015). For this reason, crime news has often been criticised for being 'unrepresentative' and presenting 'a picture of criminal offending and victimisation which is the direct inverse of that portrayed by official criminal statistics' (Greer 2010a: 202). Estimates of the precise proportions of crime news that relate to street crime as opposed to property and other crimes, like corporate crime, vary across the studies published, and according to the particular definitions and research methodologies adopted and geographical news contexts examined (Greer 2010a).

What is broadly agreed, however, is that the implications of such distortions within mediated representations of crime and justice—relative to official crime statistics—are both numerous and diverse, and can range from misinformed perceptions of 'victims' and 'offenders', and the professional practices of police, courts and corrections, through to increased concerns about risk and vulnerability, personal security and safety, as well as feelings of an imminent threat of victimisation (i.e. fear of crime and concerns about crime waves). Arguably, these concerns have increased within society—and have thereby triggered the global politicisation of fear of crime (Lee & Farrall 2008) and a sense of heightened vigilance among law enforcement and security intelligence agencies. This is especially so in the aftermath of the terrorist attacks of September 11, 2001 in the United States (Rule & Richardson 2013), and subsequent prominently reported terrorist incidents and 'lone wolf' attacks in countries that include England, Spain, India, France, Canada, Indonesia and Kenya. This returns us to the enduring and overarching question, introduced in the first chapter, of whether mainstream news media acts as a *barometer* or *shaper* of public opinion and political action (Moore 2014).

News organisations themselves have become increasingly attuned to public remonstrations of their news media practices, and the overemphasis on 'bad news' and violence within mediated representations of crime and justice. The editorial policies of the British Broadcasting Corporation (BBC) in the United Kingdom, for example, include guidance for its journalists on the news reporting of crime (see Box 3.2), acknowledging that:

> Violent crime is a small percentage of total crime but it occupies a greater proportion of our crime coverage and we should be sensitive to the fears this may create ... We should be aware that crime reporting has the potential to add to people's fear of becoming victims of crime even if statistics suggest it is very unlikely. This doesn't mean we should 'explain crime away' but we do need to pay due attention to whether we are stoking an unwarranted fear of crime ... We can help avoid unnecessary fears by thinking about how and why we are reporting crime stories, and their context (BBC 2016a).

How well journalists adhere to such guidelines and professional standards is, of course, open to scrutiny and debate.

BOX 3.2

BBC EDITORIAL GUIDELINES ON THE REPORTING OF CRIME NEWS

- We can avoid stoking unwarranted fear of crime if, over time, our news and factual programme outlets provide context to crime reporting—including not just individual events, but also the relevant trends that lie behind them.
- Avoiding unnecessary fear of crime may require us to be aware of the overall proportion of time spent on covering crime and sensitive to the cumulative effects.
- We should think carefully about the accuracy and suitability of language when reporting crimes. The factual description of crime is often sufficient to convey the reality, tragedy or horror of events, without the addition of colourful language, clichés and unnecessary adjectives.
- Providing context to the reporting of crime may require us to be cautious when using experts, make use of the BBC's own specialist advice, and take care in the use of statistics.
- When reconstructing crime for factual programmes we should take care only to reconstruct what we actually know, and avoid speculation or unfounded significant detail.

Source: BBC 2016b.

Crime journalism 'cannot be seen in isolation from its broader social contexts nor, in particular, from how contemporary political communication is conducted' (Schlesinger & Tumber 1994: 1). Yet, one of the enduring criticisms of crime news reporting is that it rarely pays attention to matters of context in its narratives of crime events, the breadth of the lived experience of the individuals involved, and the broader social issues that frame and impact upon such incidents (i.e. the social causes of crime)—even though, to some extent, this simplification is precisely what lends crime its **newsworthiness**. There are some exceptions to this rule, although they are mostly dependent on the practical constraints (and opportunities) afforded by specific news mediums and genres—for example, 'hard news' is more event-oriented and focused on the 'who, what, where, when and how' of crime news stories as compared to news features and investigative reports, which more comfortably accommodate, in terms of scope and space, thematic explorations of crime and justice and questions of 'why'. This says nothing of the way in which crime stories have increasingly been identified with '**soft news**' and as entertainment (Grabosky & Wilson 1989). Obviously, much of this is predicated on how we determine what constitutes 'news'.

SIGNAL CRIMES

The literature, even within journalism and media studies, is not entirely settled on a consensus view of how to define what is 'news' (Harcup & O'Neill 2001). In his classic study of the national news in the United States, Gans (1979: xi) defined 'news' as 'what this society tells itself about itself'. Narrowing in on the definition, Ericson, Baranek and Chan (1989, 1991) claim that 'news' is the representation of *authority* and *order*. Meanwhile, for Chibnall (1977: 23), it is simply about 'what is new, what has just happened'—highlighting precisely the event-oriented and often dramatic nature of most hard news and, in the context of crime news specifically, the tendency to focus on criminal incidents in preference to analyses of crime patterns or the possible causes of crime (Chibnall 1977; Reiner 2002; Greer 2010b). This is not always the case, especially when we consider what Innes and Fielding (2002) refer to as **signal crimes**, which by definition impact on broader publics (beyond those individuals involved in the incident—for example, victims, witnesses, offenders, emergency responders, and those known to them) as a result of their mediatisation, and can animate potentially positive social reactions to and debates about risk and vulnerability as well as other wider systemic issues that require a corrective response.

In this way, signal crimes are important 'not just in terms of the harm done to the victim, but also in terms of what they signify and communicate to a wider audience' (Innes & Fielding 2002) about the need to 'bear witness' to them and to mobilise in terms of societal response. This response can be of a punitive orientation, but it can also be socially responsible and productive, as demonstrated by the tragic death of 11-year-old Luke Batty, who was killed by his father (who was later fatally shot by police) while playing in the nets after cricket practice in the Victorian township of Tyabb, south-east of Melbourne, Australia, in February 2014. In the immediate aftermath of the incident, Luke's mother,

Rosie Batty, addressed news media with a clear message that refocused her son's death from an issue of crime and punishment to one of a broader discussion about family violence and child protection. Her words—'that family violence happens to everybody. No matter how nice your house is, how intelligent you are. It can happen to anyone, and everyone' (Batty cited in Garner 2014)—effectively served to (re)frame the incident in terms of the imperative for systemic changes, political leadership and reforms to the courts system. Rosie Batty's ongoing engagement with news media also inspired the state-based Royal Commission into Family Violence in Victoria. She was named Australian of the Year for 2015 (see Chapter 5).

Signal crimes are therefore significant within critical discussions of the construction of crime news in that the 'ways in which these types of cases are reported by journalists is important in framing social, cultural and political reactions to such incidents' and to their capacity to 'imprint to any degree on public consciousness' and within collective memory (Innes 2004: 16). In this way, they bear resonance with the media/cultural studies concept of **media templates** (see Box 3.3), given that both function as 'defining moments in the public profile of a social issue ... helping to make sense of new events (both for journalists and their publics)' (Kitzinger 2004: 8).

BOX 3.3

SIGNAL CRIMES AND MEDIA TEMPLATES

Media templates serve as a 'rhetorical shorthand' for the narrativisation of similar future events in that they allow news audiences to 'call to mind' the familiar and sometimes iconic news frames of past events (Kitzinger 2000: 75). The fatal police-involved shooting of mentally ill man Roni Levi on Bondi Beach in Sydney in June 1997, for example, has often been invoked as a media template in subsequent news discourse about police use of force in Australia, and debates about Taser use. Iconic images of the incident, captured by a professional photographer who happened to be on the beach that morning, reached international news audiences and became culturally emblematic signifiers of the critical incident, often reproduced within news media reports about other police use of lethal force incidents (Clifford 2013), such as the Taser death of Brazilian student Roberto Laudisio Curti in Sydney in March 2012. We might also point to the persistence of the Columbine High School massacre as another media template in the representation and discourse of gun violence and school shootings in the United States. In this way, both the concepts of 'signal crimes' and 'media templates' serve to establish stable, albeit mediated, reference points for public perceptions and understandings of crime and justice, as well as the social narratives and subjectivities of the individuals involved. These may be stereotypical and not necessarily accurate (e.g. trigger-happy cops, disaffected youth = outsider = potential killer), but they are amenable to challenge through a person's own 'personal experience or political perspective' and can 'be essential if we are to learn from the past and make sense of the present' (Kitzinger 2004: 73–4).

A further aspect of crime news is that the sheer quantity of stories about signal crimes and the use of particular media templates can overwhelm other types of reporting. For example, Gest (2015: 5), in commenting on how news reports in the United States may contribute to American misconceptions of crime, notes that the media cannot be blamed for all of these distortions. While '[m]ajor news organizations have reported accurately on declining crime totals', he explains, the 'overall effect of a steady diet of news stories about individual crimes is to drown out the articles on statistical trends'. Extrapolating from this, we can say that it is the combination of quantity (the number of stories that tend to focus on individual incidents) and quality (the specific manner in which crime news is framed) that serves to construct a dominant interpretative framework within which crime news is constructed and consumed.

In acknowledging the criticisms that are often directed towards news media constructions of crime (particularly its simplification), we must remember that news media professionals do not necessarily operate 'in conditions of their own making' (Kitzinger 2004: 199). What constitutes 'news' and the media practices associated with professional decisions about what stories make it into the news, on what basis, and how they are constructed— crime included—is inherently informed and shaped by a complex network of internal and external factors. These include the commercial pressures, imperatives and constraints that have become increasingly central to the corporate logic of contemporary news media organisations (Schudson 2003; Kitzinger 2004). We cannot escape that a profit motive lies behind the production of crime news, which leads news media organisations to 'create processes that make the work of the organization more efficient. Thus there is gatekeeping, ways of making decisions, and the centralization of work around events' (Shoemaker & Reese 2014: 164).

The political economy of news media is not a new phenomenon; early newspapers, for example, sensationalised crime to increase their circulation. Chermak (1995) points to the late 1880s when Joseph Pulitzer changed the news focus of the *New York World* from politics to crime and tragedy, and circulation jumped from 15 000 to 250 000. William Randolph Hearst used the same strategy to increase circulation of the *New York Journal* at the beginning of the 1900s (Chermak 1995). Meanwhile, the mid-to-late-nineteenth-century Australian press, including publications such as the Sydney scandal sheet *Truth*, often adopted a rich and expressive vocabulary, especially in their descriptions of the scandalous indiscretions of the nation's convicts and colonial outlaws (Clifford 2014b).

In recent years, however, the production of crime news (as with news more generally) has experienced a decline in the use of specialist reporters, like those who traditionally worked the police, courts and crime **newsbeats** or news rounds (Reiner 2002), which we refer to later in this chapter. This is one consequence of the highly publicised pressures on print and broadcast editorial budgets, reductions in staff numbers across newsrooms, and broader media industry changes. These have emerged from the 24/7 news cycle with its pressurised deadlines and demands for immediacy in news reporting, the subsequent presentation of complex ideas and socio-political issues as 'sound bites', and the increasing need for contemporary news journalists to demonstrate multiplatform reporting competencies and expertise. Today, journalists need to demonstrate the ability to (re)produce single news stories as multiple media texts across a number of news mediums—for example, adapting a story for print and broadcast news, online news, and as multimedia content for more innovative and engaging audiovisual forms of digital storytelling.

Within the contemporary mediascape, with such conditions and pressures as journalistic norms, it can be difficult to consistently produce contextualised crime news reporting. Under-resourced journalism can therefore lead, as Kitzinger (2004: 199) notes, to a 'proliferation of ill-informed stories which rely on emotive accounts rather than engaging with critical debate'. The political economy and commercial imperatives of news media, within this context, can at times also bring crime reporting into conflict with the coronial and criminal justice systems.

For example, in the aftermath of the Lindt café siege in Martin Place, Sydney, in 2014, public debate spilled over into Australian media headlines about the implications of exclusive cash-for-comment deals (otherwise referred to as **chequebook journalism**) with several of the hostages from the crisis. The event itself involved a 17-hour standoff between police and a lone gunman, Man Haron Monis, who held 10 customers and eight employees hostage in the café, shutting down significant sections of Sydney's central business district. During the ordeal, Monis used several of the hostages as human shields and ordered them to hold an Islamic black flag against the window of the café (misidentified in some early news reports as the flag used by the Islamic State of Iraq and the Levant, or ISIL). Several hostages made contact with news media outlets to relay the gunman's demands. Their social media profiles were also used for similar purposes. The siege ended when a heavily armed Tactical Operations Unit stormed the building in the early hours of the morning of 16 December 2014, after a gunshot was heard from inside the café. Two of the hostages were killed, along with Monis, and several others were injured. News media outlets later reported that one of the siege survivors had been paid a six-figure sum by an Australian television network for an exclusive interview, while other survivors had been approached by rival television stations for interviews (see Hasham 2015). Concerns that the 'colourful' accounts required to 'satisfy a television audience' would 'risk tainting future evidence and weakening the coronial process' were raised by both the former New South Wales Director of Public Prosecutions, Nicholas Cowdery, and former state coroner, John Abernethy, with calls for the paid interviews to be banned from broadcast (Hasham 2015).

MEDIA FRAMES AND NEWSWORTHINESS

The ways in which academics respond to the question of 'what is news' and the ways in which media professionals respond are not always in concert with one another, as we will shortly elaborate. As Hall (1981: 234) explains:

> Journalists speak of 'the news' as if events select themselves. Further, they speak as if which is the 'most significant' news story, and which 'news angles' are most salient, are divinely inspired. Yet of the millions of events which occur every day in the world, only a tiny proportion ever become visible as 'potential news stories': and of this proportion, only a small fraction are actually produced as the day's news in the news media.

This attends to another observation from our small experiment mentioned at the start of this chapter—that what is published or broadcast within news media about crime and justice events and issues is highly selective and often constructed so as to promote certain *media frames* or *news frames*. These serve to establish a definition of social problems (sometimes, this can be 'crime' itself), emphasise particular news angles and moral and causal interpretations of these problems, and propose potential solutions (Entman 1993). This reflects many of the patterns of crime news reporting that we have already identified— for example, the way in which subjectivities of individuals and groups are represented in particular ways, often stereotypical and as **binary oppositions** (such as 'victims' versus 'villains'; 'good' versus 'evil').

News frames, therefore, function in terms of the **saliency of information**, providing cues as to the information that is considered most important and is subsequently foregrounded within the news text. This is often illustrated by the prioritisation of crime stories within news bulletins or the prominence of their placement within the hard copy editions of newspapers and on the virtual front-pages of news websites—or, in the case of the scenario described around the Lindt café siege, the payment for exclusive access to a person's lived experiences of crime, violence and trauma for mediated representation and potential ratings appeal (which is consistent with the argument that 'emotion' has increasingly become a predominant and commodifiable news frame within contemporary reporting practices). In terms of a news framing analysis (see Box 3.4), this means that what is *excluded* or *absent* from a news text can be as important as what is *included* and *identifiable*.

BOX 3.4

DOING NEWS FRAMING ANALYSIS

If news framing practices involve the principles of selection and emphasis (Entman 1993), then news framing analysis seeks to unpack these by examining *how* crime and justice events and issues are *framed* within news media texts, *why* they are framed in these particular ways and *what* the potential *framing effects* of these news patterns might be—harmful or otherwise. Content *and* context are therefore important in any news framing analysis. This includes consideration of not only what is identifiable within and in relation to the news text—such as its placement or prioritisation and the *framing devices* evident within the news text (see Chapter 2)—but also the news media practices that inform its construction and the professional and socio-political environments in which this occurs and by which the construction of news texts may be affected. For this reason, the richest data often results from comparative news framing analyses, which allow for longitudinal critiques or, at the very least, opportunities to identify particular patterns or trends in news reporting across a selection of news media texts and news media outlets.

Even a simple news framing analysis can provide an invaluable opportunity to recognise and highlight the ways in which certain crime news narratives and constructions of criminality may dominate, but this does not necessarily make them 'truths' (Wykes 2001). Researchers should consider and identify the following as part of this analysis:

- the *news angle* of the story (often identifiable within the lead/introduction and reflective of the overall or dominant framing of the crime news event or issue)
- the *news values* identifiable within the crime news story
- the *publication context and stylistic conventions* (broadsheet versus tabloid; commercial radio or television station versus public broadcaster)
- *language choices* (use of emotive or meaning-laden words, colloquialisms, etc.). For example, 'youths' versus 'thugs'; 'gunned down' versus 'shot'; 'bashed' versus 'assaulted'. Are these in conflict or consonance with the rhetorical or discursive style and conventions particular to (and therefore expected of) the media outlet?
- the *selection of sources*, their *attribution* and the *positioning of their quotes*. Which sources appear earlier or later in the news story? Whose quotes dominate the news story? Are certain 'voices' absent? What are the implications of this?
- the *modes of reference* used in relation to *particular subjectivities* (e.g. 'victims' and 'villains'). Who or what is attributed as being responsible or to blame?
- the choice of *news visuals* and *image captions*, especially where these serve to reinforce or contest the dominant news frame
- other broad forms of emphasis and selection, such as the *placement or prioritisation* of the crime news story (front-page versus inside or click-through; top of the radio or television news broadcast versus somewhere in the middle)
- the *broader socio-political context* to the news event or issue with reference to public discourses and the news archive. How has the story historically been framed?
- *other potential ways of telling the news story*, using an alternative perspective or through the inclusion of absent voices or re-prioritisation of those included
- the *potential framing effects*—harmful or otherwise—of the news media coverage.

The logic and processes by which events are selected and packaged as 'news' are therefore varied and complex, but they are by no means arbitrary; as many scholars have previously identified, they form part of the *routine structures and practices* of newswork (Tuchman 1973; Chibnall 1977; Altheide 2013; Shoemaker & Reese 2014). Although routine, the processes of selectivity associated with 'newsworthiness' and news framing are not always identified by news media professionals in a conscious or systematic manner. In practice, these processes are often experienced as something far more *intuitive* and *internalised*—as a sense of what stories *feel right* to be classified and reported as 'news' (Hall 1981). This is illustrated by the concept of '**news values**', which Hall et al. (1978/2013: 57) define as the criteria of relevance in 'the routine practices of journalism', which enable news media professionals to determine 'which stories are "newsworthy" and which are not, which stories are major "lead" stories and which are relatively insignificant, which stories to run and which to drop'.

Crime events and issues that score highly in terms of newsworthiness—that is, they conform to several news values—are more likely to be reported, although this does not necessarily guarantee *sustained* news media interest or coverage (Jewkes 2011). Even crime news stories that embody a number of news values can be superseded, if another news story of greater magnitude breaks and needs to be reported in its place. This, in itself, forms part of the routine practices of news journalism; there is always the chance that a news story will be 'bumped' from the radio or television news bulletin or held over to appear in a later edition of the newspaper. In some cases, this may mean that a story loses the front-page to be repositioned further into the body of the newspaper or that the copy of a news story is cut in the interests of space. This is one of the key advantages—as many news media outlets have already identified—of an electronic news presence in that online news sites afford both the opportunity to be innovative in terms of digital storytelling, as well as the latitude to (re)publish news stories in a fuller form or with streaming updates in the case of 'breaking news', where details relevant to the story may be evolving in real-time. Take, for instance, an event like the *Charlie Hebdo* shootings in Paris, France, in January 2015 or even the 2008 coordinated shooting and bombing attacks in Mumbai, India, where there were clearly individuals who were injured, and possible fatalities, although precise numbers were unclear in the immediate aftermath of each incident as a result of the confusion caused by the scale and unexpectedness of the events.

Therefore, while news values and news frames serve as a 'core element in the professional socialisation, practice and ideology' of news media practitioners, they are rarely described in such terms by journalists themselves, nor are they 'written down, formally transmitted or codified' (Hall et al. 1978/2013: 57). As Chibnall (1977: 13) explains, they are instead 'tacitly accepted and implicitly understood' within journalistic practice and, when referred to by news media professionals, are described in more general terms as a journalist's 'news instinct' or their 'nose for news' (Niblock 2005). The identification and definition of the concepts of 'news values' and 'news framing' are, therefore, more consistent with an 'academic approach to understanding the process of news selection ... [and] the ground rules that come into operation when journalists select stories' (Harcup & O'Neill 2001: 261) and package them as 'news'. Such concepts reflect academic theorising attempts to put a name to (and, by doing so, to make observable and quantifiable for analysis) what is normatively otherwise an intrinsic and impalpable aspect of journalistic practice.

CRIME NEWS AND THE CONCEPT OF 'NEWS VALUES'

One of the earliest academic explorations of 'newsworthiness' is commonly credited to Norwegian scholars Johan Galtung and Mari Holmboe Ruge, who first identified a list of 12 news values in their study of the structure of foreign news, which was published in the *Journal of Peace Research* in the mid-1960s. While they noted at the outset, 'no claim is made for completeness in the list of factors' (Galtung & Ruge 1965: 64), scholars have since highlighted several limitations in Galtung and Ruge's work, including the hypothetical nature of the news values identified and their focus on the reporting of foreign events (Harcup & O'Neill 2001: 262). Despite this, and after decades of 'much empirical testing', as Greer (2010b: 503) notes, it is striking how well Galtung and Ruge's framework 'still stands up to scrutiny', as evidenced by how widely cited it continues to be within the fields of media criminology, and journalism and media studies.

Since Galtung and Ruge's study, there have been a number of adaptations of the news values intrinsic to journalistic practice, although many of these have been devised with a focus on general news reporting. Two of the more comprehensive reviews to analyse newsworthiness criteria in the context of crime news reporting belong to Chibnall (1977) and Jewkes (2011). For the former, a study of law-and-order news published in the British press from 1945 to 1975 revealed a total of eight professional imperatives for journalists: immediacy; dramatisation; personalisation; simplification; titillation; conventionalism; structured access; and novelty (Chibnall 1977). Suggesting there was a need to update Chibnall's taxonomy for relevance to crime news reporting in the twenty-first century, Jewkes created her own list of 12 news values, which in essence represented a distillation of both Chibnall and Galtung and Ruge's previous conceptualisations.

While these subsequent formulations have adopted several differences in terminology to that proposed by Galtung and Ruge in their classic taxonomy, the overall sentiments in terms of the criteria of relevance for 'newsworthiness' have remained the same. This is perhaps reflective of the manner in which, as Chibnall (1977: 13) notes:

> The same news values are common to most news organizations although they may not be ordered in quite the same way from one organization to the next. Each will have its own, largely implicit, news policy and will disseminate the policy to its journalists by according appropriate weightings to the news values. This will enable a paper [or online news site or broadcast news media outlet] to develop a distinctive style.

This is commonly known as a news media outlet's **house style or style guide** (see Box 3.5).

BOX 3.5

THE STYLISTIC CONVENTIONS OF NEWS

Documents related to a news media outlet's 'house style' or 'style guide' often sit within the broader rubric of the organisation's editorial policies, and provide guidance on the stylistic conventions specific to the construction of news texts. This includes rules of spelling, punctuation, pronunciation, capitalisation and visual composition. Implicit within this an innate sense of the news audience, which may share commonalities in terms of demographic profile with the news audiences of other publications, online news sites, and/or radio and television networks, but in the main will be specific to an individual news media outlet. For this reason, we can note differences in the house styles of mastheads like *The New York Times* and *The Guardian* as compared to *The Sun* newspaper in the United Kingdom. Likewise, the preferred news values will differ between each of the news media outlets.

Newsworthiness criteria or news values, as Jewkes (2011) observes, are both socially contingent and culturally and historically specific—hence, they will often reflect the specific contexts in which they are situated. The list of news values that follows reflects the taxonomy developed by Jewkes (2011) primarily, but is also informed by the reflections of other scholars, such as Conley and Lamble (2006), from the field of journalism and media studies. We have assembled the list on the basis of the news values that explicitly relate to *crime news*, informed by the case studies selected for inclusion throughout this book, and primarily with Australian news media in mind. We have kept the list and media examples deliberately brief for readers to explore their relevance within their own geographical and cultural news contexts—feel free to put them to the test, and to adapt accordingly. Readers will also note that many of the examples nominated against a specific news value in fact resonate with more than one of the newsworthiness criteria on the list.

THRESHOLD

This refers to the way in which crime events have to 'meet a certain level of perceived importance or drama in order to be considered newsworthy' (Jewkes 2011: 45). The 'threshold' of a crime news story will differ across local, national and international news contexts. A higher threshold is usually warranted for crime news to reach global audiences.

NOVELTY

A crime news event that is rare, extraordinary or unexpected will typically be considered newsworthy, although its 'novelty' does not mean the crime should necessarily be treated as frivolous. Take, for example, the Mosman bomb hoax, which featured in news headlines worldwide in August 2011 after an apparent collar bomb (it was later found to be a dummy device by bomb disposal experts) was placed around the neck of 18-year-old student Madeleine Pulver, in a failed extortion attempt by a balaclava-clad intruder who had entered the family home on the lower north shore of Sydney. Likewise, a twist or a new 'angle' on an existing crime news story will often attract further media attention.

PREDICTABILITY

A story that is predictable can be newsworthy, because it provides news organisations with an opportunity to plan their media coverage in advance, and organise their resources accordingly. As Jewkes (2011) points out, this can ensure a degree of continuity in terms of the news media coverage. Classic examples of predictable crime and justice news stories include court and coronial cases; the release of official crime statistics, government reports and the findings of Ombudsman inquiries or Royal Commissions; and public protests. Thinking more broadly, we might also consider the familiar headlines about speeding and traffic accidents around public holidays and festive seasons, as well as stories about drug use and drunkenness at large-scale music festivals and news reporting on the anniversaries of crime events, especially where the event retains a high threshold of newsworthiness (e.g. the September 11 terrorist attacks or the assassination of President John F. Kennedy).

PROXIMITY

The news value of 'proximity' has two primary dynamics: the geographical nearness (spatial proximity) of a crime event and the relevance or meaningfulness of the event to a particular news audience (cultural proximity). Newsworthiness of crime events often diminishes with distance, although international events can be 'localised'—that is, proximity can be found within them—where their threshold is high (Niblock 2005). Although the Bali bombings on 12 October 2012 occurred in the tourist district of Kuta, Indonesia, the impact for other countries, such as Australia, was significant as a result of the sheer number of citizens that were killed in the attack (88 Australians in total).

SIMPLIFICATION

One of the major criticisms of news media representations of crime is that they often reduce otherwise complex events and issues into seemingly unambiguous situations. This is typically contrasted against crime trends, which may take a longer time to unfold and can be more challenging to report. Simplification can result in a tendency to talk about crime in terms of archetypal characterisations and binary oppositions (e.g. victims versus villains; good versus evil; guilty versus innocent).

INDIVIDUALISM

Crime news stories that can be constructed within an individualistic framework, allowing events to be rationalised as the actions and reactions of people, are typically preferred to stories that demand more complex socio-political and cultural explanations. Hence, the news value of 'individualism' is closely connected to that of 'simplification' within crime news, and the more broadly cited 'human interest' criteria of newsworthiness, since these kinds of news stories can often be personalised, providing a 'human face' to the event. Consider, for example, the very familiar image of then-three-year-old Madeleine McCann, who disappeared from her bed in an apartment in Portugal in May 2007, while on holiday from the United Kingdom with her family.

RISK

Irrespective of the fact that crime is experienced by people in specific social groups and the majority of serious offences, including murder and sexual assault, are committed by people known to the victim, news media persist in presenting a picture of serious crime as random, senseless, unpredictable and indiscriminate. Perceived vulnerability is therefore emphasised over actual victimisation (Jewkes 2011).

SEX

Studies have shown that newspapers, in particular, will over-report crimes of a sexual nature, potentially exaggerating fears of violence against women (i.e. 'stranger danger'). Inversely, female offenders are often portrayed as sexual predators (Morrissey 2003). An obvious example of this is the mediated representation of Amanda Knox, who stood trial for the 2007 murder of her roommate, British student Meredith Kercher, in Perugia, Italy. Within press reports from the United Kingdom and Italy especially, Knox was portrayed as a 'sinister temptress', who regularly brought strange men back to her room for sex and left vibrators and erotic underwear on display to the dismay of her housemates. The characterisation resulted in the constant reference to the American student within news media reports as 'Foxy Knoxy'—a nickname that Knox herself had adopted on social networking site MySpace, but which had actually related to her childhood football skills, rather than her seduction technique (Clifford 2014c; 2016).

VIOLENCE OR CONFLICT

This is arguably one of the most common news values, regardless of an association with crime-related news, but often because of it. As Hall and colleagues (1978/2013: 70) explain:

> One special point about crime as news: this is the special status of *violence* as a news value. Any crime can be lifted into news visibility if violence becomes associated with it, since violence is perhaps the supreme example of the news value 'negative consequences'. Violence represents a basic violation of the person ... [and] is also the ultimate crime against property, and against the state. It thus represents a fundamental rupture in the social order. The use of violence marks the distinction between those who are fundamentally *of* society and those who are *outside* it.

Differences in opinions, perspectives and/or experiences that result in conflict and highlight opposing sides of public debate are also evident within crime news stories.

Consider, for example, these news headlines lifted from a local newspaper: 'Police union takes its anti-government campaign to the letterbox' and 'Judge takes aim at media's crime reporting'.

CHILDREN

News stories about child-victims or child-perpetrators have arguably become more newsworthy since the high-profile murder of two-year-old James Bulger by two 10-year-old boys in the United Kingdom in 1993 (we return to this case in Chapters 5 and 7). More than guaranteeing the newsworthiness of a crime story, child-victims in particular can motivate news media outlets towards what might be called 'morality campaigns', as the involvement of children results in the perception that a higher threshold of victimisation has been crossed than if adults alone were involved (Jenkins 1992). However, as Jewkes (2011) concedes, not all crimes involving child-victims guarantee newsworthiness—some, in fact, remain virtually invisible within news media (e.g. sexual violence against children within families). For a detailed analysis of news media coverage of this issue, see Kitzinger (2004).

CELEBRITY OR HIGH-STATUS INDIVIDUALS

The level of deviance required to attract news media attention is significantly lower in these cases than for crimes committed by 'ordinary' citizens, because a certain threshold of meaningfulness has already been achieved—that is, 'celebrity' is a news value in its own right (Jewkes 2011). We may instantly think of the high-profile courtroom dramas involving O. J. Simpson or Oscar Pistorius, the arrest of Reese Witherspoon for disorderly conduct, or the too-familiar mugshots of other celebrities, such as Justin Bieber, Mel Gibson and Lindsay Lohan. However, it is important to note that high-status individuals, such as politicians, can also be newsworthy where criminal offences are involved, albeit this is more often reported within local news—with some exceptions (e.g. former Italian President Silvio Berlusconi). Convicted criminals can also become 'celebrities' by virtue of the notoriety of their crimes (Jewkes 2011). Much has been written, for example, about serial killers and consumer culture, and the fact that some of these individuals were motivated to kill on the prospect of the prestige of media exposure (Schmid 2005; Jarvis 2007). We return to this idea of 'celebrity-criminality' in Chapter 5. In an Australian context, a number of real-life criminals have achieved 'celebrity status' as a consequence of their notoriety (e.g. Mark Brandon 'Chopper' Read) and the popularity of semi-fictionalised accounts of their crimes in the television series *Underbelly*. The series has been criticised for glamorising criminal and deviant behaviours (King cited in Batsas 2010).

VISUAL SPECTACLE OR GRAPHIC IMAGERY

Arguably, like conflict, imagery is one of the most important and prominent news values in terms of crime news reporting. Visual images maintain an inherent power in terms of news narratives and the media framing of individuals and crime-related issues—they provide a sense of authenticity and immediacy in the news media coverage of crime events and allow news audiences to 'bear witness' to atrocities and people's final moments. In this way, they can often provoke strong emotions and societal responses. Some can even become iconic— either fitting with or unsettling dominant moral and social norms (think about the still images from the videotape of the 1991 assault on Rodney King by LAPD officers or the closed-circuit television (CCTV) images of the abduction of James Bulger from the New Strand Shopping Centre, Bootle, in 1993). As Hall (1981: 241–2) explains:

> News photos have a specific way of passing themselves off as aspects of 'nature'. They repress their ideological dimensions by offering themselves as literal visual-transcriptions of the 'real world'. News photos witness to the *actuality* of the event they represent ... At this level, news photos not only support the credibility of the newspaper as an accurate medium. They also guarantee and underwrite its *objectivity* ...

As Jewkes (2011) suggests, the primacy of the visual within crime news media has been heightened by technological developments, such as the increased use of smartphones and the internet—although it is important to remember that news visuals have always been elemental to broadcast news (i.e. television). The rise of 'participatory journalism' or 'citizen journalism' has also played a significant role in the proliferation and availability of crime news visuals. These factors combined have shaped the contours of crime news visuals, which in contemporary crime news reporting have more prominently featured crime scene reconstructions and re-enactments; CCTV images; videos of police interviews with suspects; crime scene photographs and other visual criminal evidence; as well as views from inside the courtroom (e.g. the live news broadcasts of the O. J. Simpson and Oscar Pistorius murder trials). Other examples such as the mainstream news media's representations of the 2014 Israel bombardment of Gaza and the crash of Malaysia Airlines Flight 17 that same year have raised public concerns and questions about visual ethics and whether the relentless exposure to shockingly graphic images on social media is to blame for the increasingly graphic images in newspapers and online news sites (Posetti 2014). These developments tell us something about not only the emerging trends in mediated representations of crime and justice, but also the way in which we 'read' news.

The above list provides a useful summary of specific news values that are drawn upon in constructing crime news. As suggested, the list is contingent upon the practices of local media (including in relation to global media) and changing circumstances (including the advent of new communications technologies). It is, therefore, a relatively stable but continually evolving characterisation of what makes crime stories 'newsworthy'.

NEWS JOURNALISTS AND THEIR SOURCES

While news values may 'shape and reinforce the interpretations of law-and-order news', these interpretations receive further support from the **news sources** upon which journalists draw in their constructions of crime news (Chibnall 1977: xii). At their simplest level, sources lend credibility and legitimacy to news journalism, since they provide the information and supporting evidence that serves as the basis of a news story as well as validates its factuality—all while enabling journalists to maintain a sense of distance or independence from their news texts. In short, the 'explicit use of sources dovetails with efforts to situate the journalist as being an ideal objective observer' (Carlson & Franklin 2011: 4) and therefore adheres to the journalistic ideals (and they are only *ideals*) of 'objectivity' and 'impartiality' within news media practice.

Previous academic studies have also referred to the defensive function that news sources serve for journalists in avoiding public embarrassment and criticism—what Tuchman (1972: 664), in her classic study of news work, identifies as the assumption that 'if every reporter gathers and structures "facts" in a detached, unbiased, impersonal manner, deadlines will be met and libel suits avoided' (see also Chibnall 1977; Hall et al. 1978/2013; Ericson, Baranek & Chan 1989; Shoemaker & Reese 2014). Contemporary news, therefore, would be 'unimaginable without sources. Within all but the most trivial news stories, information arrives linked to the individuals and institutions that provided it' (Carlson & Franklin 2011: 1).

The same is true of the hard-nosed news journalism of the golden era of news rounds or 'newsbeats', as they are commonly referred to in the trade (especially in the United States), when journalists were charged with the responsibility of reporting exclusively and in-depth on specialised topics, like crime and courts, and relied almost entirely on their contacts. In Australia, veteran crime reporters like Basil Sweeney, Ced Culbert, Noel Bailey, Ken Blanch, and later, Geoff Wilkinson and Malcolm Brown did most of their work outside the walls of the newsroom (Clifford 2014b)—hence, the term 'outside men'. The 'king of Sydney's crime reporters'—the *Daily Mirror*'s knock-about journalist, Bill Jenkings—was almost as well known on the street and in the famous Thommo's Two Up School as the criminals he covered. In the foreword to Jenkings's autobiography, his former boss and publisher of the *Daily Mirror*, Rupert Murdoch, wrote: 'Every policeman knew Bill and trusted him, though he was not above working the other side of the street for tips' (cited in Mitchell 2012).

These days, newsbeats continue in some form within most newsrooms, although many have been depopulated as a consequence of the general reductions in staff experienced across a range of news media outlets. So too, the once common newsbeat practice of sources providing journalists with tips or leads on otherwise hidden tales of crime, corruption, misconduct, intrigue and scandal has become more complicated in the contemporary mediascape and as a result of legislative reforms aimed at preventing further WikiLeaks or Edward Snowden-style government and surveillance information disclosures. In Australia, there has been considerable political debate over the ramifications of both of these latter events on the freedom of the press to report on security matters that are in the 'public interest' in view of the introduction of new anti-terror legislation. Under these counter-terrorism laws, any investigation of leaks relating to 'special intelligence operations' could expose journalists or whistleblowers to criminal charges and the prospect of up to five years in prison (see Media Entertainment & Arts Alliance 2014). Similar concerns have been raised in the United States and the United Kingdom where journalists have been subpoenaed (i.e. subjected to court orders to comply with certain directions) in order to track down whistleblowers, while editors at *The Guardian* were required, by government sanction, to destroy the hard drives and memory cards used by the newspaper to store the top-secret National Security Agency (NSA) documents leaked by Snowden (Harding 2014).

These examples demonstrate that, while privileged source access to news may often be referred to in terms of the *presence* of certain voices and information within news media, it can also relate to the *absence* of others. As Carlson and Franklin (2011: 3) explain: 'Journalists seek out sources that are both available and suitable, which serves to reinforce patterned sourcing practices. As a result of repetition, the authority of some sources is bolstered— making them likely to be called on as sources again—while other voices are continually excluded'. Of course, the patterned sourcing practices of journalists should not be read without exception as entirely negative or without attention to the contextual factors that impact upon source selection, nor should the exclusion that Carlson and Franklin refer to be confused with a deliberately malevolent act on the part of every journalist. In some cases, exclusion can occur as the consequence of the time constraints associated with news deadlines. Nonetheless, as Hall et al. (1978/2013: 61) observe, the combination of these practical pressures and the professional imperatives for 'objectivity' and 'impartiality' can result in the *over-accessing* of individuals in 'powerful and privileged institutional positions' as preferred news sources. This serves to reproduce the voices of the powerful as the '**primary definers**' within news media, establishing preferential patterns of news access and setting the limits of all subsequent public and media discourse in accordance with this initial definition or framing of '*what the problem is*' (Hall et al. 1978/2013: 62; see also Cottle 2000).

This is what Howard Becker (1967) refers to as the 'hierarchy of credibility'—that is, the increased likelihood that people in high-status positions within society will have their definitions of situations and issues more readily accepted, because of the assumption that they have 'access to more accurate or more specialised information on particular topics than the majority of the population' (Hall et al. 1978/2013: 61). As Becker (1967: 241, 242) explains:

> In any system of ranker groups, participants take it as given that members of the highest group have the right to define the way things really are ... They are the ones who, by virtue of their official position and the authority that goes with it, are in a position to 'do something' when things are not what they should be and, similarly, are the ones who will be held to account if they fail to 'do something' or if what they do is, for whatever reason, inadequate.

In the context of crime news, the primary definers at the top of Becker's hierarchy of credibility include institutions of crime control and law enforcement—that is, the police (see Box 3.6)—who are seen to possess a sense of authority and integrity in terms of crime information, since they have professional expertise, based on daily personal experience (Hall et al. 1978/2013).

BOX 3.6

POLICE AS PRIMARY DEFINERS OF CRIME NEWS

Notwithstanding the fact that official sources, such as the police, are often better positioned and resourced to access news media than many other news sources (e.g. community and advocacy groups), the privilege of news access does not always necessarily equate to *favourable news* for the primary definers (Schudson 2003). In 2012, for example, the Leveson inquiry investigated relations between the police and the press in the United Kingdom on the back of the *News of the World* phone hacking scandal. Findings from the inquiry indicated that there was a perception that some senior Metropolitan Police Service officers had been 'too close' to several staff members at News International, publisher of the *News of the World* newspaper (Leveson 2012; see also Greer & McLaughlin 2012; Mawby 2014). In other contexts, this closeness coupled with police authority and expertise can produce positive and socially responsible outcomes from the media complicity inferred by the primary definers model. This was the case in the Lindt café siege, where the majority of mainstream news media outlets adhered to a police-imposed media blackout on the broadcast or publication of sensitive information, such as the hostage-taker's requests, to maintain the integrity of police negotiations and crisis operations throughout the ordeal. Contrast this with the Rizal Park hostage-taking incident in August 2010 in Manila, where disgruntled former Philippine National Police officer Rolando Mendoza hijacked a tourist bus. Negotiations, which were broadcast by foreign and local news media on television and the internet, broke down after Mendoza—who had access to a television on board the bus—saw police arrest his brother on-screen. Mendoza and eight of the hostages were killed, and others injured, after an assault on the bus by law enforcement officials (Republic of the Philippines 2010).

We will discuss the sensitivities and changes in the dynamics of police–media relations in more detail in the next chapter. For now, the key point is that where journalists turn to for news sources is neither random nor socially neutral—some opinions and some information matter more than others (see Issues for consideration below).

As we have already noted, the information demands and speed imperatives of the 24/7 news cycle have left modern-day crime reporters with less time than their antecedents and investigative contemporaries to cultivate police contacts and other sources of information about criminal activities and police investigations. At the same time, the pervasiveness of surveillance technologies, like CCTV, and social media platforms, such as Twitter and Facebook, have brought traditional news consumers closer to the action and the 'scene of the crime', in some cases, enabling citizen journalists to 'scoop' mainstream media outlets on developing crime stories (Clifford 2014b). In this way, traditional news consumers have also become *producers* and *agenda-setters* of crime news—not to mention *crime-fighters*.

This is evidenced by Milivojevic and McGovern (2014) in their analysis of the role of social media in the mediated representation of the kidnapping, rape and murder of Jill Meagher in Melbourne on 22 September 2012. The case, which captured news headlines around the world, particularly for its levels of newsworthiness and its *visuality* as a crime event, exemplified the ways in which the popularity of particular crimes and their framing by ordinary citizens online can often be enough to improve the chances of the same story being covered by traditional news media outlets, using similar news angles and preferred media frames. It also demonstrated how social media (as a news media source and a source of news for audiences) is both 'part of the solution' and 'part of the problem' within the context of potential media effects on policing practices, the processes of the criminal justice system, and their broader social environments (Milivojevic & McGovern 2014). On the one hand, social media platforms like Facebook, Twitter and YouTube facilitated the widespread circulation of CCTV footage, which was considered pivotal to solving the Jill Meagher case (Mangan & Houston 2012). They also served to mobilise the public response towards broader social justice issues, such as the prevention of violence against women (AAP 2012). On the other hand, however, social media became a catalyst for concerns about the potentially negative impacts of '**trial by media**' in the prosecution of the crime's perpetrator, Adrian Ernest Bayley, as a consequence of the creation of hate groups and the widespread circulation of prejudicial comments on Facebook (Akerman 2012; Lowe 2012).

While in-depth analysis of the Jill Meagher case is beyond the scope of this chapter, it is worth mention in the context of our discussion of the construction of crime news for the ways in which it exemplifies how 'audience fragmentation and the rise of the Internet has created new avenues for news exhibition, opened the door to non-elite media, and birthed new forms' and a shift in traditional conceptualisations of journalistic authority to 'a view of texts as collaborative and unstable' (Carlson & Franklin 2011: 7). Within journalism and media studies, much has already been written on the democratising effects of this through deployment of concepts such as 'participatory journalism' or 'citizen journalism' and the evolution of traditional media consumers as *prosumers* and co-creators of news (Rosen 2006; Couldry 2010). Likewise, albeit mostly independently of this body of work, 'a range of criminological issues' has increasingly been 'linked to the use of social media including online privacy, victimisation and secondary victimisation, and application of social media in criminal justice interventions' (Milivojevic & McGovern 2014: 24).

We argue, however, that broader scope exists for a more detailed examination of the intersections between the two in the context of critical discussions of the construction of crime news, and that this analysis must consider the increasingly hybridised and democratised models of news production that characterise the contemporary mediascape. We need only think of the increasing trend towards calls for user-generated content—videos, pictures and personal perspectives—by traditional news media outlets and their inclusion within news stories to appreciate how *diffuse* and *naturalised* this model has become (for an example, see GuardianWitness <https://witness.theguardian.com>). This is despite the fact that academic theorising is still trying to settle on appropriate ways to acknowledge and analyse the trend. As Mnookin and Qu (2013: 30) explain in their discussion of the use of social media in combination with traditional news media in the manhunt for the perpetrators of the Boston Marathon bombings in April 2013:

> There is a reflexive reaction to pit emergent social media behavior against traditional journalistic practices and norms. This defensive posture is counterproductive, for both sides. Rather than pointing out flaws to favor one model over the other, we should appreciate the interplay between them, an interdependence that ultimately produces a more participatory, accurate and compelling news cycle.

While these final claims may be arguable, there is no doubt a need to consider the complexities and contours of this relationship and to ask what its implications might be for conventional methods of theorising definitions of news, news access and source selection, the newsworthiness criteria for crime news, and the ethical boundaries and limits of crime news reporting in relation to criminological issues, such as victimisation and natural justice.

ISSUES FOR CONSIDERATION

Scholars have noted several ambiguities within the primary definers model and its reductionist approach to journalist–source relations, including 'its assumptions of elite consensus, invariably passive journalists, and static, atemporal boundaries of who may be a societal elite', particularly within the fragmentary and diffusive conditions of the contemporary mediascape (Carlson & Franklin 2011: 6; see also Schlesinger & Tumber 1994; Cottle 2000). As Kitzinger and Reilly (1997: 345) note in their study of the mediated representations of risks within news, there are also temporal dimensions to consider, including the development of 'news fatigue' and the way in which 'source strategies that work at one point in time may cease to be effective under different historical conditions'. The concept, in its strictest sense, also neglects to fully consider the potential for individuals to disrupt the conventional hierarchy of credibility through the construction of counter-narratives (often informed by lived experience) to the dominant frames established by primary definers within news media (Becker 1967). These criticisms are 'not meant to vacate inquiry connecting sourcing patterns with social control', but to more productively augment 'the assumption of power with an interest in the process by which sources acquire dominant positions within a story against other possible sources or positions and how they sustain or lose this place over time. What we gain is a set of variables and conditions to think with when we think about sources' (Carlson & Franklin 2011: 6).

Much of the criminological theorising on the construction of crime news, however, has to date focused almost exclusively on the accounts of the 'accredited experts who represent and command institutional power' (Greer 2010b: 493). This can lead to the false impression that these are the *only* sources to which journalists refer in their crime news reporting practices. Like media criminologists, news journalists also need to be familiar with a diversity of primary and secondary sources of information; sometimes to verify stakeholder claims or validate the selection of particular news angles for their stories and, at other times, by way of background data to inform their interactions and interviews with news subjects (see Box 3.7). Social media must also not be forgotten as a potential news source within this process and in the context of critical discussions of the media–crime nexus.

BOX 3.7

EXAMPLES OF CRIME NEWS SOURCES

Documents: police and court records; coronial findings; government and ombudsman reports; court lists; community research reports; **freedom of information (FOI)** requests; legislation; reference texts; academic research; correspondence; budgets; electoral records.

Statistical records: police statistics; Australian Bureau of Statistics (ABS) data; emergency services data; surveys and polls.

Digital artefacts: social media; police and emergency services websites; government websites; user-generated content (e.g. mobile phone videos); podcasts; search engines; online news databases.

Media: news archives and newspaper clippings; wire copy; letters to the editor; cartoons; photographs and videos; other news media outlets.

Public relations: **media releases**; media alerts; press conferences; official launches; ministerial announcements and speeches; media interviews.

Physical locations: courtrooms; crime scenes; Royal Commission hearings; libraries.

People: industry contacts; police officers; whistleblower leaks; criminals; eyewitnesses; citizen journalists; interest groups; protestors and activists; information from colleagues.

CONCLUSION

As this chapter has demonstrated, the media–crime nexus is a far more complex and nuanced relationship than has necessarily been theorised—especially within the context of the contemporary mediascape. News presents a version of reality that is subject to processes of selection and emphasis, and which is often in conflict with the realities of crime statistics and official criminological data.

This does not necessitate that as media criminologists we should always adopt a reductionist or negative view of crime news media and its routinised professional practices. There are real-world effects from the professional decisions and framing practices implicit within crime news journalism, but these are not always of a detrimental or harmful orientation. News media representations of crime and justice have the potential to positively mobilise publics and open up conversations about previously concealed, albeit important, social issues—as much as they can also perpetuate inaccurate stereotypes and perceptions, damage reputations and traumatise people.

The conditions under which this occurs and by which such scenarios are influenced are numerous and multifaceted. Like the news frames that are produced, these conditions are not static and remain open to contestation and advancement. But, to do this, it is important to understand what it is we are unsettling and how we can 'speak back', which requires not only an applied understanding of news media practices, but the willingness to occupy multiple subject positions and be adaptable to change.

DISCUSSION QUESTIONS

1. What is it about crime that appeals to news audiences?
2. Is too much time and space devoted to crime in mainstream news media?
3. Name three historical or contemporary crimes that could be described as 'signal crimes'. What do you think was so significant about these crimes?
4. Should we expect news media representations to accurately reflect the social realities of crime and justice?
5. Can you list three examples of news media coverage that positively contributed to public discussions about crime and justice-related events and/or issues?

WORKSHOP ACTIVITY: A COMPARATIVE FRAMING ANALYSIS

Choose a contemporary, high-profile crime that has attracted significant attention within local, national and/or international news media. Select three stories about the crime from three different print or online news media outlets (e.g. *The Guardian*, *The Sydney Morning Herald* and the *New York Post*). The stories should include at least one interviewee and news visuals or graphics, if possible. They should also reflect a period of news reporting (i.e. they should be from across a date range) to allow you to critically discuss any temporal shifts in the mediated representation of the crime. Conduct a comparative framing analysis on the three news stories, reflecting on each of the points outlined in 'Box 3.4: Doing news framing analysis', and with consideration of the 'news values' identifiable in each of the crime news stories.

FURTHER READING

Carlson, M. & Franklin, B. (eds). (2011). *Journalists, Sources and Credibility: New Perspectives*. London and New York: Routledge.

Chermak, S. (1995). Crime in the News Media: A Refined Understanding of How Crimes Become News. In G. Barak (ed), *Media, Process, and the Social Construction of Crime: Studies in Newsmaking Criminology*. New York and London: Routledge, pp. 95–129.

Couldry, N. (2010). New Online News Sources and Writer-Gatherers. In N. Fenton (ed.), *New Media, Old News*. Los Angeles: Sage, pp. 138–52.

Harcup, T. & O'Neill, D. (2001). What is News? Galtung and Ruge Revisited. *Journalism Studies*, 2(2), 261–80.

Katz, J. (1987). What Makes Crime 'News'? *Media, Culture & Society*, 9(1), 47–75.

Tuchman, G. (1972). Objectivity as Strategic Ritual: An Examination of Newsmen's Notions of Objectivity. *American Journal of Sociology*, 77(4), 660–79.

PART

II

FRAMING EFFECTS AND MEDIA PRACTICES

4

POLICE, COURTS AND MEDIA

CHAPTER HIGHLIGHTS

Introduction

Police as the 'primary definers' of crime news

Law and order in a changing media environment

Tweet justice: The infiltration of mainstream and social media within the courtroom

Cameras in the courtroom

Conclusion

INTRODUCTION

Police and courts are two of the most important sources of information for news media outlets in their coverage of crime-related events and issues. Indeed, communications between police, courts and media are as old as journalism itself. The early years of newspapers (and thus the advent of journalism), and especially the phenomenon of the 'yellow press' (older first versions of the modern-day tabloid), revolved around crime news. For journalists, the best and easiest sources of crime news, then and now, were those who dealt directly with the criminals—namely, the police and the courts.

But the nuances and complexities of these relationships have evolved with the demands of the contemporary news cycle and the emergence of mobile and surveillance technologies. These have changed the ways that not only police and courts do their jobs, but journalists too. For example, where once police agencies and courts counted on media outlets to circulate appeals for information about crimes or to translate court proceedings for lay audiences, now they have the capacity to speak directly to their publics through their own accounts on social media, including Twitter and Facebook. Likewise, with the advent of the 24/7 news cycle and the depopulation of newsrooms, journalists no longer have the time or resources to cultivate the contacts they once relied on (with 'cops' and 'crims' alike) in the golden era of newsbeat reporting (Clifford 2014b). They are now as likely to source leads for crime news stories from social media and the videos posted to YouTube by ordinary citizens—including those tragically caught up in crime-related events, like acts of terrorism—as they are to source them from more traditional means.

Whether these developments have been for the better in terms of police–media relations and court–media relations is arguable. But one thing is certain: they have created particular challenges and opportunities for law enforcement, the judiciary and media practitioners, and we explore these issues throughout this chapter.

POLICE AS THE 'PRIMARY DEFINERS' OF CRIME NEWS

In the previous chapter, we identified the ways in which journalists who write news stories about crime-related events and issues typically obtain their information from readily accessible and knowledgeable sources. Because of their professional or institutional authority and their general willingness and availability to talk to media, these sources are often preferentially and repeatedly consulted by news journalists, and their definitions of situations and issues are more readily accepted. Police are an obvious example of these *primary definers* of crime news. Reflect for a moment on what you typically see, hear and read in the news following a major crime or accident. Often, a senior officer will address the media as a police spokesperson with (an appeal for) information about the event or updates on the investigation. Police may also be proactive sources of news. Consider, for example, the police cautions about road safety and home security in the lead-up to busy holiday periods, or the health and safety advisories issued in advance of major events at which there is likely to be a police presence, such as music festivals or public protests. As Ericson, Baranek and Chan (1989: 93) explain: 'The police now accept that in relation to a particular incident or activity, a proactive approach to the news media is useful in controlling the version of reality that is transmitted, sustained, and accepted publicly'.

This does not mean that the supply of police information to media knows no bounds. There are inevitably times when police will request that journalists refrain from publishing certain details, especially where the release of information may impede police operations and ongoing investigations or prejudice legal proceedings. If the justification provided for not publishing a story is reasonable, most news editors will oblige. In some instances, they may even refrain from disclosing sensitive information, before being requested to do so (Grabosky & Wilson 1989).

On other occasions, they may go ahead and publish, despite a **news embargo**. In 2009, controversy arose when *The Australian* newspaper published details of counter-terrorism raids across Melbourne in an edition of the newspaper that then-Chief Commissioner of Victoria Police, Simon Overland, claimed had hit the streets before the raids had been executed; potentially putting the operation at risk as well as the state and federal police officers involved. Several men were arrested in the raids (dubbed Operation Neath) for an alleged plan to attack the Australian Army's Holsworthy Barracks in western Sydney as retribution for Australia's military involvement in Muslim countries (Wilson & Stewart 2009). Several days earlier, Cameron Stewart, a journalist from *The Australian*, had been contacted by an officer from Victoria Police with information about the raids, although at the time, Stewart (2012) claims, neither person knew about the Holsworthy plot. This information came to light once Stewart had contacted the Australian Federal Police (AFP) for comment on the raids story. A deal was subsequently struck between the newspaper's editor and the AFP Commissioner, Tony Negus, for *The Australian* to delay publication of the news story until after the suspects had been arrested (Rane, Ewart & Martinkus 2014).

In the furore that erupted over the miscommunication about print deadlines and the early publication of the news story, the Office of Police Integrity (OPI) investigated the leaking of the information about Operation Neath to *The Australian*. Stewart was asked to reveal his police source. This would have constituted a direct contravention of Clause 3 of the Journalist Code of Ethics and the ethical obligation to protect the confidentiality of sources (see Media, Entertainment & Arts Alliance 2015), had it not been for a Deed of Release signed by Stewart's source, freeing him of such requirements. The release meant Stewart had no other legal option but to cooperate with OPI investigators, and to reveal then Victoria Police detective, Simon Artz, as the source of the information about the raids. Although he had provided what Stewart (2012) calls 'no more than a modest tip-off', with no mention of the alleged attack on Holsworthy Barracks, Artz was sentenced to four months in prison, suspended for 12 months, for 'unauthorised disclosure of information'.

The case demonstrates just how complex and sensitive the journalist and police–source relationship can be; that it can involve as many complementarities as it can potential points of conflict. It also raises the question of 'not whether police and journalists should or do work closely, but under what conditions and in what circumstances such arrangements are benign or malign?' (Innes & Graef 2012: 161). Tensions can arise from some of the most unexpected of circumstances—for example, through language and the disjunctures between police discourse and the ways in which 'cop talk' is (re)interpreted by media and publics. Just as news has a language and rhythm of its own, so too police have a vocabulary specific to their professional knowledge and function. For example, police talk about 'information', 'intelligence' and 'evidence', but each has a specific investigatory meaning and is not the same or reducible to the other. One of the roles of crime news journalists is to translate this police-speak into news narratives for lay audiences. The same applies to court–media relations. But research has shown that, when telling stories, law and journalism use their own language. Journalism, as Johnston and Breit (2010: 8) explain, tends to be 'grounded on populist traditions', while law is 'steeped in formality' (see Box 4.1).

BOX 4.1

LEGAL DISCOURSE VS NEWS DISCOURSE

The following example, adapted from Johnston and Breit (2010), demonstrates the translation of legal discourse into crime news narrative in the 'Snowtown' case, which was a series of murders committed in South Australia between August 1992 and May 1999. Many of the murders were preceded by torture, and attempts were made by the primary perpetrators—John Bunting, Robert Wagner and James Vlassakis—to appropriate the social security payments and bank funds of each of the victims. *Snowtown*, a feature film based on the life of Bunting, was released in 2011. Note, in particular, the formality of Justice Brian Martin's description of the circumstances of the crime in comparison to the more populist language used in the broadcast television news story.

R V BUNTING AND OTHERS (NO. 3) (2003) SASC 251: PARA 346	SNOWTOWN TRIAL REVEALS 'DEGENERATE SUB-CULTURE' *THE 7.30 REPORT*, ABC TV (2003)
'… the evidence was capable of establishing the existence of an over-arching joint enterprise to which each accused was a party and pursuant to which each deceased was killed. The common enterprise began in about 1992 … The accused were linked by their common hatred of homosexual persons and paedophiles. The enterprise developed. Where possible the accused sought to benefit from the property of the deceased and to access any Centrelink benefits to which the deceased were entitled at the times of their deaths … Steps were taken to create the impression that the deceased were still alive'. (Justice Brian Martin)	'Between them, John Bunting and Robert Wagner have been found guilty of torturing and murdering 11 people in what's become known as the bodies-in-the-barrel case. Almost as shocking as the details of the crimes themselves is the grim portrait of a vulnerable underclass, which provided their victims. The victims were not chosen randomly, but rather, in the words of a senior police officer, the two were part of a group that preyed upon itself'. (Reporter Mike Sexton)

Police agencies generally have their own media policies, which govern police–media relations in many jurisdictions. However, the reliance on police by journalists for information about and definitions of crime has necessitated the development of additional resources. This is to ensure more accurate and responsible discourse about sensitive law enforcement issues and controversial social problems, especially those in which police themselves are directly implicated, such as **vulnerable people policing**. In Australia, pocket guides developed by the *Mindframe* National Media Initiative assist police officers and representatives of the courts to manage their interactions with media (and vice versa) in relation to incidents involving mental illness or a suspected suicide (see Box 4.2). These incidents are considered newsworthy, and police and courts are often the first to field news media inquiries about them (*Mindframe* National Media Initiative 2014a). Research has found, however, that the information collected by journalists from these sources can be some of the most problematic in terms of reinforcing negative stereotypes about suicide, mental illness and vulnerable individuals in the community (Pirkis et al. 2008). News stories constructed from this information will often associate mental illness with an inherent propensity for violence, focusing on specific or relatively rare circumstances, with inappropriate language a central concern. A classic example is the police reference to a mental health patient as having 'absconded from hospital', the impression being that the individual has 'escaped' and represents a threat or 'danger' to the community. In truth, mentally ill people are more likely to be the victims of violence than the perpetrators of it (*Mindframe* National Media Initiative 2014a). The differences between the ways in which police, law and media construct their narratives of crime and justice therefore have the potential to impact on not only public understandings of sensitive issues but also the roles and responsibilities of law enforcement and the criminal justice system (Mawby 2002; Nobles & Schiff 2004; Johnston & Breit 2010).

BOX 4.2

MINDFRAME FOR POLICE AND COURTS IN AUSTRALIA

Funded by the Australian Government and managed by the Hunter Institute of Mental Health in New South Wales, the *Mindframe* National Media Initiative actively encourages the responsible, accurate and sensitive representation of mental illness and suicide in media. It does so through the development of resources, strategic engagement with target sectors, education and training, and evidence and evaluation. *Mindframe* staff actively foster collaborative relationships with Australian media practitioners (from news media, screen and stage) as well as professionals from related sectors, who often act as sources for news stories, including those from the mental health and suicide prevention sectors, police and courts. The initiative also works closely with educators from Australian universities to ensure that graduates in journalism and public relations are adequately supported and equipped to respond to issues relating to mental illness and suicide. The *Mindframe* National Media Initiative resources for target sectors are designed to support these practitioners and professionals in their interactions with media so as to reduce the stigma and discrimination associated with mental illness, inform accurate reporting and portrayals of mental illness and suicide, and minimise harm and copycat behaviours.

Engaging with media on these sensitive issues, police and courts staff are advised to:

- remember their *legislative responsibilities* in callouts as well as court cases involving mental illness and suicide
- consider the *impact of the story*, particularly on bereaved individuals and traumatised witnesses, and *whether to make official comment*
- check that *appropriate language is used*, which does not stigmatise or perpetuate common myths and stereotypes about mental illness, clarifying where necessary
- ensure that actions and words reflect that *mental illness is a health concern, even when responding to a criminal matter*

- *avoid specific descriptions of the location and method of a suicide* and consider how to manage this information in the courtroom
- include information that *promotes help-seeking behaviours*
- *refer journalists to the Mindframe website and resources.*

Sources: *Mindframe* National Media Initiative 2014a; 2014b; 2014c.

The reliance on police as primary definers of news stories has raised concerns about the extent to which police control the flow of information about crime and criminality, and how they 'frame a great percentage of narratives about law and order and policing' (McGovern & Lee 2010: 459). A study by McGovern and Lee (2010) found that 67 per cent of all crime-related stories in metropolitan daily newspapers over a one-month period in Sydney were attributable to police media releases. Moreover, when newspaper reporters used the content of these media releases, they tended to do so verbatim (i.e. word-for-word) and publish them as objective news (Lee & McGovern 2013). Findings like these reinforce the persistent view that police are the dominant party in the police–media relationship.

THE RISE OF POLICE 'IMAGE WORK'

It is not always the case, however, that police play the major role in their relationships with media. This is especially the case where news media coverage is about police misconduct or controversial police actions, such as the use of lethal force against vulnerable individuals. As Lawrence (2000: 49) explains, 'particular conditions determine when one news pattern prevails over the other', which is another way of saying that context will shape content and consequence. While some studies reveal a generally favourable disposition towards mediated representations of policing, others imply that the police are more often negatively portrayed, particularly in news media (Dowler & Zawilski 2007). This can have significant implications for the perceived legitimacy of police and the public's general willingness to cooperate and collaborate with them (Myhill & Beak 2008; Novak 2009), given that evidence shows 'vicarious experiences of policing have a substantial impact on perceptions of and confidence in police' (Herrington et al. 2009: 35). The challenge, as Mawby (1999: 267) explains, is that 'the media context in which both parties operate is now infinitely more complex and accordingly more difficult for an agency such as the police to control'.

This is partly attributable to the managerialist environment in which police operate and the **mediated visibility** (Thompson 2005) of contemporary policing, which has resulted in increased public scrutiny and accountability of police, aided by technological advances and emerging surveillance and mobile media practices. The actions of frontline police officers are now routinely captured by in-car video cameras (otherwise known as 'dashcams'), closed-circuit television systems in custodial and public environments, and on the street through body-worn cameras and audio-video recording devices on Tasers. This is not to mention the smartphones of bystanders and the technical gadgetry of citizen journalists. Tim Pool, for instance, used his 'occucopter' live-streaming video and aerial drone to monitor police conduct towards protestors during the Occupy Wall Street protests in New York in 2011, while simultaneously broadcasting independent media coverage of the event via the internet (Sharkey & Knuckey 2011). Pool amassed thousands of online followers, who watched his footage, tweeted about it, shared it and commented on it. Major media organisations soon followed, taking Pool's live feed straight from his mobile phone and rebroadcasting it on their own news channels (Pool cited in Novak 2013). These kinds of surveillance and mobile media images have become so ubiquitous in broadcast and online news stories about crime, law and order that we tend not to distinguish them as anything other than what they have become—a stock-standard part of contemporary news production and mediated storytelling. While the technological advances that have underpinned the mediated visibility of policing have enhanced the capacity of publics to scrutinise the actions of police, their normative inclusion in the contemporary media environment has also made it far harder for police to control 'reputation-damaging information about their own activities and to stop it becoming publicly known via user-generated content' (Innes & Graef 2012: 158).

To contain and counter these negative representations, police agencies have increasingly engaged in what Mawby (2002) calls 'image work'—that is, professionalised **public relations (PR)** activities designed to manage the mediated visibility of police and promote and protect their organisational legitimacy. Although police have long been engaged in 'image work', their efforts have taken on a greater significance in the changing media environment with the introduction of dedicated information officers and **police media units**. Reports suggest that the Metropolitan Police, with one of the largest operations of police forces in the United Kingdom, employs more than 100 communications staff with an annual operating budget of £10 million (Turvill 2015). Responsible for the conventional tasks of responding to media inquiries and informing the public about crime-related incidents (setting the crime news agenda), the remit of these police media units has expanded to include the delivery of media training to operational police; the development of policy guidelines around media contact; and the management of in-house multimedia units, which produce audiovisual content for distribution to traditional media outlets and online news sites (Lee & McGovern 2014).

Globally, police media units have also taken advantage of the 'prime time crime market' (Huey & Broll 2012) and the popularity of long-running **police procedural** dramas, such as *Homicide* (Australia, 1964–77), *Cop Shop* (Australia, 1977–84), *The Bill* (UK, 1984–2010), *Blue Heelers* (Australia, 1994–2006), *Water Rats* (Australia, 1996–2001), *The Wire* (US, 2002–08) and *The Killing* (Denmark, 2007–12), to marry corporate branding with education and entertainment in the form of high-rating 'observational documentaries' like *Police, Camera, Action!* (UK, 1994–2010) and *COPS* (US, 1989–present). The 'factional' representations of the latter—combining images of real-world policing with the more stylised narrative and aesthetic conventions of infotainment and 'reality' television (Mason 2003)—have allowed audiences to go on a **ride-along** with police officers as they work through their shifts, giving them a bird's-eye view of the action and potentially increasing public understandings of policing and the consequences of unlawful behaviour.

Such programs claim to show us what crime and policing is *really* like (Moore 2014), despite the fact that they remain highly mediated and subject to editing processes. As Lee and McGovern (2014: 145) observe: 'When these arrangements go as planned ... the opportunities for the police to disseminate positive public images are evident'. So too are the commercial benefits. In 2009, figures obtained under freedom of information (FOI) laws and published by *The Daily Telegraph* newspaper showed that the growth of this kind of police PR in Australia had netted one police agency over $1 million from its involvement in reality television shows like *The Force: Behind the Line* and *Crash Investigation Unit*, and its consultations on other television productions featuring representations of policing practices. Not surprisingly, these commercial arrangements have attracted some criticism with accusations that they amount to little more than police spin and propaganda, given the power the police retain to vet content before it goes to air (Blacker 2009), ensuring that the representations are pro-police.

LAW AND ORDER IN A CHANGING MEDIA ENVIRONMENT

Police engagement with social networking and video-sharing sites like Facebook, Twitter and YouTube can similarly be a double-edged sword. Nonetheless, many police agencies have sought to meet their communications priorities and PR objectives through more innovative means, including the establishment of a presence on social media. The extent to which individual police agencies have embraced these communications platforms—and successfully—varies between state, national and international jurisdictions.

On the positive side, social media can enhance emergency management capabilities (e.g. in disasters) and allows police to clarify details or correct inaccuracies that may have been reported in the news. It also enables police to appeal for public information about crimes and to provide updates on the status of investigations, often bypassing traditional news media to communicate directly with the community (Dick 2011). In 2015, Detective Sergeant Tam Bui from the Toronto Police Service's Homicide Squad in Canada helped crack a two-year-old murder case by creating an innovative social media campaign, inspired by the true-crime podcast *Serial*. Over a period of several weeks, Bui used his Twitter account to reach out to new witnesses by regularly sharing clues about the murder of 24-year-old Mike Pimentel (Faruqi 2015). Pimentel had been stabbed to death early on New Year's Day in 2012 after leaving a party in Liberty Village, Toronto. Using the hashtags #mikepimentelmurder and #serial, Bui posted previously undisclosed crime scene photos and surveillance footage in an attempt to reinvigorate the investigation. On 10 December 2015, police announced they had arrested and charged a 30-year-old man with Pimentel's murder—in part, as a consequence of Bui's social media campaign and the mainstream media interest it had attracted (Toronto Police Service 2015). By the same year, police agencies like the NSW Police Force and Queensland Police in Australia had amassed more than 550 000 and 692 000 followers respectively on their Facebook pages—audiences larger than the individual Facebook followings of some of the most popular newspapers in each state, including *The Sydney Morning Herald*, *The Courier Mail* and *Brisbane Times*.

Despite its virtues, police engagement with social media can have its pitfalls. Maintaining an online presence can be a significant resourcing challenge, given the conventions of social media and the demands for two-way communication and interactivity between users. This exposes police agencies to potentially unwelcome or negative comments, making it difficult to balance online moderation and the shutting down or deletion of dissent with the ideals of fostering transparency and an open dialogue with and between communities (Lee & McGovern 2014). Police indiscretion has similarly emerged as a problem, with inappropriate off-duty disclosures and documented breaches of police social media guidelines, including racist and threatening remarks and 'friend' requests sent to victims of crime (Press Association 2014; Goldsmith 2015).

In terms of operational policing, the significant increase in the volume of information communicated via social media has created challenges for the 'golden hour' of police investigation (see Box 4.3) as well as a risk or threat selection problem, making it 'harder to decide which issues should be attended to and which should be ignored' in the first place (Innes & Graef 2012: 158). This was exemplified in the England riots of 2011, which followed the fatal police-involved shooting of Mark Duggan, a young black man, in Tottenham, London. Many of the individuals involved in the riots used social media technologies such as Twitter, BlackBerry Messenger and Facebook to coordinate their activities. While police attempted to monitor and analyse this online traffic, there were 'myriad problems' in translating the data from 'potentially interesting information into actionable intelligence' (Innes & Graef 2012: 167). Most notable, write Innes and Graef (2012: 167), was the difficulty of 'distinguishing between things that would actually happen, and rumours and deliberate mis-directions', especially the naming of locations as potential hot spots for social disorder.

BOX 4.3

THE 'GOLDEN HOUR' OF POLICE INVESTIGATION IN THE DIGITAL AGE

For police, the opportunity to collect the best evidence occurs in the period immediately following a critical incident—what is known as the 'golden hour'. As time passes, eyewitness testimonies can become confused or influenced by other information sources, and the potential for forensic evidence to be contaminated or destroyed increases. But, as the results of a study by a team of researchers from the Universities' Police Science Institute (UPSI) at Cardiff University show, with the widespread use of social media, the 'golden hour' has been compressed into a much shorter time frame and police control over information about major crimes has diminished. Where once police were able to 'seal' a crime scene 'and tightly control access to it both physically and in terms of what information was broadcast to the wider public, crime scenes are now increasingly "permeable" in that a lot of details about what has happened "leak" out via social media channels' (Innes, Roberts & Rogers 2014: 17).

To test the theory, the UPSI team analysed social media data collected from the immediate aftermath of the public murder of British army soldier Lee Rigby on a Woolwich street in south-east London on 22 May 2013, through to the conclusion of court proceedings related to the case. A fusilier and father of one, Rigby was killed in broad daylight on the walk back to his barracks after he was run down by a car driven by Michael Adebolajo and Michael Adebowale. The pair, both British of Nigerian descent and converts to Islam, attacked Rigby with knives and a cleaver, almost decapitating him. Following the attack, Adebolajo and Adebowale dragged Rigby's body into the road and waited for police to arrive at the scene. Rigby died from the multiple stab wounds inflicted on him. Both attackers were subsequently wounded by armed police officers, apprehended and taken to separate hospitals for treatment. They recovered, were convicted of Rigby's murder in December 2013, and sentenced to life imprisonment in February 2014, with Adebolajo given a whole-life term and Adebowale ordered to serve a minimum of 45 years in prison.

As McEnery, McGlashan and Love (2015: 238) suggest, the decision to 'openly commit violent murder was a provocative one ... intended to grab the attention of passers-by and onlookers'. The plan worked. Details of the incident and its location spread quickly via social media. The UPSI research team found that, within 18 minutes of the emergency call from a member of the public, and four minutes after armed police officers had shot and wounded Adebolajo and Adebowale, the first tweet was posted by a witness at the scene: 'Man taking pot shots at the police in Woolwich #wonderfulworld'. A second tweet, a minute later, identified the scene of the incident as near Woolwich library (Innes, Roberts & Rogers 2014: 17). Twitter traffic peaked within the first 24 hours of the incident, with nearly 900 tweets captured relating to the Rigby case (Roberts, Innes, Preece & Spasic 2015). Adebolajo had also actively sought out a witness with a camera phone to deliver 'a 21st-century press conference' (Halliday 2013) from the crime scene, telling onlookers 'the only reason we have killed this man today is because Muslims are dying daily by British soldiers. This British soldier is one; he is an eye for an eye and a tooth for a tooth'. The footage, which was used by a number of broadcasters in their media coverage of the incident, including news updates from the BBC, Al Jazeera and Sky News, attracted almost 680 complaints to the UK communications regulator, Ofcom (Ofcom 2014). Public concerns were raised about the graphic and insensitive nature of the footage, while other complainants argued that it 'gave one of the alleged attackers a platform to justify and explain his actions' (Ofcom 2014: 22). After investigation, Ofcom concluded that none of the news broadcasts had breached the broadcasting code. But the broadcasts had broader consequences than those of public sensitivity; as Innes, Roberts and Rogers (2014: 18) explain, they established that it is not only police who are 'struggling to respond to the rapid dynamics of the new social media environment' and the community mobilisation and collective action it enables following major crime events, but news media practitioners too.

Although comparatively slower in their uptake, the challenges of mainstream and social media engagement have been as substantive and time-sensitive for courts and the judiciary. According to Rodrick (2014: 146), most contemporary courts have 'either developed policies on the use of live, text-based communications from within the courtroom or are in the process of doing so', with some taking a more permissive approach than others. These developments have clear benefits for 'open justice' (see Box 4.4) and the timely reporting of court proceedings (Wallace & Johnston 2015).

BOX 4.4

'OPEN JUSTICE' IN A MEDIATED WORLD

The principle of open justice assumes that an accountable, impartial and well-functioning judicial system should be transparent and open to public examination, thereby engendering confidence in the courts (Rodrick 2014). This does not mean that people expect infallibility in their institutions, but that it is often difficult for publics to define what they expect when they are prohibited from observing (Rodrick 2014). The principle of open justice—in its purest form—endorses the idea that all court proceedings and the materials associated with them should be accessible to the public and for the purposes of media reporting, *without restriction*. In reality, however, the privileges and restrictions for journalists covering the courts vary markedly between jurisdictions and there is often little consistency about 'which materials are "open", about the processes to be followed, and about whether reasons need to be given by a requesting party' (Biber 2014: 74). Journalists covering the courts in Australia, for instance, are subject to different court rules and legislation across nine jurisdictions (six states, two territories and the Commonwealth) as well as the implications of publishing and sharing news stories across borders (Pearson & Polden 2015). There are, however, as Pearson and Polden (2015: 102) point out, some commonalities in the privileges afforded to journalists, including:

- the courtesy of sitting at the press bench during a trial
- being able to take notes (and sometimes recordings) and, in some cases, use social media for reporting purposes while the court is sitting
- having priority over ordinary citizens (as representatives of the broader public) for a position in the courtroom when the court is full
- having access to documents tabled in court and transcripts of court proceedings, subject to certain provisos.

Among these provisos is the recognition that there are sometimes necessary exceptions to the open justice principle, resulting in restrictions on the reporting of certain cases—for example, those related to national security, trade secrets or blackmail, allegations of sexual assault, murder or terrorism, or cases that involve vulnerable individuals, such as children and victims of domestic violence or where the court sits as a guardian of wards of the state or mentally ill individuals (Pearson & Polden 2015). Open justice may also clash with other principles, such as the right to be tried before an impartial jury, especially when the privileges afforded to journalists in terms of access to court proceedings and materials morph into 'trial by media'. Open justice, in practice, is therefore about getting the balance right, particularly as it relates to the professional imperatives and ideals of news media. As Pearson and Polden (2015: 97) argue, '[s]omewhere in between the extremes of a media free-for-all and judicial clampdown' there must be 'a legitimate and vital space for journalism, in which courts can be subjected to vigorous examination and criticism in the public interest, while those accused of a crime can still get a fair trial'.

TWEET JUSTICE: THE INFILTRATION OF MAINSTREAM AND SOCIAL MEDIA WITHIN THE COURTROOM

Live tweeting by professional journalists can inform publics about trial developments where individuals are unable to attend the legal proceedings themselves. Tweets from inside the courtroom can also add immediacy and a sensory dimension to conventional court reporting of high-profile cases, as was demonstrated in the 2010 bail hearing for WikiLeaks founder Julian Assange, when senior district judge Howard Riddle allowed journalists to use Twitter throughout the proceedings. Reporters from media outlets like American cable television news channel CNN and the United Kingdom's *The Guardian* newspaper jumped at the opportunity, posting blow-by-blow accounts of the courtroom action to their personal Twitter accounts. The tweeted commentary ranged from 'Assange attorney Geoffrey Robertson arrived at courtroom, had to bang on door to get in #wikileaks' through to 'Julian #assange in the dock. Looking more ashen then (sic) last week, wearing navy suit, open white shirt' and 'Assange remains in custody. Tells judge he understands'.

Some critics have questioned whether this style of reporting adds to public understandings of the criminal justice system, and to what extent complex legal arguments can be fairly communicated in 140 characters (Banks 2010). Concerns have also been raised about the potentially adverse impacts that live blogging and tweeting from inside the courtroom may have on the proper administration of justice. In a 2010 Judicial Studies Board Lecture, the Lord Chief Justice of England and Wales, Lord Judge, cautioned: 'we have to remember "tweets" stay on the internet, and to allow court-based tweeting is likely to increase the potential for prejudicial material regarding the defendant or a witness to become available on the internet'. He continued:

> ... even if a tweet originating in the courtroom itself may indeed be a 'fair and accurate' observation or report, the responses of other users of the Twitter system may not be.

> The publication of a defendant's previous convictions, or for that matter a victim's previous convictions, when the judge has ruled them inadmissible provides a classic example (Judge 2010).

Almost daily, courts issue **suppression orders**, which place restrictions on the publication of certain details, including the reporting of names, from civil and criminal trials. Suppression orders may relate to the more sensitive elements of a case or they can apply to the case as a whole. They are distinct from **super injunctions**, which not only restrict the reporting of certain details from the trial, but also the existence of the injunction itself. In either case, a breach can result in financial penalties, possible charges of **contempt of court** or even imprisonment. For this reason, Richardson (cited in Rule & Richardson 2013: 210) explains, 'reporters usually know far more than [what] the law will ever allow them to publish or broadcast'. However, the real-time nature of Twitter means that the effectiveness of these reporting restrictions can be stymied if journalists inadvertently tweet information that is subject to a suppression order. Retracting this information once it has been posted online or complying with court-issued 'take down' notices to remove content from news sites does not necessarily ensure the confidentiality of information or protect against wider disclosure, as the Ryan Giggs injunction controversy demonstrated (see Box 4.5). For this reason, some courts have imposed a 15-minute delay on the transmission of tweets from inside the courtroom where they relate to trial evidence or submissions made during legal proceedings (e.g. witness testimonies), while retaining the opportunity for journalists to live-tweet court outcomes and verdicts (Pearson & Polden 2015).

JUROR MISCONDUCT: THE MISUSE OF SOCIAL MEDIA

It is not only the use of social media by journalists that has come to the attention of the courts for its potentially negative impacts on legal proceedings and possible breaches of the law. In 2009, Australian news media reported that Facebook and some of its users had breached a suppression order and faced possible contempt of court charges for publishing online images of Brendan Sokaluk, the man charged (and later convicted) with arson causing death as part of the Black Saturday bushfires in the Gippsland region of Victoria (Andersen 2009). Similar web vigilantism threatened the administration of justice in the Jill Meagher murder case in Melbourne after several 'hate groups' which had been created on Facebook published potentially prejudicial comments towards the accused (later convicted) perpetrator, Adrian Ernest Bayley (see Akerman 2012; Lowe 2012; Milivojevic & McGovern 2014). The incident prompted Jill Meagher's husband, Tom Meagher, to make a public appeal for people to 'be mindful' of the fact that 'negative comments on social media' may hurt the legal proceedings. By far, however, the 'single most significant challenge that social media poses to the courts' is the potential for jurors to misuse social media during trials (Johnston et al. 2013: 9–10).

BOX 4.5

THE RYAN GIGGS INJUNCTION CONTROVERSY

Despite an injunction, in 2011, Twitter played a key role in the exposure of Manchester United footballer Ryan Giggs's alleged affair with reality TV contestant Imogen Thomas, after his name was disclosed by around 75000 users on Twitter. The British media largely held their fire on the story, in view of the injunction to protect Giggs's privacy, until UK politician John Hemming used the cloak of parliamentary privilege to name the premiership footballer—more than a month after speculation had spread on the internet. A day earlier, the *Sunday Herald* had already identified Giggs, after legal advice suggested that the injunction did not apply in Scotland, where the newspaper was published. The 22 May 2011 edition of the *Sunday Herald* featured a full front-page photograph of Giggs with a thin black line across his eyes and the word 'CENSORED' with the caption: 'Everyone knows that this is the footballer accused of using the courts to keep allegations of a sexual affair secret. But we weren't supposed to tell you that ... THE MADNESS OF PRIVACY LAWS: A SPECIAL REPORT'. Then-UK Prime Minister David Cameron subsequently conceded that the privacy rulings affecting mainstream media were 'unsustainable' and 'unfair', especially when information is otherwise widely available online. He called for a joint committee to investigate the use of gagging orders and the balance between privacy and freedom of expression (Herald View 2011). A Joint Committee on Privacy and Injunctions (2012) reported the findings of its inquiry to the House of Lords and the House of Commons the following year. The main problem, it said, was a matter of enforcement. To remedy this, the Committee's report recommended 'enhanced regulation of the media' and that major corporations, like Google, should 'take practical steps to limit the potential for breaches of court orders through use of their products and, if they fail to do so, legislation should be introduced to force them to' (Joint Committee on Privacy and Injunctions 2012).

According to Bartels and Lee (2013: 43), there are four primary ways in which jurors may use social media inappropriately, although these are not necessarily mutually exclusive:

1. publishing or distributing information about the trial
2. learning information about the case from a source outside of the court
3. contacting parties, witnesses, lawyers or even the judge in the trial
4. discussing the merits of the case or seeking opinions from other people.

The reasons for these forms of misconduct by jury members are numerous and can range from 'a well-intentioned, albeit misplaced, sense of responsibility to ensure that they deliver the right verdict' to an instinctive, impulsive and addictive mode of expression or simple ignorance towards the appropriate conduct and the instructions of the judge (Bartels & Lee 2013: 42).

One of the most well-known examples in recent years is the case of juror Joanne Fraill, who was sentenced by London's High Court to eight months imprisonment in 2011 for contempt, after she exchanged Facebook messages with the accused in a criminal trial. Fraill had also searched online for information about another defendant while she and the other jurors were still deliberating (Johnston et al. 2013). In a separate example from the United Kingdom, a juror unsure of her verdict in a child abduction and sexual assault case polled her Facebook friends on whether or not she should find the accused guilty of the crime (Khan 2008). The financial costs associated with the collapse of a court case over juror misconduct resulting from social media misuse can be substantial, with serious implications for the perceived legitimacy and integrity of the criminal justice system and for the parameters of its relationship with new media technologies.

To prevent the potential for juror misconduct, some jurisdictions in Australia and the United States have banned all communications devices from the courtroom and deliberation room (Bartels & Lee 2013). Support has also been voiced for the development of a 'juror misconduct hotline', which would allow members of a jury to report incidences of inappropriate behaviour and/or the misuse of social media by their fellow jurors (Papadakis 2013). However, this has the potential to cause significant tensions between jury members, including mistrust and concerns about vexatious claims of misconduct, 'preventing free and frank discussion and resulting in ineffective deliberations' (Bartels & Lee 2013: 43). There are also considerable administrative and resourcing costs associated with the development and maintenance of such measures. Other proposed remedies and preventative strategies include questioning prospective jurors about their social media use at the empanelment stage; requiring jurors to take an oath not to use social media throughout the trial and deliberations; the sequestration or isolation of the jury; explicitly prohibiting social media use as part of jury instructions; and improved education for judges and jurors (Krawitz 2012; Bartels & Lee 2013).

The latter extends to better understandings among the judiciary as to how social media works, given the admission that many judges are not as well acquainted with technological trends as those who appear before them, and that many have not embraced social media for themselves (Nelson 2015). According to Melbourne-based lawyer Natalie Hickey (cited in Nelson 2015), this has been borne out in **defamation** cases involving social media where concepts such as 'likes', 'news feeds' and 'walls' on Facebook and 're-tweeting' on Twitter have been foreign and 'perplexing' to many judges, requiring lawyers to submit detailed evidentiary explanations of how social media works. She explains that:

> ... users of Twitter and Instagram will be quite familiar [with the fact] that it's a bit like a ticker-tape feed or stock market prices—it rolls on a scrolling basis—and therefore has a very limited life, even if the data actually exists for a very long time. If you don't explain that to a judge then there is a risk that [they] will attribute a meaning to a tweet that may not actually be there in real life (Hickey cited in Nelson 2015).

Technological change thus can be challenging for those highest placed to make judgments over social harms—an interesting observation in its own right.

CAMERAS IN THE COURTROOM

Just as social media has played an increasingly prominent role in court cases and court–media relations, so too the importance of visual evidence such as photographs, videos, drawings—and the visual mediums of television and webcams—in the courtroom has flourished in the years since famous trials like the O. J. Simpson murder case and the police beating of Rodney King (Feigenson & Spiesel 2009). The former, along with more recent international cases such as the criminal trials of South African sprint runner and convicted murderer Oscar Pistorius (who fatally shot his then-girlfriend, Reeva Steenkamp, in his home in Pretoria on Valentine's Day 2013), and Casey Anthony (discussed in Chapter 1), has been a touchstone for long-standing debates about the merits of live broadcasting of legal proceedings. For 133 days, the trial of O. J. Simpson, a famous gridiron football player accused of stabbing to death his ex-wife Nicole Brown Simpson and her friend Ronald Goldman outside Brown Simpson's Brentwood home in California, dominated cable television in the United States—largely thanks to the Courtroom Television Network (more commonly referred to as Court TV, now truTV)—replacing daytime soap operas and creating a media vortex. It was labelled the 'trial of the century'. The live verdict and acquittal of O. J. Simpson, televised on 3 October 1995, was one of the most-watched events in television history, drawing an estimated audience of over 150 million viewers. Despite the ratings, by the end of the controversial verdict the only thing most people could agree on was that the presence of cameras in the courtroom had aggravated, if not created, the media circus that the case had evolved into (Mitchell 2002). By contrast, the filming of the Oscar Pistorius murder trial was generally positively received—particularly by media outlets (see, for example, Sky News 2014)—lending strength to the case for courts to be opened up to cameras and photographers.

Opinions remain divided on the impacts and influence of a media presence in the courtroom (see Table 4.1). Scholarly evaluations have brought little clarity to the debate by failing to conclusively determine whether cameras in the courtroom positively or negatively influence legal proceedings (see Barber 1985). Much of the research to date has relied on the self-reporting or direct observation of trial participants. 'The difficulty which arises here', write Leishman and Mason (2011: 138), 'is how accurate such perceptions are and how likely it is that legal professionals would admit to being perturbed by the presence of cameras'. Proponents of televised trials argue that cameras in the courtroom support the principle of 'open justice' by educating citizens about the judicial system, thereby improving their knowledge and restoring their confidence in the courts as well as encouraging dialogue on matters of concern (Faubel 2013–14). Opponents counter that televised trials cheapen and commercialise justice by framing news as entertainment and adding a distraction that promotes the posturing of lawyers and affects the behaviours of jurors and trial participants, including witnesses, which may result in a biased jury (Mitchell 2002; Faubel 2013–14; Thaler cited in Raptopoulos 2014). This may be precisely what television audiences want. As James Poniewozik (2011), then-media columnist for *TIME* magazine, wrote in the aftermath of the not-guilty verdict in the 2011 trial of Casey Anthony, accused of murdering her two-year-old daughter, the main lesson for media from the trial coverage was that 'there is no ratings penalty for taking a side. Viewers may want information and analysis, but at least a good chunk of them also want to hear their opinions and judgments declaimed passionately'.

Not surprisingly, some of the greatest resistance towards the widespread introduction of cameras in the courtroom continues to come from judges themselves, who fear being second-guessed and having their judicial authority diminished in the ways that it was for Lance Ito, the judge who presided over the O. J. Simpson murder trial. As Thaler (cited in Raptopoulos 2014) explains:

> He [Ito] was actually very critical of the cameras being there. But, of course, once the cameras were in ... he became infatuated with it. He would reportedly go home and turn multiple television sets on to watch the day's proceedings. I do believe that at the end of the trial, Ito was a broken man in many ways. He realized his case had gotten out of control.

In a 2001 speech to the Commonwealth Legal Education Association, The Hon. Justice Michael Kirby cited the conduct of Judge Ito as one of the setbacks to the widespread introduction of cameras in Australian courtrooms. Part of the concern, he explained, was that 'the media would trivialise the serious business of the courts—presenting short and

TABLE 4.1   Potential benefits and hazards of media presence in the courtroom

Pros	Cons
Educational imperative: informs the public of the workings of the law, police and courts.	The brevity of tweets makes it difficult to convey evidence and arguments accurately, and some court participants can alter their behaviour for the cameras.
Supports the principle of 'open justice' as it enables scrutiny and transparency of the criminal justice system and legal processes.	Can lead to sensationalism and distortion of the trial process, and misperceptions of and disrespect towards criminal justice and police practices, especially if media audiences engage only with the reporting of highlights of a court case.
Engenders a sense of immediacy and dynamism in the reporting of criminal and coronial cases.	Evidence that is challenged and subsequently ruled inadmissible or corrected may have already been tweeted/posted, rendering suppression orders futile.
Facilitates access for individuals who may be involved with or impacted by a case, but are unable to attend court in person.	A witness who is sitting outside a courtroom waiting for their turn to testify might become acquainted with evidence as it is being given by another witness and adjust their own testimony accordingly.

Sources: Adapted from Rodrick 2014, p. 147; and Leishman 2011, p. 133.

unfair "grabs" with the result that the curial issues were misrepresented' (Kirby 2001). Unlike courts in the United States, Canada, New Zealand and the United Kingdom, Australian courts continue to be disinclined to have their proceedings broadcast on television or via live streaming on the internet. The televising of cases in Australia therefore tends to be spasmodic and on an ad hoc or case-by-case basis (Rodrick 2014). There are some exceptions, such as the Supreme Court of Victoria, which audio webcasts selected sentences and judgments and streams them in real-time online, as well as making them available for listening on demand (see www.supremecourt.vic.gov.au). In 2013, the High Court of Australia also announced that it would make recordings of its full court hearings available to the public via its website (High Court of Australia 2013).

ISSUES FOR CONSIDERATION

While we have chosen to focus on news and social media in this chapter, the importance and potential 'media effects' of fictionalised representations of law and order should not be overlooked. Much has been written about the extent to which courtroom dramas and cop shows accurately reflect the realities of the criminal justice system, and the impacts of this on public understandings of policing and the law. Even as we write this book, the second series of the UK television crime drama *Broadchurch*, which focuses on the aftermath of a child's murder in a small, close-knit community and the trial of the murderer, has come under fire from the legal fraternity for its portrayal of courtroom scenes; the criticism so fervent that its writer, Chris Chibnall, was compelled to respond to the critiques in an opinion piece in *The Guardian*. He explains that the creative team wanted to take *Broadchurch* in a different direction from most legal dramas by 'favouring the experience and point of view of the victim's family' (Chibnall 2015). The decision meant that only fragments of the legal process were shown in the courtroom scenes, rather than every witness, objection, legal argument or cross-examination. He writes:

> That choice meant complex procedure had to be compressed. Hospital dramas condense seven-hour operations into two minutes of crisis. Police dramas condense investigations in the same way. Legal procedure is opaque. Murder trials often last around four weeks. So exact process and wording has to be dramatised ... That's not a scandal: it's a legitimate dramatic technique. Drama is not a literal portrayal of events. It's a depiction; it's impressionistic (Chibnall 2015).

This does not mean that fictional representations of law and order cannot and do not take their creative cues from social reality. As news does, so too other mediated representations—including those that are dramatised—can help us understand what Moore (2014: 213) describes as the 'cultural landscape of crime'.

Detective fiction, for example, became 'a recognisable genre at roughly the same point that the prison became a standard form of punishment' (Moore 2014: 214). Similarly, Rabe-Hemp (2011: 134) proposes that the 'rise of community policing has provided female officers the opportunity to adopt skills that have not previously been associated with the traditional crime fighter image of the police'. This has played out on the small screen in the form of a new wave of female-led detective series spearheaded by characters such as Gillian Anderson's DSI Stella Gibson (*The Fall*), Lesley Sharp and Suranne Jones's DCs Janet Scott and Rachel Bailey (*Scott & Bailey*), Sarah Lancashire's Sgt Catherine Cawood (*Happy Valley*), Brenda Blethyn's DCI Vera Stanhope (*Vera*), Sofie Gråbøl's Sarah Lund (*The Killing*) and Sofia Helin's Saga Norén (*The Bridge*). These contemporaries to the old-school 'cops-on-the-box' signal a shift in the predilection of crime television dramas to portray women as 'the abandoned body, the mutilated object on the floor, legs splayed and throat cut and dead eyes staring up at us, the clue that needed solving' (Gerrard 2014). But the question remains to what extent these modern-day representations of gender and policing do so without resorting to stereotyping, role reversal or replacement (i.e. denying sexuality altogether by replacing a man's role with a woman) or suggestions that a woman's success at work in the criminal justice system can only be achieved at the expense of her personal life (Martin 1996).

CONCLUSION

There are myriad more ways in which we could explore the intersections between police, courts and media, but we are constrained here by space and temporality. The repercussions of some issues relevant to the relationship have also yet to fully play out in public and institutional debates. Discussions continue, for example, about the need for legislative reforms and safeguards against inadvertent prejudicial reporting by users—journalists included—of social media both inside and outside the courtroom. So too, the education of judges about social and electronic media as a communications tool and mechanism for community engagement, and the reconciliation of the principle of 'open justice' with social media use, remain unresolved.

Yet, the pace of change is unbridled. New points of contact, opportunities and complications in the relationship between police, courts and media continue to burgeon. The number of articles published online about the emerging trend towards 'true crime' docudramas—exemplified by the highly popular podcast, *Serial* (2014), HBO's television miniseries, *The Jinx* (2015) and Netflix's 10-part series, *Making a Murderer* (2015)—offer a case in point. In each case, audiences have been invited to act as amateur detectives, questioning potential **miscarriages of justice** or, in some cases, justice overlooked. These are mediated representations with real repercussions, particularly for policing and the work of the courts. To its own degree, each series has held a mirror to the imperfections of the criminal justice system. Following the finale of *Serial*, the Maryland Court of Special Appeals filed a motion to allow Adnan Syed—whose murder conviction was the subject of investigation in the podcast's first season—to appeal his sentence and reopen the case. A petition to pardon convicted murderers Steven Avery and Brendan Dassey—the subjects of *Making a Murderer*—received an official response from the White House. Meanwhile, millionaire Robert Durst, who was profiled in *The Jinx*, was arrested for murder on the eve of the airing of the final episode as a result of an investigation stemming from new evidence presented in the miniseries. The final moments of the HBO docudrama capture Durst in an unguarded moment off-camera, having been presented with the new evidence, mumbling to himself: 'What the hell did I do? Killed them all, of course'. At the time, Durst was in the bathroom and seemingly unaware that the microphone he had been wearing for his on-screen interview with filmmaker Andrew Jarecki was still recording. Durst's comments were widely interpreted as a confession to his involvement in the 1982 disappearance of his wife, Kathleen Durst, and the execution-style murder of his close friend, Susan Berman, in Los Angeles in 2000.

According to Jeanine F. Pirro (cited in Bagli & Yee 2015), the former Westchester County district attorney, whose office investigated Kathleen Durst's disappearance for six years, the filmmakers of *The Jinx* did what law enforcement in three states could not do in 30 years. 'Kudos to them', she said. 'They were meticulous. They were focused. They were clear' (Pirro cited in Bagli & Yee 2015). But the question of whether they were ethical has barely been raised. When it has, to date it has mostly been in media commentary, rather than in-depth scholarly analysis. Despite displaying many of the hallmarks of investigative reporting, these new forms of serialised 'true crime' storytelling break many of the standards of ethical journalism, including the ideals of fairness, objectivity, disclosure, and the use of responsible and honest means to obtain materials. They often unashamedly present one-sided perspectives, blurring the lines of entertainment with the pursuit of the truth and loyalty to the public interest with sympathy for their subject(s). In the case of *The Jinx*, there is also reason to question whether the filmmakers should have used Durst's so-called confession—given that he seemingly was not aware the microphone was still switched on—or at least alerted him to their intention to use the audio in the documentary, before it aired (Dockterman 2015). Productions like *Serial*, *The Jinx* and *Making a Murderer* have therefore been criticised for, quite literally, taking the law into their own hands—the argument being, as Leszkiewicz (2016) explains, 'that they could jeopardise ongoing or potential future investigations'. This has direct and indirect implications for police and courts, among which is the 'democratisation of the criminal justice system'. But as Leszkiewicz (2016) asks: 'If audiences are so swayed by these show's subjective narratives, how truly democratic can this be?'. We must ask in return: are they really any different to the invitations currently issued to publics by police to help solve crimes? Remember Mike Pimentel, whom we discussed earlier in this chapter? Is this a classic case of 'protecting one's professional patch'?

The answers to many of these questions are yet to be fully explored and debated. This is, in itself, partly attributable to the constantly evolving and shifting nature of the environment within which police, courts and media operate and engage with one another. As we have shown, some police agencies and members of the judiciary have effectively embraced the pace of change in terms of media trends and technological developments, but many more have been slower to respond. Some of this may be attributable to history, and the general mistrust towards media that has proliferated within policing and legal circles. A cautious approach is not unwarranted. Despite the predominance of official police voices as primary definers of the crime news agenda, not all police officers believe the media always fairly represents them. While police agencies may have become 'more coordinated and better prepared' in their police–media relations, tensions remain within police circles about 'the media and openness' (Mawby 1999: 267).

So too, retired Australian High Court judge, The Hon. Michael Kirby (cited in Schulz 2010: xvi–xvii), has reflected on the damage inflicted on the relationship by increased attacks on the judiciary by mainstream media, which have served to 'damage public confidence in the institutions of law'. He further cites the way in which '[s]erious analysis of the detailed and often tedious work that judges perform has given way, all too often, to infotainment, exaggeration and personality reporting', as well as the misunderstanding and misreporting of court proceedings as a result of reduced numbers of specialised court reporters, and the frequent conflation of facts with comment in courtroom news, as additional reasons for the historical tensions between courts and media (Kirby cited in Schulz 2010: xvi–xvii).

As we have shown in this chapter, emerging media technologies offer media practitioners opportunities to innovatively and creatively construct crime news. They also present both the police and legal fraternity with a proactive means of circumventing (and speaking back to) these representations of the criminal justice system. Yet, as we have also demonstrated, these same tactics and strategies have facilitated the production of counter-frames and resistances to the preferred messages of the police and courts—in some cases, serving to undermine the integrity of the criminal justice system. As Lee and McGovern (2014: 212) observe, 'these attempts at control are imperfect'. Nonetheless, they remain an inevitability, the challenges and opportunities of which need to be negotiated by police, courts and media alike, as they continue to emerge.

DISCUSSION QUESTIONS

1. What are some of the differences between representations of policing in the news, fictional media and documentaries? How have representations changed across time?
2. Are police media units only in the business of producing police 'spin'?
3. How closely do you think most crime television dramas and 'reality' police programs reflect the realities of police work and courtroom proceedings?
4. Should judges be encouraged to make greater use of social media personally and within the courtroom? What are the advantages and disadvantages of doing so?
5. What are the pros and cons of cameras in the courtroom? What are the pros and cons of live streaming of legal proceedings in high-profile criminal cases?

WORKSHOP ACTIVITY: THE RULES OF REPORTING

Conduct an 'audit' of the jurisdiction in which you live (local, state or national) to find out what court rules and legislation journalists are subject to in their reporting of crime news and the law. What and how are journalists allowed to report and communicate publicly? Consider some of the issues discussed in this chapter, including levels of media access to court proceedings and materials, and the use of electronic equipment and social media in the courtroom. Consider also the legal context in which journalists operate by researching issues such as *contempt*, *defamation*, *freedom of information* and *source confidentiality*. You should be able to locate this information through the media policies and practices of courts in your chosen jurisdiction (available on their websites or by contacting the court registry), online free-access legal information sites, journalistic codes of ethics and reporting guidelines, and scholarly texts. Write your findings up in a table and repeat the process for another jurisdiction—compare the results, and discuss. Your audit should include consideration of the following questions:

- How many courts have social media policies?
- Are there differences between courts that deal with criminal matters versus coronial matters? Is one stricter than the other?
- To what extent is 'open justice' realised?
- How similar or different is the legal context for reporters between jurisdictions?

FURTHER READING

Barber, S. R. (1985). Televised Trials: Weighing Advantages against Disadvantages. *The Justice System Journal*, 10(3), 279–91.

Bartels, L. & Lee, J. (2013). Jurors Using Social Media in Our Courts: Challenges and Responses. *Journal of Judicial Administration*, 23(1), 35–57.

Lee, M. & McGovern, A. (2014). *Policing and Media: Public Relations, Simulations and Communications*. London and New York: Routledge.

Mawby, R. C. (2002). *Policing Images: Policing, Communication and Legitimacy*. Cullompton, Devon: Willan Publishing.

Rodrick, S. (2014). Achieving the Aims of Open Justice? The Relationship between the Courts, the Media and the Public. *Deakin Law Review*, 19(3), 123–62.

5

VICTIMS AND OFFENDERS

CHAPTER HIGHLIGHTS

Introduction

Defining victims of crime

Centring the voice of the victim

Victims and media

A walking human headline: Dennis Ferguson

Misinformation and mistaken identities

Conclusion

INTRODUCTION

We often talk about 'victims' and 'offenders' as though they are clearly distinguishable categories—opposites even ('them' and 'us'). But the reality is that such designations are not always quite so distinct or clear-cut, and they are subject to change. What it means to be a 'victim' or 'offender' in a legal sense can also differ from the ways in which individuals see themselves or indeed how society defines them. In the study of crime and its victims and offenders, there are, as Walklate (2013: 79) suggests, 'all kinds of questions to be asked about who, what, and under what conditions, victimisation [or deviance and criminality] is made visible or rendered invisible and by whom'. Insofar as this is the case, we might well ask the question: what are the key social characteristics of those who are presented as 'deviant' and/ or we are supposed to 'fear'? Equally, for whom are we meant to grieve and show compassion when it comes to the experience of crime—the victims?

These questions serve as guiding principles to the content in this chapter, where we explore the argument that, just as crime is a socially constructed problem, so too the concepts of criminality and victimisation are highly mediated in terms of their meaning and application. What makes people 'different' from each other is defined through social processes of **typification** and acknowledgment. Certain groups can be seen as problems in that their actions or appearance seem to disturb the status quo in some fashion. Others may be assumed to be vulnerable and traumatised—and, once again, treated differently—because of harms done to them.

The role of media in this process, particularly journalists, in defining social norms vis-à-vis social difference—that is, determining the visibility and invisibility of particular victims and offenders depending upon social characteristics and background—is significant, as many of the case studies in this chapter attest. We start, therefore, with an exploration of the normative definitions of 'victims' and 'offenders' in order to see how they are manifested through mediated representation. As part of this analysis, we are interested in the conditions under which such definitions can be contested and made complicated compared to mainstream media's constructions of 'victims' and 'offenders'.

DEFINING VICTIMS OF CRIME

The online *Oxford Dictionary of English* offers several interpretations of the word 'victim':

1. A person harmed, injured, or killed as a result of a crime, accident, or other event or action: '*victims of domestic violence*', '*earthquake victims*'.
2. A person who is tricked or duped: '*the victim of a hoax*'.
3. A person who has come to feel helpless and passive in the face of misfortune or ill-treatment: '*I saw myself as a victim*', '*a victim mentality*'.
4. A living creature killed as a religious sacrifice: '*sacrificial victims for the ritual festivals*'.

Criminal victimisation, however, is a far more complicated process than such definitions suggest. The contexts in which the word 'victim' are now accepted (or rejected) and how victim status is defined are manifold. Until recently, the word 'victim' was associated with someone who was sacrificed to a deity or supernatural force. It was also used to describe someone who was subjected to torture or put to death. Not until the nineteenth century did the term come to include experiences of harm or injury (Furedi 2002; Spalek 2006). This expansion in the conceptualisation of victimisation raises questions about the extent to which we are *all* potential victims now; encouraged to feel excessively fearful and vulnerable and to perceive ourselves as increasingly 'at risk'. As Walklate (2009: 6) observes in the aftermath of global events such as 9/11 and the Mumbai, India terrorist attacks of November 2008, the extensive media coverage of these 'new terrorism' crimes makes it 'difficult to escape an appreciation of the pain and the impact that they cause'. She explains: 'Media images of hostages, videotapes of beheadings, at the scene broadcasts of terrorist acts … are all intended to move us, to encourage us to place ourselves next to the victim' (Walklate 2009: 13). For Furedi (2002: 96), such developments reflect the way in which the world we live in is now defined by a 'culture of victimhood' where the 'public exposure of inner pain has become a highly prized cultural artefact'.

This is not to diminish the toll that criminal acts can and do take on people's emotions and well-being. Rather, it is to highlight the increasing visibility of the victim identity in modern society. As Furedi (2002: 100) explains:

> In the past, people who suffered from a particular violent incident did not identify themselves as victims … Even when people felt badly hurt and deeply aggrieved, their

own self-identity was not defined by the experience. In contrast, today there is a belief that victimhood affects us for life—it becomes a crucial element of our identity … Society encourages those who suffer from a crime or tragedy to invest their loss with special meaning.

While discourses about victims tend to focus on those individuals who directly experience a crime and are therefore most immediately impacted (i.e. **primary victims**), victimhood in its contemporary sense has expanded this conceptualisation to include the indirect victim (Furedi 2002). This term refers to the fact that crimes are highly traumatic events whose effects can stretch far beyond the primary victim. People who are first responders or witnesses to crime, family members, friends, neighbours, whole communities—even journalists who are routinely exposed to the vicarious suffering of others via their reporting practices—can also suffer harms and trauma from crime. They become what are known as **secondary victims** (White & Perrone 2015). Victimisation, therefore, has the capacity to affect people both directly in terms of actual harm and indirectly through fear of crime and experiences of vicarious trauma. However, statistical accounts do not always adequately capture the full range of these experiences, and can therefore understate the true extent of harm and victimisation within and across communities.

STATISTICAL ACCOUNTS OF CRIME VICTIMISATION

In Australia, for example, there is no single source of data that provides a comprehensive picture of crime victimisation. Rather, as White and Perrone (2015: 117) explain, 'there are multiple sources of data relating to different aspects of victimisation'. These include:

- national data collected from administrative records and state/territory agencies
- household and business surveys on crime victimisation and personal safety
- police records of reported offences
- data recorded through the criminal justice system
- results of academic studies on victimhood.

While in aggregate these data sources have the capacity to show a 'significant and wide-ranging experience of victimisation' (White & Perrone 2015: 117), each has its limitations, demonstrating that barriers to the accurate reporting of crime victimisation do exist. For example, police data captures only those criminal offences that have been brought to the attention of police. As we know, not all crimes are reported, especially for certain categories of offence, such as sexual assault and domestic and family violence.

What statistical datasets tell us about rates of victimisation can also operate separately from the ways in which victims are routinely characterised within media. As Greer (2007) points out, the voices of victims that resonate the strongest and are amplified by and within mainstream media represent only a fraction of those who experience criminal victimisation. Statistics show, for example, that males continue to be over-represented as victims of homicide in Australia. But this is not necessarily the picture painted by mediated representations of these crimes, which more frequently portray women as homicide victims.

Yet, according to statistics from the Australian Institute of Criminology (2015), of the 511 homicide victims in 2010–11 and 2011–12, 328 (or 64 per cent) were male; the exception being intimate partner violence, where women still constitute the majority of victims. These disparities point to the fact that 'becoming a victim is neither simple nor straightforward' (Walklate 2007: 28). Acquiring the label 'victim' is a complex process that to some extent requires an individual's victimisation to be acknowledged by others (McGarry & Walklate 2015). Writes Furedi (2002: 98): 'People who have had bad or traumatic experiences do not think of themselves as victims unless society defines them in that way'. Even then, for some, the characterisation is not a welcome one.

THE LABELLING PROCESS: 'VICTIMS' AND 'OFFENDERS'

Who or what is defined as a 'victim' or 'offender' is often instructed by and reflected through representations and news frames constructed within and by mainstream media as well as other factors, including cultural context, social divisions, personal beliefs and even the accepted norms of particular moments in time. In the same way as 'visible representations that are mediated to us of crime in society become *the* crime problem in society ... these representations [of victims and offenders] become unitary, exclusive and dominant' (Davies 2011: 41). Offender status, Davies (2011: 39) observes, is 'readily conferred upon some and victim status is equally conferred upon others'. What this false dichotomy of 'victim' and 'offender' fails to acknowledge, however, is the fluidity and contestability of such designations. Women subjected to intimate partner violence who kill their abusing partners, for instance, demonstrate that the same person may occupy both designations simultaneously (White & Perrone 2015). So too, an individual conferred a particular status can subsequently be re-labelled, shifting from 'victim' to 'villain' or from 'guilty' to 'innocent'. The latter is obvious in miscarriages of justice, such as those detailed in the documentaries *Central Park Five* (2012) and *West of Memphis* (2012), where the juveniles convicted for each crime, were, decades later, found innocent on the basis of DNA evidence. Unlike some of the cases we detail later in the chapter, in these instances media campaigns served to function in favour of those initially labelled as 'offenders'.

But research also tells us that it is possible for the victim to become the victimiser. Repeat offenders, for example, will often start off as victims themselves, especially in the case of violence and sexual abuse (White & Perrone 2015). Then, there are examples like the case of Peter Kleinig in Western Australia (WA) who, as the victim of online investment fraud, became the offender by recruiting others into the scam. Despite interventions from the WA Police advising him that he was involved in fraud, and legal action from the WA Department of Commerce, Kleinig refused to believe the investment scheme was a scam. His story is not uncommon among victims of these types of crimes, who often ignore warnings and advice given to them about their participation in suspected fraud because of the 'high levels of trust and rapport established between victims and offenders, where the offender has used an array of tricks to manipulate the victim into complying with financial requests' (Cross 2016).

'For many victims', writes Cross (2016), 'it is not just the financial losses they must deal with, but the additional trauma of offending behaviour, whether through their own deliberate actions or through their trust in their offender(s)'.

Kleinig's story reminds us that not all individuals self-identify with the status of 'victim', despite being labelled as such within their wider social arena. The application of victim status tends to be loaded with negative connotations, such as weakness, passivity and a general lack of agency (just as the application of offender status tends to be loaded with its own negative associations). This process of labelling can have stigmatising and disempowering effects, especially in societies where individual strength is valued (Spalek 2006). In response, some individuals have advocated for the use of alternative terms, such as 'survivor' (as opposed to 'victim'), in relation to experiences of crime, the argument being that 'imposing a strong, positive label on those subjected to harm will enhance their resilience and ability to regain control and power over their lives' (White & Perrone 2015: 137). Feminists, in particular, have preferred the use of the term 'survivors' of rape and/or incest, rather than 'victims'. 'This new terminology', write White and Perrone (2015: 137), 'is forward focused, implying that the status of victim is not fixed, but can be changed'.

Nonetheless, in terms of its populist application, the victim/offender dichotomy tends not to reflect such fluidity. For example, it can obscure the fact that individuals engaged in illicit activities (i.e. those who commit offences) may sometimes be genuinely deserving of protection from harm. Karmen (2010) cites the example of prostitutes, where the harms they experience—such as regular beatings from sadistic clients and being robbed on the streets or exploited by their pimps or madams—may be more serious than the offences they commit, such as soliciting in public places. Should prostitutes therefore be considered victims, who need support, or offenders who should be punished? Is there room to consider them as both? Examples like these give credence to McGarry and Walklate's (2015: 8) argument that the terms 'victim' and 'offender' are inappropriate since their use 'potentially assigns guilt and/or innocence to participants in a process in which the outcome has yet to be determined'. For this reason, Karmen (2010: 8) proposes that the designations of 'victim' and 'offender' should be 'pictured as overlapping categories somewhere near the middle of a continuum bounded by complete innocence and full legal responsibility'.

CENTRING THE VOICE OF THE VICTIM

Although victimisation dates back to the evolution of humanity itself, 'the systematic study of victims is relatively new' (White & Perrone 2015: 116). The term '**victimology**' was coined in 1947 by Benjamin Mendelsohn, an Israeli lawyer, and not long after became drawn into the discipline of criminology by Hans von Hentig, a German criminologist (White & Perrone 2015). Since its inception, victimology has grown from a relatively nebulous set of concepts and interests into a key area of concern within criminology (Jaishankar 2008). Victimologists, first and foremost, investigate the victim's plight: 'the impact of the injuries and losses inflicted by offenders on the people they target' (Karmen 2010: 2). More than this, their studies also take in broader concerns about societal conceptualisations of the 'victim'; victimisation profiles and risk distribution for various categories of crime; the impacts and fears of victims over time; causative theories on victimisation; and the relationship between victims and offenders. As summarised in Box 5.1, there are three main approaches to the study of victims and their patterns of victimisation.

BOX 5.1

VICTIMOLOGY AND ITS APPROACHES

- *Positivist victimology:* Informed by the idea that crime and victims exist in an 'objective' sense; the implication being that victimisation can be measured simply by observation and/or scientific methods (e.g. victimisation surveys).
  - Victim status is determined by criminal law or is self-evident (visible suffering) and does not extend to offenders.
  - Identifies factors relating to the potential risk of victimisation.
  - Concentrates on violent interpersonal crimes and certain types of property crimes, rather than crimes of the powerful.
- *Left-realist victimology:* Primarily concerned with the gaps in mainstream victim surveys, and with documenting particular types of victimisation.
  - Presumes that the law determines who counts as a victim.
  - Places crime victims at the centre of the research gaze in a manner that provides more precise information about the nature of victimisation.
  - Broadens the definition and scope of questions about crime by tapping into issues such as corporate crime and environmental harms.
- *Critical victimology:* Looks at victimisation as a social process, and examines how victims are created by the operation of institutions and particular forms of interaction. Victimhood is contingent upon who is doing the labelling, and how the labels are applied.
  - Concerned with uncovering the power relations that underpin how institutions confer victim status, and ignore or silence other kinds of harms by protecting the perpetrator.
  - Broader conceptualisation of crime, which includes human rights abuses.
  - Moves beyond simple descriptive categories, such as 'victim' and 'offender', to view human behaviour in the light of situational and structural contexts (e.g. who suffers from so-called victimless crimes like prostitution).

Source: White & Perrone 2015, pp. 136–7.

Another area of concern for victimologists is the ways in which crime victims are treated and dealt with by the criminal justice system. In recent times, victims have taken on a more prominent role, resulting in what has become known as 'victim-centred justice' (Goodey 2005). This is an evolving phenomenon, spurred on by victim dissatisfaction with the ability of the law to represent their experiences, the lack of participatory opportunities within the criminal justice system, and the failure of both the courts and perpetrators to acknowledge the true extent of the harms experienced (White & Perrone 2015). Within the criminal justice system, a number of initiatives have been introduced worldwide to improve **procedural justice** and the standing of victims across the pre-trial stage, at trial and during sentencing. As elaborated by White and Perrone (2015: 131), these victim-oriented services and forms of participation include:

- *Victim notification:* Victims are kept informed of the developments in the case and the hearing date, as well as court decisions relating to offender sentencing and re-entry into the community post-release from prison.
- *Victim impact statements (VISs):* These are written statements made by victims and/or their families, and are introduced to the court at the sentencing stage. VISs are designed to elucidate the victim's experiences and feelings on the harms caused by the offending. In some cases, these statements may be provided verbally in court.
- *Court orientation:* Victims are introduced to the court system so that they are able to identify the main players and feel comfortable with the court layout. Support may also be provided to victims in the form of transportation to and from the court, and 'handholding' or 'escorting' to ensure victims are not left alone and have someone to refer to throughout court proceedings.
- *Compensation:* Some forms of physical and emotional injury may be compensated via state agencies such as a crimes compensation tribunal. Alternatively, victims may receive compensation either through civil or criminal proceedings, where a court orders that compensation be paid.
- *Victim-offender mediation:* These are programs aimed at involving the victim in direct contact with the offender so that the offender can see the harm caused, and so that victims and offenders can jointly be involved in attempts to resolve the harm that has been perpetrated. This is also known as **restorative justice**.
- *General support services:* These include counselling services, youth and women's refuges and alcohol and drug services, and are focused towards both the immediate and longer-term needs of the victim(s).

Many of these victim-centred initiatives form an integral part of **victim rights**. In Australia, these have traditionally been a matter for state and territory governments, which have variously enshrined such rights in charters, declarations and legislation. As a result, the information, services and practical assistance provided have varied across jurisdictions, although more recent attempts have been made to standardise the responses to victims of crime—irrespective of where the crime occurred or where the victim lives. While charters and their implementation may vary between jurisdictions, they nonetheless share some common and fundamental principles that 'underpin an effective framework for good policy and practice in supporting victims of crime in Australia' (Standing Council on Law and Justice 2013: 3). These broadly include the right of crime victims to:

- be treated with courtesy, compassion and respect
- information about, and access to, welfare, health, counselling and legal services, where available
- information about the investigation and prosecution of the offender
- protection from the offender and protection of privacy.

As explored next, the latter has not always been maintained when it comes to the interactions of media with victims of crime.

VICTIMS AND MEDIA

In earlier chapters we established that news reporting of crime and its offenders is selective (consider, for example, the differences between media coverage of 'street crimes' versus '**suite crimes**', otherwise known as 'white collar crime'). So too, news media representations of *crime victims* can also be selective. As Greer (2007: 21) reminds us, in recent decades victims have assumed 'an unprecedented significance in media and criminal justice discourses, in the development of crime policy, and in the popular imagination'. But, in keeping with the selectivity of crime news reporting, not all victims are treated as equal within media.

Resources are most often allocated to covering victims who are considered 'ideal'. Christie (1986: 18) describes the '**ideal victim**' as 'a person or category of individuals who—when hit by crime—most readily are given the complete and legitimate status of being a victim'. People who are perceived as vulnerable, innocent or worthy of compassion (i.e. deserving) typically fit the bill—for example, children and the elderly. Those who do not fit this category include individuals who are perceived as 'undeserving victims'—for example, individuals with a criminal past or a history of habitual violence. Terms such as these are problematic in their own right. Still, it remains the case that the differential status arising from perceptions of particular types of crimes and crime victims creates 'a pecking order of sorts' (Greer 2007: 23). This is what Carrabine et al. (2004) refer to as a **hierarchy of victimisation**, where 'ideal victims' are positioned at the top and those perceived as less deserving of crime victim status (and as less vulnerable) sit at the bottom (see Figure 5.1 over the page).

Others, such as the victims of white-collar crime, may be obscured altogether within the hierarchy because they are not easily or individually identifiable, making it difficult to fit them within established media frames and news narratives of victimisation. As Greer (2007: 38) explains: 'Due to the difficult to prove and frequently diffuse nature of the harm caused by white-collar and corporate victimization, these offences … do not arouse the same

FIGURE 5.1 The Hierarchy of Victimisation

levels of fear and moral indignation as offences of interpersonal violence'. In comparison, individuals who fit the status of 'ideal victim' attract 'massive levels of media attention, generate collective mourning on a near global scale, and drive significant change to social and criminal justice policy and practice' (Greer 2007: 22).

It would be an overstatement to suggest that the media attention afforded to 'ideal victims' inevitably leads to political and legislative reforms in every instance. But it is often 'instrumental in publicly defining the cases, rooting the victims' images in the popular imagination, generating and focusing collective moral outrage and support for change, and, crucially, keeping the stories alive in both political and popular consciousness'—in some cases, long after the initial investigations have closed (Greer 2007: 33).

A clear example of this is the way in which—facilitated, in part, by the sustained media coverage around her story—Rosie Batty became a public advocate for victims of domestic and family violence in Australia, following the death of her 11-year-old son, Luke Batty, at the hands of his father. Batty rose to public prominence the morning after her son's death in February 2014 when, clearly grief-stricken, she calmly addressed the media outside her house, and started a national conversation about domestic and family violence in Australia. As author Helen Garner (2014), who interviewed Batty several months later, puts it: 'It wasn't so much what she said as her demeanour that stopped people in their tracks. There was something splendid about her, in her quiet devastation. Everyone who saw her was moved, and fascinated. People talked about her with a kind of awe'. Over the following months, Batty took no prisoners; publicly expressing her frustrations with both the government agencies whose job it is to protect women and children, and the systemic failures in responses to domestic and family violence. Her public profile was instrumental in helping to establish the state-based Royal Commission into Family Violence in Victoria and, in 2015, she was named Australian of the Year. At the time, then-Victoria Police Chief

Commissioner Ken Lay described her as the most 'remarkable victim' he had ever met (cited in National Australia Day Council 2015). Batty has been credited with activating the political leadership exhibited around the country to bring domestic and family violence to the fore (including significant funding promises), as well as the increased rates of women reporting, seeking support for and leaving abusive relationships (Medhora 2016). In many respects, Rosie Batty epitomises the phenomenon noted by Greer (2007: 32–3), who writes: 'When crime victims come symbolically to represent a problem that resonates with and potentially affects many in society—school safety, racist violence, knife crime [or, in this case, domestic and family violence]—mediatized campaigns, particularly when launched in the victim's name, are likely to garner high levels of public support'.

Rosie Batty's story is an example of how the shifting contours of victimhood have impacted on journalistic practice, as reflected by the renewed salience of victims and their personal trauma narratives as primary definers of news stories (see Rentschler 2011). More than this, however, Batty's story is an example of the ways in which the 'ripple effects' that Greer (2007) describes in relation to the public, political and legislative response to 'ideal victims' can often only be achieved as a result of the *willingness* of victims to actively engage with media. This can be a treacherous enterprise for individuals, who may not have had previous dealings with journalists, and who suddenly find themselves the centre of media attention. For this reason, crime victim support agencies in a number of jurisdictions, including Canada, the United Kingdom and Australia, have developed booklets to inform victims of their rights in dealing with media, including presenting them with the permission to say 'no' to requests for interview. *A Guide to the Media for Victims of Crime*, which is produced by Victims Services, NSW Department of Justice, cautions, for example, that there are arguments for and against talking to the media. On the one hand, doing so may raise 'awareness of the crime and prevent such events occurring again' while also offering an opportunity to publicly pay tribute to anyone who has died as a consequence of the crime (Victims Services 2014: 10). On the other hand, the guide warns that '[w]ithout media training or support from media experts, statements you make to the media may be misrepresented and can often impact negatively on an investigation' or the family and friends of the deceased (Victims Services 2014: 13).

In essence, booklets like *A Guide to the Media for Victims of Crime* are a lesson in media literacy for crime victims, helping them to become more 'media savvy' as a result of enhanced understandings of media practices and related issues, such as the:

- definition of 'public interest' as it relates to journalism
- ways in which media will approach crime victims for interview
- questions that media will typically ask crime victims
- benefits and risks in talking to journalists
- potential impacts on a police investigation
- types and amounts of information that media can legally report on at different points in time after a crime has been committed (see Victims Services 2014).

However, as Greer (2007) points out, the attribution (or otherwise) of 'ideal victim' status and the levels of media attention a victim's story receives will also be influenced by other moderating factors, such as social divisions, including class, race, gender, age and sexuality (Greer 2007). A comparative analysis of the media coverage of the deaths of Lisa Harnum and Keeli Dutton perfectly illustrates these observations (see Box 5.2).

BOX 5.2

WHOSE LIFE IS MORE GRIEVABLE?

In November 2013, Australians woke to the news that Simon Gittany had been found guilty of murdering his fiancée, 30-year-old Lisa Harnum, more than two years earlier by throwing her off the balcony of their 15th-floor apartment in central Sydney. On the same day as crowds packed the courtroom to witness the guilty verdict, the lifeless body of 41-year-old Keeli Dutton was lying on the floor of the western Sydney apartment she shared with partner, David Murray. Murray had stabbed Dutton seven times in the back and left her to bleed to death. The couple's housemate reported him to police the following evening, after Murray had confessed to him about the crime. Police subsequently located Murray, who was bleaching the apartment, while Dutton's body lay wrapped in sheets in the bedroom (*R v Murray* [2015]).

In Australia, at least one woman dies each week as a result of intimate partner violence, often after a history of domestic and family violence (Australian Human Rights Commission 2015). Each death is a significant loss, but not every victim gains the same media attention as that witnessed in the Lisa Harnum case. While news headlines were consumed by commentary about Harnum's tragic death, the murder of Keeli Dutton barely rated a mention. There were no books written about her murder as there were about Lisa Harnum's, no cash-for-comment interviews with individuals involved in the case, and none of the painstaking recreations of the crime for prime-time television viewing. How can we explain this disparity and the value judgments that appear to pervade it? The question is ethically and politically significant, because as Butler (2009: 14) puts it: 'Only under conditions in which the loss would matter does the value of the life appear'. From a media criminology perspective, the answer lies, at least in part, with the 'dominant conceptions of legitimate and ideal victims' (Greer 2007: 23).

In many respects, Lisa Harnum was the archetypal 'ideal victim'; she was young, white and photogenic, a creative and outgoing woman who had, according to friends, transformed into a Sydney socialite after falling in love with Gittany, who was considered dominant, controlling and violent. The story of their relationship, by all accounts, was defined by the very hallmarks of newsworthiness: conflict and drama. An article from *The Daily Telegraph* newspaper, published during the murder trial, summed it up with the headline: 'New pictures show smouldering beauty of Lisa Harnum as Simon Gittany admits he was a "jealous partner"' (Dale 2013). The intrigue of the case continued into the murder trial itself with a cast of colourful characters on display as well as a catalogue of harrowing evidence, including secret pinhole camera footage of the final moments of Harnum's life and her desperate bid to escape the apartment. The grainy still images from the closed-circuit television (CCTV) footage became as much a visual symbol for the case as the personal portraits of a smiling Harnum in happier times. As Greer (2007: 31) points out, photographs serve to humanise crime victims, 'adding a sense of the "real" to that which may otherwise remain abstract and difficult to latch on to or invest in emotionally'. Access to these visuals made the story of Lisa Harnum's death even more newsworthy.

By contrast, the story of Keeli Dutton was far less glamorous or accessible. The scene of the crime was not an expensive inner-city high-rise apartment, but a housing commission block almost 40 kilometres from Sydney's central business district in a suburb of some ill repute. There were no social media snapshots depicting a socialite lifestyle (in fact, an internet search reveals few news visuals of Dutton compared to those of Harnum). Instead, Dutton was a troubled mother of three, who had battled drug and alcohol problems for over a decade and had taken out an apprehended violence order against her partner not long before her death. Despite the news selectivity evident between the two cases, Dutton's story is ironically more the norm than the exception. As Speers (2015), a television reporter, wrote in the months before Murray was sentenced to 25 years imprisonment for Dutton's murder:

> So far this year, thirty three Australian women have died violent, unnecessary deaths. I am a journalist, who is married to a journalist. We practically live and breathe news. So why haven't I heard of two thirds of these women? I think I can tell you why … The news media tell stories they think people want, or need, to know. There are ways of gauging an audience's interest. And apparently, most of us just don't want to know about what goes on behind closed doors. Perhaps we think it's none of our business. Or maybe there's a lingering feeling among some, that the victims bring the violence upon themselves.

While victim participation is generally now seen as an important component in both the criminal justice system and the media's reporting of high-profile crimes, there are nonetheless 'a number of practical difficulties that have emerged as victims have been brought back into the process and given a voice' (White & Perrone 2015: 132). One of the most prominent challenges is the way in which victims' rights are often framed as only being able to be met at the expense of, or as a result of constraints upon, offender rights (White & Perrone 2015). The issue of offender rights is a controversial topic in and of itself (and certainly not a vote-winner), as demonstrated by the case of 'Australia's most hated man'—child sex offender Dennis Ferguson—and the media-inspired moral panic that erupted in the wake of attempts to reintegrate him into the community post-imprisonment.

A WALKING HUMAN HEADLINE: DENNIS FERGUSON

From the time of his release from his longest prison sentence in 2003 to his death in late 2012, Dennis Ferguson was the subject of numerous and sustained media campaigns in Australia. The dynamics of each of these episodes were remarkably familiar. As Grealy (2014: 40) explains:

> Ferguson would leave prison or previous accommodation to be settled into a new home; the media would discover this and alert his neighbours; the community would protest his presence alongside negative news coverage and talk-back radio condemnation; politicians would enter the fray; and Ferguson would be moved on, on occasion subject to new law and over time driving new approaches to post-imprisonment sex offender management.

The latter included the NSW Government's rushed introduction of new legislation, in 2009, to allow the relocation of paedophiles in public housing. This followed a campaign against Ferguson, who was at the time living in Ryde, in Sydney's north-west. At the height of the hysteria, a neighbour delivered a replica coffin to the front door of Ferguson's apartment, saying: 'Apparently you will only leave in a pine box, well we are a very caring community and we've made you one' (Killgallon cited in Kleinig, Walters & Dale 2009). The details of these hostile encounters as a result of attempts to reintegrate Ferguson featured in a 2009 episode of the ABC's *Four Corners* program titled 'Facing Dennis Ferguson' (ABC TV 2009). It was one of the few times that Ferguson had agreed to be interviewed by media (in this case, reporter Liz Jackson). The *Four Corners* episode claimed that the media frenzy he had been subjected to had been 'instrumental in heightening the community backlash against Ferguson, whenever he moved, and wherever he went' (Little 2013: 117). It was a point not lost on another ABC television program—*Media Watch*—which, the year before, had similarly argued that Ferguson was being 'thoroughly demonised' by mainstream media (ABC TV 2008). In short, says Little (2013: 117), Australian media had 'set upon Ferguson—who had no skills in dealing with the media—as a loathed criminal'.

The story of Dennis Ferguson is, in some respects, not at all exceptional: the child sex offender boasts 'a long lineage as an object of media representation and public protest' (Grealy 2014: 42). In the late nineteenth century, discourse about these individuals framed them as 'sex fiends' and 'degenerates'; by the late twentieth century, the depiction had shifted to 'sexually violent predators' and conceptions of 'dangerous non-familial offenders' and 'paedophilic strangers' (Grealy 2014). In the twenty-first century, Ferguson had become the public face of paedophilia in Australia—a metonym for sex offenders everywhere—and an ongoing governmental problem (Grealy 2014). He had been jailed for 14 years in 1988 for kidnapping three children and violating them in a Brisbane motel—not his first offence against children—and had been driven out of several Queensland communities on release from prison, before being relocated to New South Wales (Black 2009). Ferguson was, by his own accounts, a victim of child sexual abuse and suffered post-traumatic stress disorder from a lifetime of beatings and victimisation. His physical characteristics (nervous tics, wild hair, peculiar gait and aggressive outbursts) and disability (he was legally blind) served to enable and support the portrayal of Ferguson in a manner consistent with the conventional media framing of sex offenders—he was depicted as inherently evil, perverse, pathological, violent, destructive, cunning, bestial, lacking contrition and sub-human (see Kitzinger 2004; Meyer 2007). One notable front-page from the *Gold Coast Bulletin* newspaper in 2008 featured the headline 'Dob in this Monster', alongside a photograph of Ferguson, and called for readers to help get him 'locked away and to keep our children safe' (cited in ABC TV 2008). As Grealy (2014: 52–3) argues, Ferguson was positioned as 'the antithesis of childhood innocence'—and the vulnerabilities of the communities he inhabited—and his proximity to children was considered sufficient enough to 'victimise local children'.

Nothing can diminish the fact that the crimes Ferguson committed involved abhorrent and hugely traumatising experiences for his victims. But the question remains as to whether the Australian mainstream media's treatment of Ferguson constituted a breach in the balance between the need to report issues in the public interest and the right to privacy and dignity. The latter is enshrined in the Australian Media Entertainment & Arts Alliance (MEAA) Journalist Code of Ethics: 'Respect private grief and personal privacy. Journalists have the right to resist compulsion to intrude' (Media Entertainment & Arts Alliance 2015). Such principles are tempered by conditions involving substantial advancement of the public interest or where there is risk of substantial harm to people; in which case, the standards may be overridden. But this is not the only reason, says Little (2013: 113), 'why journalists should resist the impulse to side with the public protests and rail against his [Ferguson's] attempts to live in the community'. She explains: 'In the classical ethics model, no one would base that kind of decision on a utilitarian approach, but in the history of the Australian media's coverage of similar stories, we have seen what can happen when they do (see, for example, the Lindy Chamberlain case ...)' (Little 2013: 113). Here, we cannot escape the fact that one of the first rules of ethical journalistic practice is to 'do no harm'—to either the subjects of news stories or their wider communities. This applies to all, not just non-offenders. In this respect, fear-mongering in its own right, but especially in relation to highly sensitive issues such as child sexual abuse, can be extremely harmful (see Box 5.3).

BOX 5.3

CONSTRUCTIONS OF CRIMINALITY—CAN YOU SPOT A PAEDOPHILE?

Contraventions of the principles of ethical journalism in the reporting of news stories related to offenders can inadvertently impact on societal and individual safety and well-being, reinforcing inaccurate stereotypes of offenders, identifying some offenders as an exceptional population, and elevating the public's sense of anxiety or 'moral panic' about the visibility or invisibility of particular offenders. More significantly, such approaches can re-traumatise victims of crime. In September 2013, an article appeared on one of Australia's most-read websites, news.com.au (owned by News Limited), with the headline: 'Could You Spot a Paedophile? Here are the Warning Signs'. After an introduction, which effectively portrayed child sex offenders as anyone (albeit almost always men), anywhere, waiting to strike at any time, the news.com.au article assured readers that paedophiles are 'easy to pick', because they typically fall into one of nine categories or 'types' of offenders:

- the everyman
- child-related workers
- happy snappers
- close relatives and partners
- the gift-giver
- the always available babysitter
- the internet groomer
- the damaged
- the good-looking charmer.

To illustrate the point, the article included photographs of convicted child sex offenders (see news.com.au 2013a).

Perhaps not surprisingly, the news.com.au article attracted both controversy and criticism, including a complaint to the Australian Press Council (APC), which is responsible for promoting good standards of media practice, community access to information of public interest, and freedom of expression through the media. The complainants argued that the comments under the category, 'The damaged'—in particular, the warning to readers to beware of anyone with a history of sexual victimisation—were inaccurate, deeply offensive and served to marginalise victims and discourage them from speaking out (APC 2014). The APC agreed, upholding the complaint. It declared the section of the story 'so gravely offensive that it breached its principle requiring publications to balance the public interest with the sensitivities of readers' (APC 2014). The offending sections of text were subsequently deleted from the article, although the article itself remained available online.

Its updated iteration featured a link to both the APC's adjudication and the full written response from Dr Cathy Kezelman, President of Adults Surviving Child Abuse, who had publicly criticised the article for its lack of tact and sensitivity. In her response, Kezelman (cited in news.com.au 2013b) argued that the 'challenge for those reporting or speaking about child abuse in the public arena is how to increase community awareness while minimising the risks of re-traumatisation for those affected and secondary traumatisation for members of the community'. She cautioned:

> Child sexual abuse evokes very strong emotions in those bearing witness. It's normal to feel shocked and disgusted, horrified and angry, devastated and numb. It is important therefore to keep to the facts and educate rather than use information and images which invoke fear, in what is already an emotionally-charged issue (Kezelman cited in news.com.au 2013b).

In Dennis Ferguson's case, 'generalised anxieties about childhood innocence, child sexual abuse, risk-conscious parenting, and crises of faith in the criminal justice systems' were all projected onto him (Grealy 2014: 40). This is despite the fact that, in 2009, Ferguson was one of over 2000 released sex offenders monitored by NSW police (ABC TV 2009). But, as Grealy (2014: 39) notes, arguments made on behalf of Ferguson's rights to freedom and safe accommodation 'were considered rather abstract, when pitted against the immediate threat Ferguson was deemed to embody'. Because of his media visibility and the ability to identify Ferguson, it was easy for the public to despise and repeatedly condemn him (Grealy 2014). This resulted in an adversarial rights dilemma: whether to privilege the rights of the individual, who had by law completed the punishment meted out for his past crimes, or the rights and interests of the community to feel protected (Grealy 2014). Following his death, Hetty Johnston from the child advocacy group, Bravehearts, told media there would be no tears shed over Ferguson's death: '2013 is going to be a safer place without Dennis Ferguson', she said (Johnston cited in Nicholls 2012).

MISINFORMATION AND MISTAKEN IDENTITIES

While Dennis Ferguson had the opportunity for his day in court, in other instances the guilt ascribed to individuals may result without criminal evidence, or legal judgment, to support the attribution of such labels. Their 'guilt' may be a mediated phenomenon. It is not uncommon for publics to speculate and draw their own conclusions about a person's guilt or innocence in relation to a crime, often before their status has been determined in a court of law. We know this, because we have seen it happen time and again, particularly in the digital age—for example, with Sunil Tripathi, the American student who was wrongfully accused on social media as a suspect in the Boston Marathon bombings in April 2013. Tripathi had gone missing in the month prior to the bombings, which added fuel to the online theories about his involvement in the crime. The media frenzy, which erupted after Tripathi's identification by digital sleuths on sites such as Reddit, 4chan, Facebook and Twitter, only abated once the actual perpetrators of the crime—brothers Dzhokhar and Tamerlan Tsarnaev—had been identified and apprehended. Tripathi's body was later discovered in the waters off India Point Park in Providence, Rhode Island, and his death determined a suicide. This only served to compound the grief and trauma already experienced by his family as a consequence of the overzealousness of the online vigilantes.

As this case demonstrates, mainstream media can also play a part in contributing to such harms. As we mentioned earlier in the chapter, news media campaigns can work in favour of individuals misidentified as offenders (e.g. facilitating favourable outcomes to miscarriages of justice) and in public efforts to bring suspected offenders to heel (see, for example, the highly risky front-page published by the *Daily Mail* in 1997, which accused five men of the racist murder of black teenager Stephen Lawrence in the United Kingdom). But, equally so, media campaigns can serve to work against the interests of the innocent, particularly where public perceptions are informed by media misinformation (see Box 5.4). The consequences can be dire.

BOX 5.4

VANESSA ROBINSON: A MOTHER UNDER SUSPICION

In late May 2010, Vanessa Robinson's sons Chase and Tyler, aged nine and seven, were found deceased in their Mooroopna home, north of Melbourne. Vanessa Robinson was also found ill, distressed and disoriented, and was transferred to hospital. As soon as news of the tragedy broke, she became the subject of media and public suspicion, sparked by an otherwise innocuous and routine media release from Victoria Police (2010), which in part read:

> Police are investigating the suspicious death of two boys in Mooroopna this evening ... A 29-year-old Mooroopna woman is currently assisting police with their enquiries. Homicide detectives are en route to the scene.

While homicide does not necessarily equate to murder, this 'police speak' was (mis)interpreted as suggesting the investigation into the deaths of the boys was because foul play was involved. A television news report from 31 May reported as much, calling the deaths of the two boys a 'suspected murder', saying that police would not confirm whether Robinson 'may have tried to kill herself' (Dart Centre Asia Pacific 2014).

Other news reports said the deaths of the two boys had come after a 'bitter separation' between Robinson and her husband, Scott Robinson. On 1 June, Susie O'Brien (2010) of the *Herald Sun* wrote in an opinion piece:

> I don't care what difficulty you are going through as a parent, how depressed you might be or how much you hate your former partner. Get professional help. But protect your kids at all costs ... all my goodwill evaporates when I hear of children who have been harmed.

In truth, Vanessa Robinson and her husband had separated, but not bitterly, as some news media outlets had suggested. There was no estrangement between the two. Nor had Robinson harmed the children or herself in a murder-suicide attempt, as had been implied (Dart Centre Asia Pacific 2014). In fact, Robinson was unaware of the speculation and innuendo surrounding her within news media and on social media, because she was recovering in a hospital bed from carbon monoxide poisoning, and later shock. Police had determined that the tragedy had been the result of a faulty gas heater, which had been emitting the colourless and odourless carbon monoxide for several days at 500 times the safe limit; killing the boys and badly affecting their mother.

The framing of her as a murderous mother had profound 'framing effects' for Vanessa Robinson, including the intrusion on her grief and privacy, damage to her reputation and the pain of secondary victimisation. The return to her local community after what had happened was particularly difficult, she says, because she did not have her boys, she did not have a place to live, and she could tell people were talking about her and judging her—that, regardless of the facts, they considered her capable of the crime. She recalls:

> I was disgusted (by the media reports); I still can't look at them. I had reporters at my children's school the morning of the accident, telling them what I had

allegedly done to my children, to teachers and parents... I was basically treated as a criminal and I felt that the media took away the fact that I was a good mother to my children, never negligent, me and my children were a happy little family and that was all taken away from me. It still affects me today (Robinson cited in Dart Centre Asia Pacific 2014).

While Robinson's story is a lesson in what can happen when the media misinform publics, and misrepresent someone as a criminal, it is also an example of the way in which media frames can shift over time, and victims of media misrepresentation can use those same platforms to 'speak back' and lobby for change. Within three years of the deaths of her sons, Robinson had launched The Chase and Tyler Foundation to raise awareness of carbon monoxide poisoning and to advocate for legislative change to require safer monitoring and maintenance of domestic gas appliances. She and Scott Robinson also became the public faces of Energy Safe Victoria's 'Carbon Monoxide—The Silent Killer' awareness campaign. Nonetheless, the implications of Robinson's story are clear: being incorrectly branded an offender in the process of 'trial by media' can have devastating consequences for those who are the subject of such matters, as well as their loved ones.

These widespread assumptions, as shaped and informed by mainstream media frames, reflect what is commonly known as 'trial by media', a 'dynamic, impact-driven, news media-led process by which individuals—who may or may not be publicly known—are tried and sentenced in the "court of public opinion"' (Greer & McLaughlin 2012: 138). As the definition suggests, the term 'trial by media' is most commonly invoked in situations where the implication is one of guilt rather than innocence. 'In each case', write Greer and McLaughlin (2012: 138), 'the news media behave as a proxy for "public opinion" and seek to exercise parallel functions of "justice" to fulfil a role perceived to lie beyond the interests or capabilities of formal institutional authority'. One of the dangers of this rush to judgment— apart from the reputational damage it can inflict on innocent individuals, their families and their friends—is that it has the potential to elide serious and detailed considerations of risk, prevalence and causation in terms of offending by resorting to misconceptions and media stereotypes. This may, in part, be a consequence of the fact that a 'key element in the construction of a compelling crime narrative is the attribution of responsibility' (Greer 2007: 32)—the need to blame someone (i.e. an individual, the offender) or something (e.g. society, a person's upbringing, institutional influences, sometimes even media itself) for the crime. Sue Klebold (2016), the mother of one of the perpetrators of the Columbine High School massacre in Colorado in 1999, refers to precisely this phenomenon in her recollections of the aftermath of the tragedy. She writes:

> In the aftermath of Columbine, the world's judgment was understandably swift: Dylan [her son] was a monster. But that conclusion was also misleading, because it tied up too neatly a far more confounding reality. Like all mythologies, this belief that Dylan was a monster served a deeper purpose: people needed to believe they would recognize

evil in their midst. Monsters are unmistakable; you would know a monster if you saw one, wouldn't you? If Dylan was a fiend whose heedless parents had permitted their disturbed, raging teen to amass a weapons cache right under their noses, then the tragedy—horrible as it was—had no relevance to ordinary moms and dads in their own living rooms, their own children tucked snugly into soft beds upstairs. The events might be heartbreaking, but they were also remote (Klebold 2016: 60–1).

Mediated representations of victims and offenders thus serve more purposes than simply that of 'truth'—but at what cost?

WHEN CHILDREN KILL (OTHER CHILDREN)

The public can have trouble accepting that juveniles have the capacity to commit crimes of such a heinous nature. This is despite the fact that, as Allard (2016) points out, such crimes are not as uncommon as one might think. Statistics from the Australian Institute of Criminology's National Homicide Monitoring Program show that 83 people under the age of 18 years were charged with homicide in the five years to 2012, equating to around 16 murders by juveniles in Australia each year of the reporting period. Of these offenders, around 12 per cent were aged 14 years or younger. For the majority, their trials are conducted 'away from the scrutiny of the media' (Allard 2016)—sometimes due to legal restrictions related to the identification of juvenile offenders. But, for a select few, like Bronson Blessington, who was 14 years old when he participated in the abduction, rape and murder of Sydney woman Janine Balding, and the killers of James Bulger (see also Chapter 7), the gravity of their crimes can destabilise constructions of childhood and the 'innocence of youth'; provoking intense media interest, debates about criminal responsibility (whether children are born bad or turned bad through their own experiences of brutality), and even acts of public hostility and vigilantism—particularly where the case involves child-on-child homicide. These crimes, in particular, raise questions about how young offenders should be treated in the criminal justice system (see Box 5.5).

BOX 5.5

COMPARATIVE RESPONSES TO CHILDREN WHO KILL CHILDREN— UNITED KINGDOM AND NORWAY

In 1993, in the United Kingdom, two 10-year-old boys killed a two-year-old boy. When James Bulger's killers, Robert Thompson and Jon Venables, made their first appearance at the South Sefton Magistrates' Court two days after being charged with the crime, a crowd of hundreds turned out to condemn them. Some threw rocks and eggs at the windowless transport van; six people were arrested (Green 2008). The concerns catalysed by the Bulger case led to an increasingly punitive 'law and order' platform in the United Kingdom, including the introduction of the *Criminal Justice and Public Order Act 1994*, which among other things lowered the age at which a child could receive an indeterminate sentence from 14 years to 10 years (Green 2008). The killing of James Bulger was also a media sensation, and was repeatedly invoked in subsequent news stories across the world about crimes involving children. Media interest in the case surged in 2001 when both Thompson and Venables were released with new identities, having served their minimum eight-year sentences, and again in 2010 when it was reported that Venables had been jailed a second time on child pornography charges (he was released on parole in 2013).

By contrast, far fewer people heard about five-year-old Silje Marie Redergård, who was killed the year after James Bulger in the Heimdal borough of Norway's third largest city of Trondheim by three six-year-old boys, while they were playing together in the first snow of the season. In a comparative analysis of the two cases, Green (2008) highlights key differences in the public, political and mediated responses to each crime. Being below the age of criminal responsibility (15 years) in Norway, the boys involved in the killing of Redergård were neither prosecuted nor punished. Compared to the Bulger case, there was 'no mass outpouring of anger or outrage from the family, the community, or the press, no cries for vigilante justice, and no political manoeuvring by any party's politicians to politicize the incident' (Green 2008: 7). Instead, the boys were successfully reintegrated into the community by teams of social workers and psychologists to avoid **stigmatisation**. While Green (2008: 7) found that press coverage of Redergård's death was substantial, media interest was confined to the first week of the case with the incident framed as 'a tragic accident, a terrible aberration, a non-criminal act in every sense, perpetrated by innocents on the innocent'. By contrast, photographs of Thompson and Venables were plastered across the front pages of UK newspapers with headlines describing them as 'evil' and 'freaks of nature'.

As Green (2008) points out, the reactions of the families as dominant claims-makers within the news (i.e. primary definers) played an important role in how the Bulger and Redergård cases were constructed, as well as the public and political responses to them. The subdued response to the Redergård case (consistent with responses to crime in Norway more generally) allowed it to drift from collective memory, compared to the sustained saliency of the Bulger case, where the family remained outspoken about their belief that Thompson and Venables had not been sufficiently punished for their actions. These frames defined the terms of engagement for each crime; the Bulger case was constructed predominantly as a criminal justice issue, while the Redergård case was framed as a child welfare issue. And, as we know from framing theory, the definition of 'problems' within news media can dictate their 'solutions'. As Green (2008: 131) explains:

> If the cause is evil, then the solution is the removal of the evil. If the causes are multifaceted and cumulative, then the solutions are not so easy to prescribe and there are no simple means by which members of society can be made to feel at ease. When the debate is affectively bound, engagement with it must also begin at the emotional level ... Dramatic and emotional rhetoric tends to shut out much else by heating up the climate.

Like a number of other important aspects of the media–crime nexus—including the dynamics of social constructions of gendered offending and ethnicity and deviancy (which we explore in more detail in later chapters)—the question of what to do with juvenile offenders and why we respond in the ways that we do remains an ongoing focus of public debate, political negotiation and criminological study.

THE CULT OF CELEBRITY-CRIMINALITY

Lesser-examined—perhaps because of biases towards its lesser solemnity as a topic of scholarly analysis and critical discussion—is the phenomenon of 'celebrity-criminality'. Where once celebrity was associated with talent and ability, increasingly it has become synonymous with attracting media attention—even if it is only 15 minutes of fame—giving strength to the prospect of 'being famous for being infamous'. While studies have sought to examine the phenomenon of celebrity scandal and the transgressions of established public identities (see, for example, Hinerman 1997; Lumby 1999; Gies 2011), less has been written about transgression as a path to celebrity. This is despite evidence to support the idea that the 'perverse, violent and subversive nature of crime' can stimulate 'public resonance', allowing publics to live vicariously through the actions and behaviours of criminals (Penfold-Mounce 2009: 70). This has paved the way for 'ordinary' criminal identities to become household names in a manner that was once reserved for the most serious and stylised of offenders, such as gangsters and serial killers. According to Rojek (2001: 154), it has also resulted in the perpetuation of violent acts for the sake of notoriety, with convicted criminals confessing to using murder 'as a vehicle to acquire celebrity'. This parallels what Yar (2012) describes as the **'will-to-representation'**, whereby individuals stage criminal exploits for the camera, which are then uploaded and disseminated online (see Chapter 11). Coupled with the increasing popularity of true crime as a genre, which has been criticised for turning 'criminals and their activities into a species of entertainment' (Gregg & Wilson 2010: 414–15), it is not difficult to see why concerns have been raised about the glamorisation and commodification of crime, and the role of media as unwitting agents or accomplices in the perpetuation of the 'cult of celebrity-criminality'. We need only look to the case of Jeremy Meeks for evidence of this in operation.

Dubbed the 'hot convict' and 'handsome felon', Meeks became an internet sensation when his mugshot went viral after being posted on the Stockton Police Department's Facebook page in the United States in June 2014, following his arrest on weapons charges. The original booking photo of Meeks attracted more than 50 000 likes with women sending messages that promised to assist with Meeks's bail (Queally 2015). A separate community Facebook page featured Photoshopped images of Meeks as comic book heroes, including Captain America and Wolverine, as well as images of Meeks's mugshot superimposed onto the bodies of James Bond and Calvin Klein models. Despite being sentenced to up to two years in prison for his crimes, Meeks was signed by talent agency White Cross Management in 2015, while still behind bars, with plans to forge a modelling career on his release (Balthaser 2015). News of Meeks's online popularity sent internet users into a frenzy, with searches conducted for other 'ridiculously photogenic' criminal offenders. The lists developed were subsequently published on entertainment and news websites.

ISSUES FOR CONSIDERATION

The message from many of these case studies is that mainstream media can help to sustain public sympathy around crime victims as much as it can further victimise and shape public thinking about how society should respond to offenders. There are some obvious instances where the victims and offenders involved, and our preconceptions about these individuals, can intensify and even complicate our responses to crime. For example, deaths in police custody or beyond prison walls can evoke less public sympathy than similar deaths outside the system (although there are some exceptions, such as when the deaths are a consequence of police misconduct or excessive use of force). For example, when a fellow prisoner fatally bashed convicted murderer and drug trafficker Carl Williams in prison, some social media users hailed his death as a cash bonanza for taxpayers, given that they would no longer have to pay to house him in Barwon Prison. Others saw the underworld figure's death as a burden on television programming, when the Nine Network in Australia cancelled a scheduled episode of *Top Gear* to screen a documentary about Williams's life and crimes instead. In a similar vein, news stories about police killed in the line of duty will often be more sensitively and favourably framed (towards the police officer) than many other conventional news stories about frontline policing. Of course, the other obvious instance in which our responses to crime can be seen to be more complex and confronted is when children kill.

CONCLUSION

The lesson that the cases explored within this chapter teach us—both entertaining and confronting as they are in nature—is that media frames can produce real framing effects. This is true for both victims and offenders, and has particular resonance within contemporary society, where public perceptions of social difference can be shaped rapidly within and by online communities, and can bring out the worst in people. Sometimes favourable, news framing effects can also be potentially harmful and damaging in their own right—especially where the reporting and representation that underpins them lacks substance, clarity or context. Therefore, journalists, too, can fit the designation of 'offender' status as much as they may be 'secondary victims' of the experiences of crime as a consequence of their routine media practices. While mainstream media may scrutinise power, so too they exercise it and they should therefore likewise be held responsible and accountable (Media Entertainment & Arts Alliance 2015).

In exploring the social processes that work towards the 'making' of victims and offenders, our emphasis in this chapter has been on individuals. This should not obscure the fact that victimisation is not always a solitary enterprise, but can also be a collective experience. So too, crime victims can include non-humans, such as businesses, animals and the environment. In these instances, the offences committed are less likely to be reminiscent of the interpersonal violence described throughout the chapter, and more akin to those of a systemic and institutional nature. Such issues demand that we acknowledge the state, corporations and even ourselves as potential perpetrators of harm. They also require us to confront some of the stereotypes of victimhood and criminality, which are constructed socially and through conventional media images of victimisation and offending. How these emphases might, in turn, reinforce the fear of crime and serve to legitimate or de-legitimate (silence) suffering, is also an issue of policy and political relevance (Snell & Tombs 2011; Walklate 2012). Even in the context of visible harm, the nature of the construction of victimhood and criminality is highly fluid and contestable.

DISCUSSION QUESTIONS

1. How have constructions of criminality and victimhood changed over time?
2. What are some of the challenges faced by the criminal justice system in balancing the rights of victims with those of offenders?
3. In what ways can engaging with media be a benefit and a risk to victims of crime, and also offenders? What are some of the practical constraints?
4. Conduct your own research on the murders of James Bulger and Silje Marie Redergård. What factors, other than media coverage, do you think influenced the contrasting responses to these child-on-child homicides in the United Kingdom and Norway?
5. Can you locate any recent examples where individuals or groups, traditionally subject to typification as victims or offenders, have used media to counter these stereotypical representations and insert their own voices into the narrative?

WORKSHOP ACTIVITY: STATISTICAL VERSUS SELF-REPORTED DEFINITIONS OF VICTIMISATION

In terms of crime measurements and statistical analyses, 'victims' are defined differently, according to the offence category. As we know, this can deviate from the ways in which victim status is attributed in media representations, ascribed in the literature, and defined by individuals with lived experience of crime. Locate the most recent statistical dataset for 'Recorded Crime—Victims, Australia' on the Australian Bureau of Statistics (ABS) website <www.abs.gov.au>.

Note down the definitions of 'victim' for the following offence categories:

- homicide and related offences
- sexual assault
- kidnapping and abduction
- robbery
- blackmail and extortion
- motor vehicle theft.

Repeat the process using the 'Crime Victimisation, Australia' statistical dataset, also available on the ABS website. What do you notice? How do the definitions of victims from the first statistical dataset compare to the self-reported rates of crime victimisation? What are some of the challenges you can identify in terms of collecting and reporting data about crime rates and levels of victimisation? How do you think these statistics might compare to similar data on state and territory police websites?

FURTHER READING

Furedi, F. (2002). *Culture of Fear* (revised edition). London and New York: Continuum.

Goodey, J. (2005). *Victims and Victimology: Research, Policy and Practice*. London: Pearson Longman.

Greer, C. (2007). News Media, Victims and Crime. In P. Davies, P. Francis & C. Greer (eds), *Victims, Crime and Society*. London: SAGE Publications, pp. 20–49.

Kitzinger, J. (2004). *Framing Abuse: Media Influence and Public Understanding of Sexual Violence against Children.* London and Ann Arbor, MI: Pluto Press.

Walklate, S. (2013). Victims, Trauma, Testimony. *Nottingham Law Journal*, 22, 77–89.

6

PRISONS AND INNOVATIVE JUSTICE

CHAPTER HIGHLIGHTS

Introduction

Background: Prisons as bad news

Counter-frames of imprisonment

Criminological concepts and media portrayals

Conclusion

INTRODUCTION

Typically, prisons are presented in mainstream media as either being 'too soft' or 'too hard'. Austere interiors, grey walls, bars, over-crowded cells, too-hot and too-cold environments are contrasted with images of recreational spaces that are filled with televisions, pool tables, completely fitted-out gymnasiums, libraries and nutritious food. The 'reality' is much more complicated and variable, as are local conditions and facilities.

Similarly, the framing of prisoners within media discourse involves categorisations that, on the one hand, portray inmates as justifiably objects of punishment, the civil dead, who deserve whatever they encounter while inside and, on the other hand, as subjects with a humanity of their own, who experience mental and physical strains, who are victims in their own right and who deserve the chance to make good.

Responses to what occurs within prisons reveal significant ambivalence over the institutions and the people who live and work inside them. Gross miscarriages of justice, as with the extensive use of torture in Abu Ghraib prison in Iraq and the US prison at Guantanamo Bay, Cuba, frequently call forth disgust and reprobation (see Box 6.1). Yet, the ordinary brutalities of mass imprisonment and **hyperincarceration** rarely present as problematic. As long as the punishment is not seen as extreme, public sentiment is that people get what they deserve.

BOX 6.1

IMPRISONMENT AND TORTURE

The normalisation of torture and mistreatment is apparent at both the level of specific institutional practices and in regard to overarching government policy. American responses to the 'War on Terror' are indicative of this:

> On 28 April 2004, Americans were shocked to see the first pictures of U.S. soldiers humiliating and torturing detainees at Abu Ghraib prison in Iraq. The pictures have since taken on iconic status: an Iraqi detainee draped in a hood and poncho, standing on a box, his arms outstretched, with wires attached to his extremities and genitals; a bored-looking female American solider holding a naked Iraqi detainee lying at the end of a leash; naked and even dead Iraqi detainees in a variety of positions with American soldiers laughing and flashing thumbs up (Brody 2005: 144).

What happened at Abu Ghraib prison, while extreme, is symptomatic of policies adopted by the US Government in response to the terrorist events of September 11, 2001. These policies included the practice of 'extreme rendition' in which US Government agents seize a person who is believed to have ties to terrorist activities and transport them to another country where they will be tortured (Geis & DiMento 2012). They also included officially approved interrogation methods for the Guantanamo Bay prison such as placing detainees in painful stress positions, hooding them, stripping them of their clothes, and scaring them with guard dogs (Roth 2005). 'Waterboarding', a torture technique in which the victim is made to believe they will drown, was also actively used and defended under the George W. Bush regime. A recent US Senate report (United States Senate Select Committee on Intelligence 2014) suggests that many of these sorts of practices continued under Barack Obama's administration, contrary to the sentiment expressed in the banning of waterboarding by the same government.

How we *think* and how we *feel* about offenders and their punishment is socially and historically constructed. For example, the removal of punishment from the public sphere— apparent in the shift from the public spectacles to the use of closed institutions such as prisons (see Foucault 1975/1991; Cohen 1985)—has resulted in a tempering of the empathetic response towards those who commit crime. 'Out of sight, out of mind' translates into scant public knowledge about the suffering that occurs within prison. Neo-liberal values and principles that emphasise personal responsibility (for welfare, education, employment and obeying laws) further reinforce the lack of compassion for offenders, while simultaneously downplaying the need for structural responses to crime such as reducing unemployment rates or addressing the negative legacies of colonialism (Cunneen et al. 2013). Media frames can play a major part in determining 'what counts' in terms of public perceptions of punishment, welfare and personal and national security, and the emotions accompanying these perceptions.

In this chapter, we examine the ways in which crime news involving prisons oscillates between 'bad news' and 'good news' frames, depending upon broader contexts, such as the event, the stakeholders and media involved. In the main, news media frames imprisonment in very particular and, more often than not, inaccurate and negative ways, although examples do exist of more positive frames, which provide a counter to conventional reporting. How this functions forms part of the discussions that follow, where we also link these latter media portrayals and their more positive framing to particular concepts within criminology, which are presently at the forefront of policy and practitioner interest.

BACKGROUND: PRISONS AS BAD NEWS

The 'bad news' story is the epitome of most crime news reporting and fictional accounts of crime, offenders and imprisonment:

> Exciting successes and good news stories are somewhat rare in the field of criminology and criminal justice. Media representations and academic analyses have a tendency to emphasise the sad and the bad, the explosive event and the pervading sense of crisis (Graham & White 2015: 1).

Indeed, this sort of 'bad news' framing permeates mainstream news media when it comes to issues of crime and justice. Typical crime news stories focus on street crime, and the overarching message in both factual and fictional media narratives is that crime is basically about 'bad people' and the 'immoral acts' they perpetrate (often on 'innocents'). The reasons for this tendency are varied, but they include the simple observation that 'bad news' gets people's attention in a more profound manner than 'good news'. Such framing can arouse strong emotions, and subsequently is longer remembered, forgotten at a slower pace, and frequently associated with mental 'pictures' that have lasting effects (Shoemaker & Reese 2014). This is not surprising, given that 'bad news' is also largely about 'risk' and 'threat'.

Street crime, for example, is associated with personal terror and fear, and violence is seen as central. Crime is sensationalised, with important implications for the fear of crime among certain sections of the population. This fear is heightened by the way in which crime is seen to be random in nature, with anyone and everyone a possible target for victimisation. As well, there is often the idea that crime is related to morality, and specifically to the decline of that morality. What is 'wrong' is plain for all to see. Furthermore, the 'criminal' is distinctive, and identifiably different from everyone else in society. Overall, the idea is that there is a continuing 'law-and-order' problem in society, and that things are constantly getting worse.

Hogg and Brown (1998: 21) have identified the key assumptions in what they refer to as *law and order commonsense*. These include assumptions that:

- crime rates are soaring
- crime is worse than ever
- the criminal justice system is soft on crime
- the criminal justice system is loaded in favour of criminals

- there should be more police
- police should have more powers
- courts should deliver tougher penalties
- greater retribution against offenders will satisfy victims' demands.

These elements of 'law and order commonsense' form part of the routine reporting by mainstream news media on issues of crime and criminal justice.

A similar process occurs in respect to media coverage of prison issues. The normal rhythms and routines of imprisonment are generally not considered newsworthy, while unusual events, such as prison riots and prisoner escapes, constitute the staple of much media attention. Even where routine practices within prison are clearly aberrant and abnormal relative to life outside prison, these are rarely treated as of substantive media interest—unless, for instance, prisoners die in circumstances that warrant particular interest. Prison rape, for example, is frequently treated as a source of mirth rather than an abhorrent criminal act. Popular discourse and media frames thus reinforce the notion that rape in prison is simply part of the commonsense reality of prisons, an implicit deterrent factor and always a readymade source of jokes about prison (Minogue 2011). Sustained analysis of mediated representations of prisons indicates that these constructions contribute to popular misunderstandings about the nature of the prison as an institution and also underpin continued public support for an institution that demonstrably fails to either rehabilitate or deter (Mason 2005; White & Graham 2010).

As noted in previous chapters, what journalists communicate about prisons and the experiences of imprisonment is to some extent bounded by the medium itself:

> Journalists have to create stories that fit the technical needs of their newspaper, radio, television station, or website. For example, they may have to write a story of a particular length or duration, that can be understood by a particular audience, or that balances other stories being created for the same broadcast (Bloustien & Israel 2003: 41).

Likewise, journalists select stories about prison within the parameters of newsworthiness (or the 'news values') consistent with most crime news (see Chapter 3). These criteria do not always translate into 'bad news' frames. However, the inclination and tendency is towards precisely this. In part, this is due to the manner in which selling crime news is intended to generate audiences and reinforce revenues. As Bloustien and Israel (2003: 54) explain, 'the reporting of real crime has drawn increasingly upon the conventions of entertainment, tabloid media and reality TV programming. The result has been greater reliance on drama, graphics, sensationalism and a narrowing focus on particular kinds of criminal behaviour'.

Fear of crime is particularly profitable for those who have something to sell. For news media organisations, that 'something' is often fear itself, since this is a major generator of interest, and hence income. Stories aimed at mobilising deep-seated anxieties in the public are hard to ignore, and people will pay to find out about those apparent and alleged threats and risks which—while frightening to know—are nonetheless seemingly present in their lives. In a prisons context, fear is generally associated with presentations of the inmate as 'Other'—that is, a monster, a beast, a creature intrinsically considered 'dangerous'. This image is, in turn, reinforced by the separation of the offender from the rest of society.

DANGEROUSNESS AND MAKING THE INVISIBLE VISIBLE

Although the prison appears to be an intrinsic and permanent feature of our justice system (Tonry 2004), a historical review of punishment reveals that before the eighteenth century it was but one component (and by no means the most important one) in the punishment apparatus, and its purpose was vastly different from that ascribed to it today (Smart 1976; Morris & Rothman 1998).

Here, a major distinction can be made between punishment directed at the body and punishment directed at the mind of the offender. In the early days of the medieval period, for example, punishment was principally physical in nature and, since it was for the most part a public affair, it conspicuously attacked bodily integrity (Foucault 1975/1991; Spierenburg 1995). Depending upon the gravity of the offence, the courts had a wide range of punitive measures at their disposal, which Spierenburg (1995) divides into five categories of escalating severity:

- *Flogging (whipping)*: the most common form of corporal punishment.
- *Branding*: with red-hot irons or heated swords; this process inevitably resulted in a scar that permanently assigned the affected individual a criminal status.
- *Mutilation*: ranging from an incision in the cheek to blinding, and to the amputation of an ear (the most common form of mutilation), a thumb or an entire hand.
- *Merciful instant death*: including beheading, hanging (the gallows) and garrotting (strangulation).
- *Prolonged death*: that is, death preceded by torture; forms of punishment in this category included the use of horses to rip the offender's limbs apart, the throwing of offenders to beasts, burning to death, breaking on the wheel (a process where the offender had their bones broken with an iron bar prior to being stabbed in the heart), and crucifixion. Though unquestionably gruesome, such extreme forms of punishment were exceptional, and reserved for those who had committed the most heinous offences.

In addition to these forms of punishment, European jurisdictions also customarily practised judicial torture as a means of 'assisting' the inquisitorial process. Confessions were sought through, among other things, forced drinking, the application of shin or thumb screws, use of the rack, and the hanging of weights from the toes of suspected offenders (Spierenburg 1995).

It is obvious that punishment was historically designed to subject offenders to pain, but it also exposed them to public humiliation and shaming, as demonstrated by images of people in stocks and pillories situated in market squares, and the use of banishment (the forced expulsion of an offender from their community, and their relocation to a remote destination). The process of execution was particularly theatrical, often staged as a spectacle, complete with audience and detailed illustrated accounts. The ceremonial nature of the execution ritual served to intensify the shaming process, for the condemned person was subjected to a number of publicly degrading acts both before and after the execution. For example, they were marched through the streets as part of an execution procession, with church bells heralding the event, and the corpses of selected offenders were displayed in public places (such as a gallows field) until they decomposed, as a means of public warning (Spierenburg 1995; Linebaugh 2003). As the right to punish was directly vested in the authority of the king during this time, public displays of torture, execution and humiliation ultimately served to affirm the monarch's authority to rule and to punish. Crimes committed during this period were considered a personal affront to the monarchs themselves rather than crimes against the public good.

Between the early seventeenth and mid-eighteenth centuries in Europe, society began to witness a gradual decline in the use of corporal and capital punishment, especially in the case of less serious offences. The preoccupation with barbarous inflictions on the body of the offender was steadily replaced with a concern to alter behaviour by focusing on the mind. In accounting for this change in judicial focus, the influence of public opinion cannot be underestimated. While the spectacle of torture and death was formerly a popular event among the lower classes, over time it became so routine and distasteful that it offended 'a new sensibility about pain and bodily integrity' (Morris & Rothman 1998: viii).

As punishments began to conflict too acutely with the community's moral sense, the general population started identifying with the condemned, and juries consequently began refusing to convict offenders (Lewis 1953). Moreover, executions became occasions to vent expressions of public revulsion and to mock the law; for example, convicts were cheered and individuals who had been put on public display in stocks were liberated (Spierenburg 1995).

The declining confidence in public punishment prompted a move in the early modern period towards conducting punishment in seclusion; that is, *away from the public eye*. This transition from the public to the private was achieved through a variety of less spectacular punishments, such as fines, orders to keep the peace, or banishment. However, the use of penal bondage eventually triumphed, since it permitted punishment to be administered behind closed walls. Although incarceration took many forms (e.g. workhouses, transportation and imprisonment), in essence it served to deprive offenders of their liberty, separating them involuntarily from the outside world through a process of physical confinement (Spierenburg 1995).

These changes in deviancy control were identified by French philosopher Michel Foucault (1975/1991), who brought them into sharp relief by comparing two very different styles of punishment. In the first instance—a public execution in Paris in 1757—punishment was enacted through an extended ritual of atrocities in which the body of the condemned man was utterly destroyed beneath a display of authorised violence (consider, for example, the final scenes in the film *Braveheart*). In the second instance, some 80 years later in Paris, the punishment took a very different form. This time, it took place in silence, and in private, and proceeded without any overt ceremony or violence.

As noted by Cohen (1985), major shifts also took place within punishment regimes, most notably the separation of the prisoner from the rest of society (see Box 6.2). Like the history of punishment and imprisonment generally, these transformations have not been uniform or exclusive—for example, harm to the physical integrity of the prisoner still occurs intentionally in some countries, under some conditions. The exercise of the death penalty and the 'legitimate' use of torture as part of criminal justice provide evidence that the physical body still features in many punishment regimes worldwide. Moreover, even when not explicitly condoned or endorsed, the failure to provide duty of care within prison settings is itself indicative of the continuing violence perpetrated against prisoners.

BOX 6.2

TRANSFORMATIONS OF PUNISHMENT REGIMES

State involvement: from weak and arbitrary, to strong and centralised.
Place of control: from 'open' and in the community, to 'closed', segregated institutions.
Visibility of control: from public and 'spectacular', to invisible and inside.
Categorisation of offenders: from hardly developed at all, to considerable differentiation.
Professional dominance: from not at all present, to established and strengthened.
Object of intervention: from external behaviour and the 'body', to internal states and the 'mind' or 'soul'.

Source: Adapted from Cohen 1985, pp. 16–17.

Nonetheless, the separation of prisoners physically from the rest of the community reinforces the essential differences between 'good' and 'evil'. How this is done is also important to consider. This is because connotations of **dangerousness** are tied up with the architecture of the prison system itself. The notion of dangerousness is reinforced through the segregation of the 'dangerous' prison population from the rest of the community. High walls and razor wire reinforce the idea that the 'animals' are kept at bay only through intensive security arrangements. This 'othering' is enhanced by the ordinary processes of criminal justice.

The 'dangerousness' of offenders, for example, is constructed in and through the ways in which the criminal justice system processes them. The criminal justice system determines whether an offender is dangerous on the basis of three criteria (Morris & Miller 1985; Morris 1994):

- *Anamnestic prediction:* a person is perceived to be dangerous based on the seriousness and/or circumstances of the offence committed (what the offender has already done), and extrapolations from their past record of criminal activity, especially demonstrations of violent and dangerous tendencies, regarding future offending (what the offender is likely to do in the future).

- *Actuarial prediction:* a person is perceived to be dangerous on the basis of how similar individuals in comparable circumstances to them have behaved in the past—it is deemed likely they will behave as others did.
- *Clinical prediction:* a person is classified as dangerous on the intuitive judgment of professionals who have access to the offender's social history and relevant psychological and medical records.

While the first category bases its predictions entirely upon actual behaviour, in the second category, statistical prediction is based upon what other people with similar characteristics have done. In the third category, predictions are based on a professional or 'expert' analysis, and the likelihood of dangerousness upon an understanding of the offender as an individual.

The problem with concentrating on notions of dangerousness, and viewing the prison as the institution of the dangerous, lies in its generalisability—that is, the implication that all prisoners acquire the reputation of being dangerous. This still applies even when the invisible has been made more visible through mediated representation and emerging media technologies. The prison world, today, is more open to scrutiny than it was in the eras described by Foucault (1975/1991) and Cohen (1985) insofar as mobile phones, cameras, computers and microphones have provided platforms that can intrude into and communicate out of any sphere of social life, including prisons. However, as Cheliotis (2010: 170) asserts, this does not necessarily translate into a more rounded or more truthful view of prisoners and imprisonment:

> ... the mediated visibility of the prison couples with that of crime to naturalise, moralise and perpetuate the physical marginalisation of convict populations. The danger of criminal victimisation is gravely exaggerated, socially weak groups are constructed as prime target for punitive intervention from state agencies, local communities and private individuals, the prison system comes under severe criticism purportedly for coddling hardened criminals, panics are raised over the need for more and harsher punishment, whilst the imagery of human suffering so caused is either blocked or neutralised.

Examples of the construction of mediated dangerousness support these claims to some degree. Television series and movies, for example, often depict prisoners as smouldering with rage and malice (see, for example, *Oz* and *Wentworth*). This image applies also to release—if a person has spent time in prison then they must be dangerous. As Mason (2006: 263) puts it: 'Prison drama rarely provides a condemnation of the penal system, preferring instead to revert to its generic stereotype and revel in the stabbings, rapes and beatings between, and of, prisoners, whom it constructs as psychotic, violent and beyond redemption'. Such representations are drawn upon in support of populist, highly punitive penal policy.

It is important here to recall the generally non-violent profile of most prisoners before they enter into prison life (White & Graham 2010; Graham & White 2015). It is also imperative to make a distinction between those people who have a record of actual serious violent offending, and those who do not. Furthermore, we need to distinguish between a specific criminological understanding of the term 'dangerousness', which speaks to actual violent behaviour, and the more populist notion of 'dangerousness', which implies being a risk or threat to others or a problem in some way to institutional authorities, but which does not refer to formally defined serious and repeat violent offending. Dangerousness in the first instance is determined via the courts and the sentencing process. In the latter case, the idea of dangerousness refers more to overall threatening behaviour, rather than specific incidents. It is the perceived threat posed by offenders generally that is at the heart of much of the imagery associated with the prison.

The ideology of dangerousness, which becomes ingrained in the very constitution of prisons as walled edifices housing dangerous people, supports and sustains the ill treatment of prisoners. If inmates are assumed to be 'bad' and 'dangerous', then what happens to them is seen as either necessary (regardless of the brutality) or deserved (because of their deprived state). The concept of dangerousness, when attached to persons in a prison setting (most of whom have committed 'street' crime rather than 'suite' crime), thus serves to dehumanise the inmates and strip away their rights to criticise and make political demands. It is hardly likely, for example, that persons who have been classified and defined as dangerous will be listened to when they claim abuse or the infringement of rights.

The fact that prisons are generally 'closed' institutions means that most people have little direct knowledge of what goes on inside them, and have never visited a prison themselves. From the point of view of mainstream media, this means that the '... mass-produced symbols and meanings take on even greater importance when they pertain to situated experiences which most of us do *not* experience, such as incarceration' (Jewkes 2007: 447). Although news reporting of prisons is negligible in comparison to coverage of crime and policing, when journalists do turn their gaze in the direction of prisons the research suggests that this often involves lazy reporting, which is based on assumptions and stereotypes rather than prison realities (Jewkes 2007). After all, few journalists spend much time at prisons or getting to know prisoners and their personal stories and lived experience.

There are some exceptions to this. For example, 'celebrity inmates' will attract significant media attention. Offenders in this category are often distinguished as:

- individuals who have gained notoriety for their crimes (e.g. serial killers or underworld identities, like Mark Brandon 'Chopper' Read)
- famous people who have fallen from grace (e.g. Hollywood actors or pop stars who engage in riotous behaviour—like O. J. Simpson or Justin Bieber), or
- individuals who bear some 'proximity' to the media outlets covering the story, but are imprisoned in exotic places (e.g. Australians, like Schapelle Corby and the Bali Nine, caught for drug possession in Indonesia).

The exotic and the strange, the unique and the pathetic, are the substance of much news media reporting on prisons and offenders (Jewkes 2007; 2008). Yet, significant silences also exist in terms of prisoners whose stories do not get told, and whose lives are not considered newsworthy (see Jewkes 2011). In particular, what are often *not talked about* are inhumane conditions, racism within prison, drug addiction, mental illness and acquired brain injury, suicide and self-harm, overcrowding and denial of rights. Likewise, what are *less frequently* talked about are positive things happening within corrective services, life-affirming examples, and reforms that work, including innovative justice initiatives. The media framing of prisons is dominated by negative images, damning pronouncements and opinions based on ignorance and/or lack of initiative. Again, the silences in mediated representations of prisons are as important to consider and interrogate as the issues that are made visible and salient.

The framing of prisoners and prison life is not unchanging and immutable, however. Fiscal pressures and social resistance to mass incarceration in the United States, for example, have been accompanied over time by changing public discourses on the use of imprisonment. Fine distinctions supplant gross generalisations as efforts to get 'tough on crime' are modified under the rubric of being 'smart on crime' (Altheide & Coyle 2006). In essence, different types of offences and different types of crime are seen to warrant or to *not warrant* harsh sentences and imprisonment, depending upon perceptions of seriousness and commonplace occurrence. Similarly, recent debates over the closing of prison farms in Canada have highlighted the ways in which certain 'prison dramas' make visible different visions of what punishment ought to look like on the part of specific stakeholders. This particular matter was in effect made into a lightning rod issue that spoke not only to the role of prison farms, but also the politics of imprisonment more generally and to wider political debates over government, democracy and community (Goodman & Dawe 2016). The framing of prisons issues is thus not quite as straightforward as some general depictions would suggest (see Cheliotis 2010), and the next section provides indications as to when and how this more selective framing is done.

COUNTER-FRAMES OF IMPRISONMENT

Penal culture is embedded in material practices, justified in intellectual systems, and experienced in ways that are specific both to the global age and to each particular national context. In Australia, imprisonment is costly to governments, to the vulnerable people who are the main targets of the hyperincarceration impulse, and to the social fabric. But, as sustained social and historical analysis demonstrates, it is also changeable and is not the same everywhere and at every point in time (Mathiesen 1997). Social context determines both the form of punishment and its public representation in factual and fictional media (see Box 6.3).

BOX 6.3

THE EXTRAORDINARY ORDINARINESS OF PRISON IN SWEDEN

The distinctive 'situated' nature of prison and experiences of imprisonment are highlighted in literature that reveals a different common sense about punishment than what is generally known or familiar to people in Australia, the United States or the United Kingdom. The extraordinary ordinariness of prison in Sweden, for example, is demonstrated in the novel *The Girl with the Dragon Tattoo*, written by Stieg Larsson (2008). In this book, the main character, Mikael Blomkvist, is charged with an offence in the Swedish courts and is convicted and sentenced to prison. The narrative is matter of fact in its description, and no big deal is made of how this actually occurs—it is embedded in Swedish commonsense about imprisonment. As described in the book, Blomkvist is sentenced to a defined term of imprisonment (six months), and he gets to choose within a year from sentencing when he wants to serve his time. So, when he is sentenced to prison, he does not go immediately, but chooses what time best suits his personal schedule and agenda. The portrayal of this in the book assumes that this is the same for anybody in this situation. When Blomkvist does decide to go to prison, he is subject to assessments by the prison authorities with regards to therapeutic evaluations, needs analysis and potential risks. The implication is that the 'system' asks the offender what it can best do for them, rather than seeking retribution directly on the offender's person. In this instance, Blomkvist is well-educated and well-off. His needs are simple: he asks for a computer in his room (his cell) and some paper, as he wishes to work on a research project he is undertaking. He is basically left alone with his computer and proceeds to write his book. And then he is released early because the authorities say that he has completed the minimum required of his six-month sentence and that it is not doing anybody any good to keep him in prison beyond this. He walks out a free man, and one who has not been brutalised by the prison experience.

In a sense, the portrayal of imprisonment processes in Sweden in *The Girl with the Dragon Tattoo* constitutes a 'good news' story through the back door. It is, of course, a fictional account of a fictional character. Nonetheless, the message conveyed is the sensible way in which the prison system operates in the Swedish context (at least from a criminological point of view). This is in sharp contrast to the sensationalised portrayals that are the staple fare in countries like Australia.

THE PUBLIC HEALTH MODEL OF REPORTING

Constructing a 'sensible' set of mediated representations of crime and criminal justice requires a different kind of journalistic paradigm. With respect to this, it has been suggested that media practitioners adopt what is called a **public health model of reporting**. This refers to particular emphases in interpreting and (re)presenting events and issues:

> The public health model is defined as an approach that sees the causes of death and injury as preventable rather than inevitable. By studying the interaction among victims, the agent, and the environment, the public health approach seeks to define risk factors, then develop and evaluate methods to prevent problems that threaten public health (Coleman & Thorson 2002: 402).

Contrasting explanations associated with the Los Angeles riots in 1992 demonstrate the public health model of reporting in practice. In this instance, an African American, Rodney King, had been captured on a private video camera being brutally beaten by a number of Los Angeles Police Department (LAPD) police officers. Leading up to this event in 1991, there had been long-standing tension between the LAPD and sections of the African American community. The case against the police went to trial in 1992 and the police were subsequently acquitted of wrongdoing. In the riots that resulted from the verdict, some 200 of the 728 bars and liquor stores in South Central Los Angeles were destroyed. Most mainstream news media framed the stories in terms of conflicts between blacks and Koreans. Citizen groups conducted their own study and found that their neighbourhoods had more alcohol outlets than 13 other states, and that such outlets contributed to higher crime rates. In educating the local media on this point, shifts were identified in the news framing of the riots, and the predominant narrative became one of the overabundance of liquor stores—two very different explanations based upon different framings of the same incident (see Coleman & Thorson 2002).

Those journalists who reframed the issue in terms of overabundance of liquor stores did so on the basis of relying upon a citizen group doing their homework for them. In essence, the citizen group, and like-minded journalists, were carrying out basic criminological research. The findings from this research were then conveyed in simple terms to the local media in the first instance, and a counter-narrative of events was then constructed. This is an example of a public health approach to reporting insofar as the solution was embedded in the analysis and, because it was preventative, the overall solution in this case was to cut down the number of liquor stores in that particular geographical area. Incidentally, similar arguments have been consistently put forward in regards to the night-time economy, alcohol use and street violence in Australia (see Chapter 7)—namely, to reduce the availability of alcohol both in terms of outlets and the opening/closing times of drinking establishments (see Graham & Homel 2008; Sutton, Cherney & White 2014).

The importance of the public health model of reporting as applied to prisoners and imprisonment is that it mirrors criminological concerns about institutional potentials to reduce and prevent crime. Renewed interest in rehabilitation among academics and practitioners is based in part upon the prospect that offenders can change, communities can be supportive and repeat crime can be prevented, if the right measures are introduced. Similarly, as with the public health model, there is a focus on risk factors and initiatives that will strengthen the likelihood that offenders will not reoffend (Graham & White 2015).

A reporting model that provides a framework supportive of positive, preventative measures is to be welcomed by those committed to prison reform and improvement.

While attractive from the point of view of 'truth' and the provision of alternative viewpoints, there are nonetheless acknowledged limitations to the public health model of reporting. Foremost among these is the perceived difficulty that media audiences may not find the stories very interesting (Coleman & Thorson 2002). What is more appealing from an audience perspective: a story about inter-racial conflict or a story about too many liquor outlets? Some content can seem 'boring' when contrasts such as these are made. Part of the reason for this tedium is the way in which stories constructed from a public health model tend to frame the research findings as real information and publicly beneficial information; not necessarily for its values as 'infotainment'.

There are other problems as well in using a public health model of reporting. For example, time and space limitations associated with media formats will often dictate salience and therefore shape the scope and placement of content (Ericson, Baranek & Chan 1991). If a newspaper journalist only has space for 500 words for a particular news story, this severely cramps the capacity to explore the contextual factors of imprisonment. Moreover, it takes time for reporters to get good background data, and this is compounded by the fact that official criminal justice agencies frequently either do not have relevant data or will not release it. Yet, in the 24/7 news cycle, time is of the essence, especially when 'scoops' are often made on social media and through online news sites, rather than in the pages of newspapers or the news bulletins of radio and television broadcasts. Investigative reporting can also be expensive and resource intensive. A public health model of reporting thus has a number of inherent constraints and limitations.

Nonetheless, a variety of media exist that do provide research-based reporting close to this model. One solution to the problem of time and space constraints, for instance, is to allocate reporters to dedicated specialist areas or newsbeats, so that over time they can develop expertise and contacts, accumulate information and data sources, and become familiar with varied interpretations of and explanations for phenomena such as prison life, prisoner behaviour and imprisonment as a social response to crime. This requires conscious decisions about how to allocate editorial budgets and resources within particular media organisations. Indeed, this is evident in publications such as *The Huffington Post* and *The Guardian*, which regularly feature 'good news' stories about prisons and prisoners as part of their online news platforms. *The Guardian*, in particular, has run regular features on prison-related issues for a number of years. Somewhat ironically, another good source of research and ideas for mainstream media outlets is that provided through social media and other online communications platforms. For instance, *Between the Bars* is a weblog created by and for incarcerated individuals in the United States <https://betweenthebars.org>. It is designed to provide prisoners opportunities to tell their stories in their own words and give their perspective on what it is like to be imprisoned. What unites these kinds of initiatives is the importance of hearing voices from the coalface—that is, the lived experiences of prisoners and practitioners working within prisons (see Box 6.4).

BOX 6.4

PRISON LIFE AND AUTO-ETHNOGRAPHY

There are many gatekeepers involved in keeping non-prisoners, especially researchers and prison reform activists, *out* of prison, and keeping knowledge of what goes on within, *inside* the prison (see, for example, Newbold et al. 2014). Similarly, the prisoner's voice is typically marginalised in official accounts pertaining to events such as riots and prisoner deaths, if it is acknowledged at all (Scraton & Chadwick 1987; Carlton 2007). In part, this relates specifically to the framing effects of mediated representations of dangerousness, which in a populist sense can sometimes include contestations over perceptions and definitions of dangerousness between institutional and lay discourses, particularly surrounding critical incidents like deaths in police custody (see Lawrence 2000; Clifford 2012; 2013). The marginalisation of prisoner accounts is reinforced by distrust of these 'outsiders', who are deemed to be dangerous, coupled with the favouring of 'official' versions that rely upon the notion of the 'legitimate' exercise of violence or force by police and prison officers. The emergence of a 'convict criminology' group in the late 1990s offered a much-needed corrective lens to these tendencies (Newbold et al. 2014). Comprised of former inmates and those who have spent a lot of professional time within prison settings, this group uses the combined prison experiences of its members to challenge commonly held assumptions and conventional mediated representations of prisoners and prison life. The opinions and views of members of the group are not uniform. Importantly, however, they collectively and individually provide insights into the 'real world' of imprisonment, although their interpretation of this world varies in terms of correctional policy and research focus. This is frequently an emotional process for all concerned, but the existence of emotions does not invalidate 'insider' views. Rather, the passion engendered by the experience of incarceration can add much needed colour, context and contour to data collection and the representation of criminal justice processes and institutions (Newbold et al. 2014; see also Jewkes 2012). Moreover, real-life experiences can inform fictionalised accounts in ways that make representations of prison life more realistic than otherwise may be the case. For example, Piper Kerman's memoir of her prison experiences, *Orange is the New Black: My Year in Women's Prison*, became a hit Netflix show, with stories of race and power at front and centre of the series. Kerman continues to campaign to improve the prison system in the United States and, while in Australia in 2016, observed that Australia faces many of the same issues as its overseas counterpart, particularly in relation to over-representation and longer sentences based on low socio-economic status and the colour of one's skin (Reynolds 2016).

When it comes to 'good news' media frames of prisons and prison reform, a perennial question is whether or not these should be in some way sensationalist. Sensationalism sells and therefore it makes sense—from the point of view of keeping audiences interested and the profits flowing—that positive narratives are framed in ways that capture people's attention. This may include developing an alternative public rhetoric to the standard 'law and order commonsense' doctrine discussed earlier. For example, emphasising the importance of making offenders pay by having them do something constructive and meaningful can be construed as being 'hard' on crime, rather than letting them sit in prison doing nothing. Highlighting alternative and provocative images of prisoners also contradicts the normal images of prisoners as 'dangerous' and 'debased'. The sight of male prisoners undertaking detailed and intricate sewing work, or pictures of men reading to children, likewise challenge stereotypes of both inmates and prisons. Cross-national comparisons of prisons (e.g. Bastøy Prison in Norway with super-maximum security (supermax) institutions in the United States and Australia) also serve to subvert the notion that somehow things are immutable and unchangeable, and that there is no alternative to mass incarceration and hyperincarceration (see Mathiesen 1997; Cunneen et al. 2013).

The vignettes in Box 6.5 illustrate the variety of ways in which 'prison news' can be framed as 'good news' rather than as negative and pessimistic.

BOX 6.5

POSITIVE MEDIA FRAMING

These stories involve mediated representations of prisoners helping others voluntarily as part of community service (and thus paying back to their communities), and engaging in activities that undermine the notion that they are somehow distinctive, different, out of the ordinary, thugs, perverts or 'evil' (thus, reinforcing their basic humanity). Each of these portrayals serves to reframe the prisoner in a positive light as non-Other.

The offender doing something for someone else

- post-bushfire fencing and repairs
- cyclone response teams
- frontline forest firefighters

The offender doing ordinary things

- reading to children
- making clothes
- gardening

HUMAN INTEREST STORIES

These stories provide personal insight into the psyche and moral universe of those deemed to be 'bad' and 'evil'. They are framed around a morality tale of loss and gain, mistakes and pain. In their own way, they express the human vulnerability and frailty of those who have broken the law, hurt others and engaged in wrongdoing. They are stories about those who know they have done wrong and have come to regret doing so, and they hit upon one of the most basic criteria for newsworthiness—putting a 'human face' to crime and wrongdoing.

Tales of redemption (e.g. doing it for others)

> 'I thought if I can help at least one person to learn from my mistakes it would mean a lot to me, and I'm sure it would mean a lot to my victim.' (young inmate Zac cited in Khan 2013)

Tales of remorse (e.g. young men in adult prison)

> 'You've got a lot of hours to spare and think about what you've done, so there's no escape from the crimes you've done.' (young inmate Oscar cited in Khan 2013)

DOING THE EXTRAORDINARY

These stories present the prisoner as acting exceptionally in exceptional circumstances. The heroism of the act, including its unusualness, somehow brings the offender back into the fold of the righteous and the good, the world of the ordinary person. Thus, the extraordinary act in fact helps to normalise people deemed to be 'Other' in popular narratives and news discourses.

Offenders as 'heroes'

In one instance, three boys fell into a creek and were saved by three inmates working in a nearby park. As one prisoner explained: 'Just 'cause we're incarcerated doesn't mean we're bad people. We made some bad choices in our lives, but we're still, we're just like everybody else. We're just paying our debt for what we did wrong' (cited in Ashtari 2013).

SERVING VULNERABLE COMMUNITIES

These stories again emphasise the ability of offenders to do something good for others. But, in this case, they are especially poignant, because they involve working with animals. Ironically, caring for animals is widely seen as a marker of one's humanity—to care for dogs demonstrates that one is human (and not an 'animal').

Training dogs for others

- Pairing incarcerated individuals with dogs that would otherwise be euthanased because of unmanageable or dangerous behavioural issues—preparing them for eventual adoption
- Training 'service' dogs for use by people with disabilities

FUNDRAISING

These stories promote the frame of doing something for others by using physical skills and technical knowledge to assist those who have already given to their community but do not have the resources to sustain themselves. Doing something in this instance involves both making something (through building and converting) and collecting money (in the form of selling the object as part of fundraising). The work can be self-fulfilling as well as serving a wider need.

Customised motorcycles (e.g. Vermont Department of Corrections)

- Strip, restore and customise motorcycles
- Donation of completed projects to charities as fundraisers
- Recent donation of two bikes to Vermont Fallen Families, which supports people who have lost loved ones in battle (cited in Ashtari 2013)

SAVING TAXPAYERS' MONEY

These stories combine various positive elements, but especially the notion that inmate work can help to reduce costs and thus taxpayer money, or provide a community service that likewise reduces the state's burden in assisting the disadvantaged. These projects also frequently have a strong rehabilitation focus. Saving money is intertwined with narratives about food, nutrition and community giving.

'Greening justice' schemes in prisons

- Growing vegetables and fruits
- Recycling industries within prison systems

Growing for others

- Juvenile justice schemes and 'food banks'

These kinds of vignettes serve in some way to humanise the 'deviant'. As previously discussed, this can also occur in the form of stories written online by people in prison, which reveal their 'human side', although under what conditions prisoners should be provided access to the internet remains contentious (see Jewkes 2007). There are also academic developments that give voice to a different perspective on prisons and prisoners. As mentioned in Box 6.4, the last two decades have seen the emergence of what is known as 'convict criminology'—that is, a number of former prisoners have ended up studying criminology, have become criminologists, and write within the genre of convict criminology. They write about the prison experience from the inside-out, rather than from the outside-in. Their potential to contribute to 'replacement discourse' envisioned by Barak's (1988; 2007) notion of 'newsmaking criminology' is therefore significant, since their accounts are integral to (re)evaluations of the real-world of prison life, which may offer a counter-narrative to the predominant frames of news media.

CRIMINOLOGICAL CONCEPTS AND MEDIA PORTRAYALS

Much of the above discussion about mediated representation dovetails nicely with emergent concepts within progressive criminology. These concepts are associated with those strands of criminology and penology that are oriented towards rehabilitation and which support the diminishment in the use of prisons. In other words, the 'good news' framing of media stories happens to coincide with the use of certain key concepts within contemporary criminology. Many of these are interlinked with the idea of **desistance**—that is, the processes whereby, over time, offenders stop offending.

We start with the concept of **generativity**, which refers to meaningful giving in the context of community (and ultimately how this affects the attitudes and well-being of offenders towards pro-social behaviours). The key phrase here is 'meaningful giving'. It may be stated differently across different bodies of literature, but the idea is to give something back to the community—to repair the harm and engage in restorative justice (Graham & White 2015). The idea is that something is being given back, voluntarily, and both offender and community benefit from this. This is captured in mediated representations that show offenders doing volunteer work and engaging in activities that involve giving something to or doing something for vulnerable members of the community. This taps into a widespread sentiment that it is good to help the poor, the disadvantaged, the disabled and those suffering from undue and/or unexpected hardship. When prisoners do the helping, it ameliorates the harsh image and perception of them as bad people and untrustworthy neighbours. The act of giving lays the groundwork for acts of forgiving.

Another important concept in the area of desistance is the notion of a 'strengths-based approach'. This refers to approaches that value the capacity, skills, knowledge, connections and potential in individuals and communities (White & Graham 2010). Much of the discourse within mainstream criminology is a 'deficit' discourse that says 'something is wrong with you and we're going to fix it' or 'you've done something wrong and the problem lies within yourself'. These types of narratives are frequently reproduced within media portrayals of prisoners and are at the heart of 'bad news' media frames. In contrast to this, strengths-based approaches place the emphasis on what a person can do, rather than the wrongs they have done and the deficits they exhibit. An example, at a practical level, is so-called **pro-social modelling** that shows people in a positive light. Relevant media images here are those that show offenders in positive, ethical roles, exhibiting skills such as technical prowess in tailoring or motor mechanics. Basically, they are shown as competent, highly skilled and doing something productive. This is the essence of a strengths-based approach.

Dealing with vulnerability is also a strong theme in contemporary progressive rehabilitative practice. Vulnerability refers to offenders, victims and communities that suffer from some sort of harm, risk, disability or disadvantage which places them in jeopardy in terms of economic, social, cultural and political life (Bartkowiak-Théron & Asquith 2012). Many offenders who end up in prison are themselves vulnerable. In fact, most have been victims themselves, and have been subjected to various kinds of physical and psychological victimisation as well as social disadvantage. A disproportionate number of people in prison exhibit characteristics such as low education levels, low income, poor job histories, intellectual disability, mental health issues, homelessness, alcohol and other drug problems, and acquired brain injury (Cunneen et al. 2013). Women and men have also disproportionately suffered assault and violence against their person, as children through to their adult years. Institutionally, there is a variety of therapeutic interventions that are designed to assist offenders, although these are unevenly provided and of variable quality (White & Graham 2010). These kinds of matters are reflected in media images that show the vulnerable side of 'hard-core' offenders—for example, by demonstrating their affection for dogs, for their children, or for the families of war veterans. Mediated representations of the convicted killer and the hard-core 'crim' are reframed in ways that show them to have a heart and feelings. The big, burly dad engaging in a reading project for his children shows a 'softer' side as well as exposes the vulnerabilities of offenders.

Contemporary progressive criminology also places great stress on 'hope' rather than 'fear'. Fear is a substantial driver of news media reporting, since it sells well and is the staple of many of the images of prisons and prisoners. But criminologists talk of hope, because hope is essential to any chance of progress for institutions as well as for individuals (Weaver & McNeill 2010). Of course, hope is an emotion. As such, it taps into how people feel about themselves and others, and is linked to notions of self-respect and social respect. Occasionally, there *are* news stories that feature or are premised upon the notion of hope. Importantly, such stories tend to focus less on the rational than on the affective. Thus, media images convey *affective* changes in inmates, involving strong emotions and desires for change, love, reconnection and redemption. When a young man in adult prison is asked about his life, he says with breaking voice: 'I'm just so terribly sorry about what I've done' (see Khan 2013). This is powerful stuff indeed. Such a statement implies hope, because the offender has acknowledged and recognised what they have done and they want to go forward.

Community engagement is vital and crucial to the rehabilitation process as well (Maruna 2006; McNeill 2012). If bail is cut and probation reduced, then this simultaneously restricts the potential for constructive community engagement. Community engagement refers to ongoing and frequent interaction between and among all sectors of the community, including offenders. It is acknowledged that offenders are members of communities, are taken from communities and that they will return to communities. Without positive, constructive relations at the community level, then ex-prisoners, in all likelihood, will be anti-social and destroy communities on their return to them. The question this inspires is how to engender a sense of community in relation to the narrative around prisoners. Here, once again, we can refer to mediated representations of prisoners doing things in and for communities, such as bushfire relief. It also includes media coverage of community 'fun runs' that end up inside the prison. For the latter, the gates are opened and everyday citizens and residents are invited inside the prison, making for a unique and eye-opening event (Massina & White 2000).

Positive interaction at the community level allows for a sense of commonality. Ultimately, it is about knowing each 'other'. We put 'other' in quotation marks, because so often in mediated representations of prisons, the prisoner is treated solely and simply as 'Other', as if they are not one of us, the rest of the community. This also raises interesting questions about how to ensure this knowledge is transparent and involves two-way communication. Again, issues concerning access to the internet are pertinent as:

> It is not unidirectional, but would allow users to interact with individuals and groups on the outside. This might include potential employers, public sector organizations that might help inmates with particular issues such as housing prior to release, and increased contact with tutors, lawyers and family via email (Jewkes 2007: 460).

Punishment and use of imprisonment is ostensibly about the deprivation of liberty. People are sent to prison *as* punishment, not *for* punishment. Given this, there is a substantial argument to be made in favour of allowing internet access and online communications within the prison insofar as prison is not about denial of ordinary activities and human rights, but deprivation of liberty. Greater transparency and information flows between the inside and the outside have a number of potential benefits, not the least of which is breaking down the barriers and myths that sustain the prisoner status as 'Other'.

However, communication with the outside world also presents interesting quandaries and dilemmas. For example, two inmates in the Alexander Maconochie Centre, the prison in the Australian capital, Canberra, created a media stir and political outrage when photos of them posing together were uploaded to Facebook. The matter was presented as inappropriate, both for the 'bravado' evident in the photos, but also for the fact that a mobile phone was used to take the photos and post them on the social media site. This constituted a breach of prison security protocols that prohibit use of broadcasting devices because they may be used to undertake illegal activity from within the prison (Reinfrank 2015). The content and uses of communication to and from prisons thus require careful appraisal of the issues involved, and the possible remedies and solutions available.

ISSUES FOR CONSIDERATION

It is important to remember that not all 'bad news' stories about prisons and prisoners are necessarily bad. Negative framing may, in fact, be depictive of real events (e.g. assaults on prisoners by prison guards or vice versa) and real conditions (e.g. overcrowding) that require media exposure from the point of view of social and natural justice. In these instances, media stories of negative events and associations may well have productive effects. In Hobart, Tasmania, for example, the deaths of five prisoners within the space of one year led to extensive media scrutiny of the prison service. Regular news reports featuring grieving mothers and spouses also seemed to have a knock-on effect in relation to official institutional reviews and Ombudsman investigations, and certainly helped spur on the public pursuit of prison reform by family members and other activists for a number of years following the events in 1999.

'Bad news' stories, regardless of effects, are not simply more saleable and titillating. They also translate more readily into socially shared frames and ways of understanding, so they work within the confines of news reporting and its conventions. But what about other media forms? For example, the realities of prison life have also been subject to mediated representation through social documentaries (such as *Women Behind Bars*, *Hard Time: Hustle & Prey* and *Stories from the Inside*). This involves the production of images and representations from behind bars, and the active engagement of prisoners, prison officers, families and senior management. The documentary form is generally oriented towards educational imperatives rather than infotainment or sensationalism. As such, it provides for the possibility of more reflective investigation of prison-related issues and the opportunity to expose the range of human behaviours and emotions associated with living in such an institution. Rather than a 'quick dip' into the world of imprisonment, documentaries can afford the time and scope to build trust and familiarity with the environment and those who live and work within it. Different media forms therefore engender different representations and the possibility of different kinds of 'truth' about the same institution and the same people.

For example, mediated representations of prisons and prisoners, especially in fictional media, are often highly gendered. Depictions of hyper-masculinity abound when it comes to men and are likewise evident in 'butch' characters when it comes to women. Gender identities are highly stylised and stereotyped, frequently presenting a skewed and one-dimensional representation of both men and women, albeit with some exceptions (e.g. *Orange is the New Black*). The sexualisation of the prison experience similarly includes particular interpretations of hetero-normativity, including the centrality of rape in prison relations, both in terms of one-to-one intimacy and more generally as a coercive force. Different 'types' of prisoners are drawn upon to convey narratives of pathos, brutality, weakness, victimisation and domination. Violence is central to both the male and female domains, but the aggression and physicality of this varies according to different gender scripts. Media depictions of the female prisoner and the male inmate need to be scrutinised from the point of view of the kinds of social messages being conveyed about gender, power and sexuality.

CONCLUSION

This chapter has canvassed the ways in which prison issues and prisoners are conventionally portrayed through mediated representation—particularly news media—and the opportunities for counter-frames to these dominant depictions. This involves forays into both the 'bad news' and the 'good news' about imprisonment.

We wish also to make two final points. First, there is a need to go beyond single-minded approaches when it comes to media accounts of punishment, prisons and prisoners. Even mediated representations of innovative approaches and the 'good news' framing of stories can be 'single-minded' in that they will often cover one founder or leader, one initiative, one crime type or offender group, one organisation, or one jurisdiction. The challenge is to 'normalise' storytelling in ways that build context and 'setting' across themes, borders, institutions, personalities and places; to *situate* the representation of prisons and prisoners within factual and fictional media. As suggested, one way in which to do this strategically is to develop journalistic expertise over time. Getting to know the issues and building a repertoire of contacts and institutional knowledge ensures that, over time, issues of context and setting will be built into news media reportage.

From a criminological perspective, as part of this, there has to be conscious effort to make the 'Other' the not-'Other'; to reduce the social distance between prisoner and non-prisoner. This is because the more 'othering' that is done through conventional media narratives, the more difficult offenders will find it to reintegrate and resume a positive place back in their communities. **Recidivism** or repeat offending is one consequence of this—a phenomenon that puts everyone in jeopardy. Negative framing effects influence both penal policy and the substantive outcomes of that policy. But there is the potential for positive effects as well.

Finally, while we have discussed media frames of prisons and prisoners in terms of 'bad news' and 'good news' throughout this chapter, it is important not to see these as simple binaries or opposites (as only 'positive' versus 'negative'). The operations and environment of prisons and the factors that lead people to them are far more complex, and much rests on matters of definition. As Maruna (2001: 18) puts it, 'the negative is easier than the positive, but the positive is more important'. Ideally, from a media criminology perspective, what we would like to see within mainstream media is a balance between 'bad news' and 'good news' stories that reflect both the realities of prison experience and tie in with progressive reform. Conventional 'bad news' stories are easier to produce and interpret, more titillating and more confronting, albeit often less real. They can sometimes also constitute lazy journalism. Socially responsible journalism is much harder—but contributes to the making of a much better-informed and more cohesive society.

DISCUSSION QUESTIONS

1. Why do 'bad news' stories attract more media interest than 'good news' stories of prisons and prisoners?
2. What are the main elements of the public health model of reporting?
3. Does 'truth' get in the way of good stories about prisons?

4. Do 'innocence projects' and advocacy journalism, which focus on miscarriages of justice, have the capacity to change popular opinion about prisons in general, or are they seen to be solely about specific and unique individual cases?
5. Does the 'exception' (e.g. a prisoner who succeeds in their rehabilitative efforts) prove the 'rule' (i.e. that most prisoners are likely to reoffend and not be rehabilitated)?

WORKSHOP ACTIVITY 1: WRITING GOOD NEWS STORIES

Locate a local innovative justice initiative (e.g. prison community garden, offender bush rehabilitation project) and write it up as a 'good news' story for the local newspaper, applying the conventions of print news stories and the news values of crime news. In constructing the story, bear in mind the proposition and paradox that positive framing benefits women and negative framing benefits men (Shoemaker & Reese 2014).

WORKSHOP ACTIVITY 2: PRISON ARCHITECTURE

Investigate and consider the varied forms of prison architecture and how these have changed over time (e.g. from the Port Arthur or Fremantle Prison model of cramped quarters and panopticon-like surveillance to the Canberra prison model of campus-style accommodation). How does the external appearance of 'the prison' contribute to particular mediated understandings and public perceptions of prisoners and prison life?

FURTHER READING

Coleman, R. & Thorson, E. (2002). The Effects of News Stories that Put Crime and Violence into Context: Testing the Public Health Model of Reporting. *Journal of Health Communication*, 7(2), 401–25.

Jewkes, Y. (2007). Prisons and the Media: The Shaping of Public Opinion and Penal Policy in a Mediated Society. In Y. Jewkes (ed.), *Handbook on Prisons*. Cullompton, Devon: Willan Publishing, pp. 447–66.

Mason, P. (2006). Lies, Distortion and What Doesn't Work: Monitoring Prison Stories in the British Media. *Crime Media Culture*, 2(3), 251–67.

Minogue, C. (2011). Why Don't I Get the Joke? Prison Rape in the Public Discourse. *Alternative Law Journal*, 36(2), 116–18.

Newbold, G., Ross, J., Jones, R., Richards, S. & Lenza, M. (2014). Prison Research from the Inside: The Role of Convict Autoethnography. *Qualitative Inquiry*, 20(4), 454–63.

PART

III

THE POLITICS OF MEDIATED REPRESENTATION

7

YOUTH AND THE MORAL ECONOMY

CHAPTER HIGHLIGHTS

Introduction
Moral panics and young people
Sexting and social media
Typifications and particularism
Moral panics and street violence
Conclusion

INTRODUCTION

One of the hallmarks of youth crime—indeed, young people generally—is visibility. Whether it is criminal offending or shopping, playing sports or walking the mall, young people tend to do things together and in groups. They are easily noticed and occasionally some of them gain special notoriety (particularly when publicising house parties on social media that, in turn, attract hundreds to homes that normally fit dozens). When young people do something, they easily gain our attention.

For media of all forms, 'youth' and the affairs of young people is part of a staple diet. They have considerable cache in terms of news values, given their age, appearance, variability in behaviours, public presence, vulnerabilities and expressiveness. What young people do, therefore, is of interest to themselves and to wider communities of concern. But how they act and behave carries with it inevitable moral judgments, and media serves as one source of defining what is deemed acceptable and unacceptable in the worlds of the young. Whether young people agree with or respond positively (or negatively) to particular media labels is certainly a matter for concrete study and worthy of attention in its own right.

Youth experience is intrinsically context bound insofar as each young person's 'way of life' is determined by where they live and the resources available to them. As immediate social context is transformed—from within and from without—this will inevitably be reflected in the specific expressions of youth opportunity and youth culture. Three major developments in particular are reshaping the life prospects and experiences of young people (and their elders) worldwide:

- the international transfer of information, images and ideas accompanying the spread of global capitalism
- the expansion of social networking and increased use of mobile phone technologies
- radical changes and challenges to social and environmental well-being arising from present global financial and ecological trends (White 2015).

The material circumstances of diverse young women and men vary according to class, ethnic background, geographical location, national laws and civic traditions, local community resources and immediate family circumstance. Growing up is both a unique experience for specific individuals and distinctive at the level of group identification and interaction. Who people are is contingent on whom they associate and socialise with, and the material and cultural universes they occupy and/or access. All of this has implications for how youth experience is framed within media contexts.

This chapter examines the portrayal of young people in the mainstream media by considering the notion of 'moral panic' and its associated concepts. Much of the power of these media lies in the presentation of stereotypes, on a repetitive basis, in ways that generate fear of the 'Other'. Particular categories of young people are most liable to receive negative treatment and so our concern is not just with periodic (mis)representations, but also the persistence of certain images and messages surrounding particular population groups.

MORAL PANICS AND YOUNG PEOPLE

The notion of 'moral panic' refers to a concept developed by Cohen (1972) in his study of mods and rockers in England. This study showed how moral outrage was created by media in the way they demonised certain groups (in this case spectacular youth subcultures) as being deviant and a threat to the social and moral order (see Chapter 2). As Cohen (1972: 9) explains:

> Societies appear to be subject, every now and then, to periods of moral panic. A condition, episode, person or group of persons emerges to become defined as a threat to societal values and interests; its nature is presented in a stylised and stereotypical fashion by the mass media; the moral barricades are manned by editors, bishops, politicians and other right-thinking people; socially accredited experts pronounce their diagnoses and solutions; ways of coping are evolved or (more often) resorted to; the condition then disappears, submerges or deteriorates and becomes more visible. Sometimes the object of the panic is quite novel and at other times it is something which has been in existence long enough, but suddenly appears in the limelight. Sometimes the panic passes over and is forgotten, except in folklore and collective memory; at other times it has more serious and long-lasting repercussions and might produce such changes as those in legal and social policy or even in the way society conceives itself.

The moral panic is inherently media-driven, but incorporates a wide variety of stakeholders and opinion makers. Inevitably, moral panics involve societal condemnation of specific activities, whether it is the presumed link between satanic rituals and rock music, or mass shootings and the availability of guns. Ordinary events or persons are represented as extraordinary occurrences and as threats to those around them. The moral panic serves to clarify (from particular points of view) the moral boundaries of the society in which it occurs, ostensibly creating consensus and mutual concern (see Jewkes 2008).

Poynting and Morgan's (2007) *Outrageous! Moral Panics in Australia* provides a series of case studies in which specific turning points are identified when there was intensified moral indignation around particular marginalised groups of people whose actions were seen as deviant. Topics such as riots, young car drivers, rock and roll music, youth subcultures and drug use, racialised portrayals of particular ethnic minority communities, gang rapes, and disease and sexuality are all considered. The book demonstrates how the mainstream media constructs certain groups and practices as being 'dangerous', 'deviant' and 'destructive', and how this is intertwined with social responses that call forth repressive measures and collective revulsion.

Moral panics are therefore characterised by a series of interconnecting elements. They embody notions of deviance and a public awareness that there is a social issue that must be addressed. They demand collective action on the part of the public, and thus the mobilisation of concerned people to address and change specific social conditions (Goode & Ben-Yehuda 1994). As Becker (1963) observed many years ago, the social construction of 'outsiders' is achieved through the concerted action of 'moral entrepreneurs', prominent individuals who take the lead in forging a social consensus that a problem exists and that it must be dealt with in a certain way.

The difference between initial formulations of moral panic in the United Kingdom with subsequent approaches in the United States has been summarised by Critcher (2009). He suggests that British scholarly work provides a *processual model* because it focuses on the stages and processes through which a moral panic passes. For example, Cohen (1972) describes how, over time, there is a 'deviance amplification spiral' whereby low-lying deviancy associated with dress or attitude prompts harsh punitive measures, which in turn creates the conditions for higher-order acts of deviance such as violence. The initial vilification of the mods and rockers, for example, thus actually sets the scene for subsequent fights and disorder (see also Moore 2014).

By contrast, American scholars have provided an *attributional model* of moral panics, one that focuses on the qualities an episode should possess to qualify as a moral panic (Critcher 2009; see also Moore 2014). For example, according to Goode and Ben-Yehuda (1994), the key elements of a moral panic include:

- *concern* (e.g. heightened level of concern over certain kinds of behaviour)
- *hostility* (e.g. increased level of hostility towards the group, now seen as an 'enemy' of respectable society, and as responsible for the threat)
- *consensus* (e.g. substantial or widespread agreement among given group [for instance, elites] or community and/or society-wide)

- *disproportionality* (e.g. the degree of public concern over the behaviour itself, the problem it poses, or the condition it creates is far greater than is true for comparable, even more damaging, actions—that is, 'objective molehills have been made into subjective mountains')
- *volatility* (e.g. moral panics erupt suddenly and nearly as suddenly subside; they tend to be local and time-delimited).

American writers such as Goode and Ben-Yehuda (1994) also devote considerable attention to the specific stakeholders and players involved in forging moral panics (as further discussed in the next chapter). However, in this framework, the main concern (and difficulty) is ascertaining when the criteria have in fact been attained. For example, how do we gauge relative levels and types of concern, or the level of consensus (especially in a pluralistic society)? The beginning and end of moral panics can likewise be difficult to ascertain.

Yet moral panics do not have to be discrete or one-off phenomena. Nor are specific events necessarily separated from each other in media discourse. Indeed, as Poynting et al. (2004) convincingly argue, the persistence of any particular group being seen as a 'folk devil' (i.e. an object of hostility that focuses the moral and social anxieties embedded in a moment of panic) stems from the ways in which discourses are assembled over time. They point to the manner in which the 'Arab Other' has been socially constructed in media in New South Wales as one example (for a fuller discussion of this, see Chapter 8). This has involved an ongoing cycle of moral panic, the elements of which have included ideological constructs of 'crime-prone Arab immigrants, violent Muslim terrorists, Middle-Eastern queue-jumping refugees with no respect for civilised rules, and Muslims who are seen as failing to integrate' (Poynting et al. 2004: 49). Both moral panic and the construction of folk devils are complicated social processes, which operate over time and in ways that reinforce certain key messages and stereotypes.

In terms of specific targets, the presence of identifiable groups of young people in public places has been portrayed as especially disturbing by some sections of the mainstream media. As explored further in the next chapter, this has certainly been the case with regards to ethnic minority youth and so-called 'youth gangs' (Collins et al. 2000; White 2013). It also appears to be the case with certain types of drinkers, especially those identified with binge drinking, under-age drinking and drinking in public spaces.

We can also look at moral panics from the point of view of how they are constructed. Schissel (1997: 49) points out that in most mainstream media treatments of juvenile offending, the accounts of criminal behaviour tend to present *individual examples as the norm* and to simultaneously *remove the social context* for the criminal behaviours:

> What is most important in analyzing moral panics is how these accounts of criminal behaviour use individual examples as the norm, and how the criminal behaviour is decontextualized from the structured nature of society. When crimes are framed in the context of morality, poor parenting and 'poor people', the problem is reduced to the

level of individual pathology and its moral connections to privation; the legitimacy of 'normal', affluent lifestyles is reinforced, as is the legitimacy of the social order.

What, then, do we know about the nature of juvenile offending? Fundamentally, those who are criminalised for youth crimes are those from the most vulnerable and disadvantaged backgrounds (Cunneen, White & Richards 2015). In other words, youth offending is socially patterned. The phenomenon of unemployment is the biggest single factor in the transformation of young people, their families and their communities. In a wage-based economy, subsistence is largely contingent upon securing paid employment. If this is not available, then a number of social problems are often invoked, including and especially crime (Wacquant 2008). Accordingly, the social profiles of 'young offenders' tend to look basically the same throughout the youth justice systems of most advanced industrialised countries. They comprise predominantly young men with an over-representation of youth drawn from minority ethnic groups, with low income, low educational achievement, poorly paid and/or casualised employment (if any) and strained familial relations (White & Cunneen 2015). It is the most disadvantaged and structurally vulnerable young people who tend to receive the greatest attention from youth justice officials at all points of the system (Cunneen, White & Richards 2015).

Where large numbers of young working-class people congregate in particular areas, they constitute visible evidence of failing social and economic conditions within which poverty and inequality are rife, as well as the threats to social order posed by such structural failure. Such analyses are increasingly pushed to the periphery within dominant discourses that tend to privilege individual agency, underpinned by notions of marginalised young people constituting a particular type of moral category. In this way, members of the so-called 'underclass' are perceived and portrayed as morally corrupt and as a group needing to be disciplined and reformed (see especially Herrnstein & Murray 1994; Murray 1990). As well, and particularly in the light of recent urban riots in places such as England, France and Australia, youth behaviour is framed in terms of 'gang talk' that reduces complicated social issues to incidences of individual and group pathology (Hallsworth & Young 2008; Hallsworth 2013; White 2013; Goldson 2014).

The mainstream commercial media are entirely complicit in this process of issue distortion. The new 'dangerous classes' are framed within discourses of contempt and fear—a social attitude that pervades the popular media and political elites. Unemployment is reduced to 'bad attitudes' and 'bad families'. Meanwhile, local elites and civic/community 'leaders' are recruited as leading moral entrepreneurs in an attempt to regulate specific populations. They may be recruited, for example, to lead 'community' attempts to 'clamp down' on undesirable behaviour. This specific political role of local elites, however, is bolstered by the general vulnerabilities experienced by local small businesses that lend support particularly on matters of law and order:

> ... their deep and pervasive perception—supported somewhat by practical experience—is that their businesses, personal property, and physical integrity are front-line targets for street crime (e.g., armed robbery, breaking and entering, shoplifting,

mugging, etc.). For them, the visibility of working-class street culture, particularly that of various underclass strata, is a source of anxiety for their own persons, their property, their customers, and trade (White & van der Velden 1995: 69).

This anxiety translates into perpetual 'moral panics' over 'street-present' working-class young people in particular (Pearson 1983). Congregations of young people, especially if they are not spending money as consumers, may constitute both symbolic and material barriers to commerce and are conceptualised as representing disorder and decline. Young people often congregate and 'hang out' in and around commercial spaces and their very visibility, perceived lack of financial power, and behaviour (hanging around in groups, making noise) can render them an unwelcome presence, regardless of whether or not they actually transgress the law or actively engage in offensive activity (see Box 7.1).

BOX 7.1

YOUTH AS NUISANCE

Young people are sometimes perceived as persons to be 'got rid of' and thus subject to unique and targeted methods of social control. For example, the Mosquito alarm is a gadget that emits a high-frequency noise audible only to young people under the age of 25 years (Walsh 2008). It was originally designed and used in the United Kingdom in a bid to combat youths who loitered in large groups, causing nuisance to shops and residents. The Mosquito alarm is allegedly so annoying that it encourages young people to move away from an area and disperse. It has since been exported to malls in the United States, where owners hoped that it would drive youth away, especially those lounging around and presumably not spending money (Goodyear 2010), and to Australia where it is used to prevent young people from gathering in public areas late at night or engaging in graffiti (Rollason 2012; Morri 2013). The playing of loud music at the entrance to shopping centres has been used in much the same way in both the United Kingdom and Australia, and has elsewhere been described as the 'Manilow method'—given that it is often Barry Manilow tunes that are played over the loudspeakers to stop youths hanging around (The Age 2008). In the midst of Mosquitos and Manilows, one has to wonder how those young people who actually work in the shops feel about such irritants, much less those children accompanying their parents on their shopping expeditions.

Moral panics, however, are not simply fictions. They may be fictions in the sense of distorted representations of particular issues, but they nonetheless have real-world impacts. For instance, the social consequences of moral panics include such things as ostracising and penalising particular groups in society on the basis of their presumed immoral and threatening behaviour and presence (e.g. particular groups of young people).

They can involve passing legislation and stepping up police efforts to prevent or prohibit certain types of activity (e.g. certain types of drinking behaviour). They may involve the violation of human rights under the rubric of the greater good (e.g. pre-emptive police action to clear the streets). The persistence of moral panic and crime wave discourses in mainstream media also feeds a more generalised fear of crime, a phenomenon that likewise shapes how people interact and relate to one another (see Lee 2007; Poynting & Morgan 2007; Lee & Farrall 2008).

They can also have unintended consequences. For example, various studies have pointed to the ways in which the media portray certain types of youth subcultures, which in turn lead to a form of **deviancy amplification** (Young 1971; Cohen 1972; Collins et al. 2000)—that is, the sort of public labelling pertaining to some groups of young people actually generates further 'deviant' behaviour in the labelled group. Being a 'ladette' (especially if one does a ladette-to-lady course on TV) is, in its own perverse way, 'cool'. This is particularly so when publicity ensures a certain status to the activities described under the label.

In a similar vein, performing 'stupid' or 'insane' physical stunts that are then conveyed to millions via YouTube ensures the repetition of these same stunts, regardless of how many young people get hurt or injured in the process. Everyone, it seems, wants to be a 'jackass'. Reputations can also be made (or lost) through the medium of the internet and other forms of networked sociality. Conflict, for instance, can be fanned in the parallel real-worlds of young women as a result of the ways in which girls engage with social networking sites, like Facebook and YouTube, to promote, incite and normalise girls' violence. In fact, Carrington (2013) points out that thousands of girls around the world use the internet to broadcast their physical fights with other girls. Thus, there has been the emergence of online 'fight pages' and 'fight-tubes' (Wood 2016)—a number of which are dedicated to specifically hosting footage of fights between women, thereby implying an increase in female violence generally. Yet, the evidence in recent years in Australia is that young women are not becoming more violent, and that girl-on-girl violence is in fact declining (Lattouf 2016). Again, image is not necessarily the same as reality.

SEXTING AND SOCIAL MEDIA

Controversies over 'sexting' also provide an example of the complexities and consequences of moral panic in relation to young people. Sexting is a term that is used in different ways, but it 'generally concerns the digital recording of naked, semi-naked, sexually suggestive or explicit images and their distribution by email, mobile phone messaging or through the Internet on social network sites, such as Facebook, MySpace and YouTube' (Lee et al. 2013: 36). It is a phenomenon that has become a major issue for a variety of reasons, not least of all because of the instances in which young people under the age of 18 have been prosecuted for criminal offences as a result of sexting.

The availability of webcams, mobile phone cameras and video cameras has facilitated the proliferation of sexting between young people. Simultaneously, there has been increasing distribution due to texting, the internet, YouTube and Facebook. A recent online survey found that, among the respondents, 38.4 per cent of 13- to 15-year-olds and 49.6 per cent of 16- to 18-year-olds had sent a sext, while 62 per cent of 13- to 15-year-olds and 70.1 per cent of 16- to 18-year-olds had received a sext (Crofts et al. 2014).

A recent dilemma in places such as Australia has been the conviction of teenage participants involved in sexting under the crime of 'child pornography'. In some instances, this has led to young people being placed on mandatory sex offender registration lists for behaviour that many young people regard as 'ordinary' and normal for their age group and among their peers.

From the point of view of criminological analysis, cyberspace presents new challenges, of which sexting is a part. To date, however, most attention has been on responding to the challenges rather than understanding them. As Lee and colleagues (2013: 40) point out, 'the intervention in this area so far has predominantly focused on reactively managing, rather than mapping out and understanding, risk around sexting'. Recent investigations into sexting, however, are starting to unpack the complexities of sexting as a social phenomenon and the legal issues arising from it (see, for example, Parliament of Victoria Law Reform Committee 2013).

From a media/cultural studies perspective, critical commentary has registered the limitations of viewing sexting primarily through a 'risk' lens and/or through a predominantly 'adult' top-down view of the phenomenon. Some, such as Albury and Crawford (2012), argue that sexting by young people should be reframed as media production, not simple victimisation. They claim that much of the law disconnect from and moral panic surrounding sexting is due, in part, to a failure to fully appreciate the (highly conscious) use of media technologies by consenting teenagers (Albury & Crawford 2012)—that is, an individual's agency in the act.

For example, peer-to-peer sexting can have elements of both consent *and* coercion. For some participants, sexting is exciting and fun, even pleasurable; a form of social transgression that is, in its own way, exhilarating (Lee et al. 2013). For others, it depends on who is involved and how it is done. The stages of peer-to-peer sexting have been identified as: 1) requesting an image; 2) creating an image; 3) sharing an image with an intended recipient (consensually); and 4) sharing an image with others (non-consensually) (National Children's and Youth Law Centre cited in Parliament of Victoria Law Reform Committee 2013: 22). There are possible harms associated with each stage of sexting—but again, it is the social relationships and agency of the individuals involved that determines the nature of, or if there is perception of, harm.

It has been argued that the dominant public discourse about sexting involving young people tends to ignore alternative narratives in favour of moralising based upon anxiety over paedophiles and child pornography. This reinforces a coercive and highly directive approach to the regulation of adolescent sexuality and risk-taking that, in turn, generates its own unintended consequences. That is, 'the over-criminalisation of sexting by young people and attempts at its suppression have had unintended effects: they have incited sexting further into the public realm and legitimated the practice as an exciting, somewhat desirable activity for some young people' (Lee et al. 2013: 36). Reaction to sexting, therefore, can both ignore the pleasures and excitement associated with 'normal' risk-taking behaviour on the part of some young people, as well as amplify its appeal for others by over-criminalisation.

Non-consensual sexting has several different dimensions, but the bottom line is that it involves uses of intimate images that are disrespectful, inappropriate and/or exploitative. Unauthorised recording and circulation of images, and sexually exploitative sexting, are among the particular harms arising from this kind of activity.

Importantly, it has been observed that the wider 'sexualisation of culture' in ways that are heterosexual and gendered means that, in practice, sexting is not a gender-neutral activity. Research suggests that 'more young women than young men send explicit images or texts, and more young women report sending sexting messages as a result of pressure from the opposite sex' (Parliament of Victoria Law Reform Committee 2013: 41). The 'victims' of non-consensual sexting are predominantly young women, and social pressures by teen boys on girls and young women to send or post sexual images of themselves raise significant issues concerning the meaning of 'consensual' in the first place.

Nonetheless, specific harm is best assessed through examination of particular instances, and the conditions and circumstances underpinning the specific stages of sexting. As formal hearings in Victoria illustrate, young people may be aware of the risks but choose to participate in sexting anyway, since it is part of their social experience. Those who engaged in it often saw their behaviour as a normal and common practice among their peers, and that the wrong occurs when a sexting message is treated disrespectfully by someone within the peer group (see Parliament of Victoria Law Reform Committee 2013).

Sexting is not the only youth issue related to social media that generates public reaction. For some young people, the digital world offers a more attractive alternative space to their non-digital world, and they spend as much time as they can there. Some researchers have labelled this 'digital addiction'. The phenomenon can take the form of excessive video game playing, accessing particular websites (pornographic sites and gambling sites, for example) or becoming obsessed with chat rooms (Young 2004). In a similar vein, the notion of 'digital drift' refers to the ways in which criminal commitments may form through using the internet and related communication technologies. In particular, it describes how such movement allows individuals to limit their involvement in particular associations or networks while simultaneously allowing them to commit crimes more autonomously through facilitating self-instruction online (Goldsmith & Brewer 2015). There are also cyber-safety issues related to the phenomenon of 'gate-crashing', such as when the location of a party is posted on social media (usually Facebook) and hundreds of 'strangers' show up. Concern has also been expressed about particular young people's use of social networking sites in relation to privacy, disclosure and breach of confidence; intellectual property rights, especially copyright infringement; defamation; and criminal laws, including harassment and offensive material (de Zwart et al. 2011).

Investigation of the intergenerational dynamics shaping attitudes towards and usage of social networking services and cyber-safety (including in regards to sexting) have attempted to refocus attention on the ways in which young people themselves relate to new information technologies. For example, conventional approaches to promoting cyber-safety among young people tend to focus on risk management, typically through educational and regulatory approaches. Most cyber-safety programs are delivered through the school setting, which is typically removed from other settings (such as family and work) and social relationships (with peers, parents and other adults) in which young people regularly engage (Third et al. 2011). Thinking about the issues in this way means that responses to cyber-safety need to acknowledge young people's expertise in the use of modern communications technologies and the internet (Third et al. 2011). The emphasis, therefore, should be less upon risk management and regulation focused on young people and more on strategies that incorporate 'real-world' experiences and knowledge acquisition. Rather than being top-down in orientation and reflecting generational assumptions and fears, such principles must begin with the idea that young people are more knowledgeable than previously assumed when it comes to safety and security online.

TYPIFICATIONS AND PARTICULARISM

With young people, it is not the severity of an issue that dictates the moral panic; rather, what counts is who mobilises around and behind the particular event or issue. In short, it depends on who jumps on the bandwagon, and how public, political or elite opinion is mobilised, that dictates the public contours of a moral panic. The severity of any particular issue, therefore, does not necessarily translate into the prominence given to that particular issue. The key question is why certain issues become 'known' more so than others. State intervention and social movement action around specific issues similarly rest upon the fact that these specific issues have become important enough to generate widespread, concrete social responses. What becomes prominent as a social issue reflects a social process in which certain claims—about people, events and impacts—are brought into the public domain and gain ascendancy.

Why are certain events chosen for concerted media attention but other equally tragic or difficult or troublesome events are not—even though they occur at the same time—and how are these events portrayed if chosen? From a journalism and media studies viewpoint, the answer to the first part of the question lies in 'newsworthiness'—that is, the selection and salience of issues. For the second part of the question, the issue is more about 'framing'—that is, the way in which media representations are packaged for interpretation. Here, criminology generally talks about the social processes of typification and how through these processes what is considered normal and what is considered deviant becomes naturalised as everyday perceptions of the nature of social reality:

> The construction of a commonsense consensual view of society is 'achieved' through continual processes of typification. Through these processes, what is 'normal' and what is 'deviant' become naturalised as everyday perceptions of the nature of social reality. By highlighting what is 'abnormal' or 'deviant', the media both passes judgement on what is seen as 'bad' behaviour and implicitly reaffirms the presumed status quo (White 1990: 106–7).

In other words, we get so used to *typifications* of certain people, in certain ways, good or bad, that it becomes part of our everyday commonsense; it becomes naturalised.

For their part in this process, Lea and Young (1984: 64) argue that mainstream media 'selects events that are atypical, presents them in a stereotypical fashion, and contrasts them against a backcloth of normality which is over-typical'. What quite often exists, then, is a conjunction of misrepresentations and distortions. The power of the moral panic is embedded in this process; atypical events (such as a one-punch event where somebody is killed) are taken, presented in a stereotypical fashion (this is happening everywhere, with young men the innocent victims), and contrasted against the backcloth of a normality that is over-typical (this does not happen or should not happen in this country). What we end up with is a series of media stereotypes (see Box 7.2).

BOX 7.2

MEDIA STEREOTYPES OF YOUNG PEOPLE

- The *ideal* young person:
  - Commercial advertising: healthy, wealthy and fun-loving; freedom, mobility, affluence.
  - The 'exceptional' young person: achievements gained through exceptional talent or by serious hard work.
- Young people as a *threat*:
  - Challenging convention: lack of respect for authority, drugs and alcohol, alternative dress/hair/music.
  - Juvenile offenders: vandals, hoons, larrikins, youth gangs.
- Young people as *victims*:
  - Problems of youth: suicide, homelessness, unemployment; objects of adult pity.
  - Middle-class youth: controlled by drugs/alcohol.
- Young people as *parasites*:
  - Do nothing: lazy, lacking incentive, wasting their time, hanging around.
  - Taking everything: reliant upon adults, on welfare, getting handouts, leeching off others, including parents.

The media stereotypes in Box 7.2 were actually observed several decades ago (see White 1990) and yet they have hardly changed since. Basically, a look at the stereotypes of young people in the media will likely produce this kind of list.

These stereotypes are not necessarily new, and tend to be based upon myths that go back several centuries. For example, the 'hooligan' has historically long been part of popular folklore, and is represented today in the form of 'louts', 'larrikins' and 'gangs' (Pearson 1983; White 2013). So too the drug problem perennially is construed as the 'youth' drug problem. A 1937 US Government docudrama, for instance, exclaimed that: 'Organized gangs are distributing drugs to every school in this city ... dope peddlers infest our high schools ... in every community and hamlet in our country. Hundreds of new (drug) cases involving our youth come in every day ... Drug-crazed teens have murdered entire families' (Males 1996: 260). The scourge of 'ice' (crystal meth) has been presented in much the same way in Australia, and is likewise seen predominantly as something destroying the lives of young people. This is dramatically reinforced by crime drama television series, such as *Breaking Bad*, and graphic advertisements featuring violent episodes in hospitals that are attempting to provide care to ice addicts.

Dating back to the early twentieth century, adolescence has consistently been presented as a period of storms and stresses, as a special time of life, when people are a bit confused and need assistance in order to grow up properly (Hall 1905). This theme was evident when, in 1987, *The New Physician*, a US magazine, commented on teen suicide: 'Adolescence is a time of turbulence marked by rapid physical, sexual, social and emotional development. It is a time of confusion and rebellion' (cited in Males 1996: 33). That phrase alone could be used to describe most of our lives at almost any point. For example, there is much media talk about the time of changes for women, about the time of changes for men, occurring as they move into middle age, and these could easily be seen as 'the time of changes is a time of turbulence marked by rapid physical, sexual, social and emotional development', in varying ways. Nonetheless, a look at the rate of suicide for teenagers in the 1980s shows that teen suicide rates were 'only one fourth those of physicians' (Males 1996: 33).

Analysis of how youth are presented in media presents a picture in which white, middle-class young people are considered 'good' and minority or Indigenous, working-class young people as 'bad' (White 1990; Sercombe 1995). When the so-called 'good' young people are implicated in crime this is seen as something that stems to events beyond their conscious control (e.g. unscrupulous drug dealers). When 'bad' young people are arrested for a crime, this is seen to be entirely their own fault and to reflect their essential evilness (e.g. they indulge in drugs by choice). The class, gender and ethnic inequalities in the way the media portray young people and crime warrants ongoing analysis and critique. Different discourses are used to frame issues and individuals in different ways. For example, often it is the white, middle-class young people who are called 'kids', but if someone happens to be Indigenous or working-class, they would be called a 'druggie'.

We can also look at media in terms of how they portray young people literally—in other words the impact of photography and the way in which photography does not speak for itself. The expression 'a picture is worth a thousand words' is not quite as simple as it may first appear. For example, the words underneath a picture can completely transform the ordinary meaning of a photo (see Box 7.3). A classic case of this is from 22 November 1993, when the *Herald Sun* newspaper presented the photos of three ordinary-looking young boys. Even though this is an Australian publication, it was a representation of a case from the United Kingdom in which two older boys had killed a younger boy. All three photos, in another context, would have been seen as pictures of just three ordinary children. A small inset photo featured two-year-old James Bulger (the victim). The larger photos included 10-year-old Jon Venables, captioned 'cunning and wicked', and 10-year-old Robert Thompson, captioned 'a cold, evil smile' (the perpetrators). Linking the photos of the two older boys were the large underlined words of a police officer: 'I believe human nature spurts out freaks. These two were freaks who just found each other. You should not compare these two boys with other boys—they were evil'. The message is clear.

BOX 7.3

WORDS AND IMAGES

In our own teaching, we occasionally use an exercise where we put up two sets of photographs. One is a set of photographs without captions, comprised of just mugshots of people who have committed a crime. These are taken from a local newspaper. Then we put up another set of photographs, uncaptioned, again from the same newspaper, with exactly the same kind of mugshot (the original caption was 'I want work'). These images related to a campaign where newspapers would post profile shots of people and describe what work the person wanted. We just clipped off the subheading or the caption underneath each of these and put them at random together into one slide. We then invited the class to identify who was the criminal and who was the person wanting work. Guess what? They could not do it. Students could not distinguish between the two, because basically all the images looked the same. Without the caption, they could not interpret whether the person was in the 'mugshot' because of a crime or because they wanted to work. This highlights the way in which the captions to photographs, including those used by and in media, 'tell us, in words, exactly how the subject's expression *ought to be read*' (Hall 1981: 229).

The influence and importance of visual captions in framing is found in how they set up expectations. We end up 're-seeing' the people because of the caption, even if the message is something the original photo did not intend. For example, the original photo in the case of both of these 10-year-old boys complied with the conceptions of the 'normal' child and its connotations of innocence. Indeed, one of them was a school photo. It is the caption, which disturbs these images and frames them through an oppositional discourse, that emphasises abnormality. A disjunction exists between appearance and being, and Thompson and Venables, in the words of Young (1997: 115) '*appear* to be children but they are not: they are more like evil adults or monsters in disguise'. As with horror movies, there is a veneer of normality but underneath this, evil lurks.

Another phenomenon related to moral panics is the introduction of specific types of legal reform that break with usual practice. To explain this, we can examine a recent moral panic in New South Wales (NSW) pertaining to rock throwing, especially off overpasses on major highways; one such incident led to a person being killed because of the thrown objects. After a number of high-profile incidents in Sydney, the NSW Attorney-General introduced a Bill related to rock throwing. The second reading of the Bill said: 'The bill recognises and responds to well-founded community concerns about the abhorrent practice of rock throwing by introducing a new five-year, stand-alone offence for throwing objects at vehicles or vessels' (cited in Loughnan 2010).

This has been called **particularism**. Particularism has been defined as the practice of the drafting of offences where the particular wording of offences provides the definitional detail that exemplifies rather than delimits the wrongdoing (Loughnan 2010). The result is that new specific offences are created (such as 'rock throwing') that could have been covered underneath a general overarching principal offence (such as 'assault'). Particularism arises out of moral panics. In this instance, there was one tragic death in NSW that generated the moral panic. The response of politicians was to create new criminal laws specific to that particular kind of behaviour, rather than using existing laws that cover general behaviour of a similar nature. The consequence of particularism is that it cannot distinguish between different kinds of offences and degrees of wrongdoing. The offence of 'assault', for example, allows for gradations of harm and seriousness, and degrees of moral culpability, with suitable penalties to match. An offence termed 'rock throwing' describes the factually proscribed conduct, but does not allow for these finer moral distinctions.

The concept of particularism is important because, as will be discussed below in reference to 'one punch' laws, NSW continues to do exactly the same thing time and again—that is, the Parliament names a law and constructs a new criminal offence that is very particular to a specific type of action. In our example, it is the moral panic over rock throwing that led to the creation of a new law even though the harm caused by the rock throwing was already covered under existing criminal laws (i.e. 'assault'). However, the way in which the new law is constructed and framed does not tell us anything about the immorality of rock throwing as such. This is because it is not situated within a general concept of harm within which such distinctions are able to be made.

To put it differently, the criminal law is premised on establishing the difference between right and wrong, to set differentials in terms of the seriousness of offences, and to assert that certain acts are an affront to moral standards and values of the community. The criminal law is thus meant to convey the seriousness of an act or omission. It is not clear that the offence of rock throwing delineates something morally (as opposed to factually) distinct about the proscribed conduct—all rock throwing is treated the same. Conversely, the crime of 'assault' does do this, because it distinguishes between kinds of offences and degrees of wrongdoing. By contrast, while not all rock throwing leads to tragic conclusions, the offence is treated the same regardless.

MORAL PANICS AND STREET VIOLENCE

The search for audiences by mainstream media, and indeed social media, has exacerbated the processes of **tabloidisation**, which emphasise entertainment values, the power of the visual and news as entertaining spectacle. Broadsheet newspapers have historically favoured news stories that are supported by expert opinion and research-based evidence, rather than eyewitnesses and less reliable sources (although even this is changing). Images and headlines count in the media wars, and so the tabloid format has acquired a certain ascendency, even in regard to the so-called 'quality press'. This is perhaps most dramatically illustrated in several years of tabloid coverage of alcohol-related violence and disorder in Australia.

The headlines are familiar (see Wadds 2015):

> 'Another Drunken Night on the Streets—OUR DRUNKEN NIGHTLIFE' (2007)
> 'Never-Ending Violent Season Thrust Upon Us' (2007)
> 'The Worse for Drink: Public Violence Soars' (2007)
> 'Drunks Add to Social Fears' (2008)
> 'We are Living in Fear of Drunken Violence' (2008)

Things started to come to a head, in terms of moral panic and institutional consequences, with the death of Thomas Kelly in Sydney in July 2012. The death of the 18-year-old set off intense public debate about street violence and 'king hits'. For this crime, 19-year-old Kieran Loveridge was charged with murder. The newspapers lamented that:

> Another Saturday night, another cohort of young men bashed, stabbed, even killed, as our streets become no-go zones ... where an innocent word or sideways look can bring the wrath of the unhinged down on a young man out having a good time with his mates (Devine 2012).

A flurry of similar dystopian articles hit the streets (Wadds 2013; 2015):

> 'Cross Marks Spot Where Violence is All Too Common' (2012)
> 'Young Man Senselessly Murdered in Random Act of Madness—Kings Cross Bashing' (2012)
> 'Unprovoked: Teen Talking on Phone Fatally Punched on First Night Out in Kings Cross' (2012)
> 'Enough is Enough with Kings Cross Lawlessness' (2012)
> 'Crossing the Line into the Danger Zone' (2012)

But news media and social media coverage of the night-time economy (NTE) is ambivalent. On the one hand, the commercial viability of the NTE rests upon the portrayal of the city after dark as a liminal and transgressive leisure environment—where 'things happen' (violence, drug-taking, binge drinking, sexual exploration): this is precisely its appeal! From Kings Cross in Sydney to Northbridge in Perth, certain areas are attractive to tourists and locals alike because they offer variety and opportunity in activities. On the other hand, moral panic, harsh regulation and interventionist policing threatens to upset the alluring mix of threat, risk and excitement that is so central to the viability of the NTE.

One result of this tension between 'attraction' and 'repulsion' is that news media often engage in individualised and decontextualised treatment of specific incidents and issues. The same response is also evident in political responses based upon 'particularism' as described above. For example, on 8 November 2013, Kieran Loveridge was sentenced to a total of seven years and two months for the combined manslaughter of Thomas Kelly and four other unrelated assaults. Considered by some as too lenient, the sentence triggered outrage across news media headlines; so much so that, by 12 November, the NSW Attorney-General had announced a proposed so-called 'one punch' law for NSW, based on a Western Australian 'one punch law', but instead of carrying a maximum penalty of 10 years, it was proposed that, in NSW, the maximum penalty consist of 20 years imprisonment.

Experts disagreed with this reaction to the incident, and criticised the proposal as basically being wrong in law. According to the former Director of Public Prosecutions of NSW, Nicholas Cowdery, the specific case prompting the law reform was never a case of murder. He pointed out that:

> 'One punch manslaughters' are a common feature of the criminal justice process. It is not murder because the mental elements of murder cannot be proved—intention to kill, intention to cause grievous bodily harm or recklessness (which requires proof that the offender turned his (sic) mind to the possible consequences of his action before he acted). The Crown would rarely be able to prove (especially without any admissions), in a case of an intoxicated and volatile offender, that he had a specific state of mind when he acted (Cowdery 2013).

Moreover, Cowdery queried who in fact was in the best position to judge this or any other case associated with NTE activities:

> The person in the best position to know if the sentence imposed upon Loveridge is the right sentence is the sentencing judge. He has read all the relevant material. He knows the law. He has heard the submissions of the representatives of Loveridge and the community. He has assembled all the competing considerations in his Remarks on Sentence and imposed a sentence that he considers appropriate and within the proper range for such offending (there can never be just one, single, correct sentence for any serious offence) (Cowdery 2013).

While experts and experienced members of the bar argued the merits or otherwise of impending legislation and specific cases, it was not long before a media tornado was building again. This saw the widespread appropriation of the term 'coward punch' by media outlets and social commentators. The occasion for this was when 18-year-old Daniel Christie was assaulted in Kings Cross on New Year's Eve, and subsequently died. A 25-year-old man, Shaun McNeil, was charged with maliciously inflicting grievous bodily harm over the attack. Soon after, the family of Daniel Christie released a statement expressing their gratitude for the support of doctors, the police and the general public. They called for the term 'king hit' to be replaced by 'coward punch'. Immense media pressure was then put on the NSW Government to act quickly, symbolically and forcefully in response to the Thomas Kelly and Daniel Christie cases.

Much was made of the fact that such events had occurred over and over again. For example, Paul Stanley lost his 15-year-old son Matthew in 2006 after he was fatally punched outside a party in Brisbane. A headline from *The Guardian* eight years later ran: 'It's a "coward's punch": man whose son died at party says "king hit" hides truth' (Hurst 2014). Reports across news media pointed out that king hits had claimed 91 lives in Australia since 2000 (see, for example, Needham & Smith 2014). NSW had the highest toll with 28 victims. Soon after this extensive media push, NSW saw the introduction of 'one punch' laws.

Specifically, on 30 January 2014, the NSW Parliament added two new offences to the *Crimes Act 1900* (NSW), sections 25A and 25B:

- Assault causing death; and
- An aggravated version of that offence where the offender is intoxicated at the time of committing the offence.

Maximum penalty: imprisonment for 20 years.
Aggravated maximum: imprisonment for 25 years.

These changes largely ignored the recommendations of law reform commissions in Australia (especially Western Australia and Queensland) that had expressly recommended against their introduction (Quilter 2014). Commentators criticised this particular Act on the basis of technical difficulties in the Act itself (e.g. such as defining 'intoxication') as well as the lack of a definitional or operational gap requiring such law reform (Quilter 2014). For example, in regards to convictions for one-punch manslaughters, it is notable that in 18 cases of what may be called 'one punch' manslaughters from 1998 to 2013 all but one proceeded to trial with the offender pleading guilty to manslaughter (Quilter 2014).

Media frenzies such as this basically lead politicians to enact bad law. As Garland (2001: 112) puts it, responses tend to be 'urgent and impassioned, built around shocking but atypical cases, and more concerned to accord with political ideology and popular perception than with expert knowledge or the proven capabilities of institutions'. In this instance, the increase in media reporting on the topic of 'pubs and violence' since 2003 has not been matched by figures from the NSW Bureau of Crime Statistics and Research (BOCSAR), which show that if anything there has been a marked decline in non-domestic assault incidents recorded by NSW Police in Kings Cross over the past five years (New South Wales Bureau of Crime Statistics and Research 2014). Bad law is thus founded upon bad news that actually distorts overall trends.

Statistics produced by NSW BOCSAR showed that there was no statistically significant upward or downward trend in the monthly numbers of recorded criminal incidents for 'assault–non-domestic violence' over the same period of time that the media frenzy and political concern about drunken violence was at its high point (Wadds 2013). In fact, Kings Cross statistics showed a 3.3 drop in average annual per cent change over 10 years from 2002 to 2011. As Table 7.1 demonstrates, assaults have remained stable and/or declined over the years, regardless of media pronouncements to the contrary and legislative intervention.

TABLE 7.1   Kings Cross violence 2002–11

Non-domestic assault incidents recorded by NSW Police				
	On licensed premises		Off licensed premises	
	postcode 2011	KC LAC	postcode 2011	KC LAC
2 year trend average annual % change	−20.2	−19.6	Stable	Stable
5 year trend	−5.5	Stable	Stable	Stable
To August 2013				

Source: NSW Bureau of Crime Statistics and Research (BOCSAR) 2014.

To consider whether crime is increasing, there is a need to also put things into a wider context and perspective. For example, in medieval and early modern England, levels of violence were dramatically higher than today. In Oxford in 1340, for example, there were 110 murders per 100 000 people, while at present the rate is about 1.9 per 100 000. The general rate for murder during the twentieth century is one-sixteenth of the level in the convict period; one-thirteenth of the gold rush level; one-quarter of the 1870s; and one-half of the 1890s (Grabosky 1989). Things are not necessarily 'getting worse' at all.

Yet underlying the moral panic over street violence and alcohol-related violence are certain shifts in the nature of violence and its contexts. For example, the 'traditional' violence of young working-class men was typically based upon long-standing traditions of male working-class leisure and entertainment. A 'top night out' (Tomsen 1997) might include elements such as getting pissed and having a punch-up, doing things with their mates in their own territory and neighbourhoods, where conflict occurs there being defined 'rules of engagement', and returning to the same pub or places regularly. By contrast, 'contemporary' violence takes place in the NTE characterised by mass congregations of people, multiple alcohol outlets and an anonymous presence. The party culture associated with this can include elements such as getting paralytic and punching anyone, doing things in unfamiliar and uncertain territory, engaging in conflict where there are no defined 'rules of engagement', and having a series of one-off encounters and visits (see White 2013).

Underlying present-day street violence are certain social structural features pertaining to contemporary Australian society (see, for example, Flynn, Halsey & Lee 2016). Moral panics that exaggerate and that have certain social and legal consequences can be distinguished from more embedded social problems that demand going beyond individualising cases, decontextualisation and sensationalism. The particularism of law reform spurred by moral panic, for instance, leaves no opportunity for the emergence of considered opinion that further criminalisation or draconian penalties may not in fact be the best regulatory tool for addressing the problem of alcohol-related violence (Quilter 2014). The 'truth' inherent in any moral panic ought not to blind us to the deeper issues and strategic responses needed to address their essential message. Violence in particular instances can indeed be 'bad' and have profoundly negative consequences. But this violence always occurs within a particular social, economic and political context.

Table 7.2 presents a schematic overview of conventional media and social issues relating to alcohol and violence. The top part identifies a series of 'moral panics'. These, it is suggested, tend to be event-driven—that is, they are sparked by specific incidents, incidents that may and quite often do reoccur on a regular basis. They are the prime fodder for mass-circulation daily newspapers and current affairs television.

The bottom part of the figure alludes to 'social problems'. These, it is suggested, are structurally and culturally embedded into the core fabric of Australian society. It is these that garner less attention in public debates about alcohol and violence, but which nonetheless constitute the most significant and profound aspects of these debates. These are the issues sometimes put into the too-hard basket, and which seldom feature in day-to-day portrayals of the alcohol–violence nexus.

TABLE 7.2   Perceptions and interpretations of issues

Perception	Impetus for action	Spotlight issue
Event driven		
alcohol-related violence is increasing	'moral panics' (e.g. binge drinking)	alcohol consumption and misuse
female violence is on the rise	'moral panics' (e.g. ladettes)	gender roles and problematic heterosexism
street fights and pub brawls	'moral panics' (e.g. glassing)	mindless thuggery and inappropriate behaviour
Structurally embedded		
violence is prevalent	'social problem' (e.g. chronic violence)	violence is bad within society, but may not be increasing as such
violence is overwhelmingly male in nature	'social problem' (e.g. masculinity)	violence and social identity
alcohol-related violence is typical not abnormal	'social problem' (e.g. drink and fight culture)	drunkenness and violence is a harmful form of recreation

Source: White, Wyn & Robards 2017.

Interestingly, research in the Netherlands shows that different sections of the media treat youth crime differently, more or less in line with the 'moral panics' and 'social problems' division suggested in Table 7.2. For example, it has been pointed out that: 'Youth crime coverage in popular media and new media goes hand in hand with a stronger episodic focus over time, while the elite press covers youth crime increasingly thematically' (Ruigrok et al. 2016: 15). Even though the framing of youth crime differs in this respect (as incidents only and with too little context *compared with* focus on causes and possible remedies), it is still the case that sections of the mainstream media reinforce the fear of youth crime. This is so, regardless of the fact that the number of registered juvenile suspects has been declining markedly at the same time. Moreover, mainstream media tend to support the idea that repressive measures are needed, in the first instance based on news coverage about youth crime that is exaggerated compared to the facts, and in the second due to news coverage that is dominated by governmental sources that argue for punitive measures (Ruigrok et al. 2016). Even though the conclusions are arrived at by separate and different types of media framing depending upon the media in question, the net result across the board is to create a similar overarching frame; one that emphasises fear and repression.

A media-fuelled moral panic around teenage drinking will privilege questions of alcohol use over and above those of violence. A concern with violence, on the other hand, will focus attention and energy on the dynamics and causes of the violence. In more specific terms, alcohol-related violence may be interpreted simply and solely in terms of licensed premises and night-time districts. Each of these foci may, in their own right, tap into an important social issue. However, jumping on a moral panic bandwagon that sees issues through a narrow and sensationalistic lens may well distract from seeking solutions that can address the more profound underlying social problems.

Finally, it is notable that moral panics over 'king hits' or 'coward punches' seem to also have a racial dimension. The 'signal crimes' as defined by and within news media tend to feature 'white' young men. By contrast, Graham (2016) points out how, in Queensland, 40-year-old Trevor Duroux died in a one-punch assault on the Gold Coast—but there was not one single story in the media about this event. This occurred one month before 18-year-old Cole Miller died and made headlines in Brisbane. After considering the two cases carefully, Graham (2016) concluded that, apart from their age, there was one major difference between the Trevor Duroux and Cole Miller cases—Duroux was an Aboriginal man.

ISSUES FOR CONSIDERATION
THE COLOUR OF JUSTICE

Media reporting of young offenders is frequently racially biased, particularly in regards to Indigenous young people and young men of colour. What is less commented on is the systematic way in which the Australian state intervenes in the lives of the 'colonial subject'.

For example, the concept of 'hyperincarceration' is based on the notion that there is a broad complex of law, policy and practice that frames the use of imprisonment, and that increases in imprisonment are not undifferentiated, but very selective (Cunneen et al. 2013). While it may make sense to talk about 'mass incarceration' in the context of US penal developments (Garland 2001; Wacquant 2009), this is less accurate or insightful when it comes to conceptualising what is occurring in the Australian context. Here, what is striking is that increased imprisonment has been targeted at particular racialised groups, most dramatically evident in Indigenous over-representation figures, as well as other marginalised groups within the wider society, such as people with mental health disorders and drug and alcohol addictions (Cunneen et al. 2013).

Cunneen et al. (2013) argue that the rapid increases in imprisonment rates across Australian jurisdictions since the mid-1980s can be seen as predominantly composed of Indigenous men, women and young people. This is the essence of hyperincarceration in an Australian context. Indeed, penal culture in this country hinges upon the nature of the colonial subject as 'Other'. The history of Australia is a history of colonial penality in which subjugated populations have suffered more than two hundred years of imprisonment and punishment. Mainstream punishment has always been directed against particular subjects and, in the Australian context, penal excess has been marked by racialised penal regimes developed specifically for Indigenous peoples (Cunneen et al. 2013). The (limited) introduction of Indigenous sentencing courts and similar types of 'alternative' forms of punishment systems belies the long-standing, continuing and growing over-representation of Indigenous people within the harshest parts of the criminal justice system nationally.

The overarching focus of juvenile justice today seems to be less about the welfare, support and/or rehabilitation of young people than about making them accountable and ensuring a modicum of community safety (Cunneen, White & Richards 2015). A hybrid system that combines punitive features (such as juvenile detention) with reparation philosophies (such as juvenile conferencing) makes sense only insofar as it reflects a differentiated profile of young offenders. The serious and persistent offender is liable to be punished up to and including the use of detention. The low-risk offender is asked to make amends for their wrongdoing by repairing the harm and perhaps making an apology. Meanwhile, the potential offender is dealt with through deployment of risk assessment technologies and ongoing surveillance in order to prevent future deviation. All of this is overladen by clear racial and class biases in the system (White 2015).

Popular images of criminality and offending behaviour provide for a racialising discourse at the centre of which are Indigenous young men (Cunneen et al. 2013). This translates at an empirical level into high rates of intervention and incarceration, even when the system as a whole is contracting. For example, recent figures on the number and rate of young people under supervision in Australia (both in the community and in detention) show a fall in the number of young people under supervision in 2012–13. Yet, of those under supervision, young people aged 10–17 years from the areas of lowest socio-economic status were more than five times as likely to be under supervision as those from the areas of highest socio-economic status (Australian Institute for Health and Welfare [AIHW] 2014a). Between 2008–09 and 2012–13, the level of Indigenous over-representation in supervision on an average day *increased* in all states and territories for which data were available, except in South Australia and Tasmania (AIHW 2014a). Furthermore, in 2012–13, Indigenous young people were 17 times as likely as non-Indigenous young people to have been under supervision and they were also, on average:

- younger (27 per cent were aged 10–14 years, compared with 13 per cent non-Indigenous)
- more likely to complete multiple periods of supervision (22 per cent, compared with 14 per cent)
- spending longer, in total, under supervision during the year (195 days, on average, compared with 180) (AIHW 2014a).

To put these figures into further perspective, the Indigenous youth population comprises less than 5 per cent of the total youth population in Australia. Yet, 49 per cent of all young men held in youth detention were Indigenous (i.e. almost half), and 54 per cent of all young women held in youth detention were Indigenous (i.e. more than half) (AIHW 2014b). Indigenous young people under supervision were more likely than non-Indigenous young people to have lived in remote or very remote areas before entering supervision (10 per cent compared with less than 1 per cent), and also more likely to have lived in areas of lowest socio-economic status before entering supervision (44 per cent compared with 35 per cent) (AIHW 2014c). There has been no 'moral panic' over this hyperincarceration, which in itself indicates a normalisation of expectation and reliance upon stereotypes as implicit justifications of the socially unjust.

Yet, a 2016 *Four Corners* exposé of torture and mistreatment of largely Indigenous young people at Don Dale Youth Detention Centre in the Northern Territory did prompt the immediate establishment of a Royal Commission into the abuse (Meldrum-Hanna & Worthington 2016; Oaten 2016). Interestingly, much of the public debate surrounding this event and the response of Prime Minister Malcolm Turnbull revolved around extending the terms of reference of the Royal Commission to include all youth detention centres in all states and territories. This in itself indicates the growing unease among many Australians about who fills these centres—and the lack of action in regard to this.

STIGMATISATION AND YOUTH VULNERABILITY

Within criminology, labelling perspectives look at the impact of the application of certain labels (e.g. 'bad', 'criminal' and 'delinquent') in fostering deviant behaviour (White, Haines & Asquith 2017). Public labelling, it is argued, may affect individuals' self-identity and transform them so that they see themselves in the light of the label. The process of labelling is tied up with the idea of the self-fulfilling prophecy. That is, if you tell someone sufficiently often that they are 'bad' or 'stupid' or 'crazy', that person may start to believe the label and to act out the stereotypical behaviour associated with it, thereby further reinforcing the label.

A further aspect of the public labelling process is that stigmatisation may occur. This involves the application of a negative label that becomes the 'master' (or dominant) definition of the person to whom it is applied. Regardless of current behaviour or past experiences, a person may become known to the wider community mainly or solely in terms of the label applied to them. A negative label, such as 'criminal' or 'delinquent', can colour the perceptions of people with whom the individual interacts and influence how the community in general treats that person (Goffman 1963). Where such stigma exists, a situation may arise where the 'deviant' begins to live up to the dictates of the label and to change their identity and behaviour accordingly.

Labelling theories in criminology have had their greatest impact in the specific area of juvenile justice. This is not surprising, given the general view that young people and children are more impressionable than older people, and therefore more likely to respond to any labelling that might occur. Whether they are good or bad, negative or positive, constructive or destructive, labels, it is argued, do affect and have consequences for subsequent behaviour. This approach sees crime and deviance as socially constructed categories (rather than objective phenomena) that are maintained, perpetuated or amplified by the labelling process. The process of social reaction defines not only acts, but also people. Criminality is thus something that is conferred upon some individuals, and on some types of behaviour, by social control agents that have the power to do so, and have sufficient authority and credibility to make the label stick (i.e. cause the label to be internalised so that it shapes personal identity and action).

A key feature of many moral panics pertaining to young people is that they reinforce negative stereotypes for already vulnerable groups. This is certainly the case for Indigenous young people. Others are affected negatively as well, not only by stigmatisation, but also by becoming entwined in deviancy amplification. Media treatment of homeless people, drug-using street young people, children and young people in state care and so on tend to reinforce images of pity, transgression, risk and community insecurity. The outcome is a control agenda for those who do not fit in to the existing social institutions of family, school and leisure.

This is evident to some extent when examining the relationship between institutionalisation and incarceration. The facts bear out that frequently it is the most vulnerable children and young people who are the most feared and who are the most penalised. Each type of vulnerability goes hand-in-hand with another, forging a picture that is tragic in its gross outline. For example, each year, at least 100 000 children and young Australians access homelessness services; 30 000 have a notification of abuse or neglect substantiated by a child protection agency; 70 000 are proceeded against by police for criminal activity; and 14 500 are supervised by juvenile justice agencies in the community or placed in juvenile detention (AIHW 2012). In a nutshell, people with involvement in one of the three sectors (supported accommodation, juvenile justice, child protection) are more likely to be involved in another of the sectors than the general population. This means, for example, that young people with a child protection history enter juvenile justice supervision at a younger age (AIHW 2012).

CONCLUSION

This chapter has considered the application of the concept of 'moral panic' in regard to the behaviour and activities of young people. Closely associated with this concept are the notions of deviancy amplification and stigmatisation. News media often frame issues in ways that particularise and decontextualise, with the consequence that specific events are separated from wider structural causes and contexts. Specific groups of young people are singled out for negative treatment, again with institutional consequences that affect their lives in profound and long-lasting ways.

Media may present distorted views of crime and crime control, but the social impact or ramifications of such distortions are certain to be complex and multidirectional. Big questions remain as to the specific effect of media on particular individuals and groups of people. What evidence is there to support or deny particular 'media effects' in concrete cases? To what extent are images promulgated by media a contributory factor in or major cause of criminal, harmful or deviant behaviour? For example, do movies about gangs create gang-like responses among groups of teenagers? How do action movies, war video games and DVDs that feature horror and terror themes (and, we might add, the nightly news) sensitise or desensitise viewers to real-world suffering and atrocities?

It is not only attitudes and beliefs that may be conveyed and that may be influential. Crime fiction, both print and visual, often provides detailed information about how particular crimes are committed (and solved). Knowledge and techniques are important components of the processes that underpin harm and victimisation. The 'how to' can be just as important as the 'why to' when it comes to engagement in specific acts that do harm. Crime, too, is learned behaviour, and media can be a significant, if not entirely reliable, teacher. In an era where we are now witnessing teenage killers who have been radicalised via the internet, such questions remain important.

DISCUSSION QUESTIONS

1. In some instances, the sex, drugs, violence and excitement of criminality—at least as portrayed on screen—could well be seen as attracting rather than dissuading people from a 'life of crime'. Discuss.
2. How do specific individuals and groups of young people respond to the negative (or positive) media portrayals of their activities? Is stigmatisation necessarily something to avoid (especially if one's street credibility depends on it)?
3. Do media construct what is 'normal' as well as what is 'deviant'?

4. In what ways do social media construct and contribute to moral panics? Discuss in relation to the notion of 'coward punches'.

5. What evidence is there that news media can have positive pro-social effects on young people, especially in regards to their behaviour in the night-time economy?

WORKSHOP ACTIVITY: THE CYCLE OF JUVENILE JUSTICE

It has been argued in the United States (see Bernard & Kurlychek 2010: 4) that there is a cycle of juvenile justice involving four interrelated elements, each representing a stage or time period of concern:

- Juvenile crime is thought to be unusually high and is blamed on lenient treatment.
- Juvenile crime is thought to be unusually high but officials are forced to choose between harshly punishing the juvenile offenders and doing nothing at all.
- Juvenile crime is thought to be unusually high and is blamed on both harshly punishing and doing nothing at all.
- A major reform introduces lenient treatments for juvenile offenders so as to create a middle ground between harshly punishing and doing nothing at all.

Provide examples from your local context where media have engaged in specific types of campaigns, including inspiring moral panics, in regard to each part of this cycle.

FURTHER READING

Cohen, S. (1972). *Folk Devils and Moral Panics: The Creation of the Mods and Rockers*. London: MacGibbon and Kee Ltd.

Crofts, T., Lee, M., McGovern, A. & Milivojevic, S. (2014). Sexting and Young People. *Legaldate*, 26(4), 2–4.

Cunneen, C., White, R. & Richards, K. (2015). *Juvenile Justice: Youth and Crime in Australia*. Melbourne: Oxford University Press.

Pearson, G. (1983). *Hooligan: A History of Respectable Fears*. London: Macmillan.

Ruigrok, N., van Atteveldt, W., Gagestein, S. & Jacobi, C. (2016). Media and Juvenile Delinquency: A Study into the Relationship between Journalists, Politics, and Public. *Journalism*, 1–19: DOI: 10.1177/1464884916636143.

8

RACIALISED VIOLENCE AND HATE CRIME

CHAPTER HIGHLIGHTS

Introduction
Ethnicity, deviancy and the media
Islamophobia and the Arab Other
Conclusion

INTRODUCTION

The aim of this chapter is to critically consider issues pertaining to race and ethnicity by examining the place and role of racism in mediated constructions of crime and deviancy. We see 'race' not as a biological given, but as a social construct, based upon perceived differences between groups on the basis of factors such as physical features, cultural background, language, religion and country of origin. Ethnicity is a related, but separate, concept. It refers to cultural attributes within social groups that form the basis of a shared sense of identity both within the group itself and by those outside of it. Commonalities may include physical appearance, religious allegiance, language, custom, attachment to an ancestral homeland or some combination of these (White & Perrone 2015).

Racism can be seen as a combination of beliefs and behaviours that involve aggressive, abusive and offensive attitudes and actions towards members of other groups based on a belief that some races, religions and ethnic groups are inherently superior to others. The most harmful sorts of racism involve crime—for example, hate crime, sometimes described as bias crime or prejudice-related crime, is violence, bigotry and hostility that are directed at vulnerable individuals or groups on the basis of their actual or perceived sexuality, disability or membership of a racial, ethnic or religious minority group. Often the motive behind the violence is the intimidation of the group as a whole (Cunneen, Fraser & Tomsen 1997; Garland 2011). According to Perry (2009), hate crime is intended to emphasise the 'othering' of those visibly different, and both reflects and reinforces existing hegemonic power structures and hierarchies of domination and subordination. Violence includes assault, homicide, vilification, harassment or attacks on property, including firebombing and graffiti. In Australia, most hate crimes have been directed against minority groups, including gay men and lesbian women, disabled communities, Indigenous Australians and non-English-speaking background (NESB) migrants, especially the Jewish, Muslim, Asian and Indian communities (Mason 2011; 2012).

The pattern of hate crime is quite distinct from other forms of violence in that, unlike most violence, which occurs between people who have some form of relationship with one another, hate crime often involves the targeting of people who are strangers to the assailant and have had no engagement of any kind with them. It is the perception that the victim belongs to a particular out-group that leads to the violence, rather than their individual characteristics or behaviour (Human Rights and Equal Opportunity Commission 1991; Garland 2011; Chakraborti & Garland 2012). At the same time, hate crimes also include attacks on individuals who are known to perpetrators, but the motive for their attack is not tied up with *who they are individually*, but rather *what they represent*—their perceived membership of a particular hated group (Tomsen 2009). In either scenario, the intention is to send a threatening, symbolic message not only to the immediate victim, but to the wider group or community to which they belong (Garland 2011).

The origins and dynamics of racism vary depending upon national, historical and regional context. In other words, racism impacts upon vulnerable groups and communities, but the reasons for this are not the same. For example, colonialism refers to the invasion of one people's territory by another, with subsequent physical, spiritual and economic displacement, and theft of the land of the original people. In Australia, colonialism has had a severe impact on Indigenous cultures and ways of life, as discriminatory policies and practices continue to affect the life chances of Indigenous people within mainstream social institutions. On the other hand, another source of racism relates to processes of immigration, involving the movement of people from diverse parts of the world to settle in a new place, in which there are dominant ethnic groups and minority ethnic groups, and subsequent experiences of prejudice and discrimination. In the United States, for example, not only are issues of colonialism (e.g. in relation to Native American people) and immigration (e.g. in relation to Mexican migrants) strongly associated with racism, but a history of slavery has had an enduring negative impact on African American communities.

Race and ethnicity are therefore basically about identity and differing relations of power based upon identity. Yet, identity is itself an ambiguous and complex phenomenon as attested to by the global images, presence and contexts of youth gangs (see Box 8.1). While there are both commonalities and differences worldwide in gang dynamics, the circulation of certain ideas and images has had manifold consequences across the globe.

To some extent, identity involves elements of choice in who we are (e.g. 'Australian' and/ or 'Vietnamese'), and various hybrid identities (e.g. based on the one hand on where we live, e.g. Australia, and on the other hand on family traditions and cultures, such as being Jewish or Muslim or Christian). Being vilified or privileged in popular discourses also shapes our identity and self-image. For instance, being cast as 'ethnic minority' often implies that some people are 'ethnic' and some are not—even though everyone is connected in some way to a particular ethnic community (or several different communities). Moreover, as this chapter explores, the social construction of minority status is frequently associated with mediated images of deviancy and criminality. A white Anglo-established Australian, however, is often presumed to be the 'standard' or 'norm' by which national identity is ultimately judged, regardless of the actual nature of a multicultural, poly-ethnic Australia.

BOX 8.1

YOUTH GANGS IN A GLOBAL CONTEXT

Different gangs tend to adopt specific forms of (subcultural) jargon, hand gestures, forms of dress, membership rules and insider/outsider relationships and rituals. They do so in the context of the wider 'gang' imagery that provides the grounding upon which identity is constructed. What is built by the young people themselves will share commonalities with their wider cultural narrative ('gang'), specific terminologies within this narrative ('Bloods and Crips'), and elements of biographical and geographical being associated with the gang motif (this is my 'turf').

Yet, gang style and gang images are essentially localised in their re-representation and reconstruction in the lives of particular groups of young people. To put it differently, young people might appropriate 'universal' images, yet they transform these into unique forms and practices that make sense to them within their immediate milieu:

> Despite the similarity in names and gang style, there are important differences between Crips in the USA and Crips in The Netherlands. The latter are far less organized, are not organized around drug sales, are not territorial, and engage in much lower levels of violence. In other words, European Crips have more in common with Crip gang style and affectation than organization or behaviour (Decker, van Gemert & Pyrooz 2009: 401).

Here we have a case of ostensibly similar gang images, symbols and culture that, in reality, are quite different. Along the same lines, the terms 'Bloods' and 'Crips' are also used in New Zealand and Australia, where they essentially comprise ethnic markers: the Bloods refer to Samoan young people, the Crips to Tongan young people (White 2013). The colours each group wears (Bloods, red, Samoan; Crips, blue, Tongan) are immediate and striking signs of ethnic, and indeed, original island origin. The relationship to US Bloods and Crips is tenuous, and the terms have basically been appropriated less as a gang identifier and more as local descriptions of ethnicity.

For the purposes of this chapter, our interest is mainly in how media routinely perform a sort of ethnic selectivity in presenting and interpreting events. For instance, contemporary media images and treatments of certain ethnic minority communities in Australia are generally negative. This was demonstrated in various youth studies undertaken in the 1990s that showed this was especially the case with respect to *groups* such as Vietnamese, Lebanese and Pacific Islander people, although other groups have also felt singled out for negative and stereotyped media treatment (White et al. 1999). The trend has continued today, albeit with different groups in the firing line, such as Sudanese community members. It is frequently the case as well that particular *events* are seized upon by mainstream media to reinforce the 'ethnic' character of deviancy and criminality in ways that stigmatise whole communities (e.g. gang rapes in Sydney) (Poynting & Morgan 2007).

ETHNICITY, DEVIANCY AND THE MEDIA

The persistence of any particular group being seen as a 'folk devil'—that is, an object of hostility that focuses the moral and social anxieties embedded in a moment of panic—stems from the ways in which discourses are assembled over time. For instance, consider the manner in which the 'Arab Other' has been socially constructed in news media in New South Wales. This has involved an ongoing cycle of moral panic, the elements of which have included ideological constructs of:

- crime-prone Arab immigrants
- violent Muslim terrorists
- Middle Eastern queue-jumping refugees with no respect for civilised rules
- Muslims who are seen as failing to integrate (Poynting et al. 2004: 49).

These constructs actually resonate with similar and long-standing types of moral panic going back well over a century in certain parts of the world. For example, from around the mid-1800s onwards, most major cities in the Western world witnessed the emergence of, and moral panics over, groups of young people on the street (Pearson 1983). Variously branded—from 'street Arabs' in London, to 'hoodlums' in San Francisco, to 'larrikins' in Melbourne—the banding together of large groups of young men was essentially linked to urbanisation and industrialisation. Social formations of this type were the child of the industrial revolution, a revolution that placed great masses of people together into urban conglomerations for the purposes of manufacture and trade.

Some commentators in the mid-nineteenth century divided humanity into two broad races, using language such as the 'nomadic' and the 'civilised' to suggest fundamental difference. It is but a small step to see the 'nomad' as the 'street Arab'—that transient person for whom the street itself constitutes home. The 1840s is replete with descriptions of 'predatory hordes' of young people on the street, who appear to almost belong to another race, which in the context of British imperial power opens the door to peculiar forms of naming the 'Other':

> And perhaps it goes without saying that so un-civilised, un-Christian and un-English were these young thieves and rascals that they were known flatly and uniformly in this era as 'street Arabs', 'English Kaffirs' and 'Hottentots' (Pearson 1983: 159).

Importantly, then, words such as 'street Arab' connote not only difference, but *foreign-ness*.

One hundred years or so later, the character of the street has changed, and so has the nature of the moral panics over street-present youth. In high immigration countries such as Australia today, ethnicity is seen to be central to group formation and more generally to the gang phenomenon. This is so both at the level of popular image—as reflected in media fixations with 'ethnic youth gangs'—and in regard to the social activities of large groups of (mainly) young men at the local neighbourhood level. Who a person is, in terms of social identity, is largely determined by ethnic and class background, and gender. Who that person hangs around with is likewise shaped by ethnicity, among other social factors.

Congregations of ethnically identifiable young people have frequently been publicly associated with images that are negative, dangerous and threatening (Asquith 2008). The media have tended to emphasise the 'racial' background of youth groups, and their presumed criminality, to the extent that identification with a particular ethnic group becomes equated with 'gang membership'. The extra visibility of young ethnic minority people feeds the media and public's moral panic over gangs, as well as bolstering a racial stereotyping based upon physical appearance (White 2013). At the time of writing, headlines such as the following pervaded Australian news:

> 'Melbourne Home to More than a Dozen Race-based Street Gangs'—*Herald Sun*, April 2016
> 'Migrant Groups Going Gang Busters'—*The Australian*, April 2016
> 'African Youth Crime Concern'—*The Age*, April 2016
> 'Fear of Cronulla-like Unrest as Refugee Lawlessness Grows in Melbourne'—*The Sydney Morning Herald*, April 2016

Research demonstrates, however, that crime is more of a socio-economic issue than a cultural one (Collins et al. 2000). There is very little reliable evidence that shows that 'ethnic crime' as such is a problem. Instead, its roots appear to lie in factors such as inequality rather than ethnic background (Cunneen, White & Richards 2015). What is a problem, however, is the 'racialised' reporting of crime in which news media uses ethnic identifiers in relation to some groups, but not others (such as Anglo-Celtic Australians). Moreover, the 'explanations' for such 'ethnic crime' tend to pathologise the group, as if there is something intrinsically bad about being, for example, Lebanese or more generally Middle Eastern. These distorted images also suggest that the origins of the criminality stem from outside Australia and are related to immigration policies and 'foreign' ideas and cultures, rather than the social and economic inequalities within the country. This racialisation has a major impact upon public perceptions of the people and the issues, as well as on the response of state agencies, such as the police.

In a similar vein, the dominant construction of Aboriginality within news media is largely negative and tends to be associated with stereotypes such as the long-grasser, juvenile joyrider, petty thief and drunk (Jakubowicz & Goodhall 1994; Sercombe 1995; Trigger 1995). In their analysis of the images of Indigenous people in media, Jakubowicz and Goodhall (1994) argue that positive images tend to be limited to rural and remote locations where the traditional way of life is romanticised. In contrast, images of Indigenous people in urban settings are presented in the context of criminality and disorder. Whatever the setting or the subtext, the images are largely marginal to mainstream Australian culture so that Indigenous people are presented to the white gaze as separate and 'Other', as people who do not belong to ordinary, modern life. These stereotyped images do little to promote understanding of the wide and varied experiences of Indigenous people. Similar distortions are apparent when it comes to the notion of youth gangs.

YOUTH GANGS AND DEVIANCY

The concept of 'gang' is highly contentious and controversial (White 2013). The ambiguities surrounding what a gang is and what gangs do are precisely why the term is both powerful and predictable in public discourses of disorder and danger. Gangs connote predatory and violent action, usually by groups of young men. The concept encapsulates notions of aggression, viciousness, chains of brotherhood forged in combat, and codes of obedience and behaviour that discipline individuals to the group's norms and values. Yet, simultaneously, the idea of gangs has a certain appeal, based on images and portrayals that emphasise shared purpose, strong group bonds, explosions of excitement and adrenaline, and financial and social gratification in the here-and-now. Even the fictionalised accounts of gangs embody these aspects of uncertainty and complexity when it comes to their good and bad features.

One of the main reasons why young people join or form youth 'gangs' is for their own protection and/or to establish their own powerful identity in the face of prejudice, racism and social inequality (White 2013). Sydney-based research, for example, has found that there was an intersection of masculinity, ethnicity and class—in such a way as to affirm social presence, to ensure mutual protection and to compensate for a generally marginalised economic and social position (Collins et al. 2000). Assertion of gang membership can thus be interpreted as attempts by the young men to 'valorise' their lives and empower themselves in the face of outside hostility, disrespect and social marginalisation. Australian gang studies have largely concluded that the rationale for most youth formations is primarily 'fun' (i.e. as part of a social network), rather than 'business' (i.e. as part of a criminal network). Nevertheless, while the purpose for a group forming tended to be social, rather than criminal, each type of group may, to a lesser or greater extent, engage in illegal activity, fights or drug use. This, however, is not driven by the agenda of the group as such, nor is it particularly unusual for Australian teenagers and young adults generally. Much of what happens on the street is contingent upon specific circumstances and events (White 2013).

The present-day concern with the question of gangs mostly stems from negative media treatment of young people, which more often than not is framed in terms of the threat posed by gangs. This is reinforced politically by populist accusations that youth gangs are a major social evil today (Hallsworth & Brotherton 2011). Branding certain young people as 'gangs' has allowed for widespread vilification of particular groups of street-present young people and created political space for the imposition of draconian forms of social control over their behaviour and, indeed, their very presence in the public domain. Moreover, exceptional and dramatic events, such as the England riots of 2011 and Cronulla riots of 2005, provide platforms for the exposition of a form of 'gangs talk' that reduces complex social problems to simple answers and solutions (Hallsworth & Young 2008). Gangs are easy to blame.

The content of 'gangs talk' in recent years and in a number of countries has been imbued with a distinctive 'racial' or 'ethnic' character. Ethnic minorities, people of colour and immigrants have become socially defined through the language of 'gangs', and have steadily been subjected to coercive rather than enabling forms of state intervention. Australian research has shown that in virtually every location around the country, ethnicity is central as to which groups are deemed to be 'gangs' and to who the gang members are (White 2013). The media is directly implicated in both the formation and continued encouragement of youth gangs and much of the coverage of youth crime is couched in the language of 'youth gangs', and especially 'ethnic' youth gangs. The latter is especially the case in Australia, but is certainly not unique to this country (see, for example, Hagedorn 2008; van Gemert et al. 2008; Goldson 2011).

The mediated coverage reinforces the perception that groups of young people are 'out of control' and 'terrorising' ordinary citizens. Thus, any portrayal of 'youth' tends to be linked to criminality, and media discourses on 'law and order' frequently portray youth groups as criminal gangs. Moreover, in order to sell a story, news media often attempt to involve young people directly through interviews and pictures (Collins et al. 2000). If there is no gang as such, then at times young people have been asked to 'pretend' to be gang members 'for the camera'. Not only is this unethical and a gross misrepresentation of actual youth group formations, but it can, ironically, lead to identification of some young people with gang membership—that is, the thrill and excitement of media attention may amplify the desire to be seen as a gang member. Reputation and status thus may be artificially created, but have material and longer-lasting consequences for the young people and communities involved.

Gang membership is also shaped by how others outside of immediate social networks perceive youth group formations. Whether it be media, politicians, law enforcement officials or academics, the portrayal of certain groups of young people as 'gangs' may well produce the very thing that is being described. In other words, most gangs are not that organised, but treating them as if they are has potentially serious social ramifications: 'Treating them like cohesive groups may create a self-fulfilling prophecy ... It can provide the group with a common point of conflict as well as a label and identity, setting a self-fulfilling prophecy in motion' (McGloin 2005: 608). If a particular group is called a 'gang' enough times, then the group may well transform into the very thing that it has been named. This is particularly relevant in regards to the so-called 'Gang of 49' in Adelaide. A group of 49 Indigenous young people were basically lumped together into one social category, sensationally by news media ('gang') and administratively by the police ('Aboriginal'). Eventually, the labelling process itself contributed to a 'real' social problem that government authorities felt compelled to address (Kitik 2009).

Significantly, research indicates that where young people themselves claim gang membership, they tend to engage in substantially more anti-social and criminal behaviour than those who do not profess to be gang members (Esbensen et al. 2001)—that is, who someone says they are has implications for what they do and with whom. Group identification is thus intertwined with group activity. Access to media and communications technologies (e.g. mobile phones, social networking sites such as Facebook and MySpace), and exposure to modelling of risky fighting behaviours through entertainment media (e.g. 'cage fighting'), also have an impact on group decisions and fighting patterns within and between identifiable ethnic groups. In the public eye, some groups are presented as more problematic than others.

Deviancy amplification is also apparent in regard to youth gangs. The uniformly problematic images associated with gangs tend to impose and impact negatively on young people (while simultaneously spurring youth to become that which is problematic). For example, the social consequences of moral panics around youth gangs typically include ostracising and penalising identifiable youth groups—especially migrant and ethnic minority youth—on the basis of their presumed immoral and threatening behaviour, often through the implementation of legislation and stepped-up police interventions to prevent or prohibit street presence and certain types of activity. Moral panics over gangs usually include popular representations of stereotypical gang characteristics (e.g. the colour gangs of US Hollywood ilk) that frequently fail to capture and/or accurately represent nuanced differences in street level youth group formations (White 2013). Nonetheless, the dissemination of such matter has been enhanced by the advent of the internet. Often, what is conveyed is simply wrong or just plain racist (Goldson 2011).

Such representations tend not only to induce panic, fear and anxiety, but they also impact worldwide on the ways in which young people see themselves and their activities; how they behave and make sense of their lives (Hagedorn 2008). Paradoxically, at this level, the gang image is not necessarily seen as 'bad', but rather as something to which to aspire or emulate; the 'gangs' moral panic itself can serve to amplify the excitement attached to the label. For marginalised and often criminalised young people, transgression can be very appealing, especially as it both inverts the negativity of the label (being instead a sought-after status) and reinforces notoriety (since it feeds back into the very thing that is popularly detested). Street credibility and peer respect is fashioned out of precisely the process that most turns the state against the young people in question—the appearance of gang affiliation.

So too, the internet, and the many gang sites online, provide a ready forum for transfer of information, images, ideas and attitudes. Online sites are particularly significant as what is being conveyed includes not only the usual hyper-masculinity trappings, but also affective attributes such as the sense of anger and injustice at being 'on the margins'. Gang membership becomes an important part of social connection and social belonging, at many different levels.

ISLAMOPHOBIA AND THE ARAB OTHER

From the point of view of mainstream media and politicians, young Muslim men—of 'Middle Eastern appearance'—have become the bête noire of sensationalised reportage and political intolerance. From rape gangs to terrorists, the public discourse has vilified Lebanese (Australian) young men in particular (Poynting et al. 2004; Poynting & Morgan 2007). This has been occurring for a number of years, at least back to the time of the first Gulf War in the early 1990s. Lebanese young Australians are the 'larrikins' of modern-day 'outrages'.

The public presence and visibility of Lebanese young people, particularly in western Sydney, forms part of the reason why they have become so prominent in Australian media-driven moral panics. Lebanese Australians have established residence in great numbers in suburbs such as Bankstown. Given their overall socio-economic situation, they now constitute the new 'dangerous classes' of late capitalism and are perceived as a breeding ground for criminality, immorality and social deviance.

Young people hang out in parks and on the street. They engage with rap music, as producers and consumers. They drive around in convoys of cars seeking thrills and excitement. They gather together to socialise—and to fight. They use public space to entertain and to be entertained. This is neither new nor peculiar to this particular group of young people.

But there are important contextual factors that shape the specific content of this particular racialisation process. The post-World War II era witnessed the integration of many new population groups into the Australian social and cultural mosaic, albeit under terms mainly set by the dominant white Anglo majority. This process has generally been characterised by a period of various public oppositions to the new settlers in the first instance, followed by a gradual transformation of the 'Other' into the 'ordinary'. One might consider here, for example, the social history of Greeks and Italians, who were considered initially as 'folk devils'. This contrasts to their place today as *bona fide* citizens and respected contributors to a proudly cosmopolitan Australia.

The experience has been different, however, for recent Muslim and Arabic immigrants, at least within the Sydney context. In this instance, the transition has been troubling, is in a constant state of flux and has not yet been completed. The settling-in process has been interrupted and distorted by overseas events—such as the Gulf Wars and particular terrorist attacks (New York, Washington, London, Madrid, Bali, Paris, Brussels)—and by issues surrounding the wearing of the hijab and burqa that have negatively impacted upon the place and status of Muslims in wider Australian society and fuelled fear of the 'Other' at several levels.

This is also a catch-22 associated with this racialisation process. Racism permeates the lives of many young Muslim and/or Arab men, as it does other ethnic minority groups in Sydney and elsewhere. Coupled with economic, social and political marginalisation, it is no wonder that violence of varying kinds features prominently in their lives. The central paradox for these young people, however, is that the more they try to defend themselves, the more likely they are to be targets. The more they resort to membership of street groups and engagement in fighting to assert themselves, the more they will be treated as 'outsiders' and as deviant. These kinds of images and representations circulate at the global level and reinforce 'folk devil' reputation in the same moment as representing fundamental shifts in the nature of moral panic (see Box 8.2).

BOX 8.2

GLOBAL MORAL PANIC AND ISLAMOPHOBIA

In the global 'West', the racialised 'Muslim Other' has become the pre-eminent 'folk devil' of our time. Morgan and Poynting (2012) argue that this is a global process, involves popular demonology, and is oriented towards the containment of communities of deviance associated with this demonisation. The nature of moral panic has been transformed in three key ways (see Morgan & Poynting 2012):

- First, from 'self-limiting, temporary and spasmodic' to there being connection between discrete moral panics insofar as the process of producing 'folk devils' is ongoing and cumulative. In other words, there is a 'global stock' upon which each 'splutter of rage' draws, engendering cycle after cycle of panic, of a variety of scope and localities.
- Second, from 'local or national panic' to the presentation of the threat to 'our civilisation' as transnational. That is, contemporary Islamophobia is grounded in popular anxieties around transnationalism, in which there operates a global cultural space in which this alternative transnational imagined community is nourished.
- Third, whereas traditional media were the key players in moral panic, the mediascape has passed through epochal changes, involving temporal as well as spatial compression. For instance, news media today is now global and virtually instantaneous, plus there is now social media and the advent of 'citizen journalists' who contribute to the process of producing—and challenging—contemporary panics and folk devils.

The overarching nature of these global moral panics is transforming life at the community level in, at times, quite dramatic ways. In the light of these trends, Morgan and Poynting (2012) claim that globalisation can often accentuate nationalism and xenophobia. It does this through regimes of surveillance and the blurring of boundaries between policing and counter-terrorism; through authorities turning a blind eye to racist vilification and violence—a form of 'permission to hate'; and in struggles over the symbolic presence of Islam in Western cities (such as banning the building of mosques, minarets, Muslim schools and prayer rooms, and challenging the right of Muslim women to wear the 'veil' (hijab, jilbab, niqab, burqa).

Public scaremongering that attempts to link halal food certification with Muslim terrorist groups began as social media campaigns, but has recently gravitated towards mainstream media as well. As one commentator observes, this represents a shift in the representations of Muslims from a visible, alien presence to a hidden, covert threat—they are increasingly targeted not for 'standing out' as misfits, but for 'blending in' as the invisible enemy (Hussein 2015). Whether cast as a visible or invisible threat, the Muslim as enemy is a prominent theme in such media coverage (however, see also Box 8.3).

BOX 8.3

#WISH SOCIAL MEDIA CAMPAIGN

An example of a counter-narrative to conventional mainstream media representations of Muslims is the #WISH (Women in Solidarity with Hijabis) social media campaign, which sprang up in 2014. The campaign encouraged women from diverse backgrounds, including non-Muslims, to take a photograph ('selfie') of themselves wearing a hijab and upload it to social networking sites as a symbol of support for Muslim women and religious freedom, and as a counter to rising Islamophobia (including calls to 'ban the burqa'). In Australia, a Facebook page for the campaign was established by lawyer Mariam Veiszadeh, who had come to the country as a refugee from Afghanistan. Within 24 hours, the page had reached global audiences and spawned a number of derivative campaigns. In Sweden, for example, women posted images of themselves in headscarves on social media platforms, including Twitter and Instagram; again as expressions of solidarity (see #hijabuppropet). In the United States, female religious leaders—a Jewish rabbi, an Episcopal vicar and a Unitarian reverend—similarly covered their hair with scarves in support of 'Wear a Hijab' day (Nomani & Arafa 2015). The point of these types of interventions is to pre-empt and respond to increasing violence and racial slurs being directed against visibly Muslim women in Western countries.

Yet, while the sentiments are laudable, the campaigns are not without their own particular controversies. For instance, some mainstream Muslim women view the hijab as a symbol of oppression and the efforts of conservative Muslims to dominate modern Muslim societies. They argue against the interpretation that the hijab is merely a symbol of modesty and dignity adopted by faithful female followers of Islam. They further campaign for the right not to wear the hijab and to let individual women make their own choices about such things. As Nomani and Arafa (2015) observe:

> In 1919, Egyptian women marched on the streets demanding the right to vote; they took off their veils, imported as a cultural tradition from the Ottoman Empire, not a religious edict. The veil then became a relic of the past. Later, Egyptian President Gamal Abdel-Nasser said in a speech in the early 1960s that, when he sought reconciliation with members of the Muslim Brotherhood group for attempting to assassinate him in 1954, the Supreme Leader of the

> Brotherhood gave him a list of demands, including, 'imposing hijab on Egyptian women'. The audience members didn't understand what the word hijab meant. When Nasser explained that the Brotherhood wanted Egyptian women to wear a headscarf, the audience members burst out laughing.

Looked at historically and contextually, then, the wearing of the hijab is closely associated with particular kinds of politics—both 'for' and 'against' Muslim women.

The mediated formation of 'suspect communities' is evident not only in Australia. For example, the position of Moroccan youth in the Netherlands is highly racialised in the local media. There is a steady diet of stories in the media about misbehaving Moroccan youngsters above and beyond that of other ethnic minorities: stories of the variety 'Moroccan youths make my life a misery'. The language is one of vilification:

> Although the stories are typically overblown, the trouble of Moroccan youth is now accepted as social fact. Terms that refer to this such as street terrorism, beach terrorism and street terror have become commonplace, invariably in relation to Moroccan youngsters (Pakes 2012: 39).

The threat apparently posed by the 'Other' is twofold. On the one hand, it is seen to be a cultural threat, based on the perceived influence and threat of the Islamic faith, so the target is those associated with this religion—namely, Moroccan youth or, in Australia, Arabic/Lebanese youth. This form of xenophobia is sometimes defended on the basis of libertarianism in which the so-called 'freedom' of the West is juxtaposed to the un-freedom of Islam.

Yet, the presence of politicians, singers, football, comedians and actors in mainstream Australian social life belies these sweeping generalisations. The award of the 2016 Gold Logie to Waleed Aly, co-host of the news and current affairs television panel program *The Project*, was both a signal moment for Australian Muslims in demonstrating popular acceptance as bona fide contributors to Australian society, and a poignant reminder of how exceptional the moment really was. This is because Aly's nomination for the award had been branded a controversial inclusion by some quarters of the mainstream media (Idato 2016); sentiments that dominated media coverage in the lead-up to the event. Aly nonetheless won the gong for Best (Most Popular) Personality on Australian Television and gave a gracious, powerful and generous acceptance speech.

On the other hand, the threat posed by the minority 'Other' is seen to stem from inherent problems of crime and disorder. Here, it is the presumed daily nuisance and criminality of Arabic and Muslim youth that is seized upon, to be followed by calls for more security, less crime, less immigration and less Islam. But the actual discriminations in criminal justice, the age profile of community and the impact of harsher sanctions means that communities that are entrenched within the national fabric begin to lose confidence in their place within the wider society. The impact of racialisation of social issues and racialised constructions of social deviancy is predictable: the radicalisation of those young people who feel ostracised and excluded from mainstream Australian society. The phenomenon of home-grown terrorism begins at home.

In the cacophony of voices condemning the evils of terrorism and commenting on the threats posed by Muslims, it is sensationalism—not sensitivity—that is the order of the day. Former Australian Prime Minister Tony Abbott exhorted Islam to change, to undergo a reformation and enlightenment—his words thereby alienating Islamic neighbours such as Indonesia and enraging Australian Islamic communities who view such ill-informed comments as grossly disrespectful to their beliefs and traditions (Henderson 2015). Meanwhile, Muslims who do enter public debate are only allowed to do so as 'one-dimensional Muslims' according to psychologist Hanan Dover (2015). From her own experiences, Dover concludes that there is little room for nuance in understanding and explaining radicalisation, and no acknowledgment of professional credentials when she wears the hijab. Rather, she says, 'It's either condemn, or be condemned. We must confess our loyalties and not much else' (Dover 2015: 1). The pre-existing script demands that each Muslim 'condemn ISIS'; any attempt to offer sophisticated analysis and insight into youthful behaviour is dismissed or distorted. Islamophobia thus is ingrained in tabloid-style media coverage of people and events that stigmatise and inflame.

CASE STUDY:

THE CRONULLA RIOTS

In December 2005, riots occurred at south Sydney's Cronulla Beach, the nearest beach suburb to the city's working-class western neighbourhoods. This event involved several thousand people rioting, in the process damaging property and violently attacking anyone who had a 'Middle Eastern' appearance. Many participants wrapped themselves in Australian flags. Many, too, participated in shouting out the highly offensive words 'Fuck the Lebos' in unison, as a common theme to the aggression.

The next day saw reprisal attacks. Dozens of carloads of people from the community, targeted the previous day, retaliated by engaging in similarly 'random' violence throughout the beachside suburbs. The point is that there exist highly volatile relations between 'Lebanese' and other young people across major parts of the city. This negativity had been brewing for a number of years, in part fostered by the territorial segregation of particular groups into racialised patterns of disadvantage (Jakubowicz 2006). Where one belongs is increasingly socially constructed in relation to specific 'ethnic locales'; areas defined by particular combinations of economic, social and cultural characteristics.

The trigger for the Cronulla riots was a punch-up involving young men from Middle Eastern backgrounds and off-duty Anglo surf lifesavers at the beach the week before. News media frequently plays a major role in reflexively creating violent events by publicising them in advance, sensationalising them when they occur, and exaggerating the enormity of particular events relative to 'the Australian way of life'—hence the stimulation and provocation to violence is, to some extent, inspired by media itself. This is exactly what occurred in the case of the events at Cronulla (Noble 2009).

Indeed, the Sydney media did a lot to foster the idea that 'trouble' would take place on the weekend in question. Not surprisingly, lots of 'troublemakers' showed up expecting precisely the very thing that was being warned against. At least a portion of the crowd was actively looking for violence. For these young men, the attraction was the violence, not the public issues surrounding the beach as such. The advance notice that there would be a crowd gathering at the beach opened the possibility for violence to take place. It was on the agenda from the outset, and the crowd became the social vehicle through which the desired collective violence could ensue.

The violence that occurred was not socially neutral, however. It was targeted at Lebanese people and others of 'Middle Eastern appearance'. In popular discourse, the riots were ultimately blamed on Lebanese youth. Whoever engaged in violence was thus less problematic than the source of inspiration for the violence—the so-called Middle Eastern gangs. If not for their presence and if not for their actions, there would not have been any riots—so went the script for the continuing moral panic about 'the Lebanese'. It was their 'way of life', their values and morals, their actions and behaviour, their religion that, yet again, was publicly scrutinised, vilified and mythologised. What this particular event signified is a strong and very particular racialisation of street life, including and especially in regard to group conflict.

Moral panics can be differentiated by dimensions of motive and responsibility (see Goode & Ben-Yehuda 1994). For example, they can be distinguished in terms of *grassroots* panic (reflecting widespread public sentiment and attitudes), *interest group* panic (reflecting sectoral material interests and status gains) and *elite-engineered* panic (reflecting political and corporate interests). The Cronulla riots exhibited elements of all three forms of motivation and responsibility, and involved multiple media platforms in their construction. However, while social media, for example, allows for anyone to be involved in framing an event, this does not mean that events will be framed in multiple ways (see Ruddock 2013). Indeed, Wright (2015) argues that a common feature of moral panic is that of 'enacted melodrama'. This refers to the notion that, during such events, 'everyday citizens experience the role of the suffering victim, where ordinary outsiders are shaped into extraordinary villains, and where moral entrepreneurs "step in" to become heroic' (Wright 2015: 2). A melodrama basically tells the story of 'good' versus 'evil'. In the case of the Cronulla riots, at least for some, it was the rioters who assumed the mantle of 'the good', battling the 'evil' of Lebanese outsiders. This narrative was a central frame to the event, and was reinforced and reproduced by grassroots, interest group and elite opinion shapers.

The substantive content of the narrative emphasised social difference (white Anglo Australians as 'us' and Australians of Middle Eastern appearance and Lebanese

Australians as 'them') in ways that attached negative labels to the migrant outsiders and heroic labels to the established Australians. Symbolically, the 'beach' is an Australian icon, and therefore 'protection' of the beach was the imagery that was drawn upon to justify the congregation, the aggression and the passion of the day. Words were used to position people within hierarchies of citizenship and social belonging, with hate speech employed to demarcate not only the 'villains', but the 'no-go zones' for them as well. 'This is OUR beach' proclaimed some of the protestors, establishing identity and possession, citizenship and legitimacy in one brief statement.

The resonance of such claims for a much wider audience can be explained in terms of a conjunction of forces, events and interventions. At the grassroots, there was fertile ground for panic over 'the Lebanese', which had been laid over many years and across many social platforms. Media, politicians and white supremacist groups had been banging the racism drum for several decades. This is captured in the book *Bin Laden in the Suburbs*, which provides a detailed investigation of the ways in which the 'Arab Other' has, especially in Sydney, been reconstructed as 'terrorist', 'criminal' and 'illegal' (Poynting et al. 2004). Specific moral panics, including those surrounding the actions of a particularly nasty 'rape gang', have served to entrench a popular resentment against specific population groups (Poynting & Morgan 2007), thereby reinforcing the underlying 'permission to hate'. When the Cronulla Beach issue first came to public attention, there appeared to be a modicum of grassroots support for the notion that 'something needs to be done'. Much of this was framed in terms of those who were deemed to be 'un-Australian'. A series of gang rapes by young Muslim men in Sydney during the late 1990s and early 2000s led to media frenzy over the alleged 'unassimilable' attitudes of Muslim/Arab men towards women. Thus, in one fell swoop, all Muslim/Arab men were tarred with the same criminal brush.

In response to the original fight on the beach, some sections of the commercial media went into hyper hate mode. This was bolstered by the interchange and overlap between social media and public media. For example, an anonymous SMS was sent out, and then re-broadcast by Sydney radio personality Alan Jones (see Asquith 2008; Asquith & Poynting 2011). The SMS was a prime example of hate speech, and established the linguistic parameters of much debate that was to follow:

> Aussies ... this Sunday, every Aussie in the Shire get down to North Cronulla to support Leb and wog bashing day ... Bring your mates and let's show them that this is our beach and they are never welcome back (Anonymous SMS read out by Alan Jones, 8 December 2005, cited in Asquith & Poynting 2011: 100).

It was the combination of the mass distribution of this SMS and, in particular, Jones's constant repetition of the SMS that led to the unique conditions of a 'white' race riot.

Close analysis of the verbal and textual hostility employed by rioters, politicians and media in Sydney in December 2005 exposes the essential ways in which such hate speech works (Asquith 2008). For instance, the linguistic conventions surrounding the Cronulla riots included certain specific elements (Asquith & Poynting 2011):

Naming

This refers to hate speech that involves a process of 'naming' someone, recognising them within a hierarchy of subject positions, with the aim to isolate, separate and rank individuals according to their visibility as 'Other'. It is manifest, for example, in naming Muslims as 'terrorists' and Jews as 'manipulators' (see also Asquith 2008).

Pathologising

This refers to the process of labelling the 'Other' as dirty or impure. In the public discourses concerning Cronulla, the idea that 'this place is a mess' (too much garbage) was seen to stem from the presence of outsiders. This in turn led to a T-shirt printed especially for the Cronulla riots, which claimed the wearer to be part of the 'Ethnic Cleansing Unit'. Alan Jones added his opinions to the emerging panic. For two days, he likened immigration to being invited into a family home, and claimed that Lebanese Australians were trashing the invite: 'but you're not going to sit down at the table and start spitting on my mother or putting your feet under the table, or bringing dog manure in with you' (Jones cited in Asquith & Poynting 2011: 103).

Criminalising

This refers to the labelling of the 'Other' as criminal. Again, Alan Jones was at the forefront of the vilification: 'This is gang stuff mate ... it's a gang problem', and 'All across Sydney there is universal concern that there are gangs, the gangs are of one ethnic composition' (Jones cited in Asquith & Poynting 2011: 107).

Terrorising

This refers to the making of threats to bodily harm as a means to silence the 'Other'. This was linked to the idea that it is legitimate to engage in unauthorised policing of the target of vilification: '... now the Police can't do the job, even though we've put faith in them and we want them to do the job, that means to me the next step is vigilantes and personal protection by ourselves' (Jones cited in Asquith & Poynting 2011: 107). During the week leading up to the riots, Jones also invited Australia's biker gangs to defend the beach against the 'Lebanese thugs', and stated that '... you gotta scare, there's got to be an element of fear in this' (Jones cited in Asquith & Poynting 2011: 110).

Sections of the Sydney media, in conjunction with grassroots social media and the actions of special interest groups such as white supremacists, created the conditions for the Cronulla riots and their aftermath. They did this through selective framing of the issues and systematic 'othering' of particular groups, through naming, pathologising, criminalising and terrorising. The result was violence—symbolic, cultural, social and physical. Hate crime and hate speech are inextricably intertwined.

The event at Cronulla was not only reported on; it was actively constructed in, by and through the panic storm whipped up by anonymous social media, well-known radio talk show hosts and the local press. It was thus preceded by discourses and narrative frames that virtually guaranteed that a riot would occur. Intrinsic to these discourses was the sense of indignation that goes beyond empathy. Over 4000 people showed up at 'their' beach to protect 'their' way of life from the perceived 'foreign' villains. In the lead-up to the riots, the varied media presented such 'defenders' as unofficial heroes and as necessary antidotes to the poisonous presence of outsiders and interlopers, who were seen to be victimising 'ordinary' beachgoers.

The violence of the day, however, shocked many onlookers out of any pretence of enacted melodrama. The overt racism was similarly confronting for many. This was not the coded racism of Alan Jones, but full frontal explicit racism. Many of those actually living in Cronulla found it profoundly embarrassing. From their point of view, it was non-Cronulla outsiders who had come into their living spaces and caused the problem. Yet, to the rest of the country, the narrative was that Cronulla is a particularly racist place, which is why it played host to such an event.

Ten years later, certain lessons had been learned. Racial vilification charges were levelled against those who wanted to positively 'commemorate' the 2005 riots. Police were mobilised to prevent any possibility of its reoccurrence. The spokesperson espousing anti-Islamic rhetoric was portrayed as singular, lost and something of an idiot (see Purtill 2015). Yet, simultaneously the same decade saw the rise of militant jihadism drawing in young men and women from Muslim backgrounds around the world, including Australia, as well as resurgent anti-Islamic groups, such as Reclaim Australia. While the locations have changed—from Cronulla to Bendigo, Victoria (where outside activists travelled from far and wide to protest against construction of a new mosque in 2015)—many of the same forces and the same faces are still evident. And new enacted melodramas are played out across new forms of moral panic, utilising all manner of leading-edge technologies and social media. For the extremists on the other side, it is a win-win situation, as hate begets hate and exclusion bolsters further exclusion. For the majority middle, the threats and insecurities will only intensify unless an inclusionary communal agenda is once again prioritised and given political weight.

The prevalence of Islamophobia and the events at Cronulla both point to the substantial social impact of new information technologies in conveying messages of hate and exclusion, and infiltrating all spheres of communications. This is a lesson that has not been lost on far-right racists or fear-mongering jihadists. Platforms such as Twitter and Facebook provide ready access for transmission of hateful messages (verbal, written, visual) that are ubiquitous, itinerant and difficult to suppress. From the point of view of research and social action, issues of online hate speech are complicated, urgent and transnational. There is a need to monitor how online hate speech emerges and spreads, and to develop technical and social strategies that can provide a robust response to online hate speech (Ichou 2015; Gagliardone et al. 2015). Crime and violence are directly and indirectly a consequence of and implicated in maledictory speech. 'Sticks and stones may break my bones but names can never hurt me' has never been further from the truth.

ISSUES FOR CONSIDERATION

Hate crime is basically about perceptions—of membership of certain groups, and the implication that membership means an individual is like 'them' rather than being associated with 'us'. Gay bashing, for example, may involve the targeting of men who 'look gay' and/or are 'effeminate', regardless of whether or not they actually are gay. Even when seemingly sympathetic to victims of apparent hate-crime attacks (through employment of 'tragic frames'), the mainstream media nonetheless may well reproduce a discursive system of prejudice that contributes to such violence in the first place. It does so through, for example, an emphasis on the scapegoat process (e.g. the attention devoted to character flaws of the chief antagonists, which is then accompanied by their subsequent dehumanisation in media accounts) that can function rhetorically to alleviate a public's guilt concerning anti-gay hate crimes. Simultaneously, media stories may also reaffirm a set of discourses that socially stigmatise gay, lesbian, bisexual and transgendered persons (e.g. the use of terms such as 'homophobia' that place the onus on the oppressed rather than the agents of oppression, thus making *them* the instigator of the action) (see Ott & Aoki 2002).

There are other facets to the identity politics of hate crime that are worth further consideration as well. For example, perversely, the lack of cultural awareness exhibited by those wishing to purge the 'Other' (in this case, 'the Lebanese') at Cronulla also had implications for who were attacked. The violence was such that anybody who was (apparently, to the mob) of Middle Eastern appearance was targeted, and people of Indian ethnic background were thereby punched and assaulted because, to the mob, they were 'seen' as being Middle Eastern. The nature of racist violence and hate crime is that it is often imprecise because it is about lashing out at certain presumed targets. A Sikh Indian can be attacked because they are deemed by the ignorant and the indignant to be a Middle Eastern Arab. The reality is that the victim is actually part of a completely different religion and from a different part of the world.

In the weeks and years that have followed the Cronulla riots, there has been grassroots push-back to the populist media framing of Islamic communities as outsiders, socially deviant, oppressive and threatening. Within media studies, much existing research tends to focus on textual analysis, especially in relation to media racism, the experiences of 'ethnic minority' media producers in mainstream institutions, and the importance of news media in negotiations of identity. However, people in culturally and linguistic diverse communities are also attempting to intervene in mainstream news media themselves. For example, in response to the negativity of 'othering' processes affecting many in their local community, people in Bankstown, Sydney, developed community-based media interventions that aimed to shift the mainstream news agenda. The notion behind this is that: 'Through media skills training, forums, events and cultural production, Arab and Muslim Australians in the Bankstown area positioned themselves as the *subjects* rather than the *objects* of news' (Dreher 2003, emphasis added). As pointed out in Box 8.3, social media campaigns initiated to provide support and solidarity for Muslim women from non-Muslim women are also important to the building of counter-narratives.

Humour can help defuse situations and/or transform perceptions as well. For example, in parts of Sydney in recent years there have been billboards and bus shelters with messages such as:

Words on a black and white surface:

> 'Crime. It ain't ethnic.' [Message: that it belongs to no one and everyone]

Two women wearing a head scarf, a blurred photo:

> 'It's amazing how some clothes attract so much attention.' [Message: women are usually portrayed as objects, wearing few clothes]

Shortly after the Cronulla riots a short video was made by local filmmakers. It poked fun at the event in a rather unique way: A 'bogan' and a 'Lebanese' both end up at the 'wrong' beach; they end up talking about cars and music systems; the 'bogan' grabs a cricket bat out of their car boot (it was brought by the former to hit people like the latter) and they end up playing beach cricket. [Message: it's all about common ground and commonalities].

Taking serious issues seriously sometimes requires less than serious responses. This, too, is one of the ironies of recasting identification in more inclusive ways and resisting attempts to portray groups as 'folk devils' (see Box 8.4).

BOX 8.4

BLACK COMEDY ABOUT CRONULLA

A new 'black comedy' called *Down Under* was due for release in 2016 (see Maddox 2015). The film takes place the night after the first violent clash at Cronulla Beach and centres on three carloads of hotheads—two from Sutherland Shire (the home of Cronulla Beach) and one from Lakemba (located further inland)—who are out for retaliation. As the writer-director of the film, Abe Forsythe, commented: 'If you get to the base level of racism and look at it, you realise how ridiculous it is'. This forms the basis for the humour in the film. According to Forsythe: 'We don't talk about this stuff enough. It's just easier to brush it under the carpet and pretend it hasn't happened. But racism in all its forms—from the overt racism that happened on the beach that day to the casual racism which just happens all the time—I find quite troubling'. As the newspaper article reporting on the film then observed:

> One example happened during filming when a Middle Eastern cast member with a full beard, who was getting out of a car at the set, was confronted by a group of youths chanting 'Aussie, Aussie, Aussie' (Maddox 2015).

Making the comedy film was therefore no laughing matter—in more than one sense.

CONCLUSION

This chapter has provided an introduction to the mediated world of racism and violence. From a criminological perspective, portrayals that stereotype particular ethnic minorities as 'gangs', 'criminals', 'terrorists' and 'illegals' not only distort the actual realities of these communities, but also provide populist grounding for 'permission to hate' which, in its most extreme forms, involves criminal acts such as assault and murder. In a world where extremism is a social problem, and where extremists do engage in terrible acts of destruction and killing, the language of hate feeds the very thing that we most fear. Exclusionary language that vilifies and separates creates the conditions for alienation, marginalisation and detachment from the mainstream. Under such circumstances, more crime, not less, is the likelihood.

DISCUSSION QUESTIONS

1. What is 'hate crime'? Who are the most likely targets of hate crime, and why?
2. Racism is always a mediated phenomenon that ultimately depends upon questions of identity, and issues pertaining to 'who' and 'where'. Discuss.
3. What is 'Islamophobia'?
4. What were the different motivations and responsibilities that underpinned 'moral panic' in regard to the Cronulla riots?
5. Outline the key elements of 'enacted melodrama' in relation to the Cronulla riots. How do we know who the 'heroes' and 'villains' are, and who the 'victims' are?

WORKSHOP ACTIVITY 1: DRIVING THE MORAL PANIC

Moral panic is generated by *grassroots* campaigns organically emerging at the local community level, *special interest* groups that emerge around particular issues, and *elite* groups that provide impetus for the moral panic as a defence of the status quo. Provide examples of different moral panics predominantly linked to each of these three social forces.

WORKSHOP ACTIVITY 2: PRESENCE AND NON-PRESENCE

*   What are some of the 'visible' signs of difference that are used against vulnerable and minority groups as part of negative moral panic discourses?
*   In what ways are vulnerable and minority groups portrayed as constituting an 'invisible' threat or enemy? To whom or what are they portrayed as being a threat?

FURTHER READING

Asquith, N. (2008). Race Riots on the Beach: A Case for Criminalising Hate Speech? Papers from the British Criminology Conference, vol. 8: 50–64. British Society of Criminology.

Asquith, N. & Poynting, S. (2011). Anti-Cosmopolitanism and 'Ethnic Cleansing' at Cronulla. In K. Jacobs & J. Malpas (eds), *Ocean to Outback: Cosmopolitanism in Contemporary Australia*. Perth: UWA Publishing.

Gagliardone, I., Gal, D., Pinto, T. & Sainz, G. (2015). *Countering Online Hate Speech. UNESCO Series on Internet Freedom*. Paris: United Nations Educational, Scientific and Cultural Organization.

Ichou, R. (ed.) (2015). *World Trends in Freedom of Expression and Media Development: Special Digital Focus 2015*. Paris: United Nations Educational, Scientific and Cultural Organization.

Wright, S. (2015). Moral Panics as Enacted Melodramas. *British Journal of Criminology*, 55(6), 1226–44.

9

CRIMES OF THE POWERFUL

CHAPTER HIGHLIGHTS

INTRODUCTION

The problem of crime is generally framed by the problem of disadvantage—that is, most official crime statistics and the work of most criminal justice agencies are oriented towards working class or street crime. It is poor people who are most likely to engage with the criminal justice system, and it is poor people's crimes that remain the central focus of most criminological theory and practice.

As well, there is often the idea that crime is related to morality, and specifically to the decline or absence of a moral sensibility in the offender. What is 'wrong' is plain for all to see. Furthermore, the 'criminal' is distinctive, and identifiably different from everyone else in society (the exception being paedophiles and serial killers, who are hard to distinguish from 'ordinary people' including next-door neighbours). Overall, the idea is that there is a continuing law-and-order problem in society, and that things are constantly getting worse. Similarly, there is a skewed focus on crimes such as street assaults and on extraordinary or bizarre events, such as school shootings.

Meanwhile, the destruction of the environment, white-collar and corporate crimes, and state crimes tend not to receive the same kind of coverage or treatment by mainstream media outlets. There is a large silence when it comes to crimes of the powerful. And if criminal or immoral activity is detected, discovered or exposed in some way, this is rarely framed as typical, normal or part of the fabric of the social order. Rather, elite deviancy is generally approached as 'accidental', 'one-off', 'unusual' and 'rare'. Yet, criminological analysis of crimes of the powerful suggests otherwise.

This chapter shifts the analytical gaze from those crimes commonly reported within media to those that are less-frequently covered: crimes of the powerful. We turn our attention to those crimes committed by powerful individuals and the institutions of power, in particular, corporate and state crime. Public debate about 'law and order' continues to focus on traditional rather than white-collar crimes. This is partly explained by the ability of the wealthy and the powerful to normalise their activities, so that their crimes are not recognised as 'real' crimes and harms, but are instead seen as acceptable, even necessary, to the doing of business or the running of the state (or, indeed, to doing both simultaneously). It is also due to the character of these crimes, which do not necessarily fit with the news values and master narratives common to mainstream media, and as such may also not suit audience preferences. In some instances the relative lack of suitable attention to such crimes derives from the shared economic interests of media companies and their corporate owners—interests that may intrude upon what is deemed newsworthy.

CRIMINAL FICTIONS

Sutherland (1949: 9) is acknowledged as one of the first persons to define the phenomenon of white-collar crime, describing it as 'a crime committed by a person of respectability and high social status in the course of his (sic) occupation'. The point Sutherland was making is that crime in the business sector is just as real and damaging as crime among the disadvantaged. In many ways, it is more serious because the sums involved are staggeringly high—far higher than the conventional crimes associated with the working class (Tombs & Whyte 2015; Rothe & Kauzlarich 2016).

Crimes of the powerful occur within the contemporary context of neoliberal global capitalism. **Neoliberalism** describes a broad political and economic orientation that emphasises individual responsibility for one's own actions within the institutional framework of strong private property rights and unfettered commodity markets. Contemporary neoliberalism ostensibly favours market forces over state intervention, and it views inequality as a natural outcome of competition between individuals. At an abstract level, each person is seen to be personally responsible for his or her own welfare and life chances. In practice, economic power tends to already be monopolised and concentrated in ways that foreclose any possibility of fair or free competition. Nonetheless, the idea dominates the reality.

The main economic policy and practical trends associated with neoliberalism include reduced trade protection, user-pays, privatisation and deregulation (Harvey 2005). The net result of neoliberalism is impoverishment for many at the same time that social privilege has skyrocketed for the few. Accompanying the dominant economic policies and practices of the past three decades, there have been major shifts in wealth and power on a world scale in favour of a handful of large corporations (Tombs & Whyte 2015). Neoliberalism as a practice, policy and ideal has basically been built upon a falsehood. Powerful sectional interests already substantially own and control the bulk of the world's resources (including natural, financial and technical capital) (see, for example, Harvey 2005). There is no 'free market' as such. Land, water, food and energy are under the control of a small and shrinking number of private firms and the community outside is both growing and increasingly subjugated by this concentrated ownership and control.

In criminological terms, the crimes of the powerful can be distinguished on the basis of particular sets of actors and institutions (Rothe & Kauzlarich 2016). These actors and institutions interact across interrelated sectors. The criminality of the powerful includes:

- corporate crime (large businesses and industry conglomerates)
- state crime (government agencies and officials)
- state-corporate crime (collusion between companies and states)
- international financial institutions crime (arising from the activities of agencies such as the International Monetary Fund and World Bank)
- organised crime (organised criminal networks including the Mafia and Yakuza)
- militia and insurgency crime (rebel groups, religious-based fanatics).

A defining feature of crimes of the powerful is that such crimes involve actions (or omissions, failures to act) that are socially harmful and carried out by elites and/or those who wield significant political and social authority in the particular sectors or domains of their influence.

Class analysis provides one interpretive lens by which to understand the dynamics and nature of crimes of the powerful, especially corporate crime (White 2008). For example, accumulative and augmentative forms of criminality are closely linked aspects of class position. **Accumulative criminality** refers to corporate or organisational crime, as a direct link and natural flow-on of the capital accumulation process (i.e. profit enhancement and cost minimisation). **Augmentative criminality** refers to the closely connected but distinct personal wealth-enhancement component in the criminality process that flows from the access and advantage gained from ownership and a controlling position in the capital accumulation process. In the case of owners of capital, the personal augmentation of wealth through criminality may be the basis for accumulating capital, or for hiding accumulated capital (and vice versa). In the case of managers of capital, accumulative criminality (as a necessary feature of corporate business success or to stave off failure) may be the basis for expanded personal wealth (e.g. bonuses) or a calculated necessity in job retention.

Through their public relations and marketing departments, and entrenched relations with the advertising industry, big corporations have strategic power to persuade the general public that their company, their brand and their commodities are good, essential and benevolent. Yet the reality of corporate criminality, and the policy context within which this flourishes, tell a different story.

The initial difficulty, however, in determining the crimes of the powerful is that laws reflect the interests of the ruling elites and classes in any particular society. As such, many types of harm may not be incorporated into criminal law if to do so would go against these elite interests. Crimes of the capitalist class, for example, incorporate white-collar and corporate crimes that have significant structural effects in terms of deaths and financial losses. Nonetheless, they are rarely perceived by the general public as being of special interest to them personally (except in the case of events such as preventable workplace deaths—that is, industrial homicide). Broadly speaking, state crime refers to crimes involving the state acting against its own citizens, or against the citizens of another state as part of inter-state conflict. State crimes include those committed on behalf of the state or through using a position within the state to engage in socially harmful activity (White & Perrone 2015). Neither type of crime is dealt with in the same manner as working-class and street crime (see Box 9.1).

BOX 9.1

CRIMES OF THE POWERFUL

Typical crimes, motivations and criminal justice responses to crimes of the powerful include:

Typical crimes	Examples
Economic	Breaches of corporate law, environmental degradation, inadequate industrial health and safety provisions, pollution, violation of labour laws, fraud, embezzlement
State	Police brutality, government corruption, bribery, violation of civil and human rights, misuse of public funds

Motivations	Examples
Maximising profit	Structural imperative to minimise costs and maximise economic returns in a competitive capitalist market environment
Augmenting wealth	Attempts to bolster one's own personal position in the economic and social hierarchy
Social control	Violation of privacy and of human rights is justified in the name of national interest, and whatever legal, coercive and propaganda means are necessary will be used to ensure public order, to quell dissent and further private economic interests

Criminalisation	Examples
Shaping definitions	Capacity to influence what is defined as harmful, and the definitions of certain acts as being civil or criminal harms
Protecting interests	Capacity to mobilise best legal assistance and intricate knowledge of the law
Sentencing	Use of stereotypes and criminal histories to mitigate against harsh punishments due to the nature of the offence (not seen as serious) and offenders (upstanding citizens)

Source: White 2008.

Compared with the amount of theorising that has occurred in relation to crimes committed by young, working-class males, there have been relatively few attempts to explain crimes of the powerful, such as corporate crime. One critical observation, however, is that the existence and extent of crimes of the powerful challenge any simplistic explanation of crime in terms of poverty or psychological pathology. Broadly speaking, corporate crime is typically explained in terms of structural features (e.g. the demands of business competition), cultural processes (e.g. the normalisation of illegal behaviour) and the operation of the institutions of criminal justice (e.g. the low likelihood of getting caught). For example, survival of corporations—and the individuals within them, especially managers—depends on the achievement of profits. Where the capacity to make profits is blocked by environmental factors, such as government regulations or the price structure of competitors, companies will face considerable pressure to use illegal means to overcome the blockage. This, together with opportunities for illegal behaviour, weak law enforcement, and an ideological blurring between 'entrepreneurialism' and illegal behaviour, leads to engagement in illegal acts. Crime is therefore a rational response to a rational objective. From this perspective, corporations are inherently '**criminogenic**' (see Box 1983; Bakan 2004; Glasbeek 2004; Tombs & Whyte 2015; Rothe & Kauzlarich 2016).

Glasbeek (2003; 2004), for example, observes that there are several interrelated legal fictions relating to corporations that foster and sustain systemic corporate wrongdoing. These include the ideas that:

1. the registered corporation is deemed to be a separate legal person, acting in its own right
2. because the corporation needs others to think and act, it cannot be guilty of a criminal offence
3. corporate wrongdoing pays, because the structured criminogenic nature of the corporation is almost always avoided in cases where real people are actually prosecuted (Glasbeek 2003; see also Clough & Mulhern 2002; Tombs & Whyte 2015).

The bottom line is that corporations commit an enormous number of offences, and they reoffend regularly. Such evil-doing is not exceptional behaviour, but the norm.

The costs of corporate crime are enormous and certainly outweigh the costs of traditional crime (see Friedrichs 1996; Shover & Wright 2001; Rothe & Kauzlarich 2016). These costs are both financial and physical in terms of damage to individuals and the environment. There are also serious social costs as a result of the violation of community standards and the creation of an atmosphere of cynicism and mistrust towards 'big business' in the community (Rosoff, Pontell & Tillman 1998). Although corporate crime is often perceived as a 'victimless' crime, the reality is quite different. For example, the release of toxic chemicals into waterways, the inadequate testing of products, failure to acknowledge or release research results, and poor industrial safety standards can affect millions of people as well as whole communities and the surrounding environment.

Thus, crimes of the powerful are intrinsically linked to the operation of the system as a whole. In other words, such harms are inseparable from who has power, how they exercise this power, and who ultimately benefits from the actions of the powerful. Powerful social interests not only perpetuate great harms, they also obscure and mask the nature of harm production. They are also best placed to resist the criminalisation process generally. This applies to corporate crime as well as to state crime and other crimes of the powerful.

For instance, a key issue in regards to state crime is the covering up of abuses and crimes by government officials. If something is exposed as a problem or as wrong, it threatens government and state officials with a loss of power. The response, in some cases, is to engage in perjury—that is, to lie or pervert the course of justice (e.g. by shredding records). Other responses are to deny any wrongdoing has occurred or to hide behind secrecy provisions. For example, serious harms were caused as a result of nuclear testing at Maralinga in South Australia between 1956 and 1963. A total of seven British nuclear tests were performed at the facility co-funded by the British and Australian governments. These tests and hundreds of minor trials were subject to extreme secrecy and were not revealed by Australian journalists until the late 1970s. The nuclear fallout threatened the health of personnel at the site and damaged local Indigenous people (the lands were previously inhabited by the Pitjantjatjara and Yankunytjatjara people), as well as their culture and environment. However, information about the tests was classified as top secret and it was decades before the full extent of the safety issues came to light and the inadequacy of information provision by the British Government to the Australian Government was revealed (Grabosky 1989).

Furthermore, one of the problems in dealing with and discussing state crime is that it is not only governments and perpetrators who deny its existence, but citizens as well (Cohen 1993). Cohen (2001) provides a sustained analysis of how it is that, contrary to United Nations Conventions and everyday moral standards, governments deny their responsibility for acts such as genocide, torture and massacres—and how, so often, ordinary people allow this denial to occur. Appeals to national loyalties, ethnic identifications and simply following orders are only some of a wide range of justifications put forward to justify the unjustifiable. Such justifications are reinforced across a series of media platforms. For example, state crimes such as torture and indiscriminate killing are justified and glorified in television series (such as *24* and *Homeland*), in movies (such as *American Sniper* and *Zero Dark Thirty*) and video games (such as *Battlefield* and *Call of Duty*). Although people do not necessarily equate these dramatised media texts to real life, they nevertheless contribute to a cultural field within which 'anything goes' when it comes to interpreting the so-called national interest.

Corporate criminality, as perhaps the predominant form of crimes of the powerful, is characterised by its invisibility as much as by its ubiquitous nature. It is nowhere, yet everywhere. There are a number of reasons for this. Many corporate crimes are not publicly observable in the way that many traditional crimes, such as assault or offensive behaviour, are. They may involve conversations behind closed doors, transactions in cyberspace and offshore accounting practices. They also do not exhibit the same kind of typification of offenders evident in the case of street crimes. Rarely does the corporate offender fit the societal image of the street offender—the thief, murderer or rapist—so often depicted in mainstream news media. Moreover, when subject to prosecution and conviction, they frequently draw upon 'good character' stereotypes (e.g. as a high status citizen who regularly donates money to charities) to neutralise responsibility, the harm they have caused and/or they penalty they might face (White & Perrone 2015).

Another aspect of corporate crime is that such harm may be defined as a regulatory infraction (e.g. failure to exercise due care when it comes to occupational health and safety) rather than a crime (e.g. industrial homicide). Indeed, very few crimes of the powerful—occupational (i.e. performed by individuals in high-status jobs for their own advancement) or organisational (i.e. performed by high-status individuals for the company's or state's advancement)—constitute 'signal crimes' (Innes 2004). That is, they do not evoke and symbolise wider problems in society (which can be contrasted, for example, with graffiti, which is seen to be an indicator of a wider lack of community spirit or social decay) (Innes 2004; Levi 2008; Rothe & Kauzlarich 2016).

From the point of view of media, corporate and state crime tend to escape notice or to have different connotations due to three broad social processes. First, such crimes are constructed in ways that basically abrogate any responsibility at a firm or structural level. The events are portrayed as one-off, and the perpetrators as 'bad apples'. Second, the powerful actively protect their images and reputation through both public relations exercises (the 'positives') and use of legal measures to prevent others from being critical of them (stopping the 'negatives'). Third, the powerful mobilise resources in ways that involve intentional deceit around key public issues and that will support their marketing efforts, both in furtherance of specific sectoral interests.

Asking why crimes of the powerful are *not* covered also requires acknowledgment that such crimes are not easily identifiable and are therefore less easily recognised as 'newsworthy'. Moreover, crimes in which victims are more diffuse (as with banking fraud or tax evasion) and perpetrators are not singularly identifiable (as in crimes involving large complex organisations) means that crimes of the powerful often do not lend themselves to stories featuring a 'personal angle' and thereby a 'human interest' dimension.

ACCIDENTS AND EXCEPTIONS

But, there are exceptions. Some instances of corporate wrongdoing are so immense and so visible that they cannot be hidden from public and media scrutiny. The oil spill associated with the *Exxon Valdez* off the coast of Alaska; the BP Deepwater Horizon oil rig explosion and subsequent pollution in the Gulf of Mexico; the death of thousands of people due to lax safety precautions at a Union Carbide plant in Bhopal, India; the terrible and tragic human consequences of pharmaceutical product Thalidomide used by pregnant women; and the collapse of financial giant Enron (which we will return to shortly)—all of these captured the public imagination and generated critical commentary along with angry citizen responses. The dilemma is that these 'monster' cases can nonetheless obscure the everyday incidence of corporate crime, given that they are presented as exceptional events and atypical of how most corporations operate.

There is also evidence to the contrary, as demonstrated by the widespread nature of financial services fraud, chronic food crimes such as food poisoning, safety crimes involving the death and maiming of employees, and the prevalence of air pollution in major cities (see Tombs & Whyte 2015). Few of these harms are criminalised, and it is even rarer that specific industries and firms are held to account. From a media perspective, a vital issue is the way in which news media, in particular, determine what counts as news and what does not. As part of this agenda setting, it is important to acknowledge that it is not so much that mainstream media succeed in telling the public what to think, but that they are successful, to some degree, in telling them what to think about (Mazur & Lee 1993: 682). A large part of this framing centres on the concept of 'accident'.

Typically, corporate crime that involves spectacular effects (such as the global financial crisis of 2008 through to the nuclear meltdowns at the Fukushima nuclear power plant in Japan after the earthquake and tsunami in 2011) is mediated in news coverage, internet reports and fictional retellings in ways that diminish responsibility. What are stressed are the unusual circumstances surrounding specific events or outcomes, rather than the regularity of poor oversight and chronic vulnerabilities associated with everyday financial transactions and material commodity production. The Deepwater Horizon catastrophe is seen as a one-off or rare event, even though there is ample evidence that oil spills are a recurring problem and that the consequences of 'accidents' in high-risk industries have a large societal and ecological impact (van Gulijk 2014). Rather than rare, oil spills are persistent and frequent—but they continue to be portrayed as singular and seldom.

In regard to environmental harms, Walters (2013: 137) also observes that the nuclear disasters at the Chernobyl (in Ukraine, then part of the former USSR, in 1986) and Fukushima power plants, as well as the Deepwater Horizon oil spill off the coast of Louisiana, United States, are:

> ... often presented in media and political discourses as 'accidents' associated with high risk commercial industries. This categorization serves to embed a discursive public consciousness about the origins, practices and outputs of 'necessary' industries. As a result, 'accidents', 'spills', 'leaks', and 'meltdowns' perpetuate a social and political tolerance that accepts environmental harm and human injury as an unfortunate bi-product of essential capitalist enterprise. Such catastrophic events become part-and-parcel of industries that provide the essentials of our daily lives.

Here we have what could be called a 'reverse moral panic' in the sense that the routinisation of 'accidents' ensures a dip in media coverage and public concern rather than a spike (as with traditional moral panics involving youth gangs or racialised crimes). In similar fashion to how the connection between discrete moral panics produces a global repertoire upon which each emergent moral panic draws, so too the narratives surrounding preventable corporate harms provide stock answers to similarly recurring questions.

Corporate harms are thus treated as simply an 'accident' and/or as part of the trade-off between health and well-being, and a consumerist lifestyle. Moreover, everyday harms, threats and vulnerabilities become seen, and accepted, as natural and necessary

(Tombs & Whyte 2015). In this sense, the image and practice of the corporation is treated as being outside of history—the corporation presents as an ahistorical entity that has always been here and always will be: 'there is no alternative'. This is regardless of actual history and the actual development of the corporate form, in collusion with nation-states, over the past 200 years (Bakan 2004; Tombs & Whyte 2015), and the variability and volatility of specific corporate-state interactions during this time.

The noise and furore around particular high-profile events implies that 'something is being done', to remedy the immediate problem, to prevent future occurrences and to punish the specific offenders (both human and corporate). How many people, animals and eco-systems are affected by these events? The figure would be in the tens of thousands, or even millions. But how many individuals are actually sent to prison because of the deaths and destruction caused by their behaviours and actions? How many corporations are de-registered and relegated to the dustbin of history? The answer is 'very few'.

As illustrated in the serious frauds in the banking and finance industry in 2012 in Britain—one that involved household-name UK banks and that was systemic and widespread—the use of a *scapegoat* alleviated the pressure for deep regulatory reform and more intense criminal justice intervention and prosecutions. A scapegoat takes the blame for wider communal sins and wrongdoing. The scapegoat in this instance was a junior City trader, presented to the public as a sole, rogue trader, who was sentenced to seven years imprisonment for off-the-books trading (Tombs & Whyte 2015). The banks and finance industry survived, and continue to flourish. And while the systemic corporate crime and misconduct continue, the media silence is deafening.

EXPLAINING THE SILENCES

Discussion of 'moral panics' as these pertain to prisoners and prisons, hate crime and ethnic minorities, and young people and public space, tends to focus on the specific mechanisms that present particular mediated images. It is oriented towards explaining how and why people mobilise in particular ways in relation to specific 'deviant' groups and public presences.

By contrast, a key question for critical criminologists when it comes to crimes of the powerful is how to explain the *absence of public outcry* over corporate wrongdoing and the general lack of concern about entrenched harmful practices and social and ecological injustices. For some, the issues revolve around what news media—as corporate watchdogs— are not reporting on and what the consequences of these decisions are or might be (see Brisman & South 2014). The Enron scandal provides a timely reminder of these (see Box 9.2). In part, the answer lies in how issues are socially constructed in and by mainstream media, and who actually owns and controls these media organisations. In the first instance, the medium itself shapes what and how information is presented. In the second, the main issue is one of particular social interests that drive media outputs.

BOX 9.2

MEDIA AS A SOURCE FOR CORPORATE WRONGDOING— THE ENRON SCANDAL

The Enron scandal, revealed in October 2001, eventually led to the bankruptcy of the Enron Corporation, an American energy company based in Houston, Texas, and the de facto dissolution of Arthur Andersen, which was one of the five largest audit and accountancy partnerships in the world. In addition to being the largest bankruptcy reorganisation in American history at that time, Enron was cited as the biggest audit failure. Before its collapse, Enron marketed electricity and natural gas, delivered energy and other physical commodities, and provided financial and risk management services to customers around the world. Enron was once ranked among the largest energy companies in the world.

Most of the company's top executives were tried for fraud after it was revealed in November 2001 that Enron's earnings had been overstated by several hundred million dollars. The charges included a broad range of financial crimes, including bank fraud, making false statements to banks and auditors, securities fraud, wire fraud, money laundering, conspiracy and insider trading.

In the case of Enron, the media actually missed the story originally, because before its collapse the company had been a media darling. This relationship reflected an association that is common between corporations and mainstream news media; namely, inter-dependency, where each needs the other for informational and reputational purposes. However, even for a corporation that falls out of favour with mainstream news media, the consequences can be significant. Thus, the deluge of media interest did occur, but only after an unfortunate silence.

Not only did the mainstream media eventually jump on the bandwagon by reporting on the wrongdoings at Enron, multiple media sources also provided important research data for a subsequent analysis of its corporate culture (Knottnerus et al. 2006). This research exposed the daily work rituals at Enron's corporate headquarters, and encompassed four key aspects: *risk* (such as hiding risk, leading to an elevation of unethical behaviour); *gratification* (there were lucrative bonuses, encouragement of ambition, and approval of 'sexual shenanigans' involving employees); *pride* (conceit about the firm, widespread notions of invincibility, and an attitude of indestructibility); and *fantasy imagery* (that included an in-house film spoof for a sales event, and frequent use of *Star Wars* imagery both good and bad— in some instances, insiders described themselves as part of the 'Evil Empire', in others as 'Jedi Knights'). As media sources revealed, these themes shaped Enron employees' cognition, patterns of behaviour and social interaction, and led to the normalisation and reproduction of deviance.

The shaping of public views, attitudes and perceptions is achieved through diffusion of many different ideas and forces. While not all audiences and publics respond in the same way to media representations (Brisman & South 2014), there are nonetheless overarching narratives and media practices that orient interpretation and understanding in very particular directions. A brief study of environmental issues illustrates this point, and the ways in which, in media framing, it is important to consider not only what is *included*, but also what is *absent*.

MEDIA SILENCES

We have already discussed the way in which news media consists of a range of specific forms, such as the printed press (newspapers and magazines) and broadcast media (including free-to-air television, subscription television and radio), not to mention online and multimedia journalism. The specific medium utilised to convey information also influences the content of the message being delivered. In other words, the content must fit the format, and is therefore always relative to these conventions (Ericson, Baranek & Chan 1991). For example, TV news depends on short, sharp sound bites, and has a strong emphasis on the visual. If there is no footage, there may be no story. In a similar fashion, radio news relies on audio. So the medium itself determines what makes it into the news bulletin, the length of the story and its presentation.

Regardless of medium, there seems to be a longer-term trend that has entrenched the media practice of replacing complex information with symbols, images and catchwords. Arguably, contemporary audiences have been trained to want nothing else (or perhaps it is their appetite that drives the trend). The emphasis is on theatre and spectacle, images and style, rather than meaning and context. Entertainment and 'infotainment' seem to be privileged within contemporary news media. One consequence of this is a persistent lack of 'historical' sensibility: each day brings an apparently 'new' event (this has been exacerbated by technological advances and the emergence of the 24/7 news cycle).

The gaining of a collective definition of social problems via media involves issue selection. This is partly determined by the nature of the medium itself. It is also related to notions of what is 'newsworthy'. Disasters, for example, are eminently newsworthy. They command attention and offer much in the way of televisuality. They tend not to be politically threatening. More complex and diffuse issues, such as global warming, are harder to present in simplistic form and in ways that capture public interest (although Al Gore, former Vice President of the United States and Nobel Peace Prize winner for his film *An Inconvenient Truth*, which addressed the issue of climate change, would no doubt argue that this is not the case). The content of media coverage tends to be event-centred, focusing on milestones, catastrophes and court actions, rather than being exploratory and explanatory of trends. The activist who risks life and limb against the Japanese whaler makes a good and sensational story. After all, mainstream news media constitute big business and the bottom line for those who own these media outlets is sales and profit (this is not necessarily 'top of mind' for journalists working at the coalface of news production). For environmental claims-makers, this adds pressure to be dramatic rather than prosaic in their approach to conveying information about issues (Hannigan 2006).

The nature of news coverage of environmental issues is contingent to a great extent on who owns and controls the media. In particular, commentators have pointed out the close ties between media ownership and environmental coverage (see Box 9.3). NBC television in the United States, for example, is owned by General Electric (GE). The latter has major economic interests in nuclear energy. Not surprisingly, this is promoted through the means of NBC TV. Moreover, GE funds conservative think-tanks, which are then used as a source of 'independent' experts for NBC, on issues such as nuclear power (Beder 1997). In 2010, a story ran on several television networks about the fact that GE made profits in the United States of $5.1 billion, but paid no taxes. The story did not feature on the GE-owned NBC nightly news or the network's flagship public affairs program *Meet the Press*. It was a case of the missing news story linked to corporate ownership (Buist & Leighton 2015).

BOX 9.3

POWER, IDEOLOGY AND INTERESTS

Questions of ownership and control have long been the concern of radical critiques of both corporate criminality and media organisations—for example, arguing the case of media as propaganda, Herman and Chomsky (1994) provided a political economy of the commercial media in which 'size does matter'. They pointed to the sheer size of media corporations, the continuing concentration of media ownership, its profit orientation, the relationship of media corporations with advertisers and governments, which in turn skews media content, and their support for the dominant pro-business ideologies sustaining the system as a whole. Acknowledging that the news industry, in Australia in particular, is dominated by a small number of corporations (many still family-owned), the issue is whether this also translates into a narrow range of viewpoints. This is an empirical question and open to investigation, but certainly the topic of 'proprietorial bias' continues to be a source of consternation among audiences and journalists alike (Moore 2014).

Explaining the specific content of crime news likewise reflects these general concerns. Three broad perspectives concerning the link between power, interests and content have been identified (Chagnon 2015):

• First, some argue that the news is a prime hegemonic force, which is effectively controlled by elite interests and/or dominant ideologies. Crime news, as with other news, is mostly a product of top-down power exercised in the interests of the ruling capitalist class and power elites.

- Second, others argue that the major influences on the news are professional and organisational factors—linked to the direct production of news coverage itself—and thus are the product of 'deliberate and reflexive action by journalists' (Chagnon 2015: 108).
- Third, there is a position that is a hybrid of the first two. It is argued that media content is multidimensional and pluralistic, albeit shaped by both ideology (that is promulgated by elites as well as ambiguously incorporated by individuals) and the contingencies of contemporary news production (such as company expectations for ever quicker and cheaper news production).

In more sophisticated analyses, ideological processes are theorised as complex yet pervasive, and professional practices likewise situated in the context of personal values as well as institutional pressures (Chagnon 2015). Hence, there are many and variable influences that help to shape news content, although these can largely be explained by what is happening at the structural (the nature and dynamics of capitalist society) and institutional levels (the nature and dynamics of commercial media organisations).

In a similar vein, the death of 96 Liverpool Football Club supporters at an away game at Hillsborough Stadium in 1989 was first described as 'accidental death'. Finally, however, after 27 years of agitation and investigation, a 2016 coronial inquiry deemed the deaths to be an 'unlawful killing' due to police actions and ineptitude. For years, efforts had been made to transfer the blame from the police to the innocent victims by spreading lies, doctoring evidence, pressuring witnesses and suppressing the truth—for example, 164 witness statements were altered and, of those, 116 were changed to remove criticism of the police (Magnay 2016). The findings made the front-pages of newspapers worldwide, but *not* those of *The Sun* and *The Times* in the United Kingdom—two of the staunchest supporters of the status quo and thereby the power, authority and legitimacy of the police come what may.

Direct ownership is only one way in which economics impinges upon environmental reporting. Another is the influence of advertisers on the content presented by private media providers. Revenue for mainstream media is part-driven by advertisers. Advertisers are often companies that want to sell something to the public, and which therefore have a vested interest in promoting consumption and economic growth. Stories that threaten specific corporate interests and images, and those that de-legitimise the economic imperative over the ecological, are more apt to not see the light of day.

On the other hand, there are market opportunities to develop environmentally oriented television that is not about information as such. Nature programs and programs about exotic animals and plants might well fall into this category. They bring the rest of the world into the lounge rooms of the relatively affluent, but in ways that do not compel audiences to engage in anything more than non-demanding action (e.g. provide a donation to a wildlife protection fund). It is the unusual and the spectacular that is emphasised, not the mundane and the ordinary.

Another aspect of environmentalism and mainstream media is that, for 'hard news' in particular, sources of information often include what is provided by company public relations people via media releases, media conferences and other staged events. News frames thus reflect the power of these news-makers as 'primary definers' (Hall et al. 1978/2013). Likewise, it has been observed that large corporations that tend to run green advertising campaigns are almost never examined for their environmental record (Beder 1997). Being green, it seems, is in the eye of the beholder—as determined by the beholder.

One theme of this chapter is why it is that some types of human activity are more likely to be subject to criminalisation than others. Specifically, the concern is to identify those elements that together result in activity being deemed harmful, and thereby worthy of investigation and prosecution. The study of environmental problems is the study of real, existing problems. But these *become* social problems as the products of a 'dynamic social process of definition, negotiation and legitimation' (Hannigan 2006: 31). The problems may be 'real', but the definition, magnitude, impact, risk and origins of phenomena such as pollution, climate change and toxic waste are open to interpretation and dispute. Much the same can be said about corporate crime in general.

As with financial crimes, food crimes, state crimes and other harmful transgressions, there are some dramatic problems facing the planet when it comes to environmental issues. As we know, though, the severity of any particular issue does not necessarily translate into the prominence given to that particular issue within media. State intervention and social movement action around specific issues similarly rest upon the fact that these specific issues have become important enough to generate widespread, concrete social responses. The absence of such—as with crimes of the powerful—is partly due to constructed silences in relation to such crimes. It is also a matter of emphasis or salience.

What becomes prominent as a social issue reflects a social process in which certain claims—about nature, about environmental harm, about social impacts—are brought into the public domain and gain ascendancy. In this regard, it is important for the researcher to 'ask where a claim comes from, who owns or manages it, what economic and political interests claims-makers represent and what type of resources they bring to the claims-making process' (Hannigan 2006: 69). Hannigan (2006) provides a useful analytical model that describes just this process (see Box 9.4).

BOX 9.4

ANALYSING CLAIMS ABOUT ENVIRONMENTAL PROBLEMS

There are several key tasks in constructing environmental problems. For Hannigan (2006), the first is *assembling*. This determines the claim and supports it with requisite information and evidence. It involves discovering and naming the problem and constructing 'proof' through appeal to scientific evidence. The more systematic and streamlined the knowledge claims, the more likely they can overcome pitfalls associated with lack of clarity, ambiguity and conflicting scientific evidence. A typical proposition might be, for example, that 'fish farming is bad for the environment'. Protagonists on both sides of this proposition would then engage in assembling their case, using whatever scientific and other evidence they could marshal in support of their position.

The task of *presenting* refers to the process of commanding attention and legitimating the claim. The central forum for this is news media, and the message is usually portrayed as a moral claim: fish farming is 'bad', and we should stop it now (or conversely, it is 'good' and should be encouraged). This task requires a communicator, someone who can gain public attention. This can be achieved by use of dramatic verbal and visual imagery, such as pictures of diseased fish or human victims of contaminated salmon. The key is visibility and keeping things in the public sphere.

The third task is that of *contesting*. This means being able to invoke action and mobilise support for the claims being made. This takes the issue into the political realm, and brings with it consideration of legal matters such as burden of proof and potential legislative change. Getting scientists on board, networking with like-minded people and organisations, and initiating public rallies (e.g. of fishers, of consumers, of commercial operators) is all part of the process. It can be undermined by cooptation (e.g. allowing fish farms, but only under these rules), issue fatigue (people do not want to hear about it anymore) or countervailing claims (fish farms are vital to the food supply of people in China, Vietnam and other places).

The success or otherwise of claims-making in regards to corporate crime and state crime also rests with the ability of the powerful to resist such claims through legal and extra-legal means.

SILENCING OPPOSITION

The silences surrounding crimes of the powerful are partly secured by silencing opposing voices. This can take several different forms. Governments can imprison whistleblowers and those who oppose existing public policy. This is precisely the case in relation to reporting what is happening in the holding camps in which asylum seekers wishing to come to Australia are held, in offshore places like the detention centres in Papua New Guinea. Human rights abuses have occurred in these camps. Yet, Australian laws now prohibit anyone from exposing these injustices under the rubric of 'the national interest'. It is against the law to speak or write about what are arguably state crimes.

Litigation is a method used by companies to stop critical comment and social protest. For example, a favoured tactic familiar to residents of Tasmania is the SLAPP (strategic lawsuit against public participation). The precise character of a SLAPP may vary from situation to situation, depending upon the players and the issues involved. Generally speaking, however, a SLAPP refers to:

- a civil lawsuit filed against private individuals or organisations that have spoken out on issues of public interest or social significance
- a strategy aimed at intimidating an individual from engaging in particular behaviour believed to be detrimental to the SLAPP filer
- an intent not to win the legal case, but to silence the critic by dissuading citizens from speaking out on matters of public interest (see Beder 1997; Walters 2003).

Beder (1997: 64) quotes a US trial judge on the dynamics of a SLAPP:

> The conceptual threat that binds [SLAPPs] is that they are suits without substantial merit that are brought by private interests to 'stop citizens from exercising their political rights or to punish them for having done so' ... The longer the litigation can be stretched out, the more litigation that can be churned, the greater the expense that is inflicted and the closer the SLAPP filer moves to success. The purpose of such gamesmanship ranges from simple retribution for past activism to discouraging future activism.

SLAPPs are thus generally seen as strategic lawsuits that are commonly filed by larger corporations to prevent the public from intervening in disputes and to protect themselves against any claims that could jeopardise their image or reputation. Typically, such suits 'are cloaked as claims for defamation, nuisance, invasion of privacy, and interference with contract, to name a few' (Society of Professional Journalists 2008).

Ogle (2007) emphasises the need to distinguish a SLAPP as an effect, rather than an intent. He argues that George Pring and Penelope Canan, who first coined the term in the United States, used it to refer to the effect of the suits. They acknowledged that legitimate litigation could be a SLAPP suit if it had the effect of 'chilling public debate' (Pring & Canan 1996). For Beder (1997), however, there is the implication that SLAPPs refer mostly to suits without merit or suits brought for the express purpose of silencing debate.

This is a crucial distinction. First, if SLAPPs are analysed in terms of effect rather than motivation, then it provides a more legally neutral and inclusive definition. As Ogle (2007: 71) observes: 'The effect on public participation is the same regardless of the merit of the case or intention of those suing, so the real issue around SLAPP suits is their impact not just on the defendants, but on the broader community's right to public participation. SLAPP suits can effectively intimidate people—literally scare them into silence on issues of public concern'. Second, if motive is hard to discern, then accusations of using legal action as a SLAPP can themselves lead to further lawsuits. In other words, calling a suit a SLAPP (when narrowly defined in terms of motive) can call forth a countersuit because it is defamatory (since the label, as narrowly defined, carries the imputation that the plaintiffs would abuse the legal system). For present purposes, therefore, SLAPPs are defined in the broader sense of the term.

SLAPPs have other attributes as well. For example, they can involve actual lawsuits. They can also involve the threat of lawsuits. SLAPPs tend to be directed at individuals. They also tend to be aimed at prominent spokespeople and leaders of community groups. In the Tasmanian context, SLAPPs have also been used (or threatened) in attempts to stifle the publication of material critical of the Tasmanian Government in relation to forestry issues. The Gunns writ (see Box 9.5) certainly constituted one of the most sustained private attacks on environmental activism of its kind, but it was by no means unique in Australian litigation (see Ogle 2005; 2007).

BOX 9.5

THE GUNNS20 LAWSUIT

On 13 December 2004, Gunns Limited issued a writ in the Victorian Supreme Court against 20 environmental activists. At the time, Gunns Limited was Australia's largest fully-integrated hardwood forest products company. It owned 175 000 hectares of freehold land and managed in excess of 90 000 hectares of plantations. The company employed over 1200 people and had a turnover in excess of AUS$600 million. The company sued the group of environmentalists, protesters and Greens MPs for AUS$6.3 million. In this first version of the lawsuit, the company claimed damages for financial loss allegedly suffered as a result of protest actions related mainly to the activities of the company in Tasmania. Examples cited in the writ included:

- the Styx Valley tree-sit campaign the previous year (in Tasmania)
- a protest and 'lock-on' at the Triabunna woodchip mill (in Tasmania)
- a letter-writing campaign that saw more than 7000 people write to Japanese woodchip customers urging them not to buy Gunns woodchips
- a media campaign urging four major banks to end their association with Gunns Limited
- a lobbying campaign to have Gunns removed as a finalist from the Banksia Environmental Awards
- a claim by the group, Doctors for Forests, that the Burnie woodchip pile in northern Tasmania could harbour legionella.

The writ claimed that the overall campaign against Gunns constituted a conspiracy to injure Gunns by unlawful means and through interference with Gunns' trade and business by unlawful means.

One outcome of the Gunns action was heightened publicity about *all* of Gunns' activities, accompanied by greater public scepticism about the veracity of its claims across a range of issues. For example, in June 2005, submissions relating to the draft scope guidelines for an integrated environmental impact statement were being accepted on a proposed $1.3 billion Tamar Valley [northern Tasmania] pulp-mill project to be built and operated by Gunns. However, on the day that submissions closed for comment, Gunns revealed that it wanted to expand the original project site area from 100 hectares to 650 hectares—a sixfold increase in the size of its proposed mill site. Not surprisingly, this generated considerable criticism and protest from green groups and environmental activists. It attracted front-page headlines, and was the subject of a cynical editorial cartoon in the Tasmanian newspaper *The Mercury*, although the northern newspapers (*The Advocate* in Burnie and *The Examiner* in Launceston), long-standing supporters of Gunns and the pulp mill, were more muted in their response.

Another consequence of the Gunns20 lawsuit was popular outrage at the use of this kind of tactic. Shortly after the writ made the headlines, car stickers in the shape of the Greens' green triangle began to appear all over Hobart (and beyond) with the slogan 'So Sue Me'. Basically, the reaction was to make fun of Gunns for taking the action—but, as well, there was a strong undercurrent of consternation and anger against the company. Another result of the lawsuit was the making of a documentary, *Defendant 5*, which chronicled the personal struggle of Heidi Lee Douglas as she battled against the large corporation. Shown on ABC TV in December 2014, the documentary communicates the trauma inflicted by the Gunns lawsuit. Public debate and disgust over the writ also translated into financial penalties for Gunns Limited. Within a year of the lodging of the original writ, Gunns' share price had plummeted by some 30 per cent and the company had lost orders for woodchips from two Japanese customers, a trend that continued until the demise of the company itself (see Gale 2011). In 2010, the company abandoned the Gunns20 litigation.

Given the relatively small community in Tasmania (the overall population of the state is around half a million people), it is not surprising that strategic action against public participation takes more than one form. Specifically, attempts to quell dissent or silence critics can occur *informally* (and often privately) via phone conversations, 'gossip' networks, chance street meetings, advice from 'those in the know' and so on. A 'friendly' word of advice or veiled threats are not uncommon in and out of the corridors of power. Such warnings also occur *formally* (and both publicly and privately) via legal action, public condemnations, involvement of statutory bodies, input of professional associations, and so on.

The use of SLAPPs has been heavily criticised because of the way in which they allow large corporations to stifle public discussion, including criticism, about their business activities. Commentators in Australia such as Beder (1997), Walters (2003; 2005) and Ogle (2007) have signalled the fundamentally un-democratic nature of such suits. Moreover, they have called for vigilance, community agitation and new legislative safeguards to prevent their use now and into the future.

GREENWASHING AND CONTRARIANISM

In a manner analogous to the denial of human rights violations (see Cohen 2001), crimes of the powerful call forth a range of tactics on the part of nation-states and corporations, which, ultimately, legitimate and justify certain types of harmful activities. For example, this may take the form of '**greenwashing**' media campaigns, which misconstrue the nature of collective corporate business in regard to the environment (Athanasiou 1996; Beder 1997, 2004). Much money is spent on engendering a green spin that presents even the most environmentally destructive companies as being environmentally virtuous.

The form that greenwashing takes varies from the purely decorative (such as printing annual company reports on recycled paper) to assertive public relations campaigns that extol the ecological virtues of even the most 'dirty' of industries or companies. The idea is to make a business appear more environmentally and socially responsible than it actually is. For instance, the large oil company Chevron claims in its advertisements that it cares deeply about the environment and the communities in which it operates (using the slogan 'we care'). This campaign occurred at precisely the time that it faced a US$18 billion judgment for polluting the Ecuadorean Amazon and injuring its people (Cherry & Sneirson 2012). Or, in an early example of greenwashing in the United States:

> When a scandal-ridden company called Nuclear Engineering Inc changes its name to U.S. Ecology, wins the contract to build a hotly contested radioactive waste dump, and distributes slick brochures explaining the dump's displacement of a threatened desert tortoise as 'A New Home for Endangered Friends', it is obviously the logic of appearance that sets the terms (Athanasiou 1996: 232).

Greenwashing also involves tactics such as manipulation of statistics (so as to, for example, disguise the level and extent of pollution generated by a factory or company), the creation of 'front organisations' (intended to defend certain industries and activities), funding of sceptics and contrarian commentators, and appeals to in-house expertise as the only way in which to respond to looming environmental and social issues. Environmental awards are also another popular measure to instil the notion of environmental virtue. Companies can present themselves as being green and good by virtue of such awards.

For governments, denial of harm is usually associated with economic objectives and the appeal to forms of economic development, which fundamentally involve furthering specific company interests even if they involve environmental degradation and threats to human health and well-being (for examples, see Harvey 1996; Brunton 1999; White 2008; Tombs & Whyte 2015). Government action can also take the form of denying access to legal representation by restricting the provision of free legal services on matters of substantial public concern (Kuehn 2000).

Again, drawing upon examples dealing with the environment, the lack of concerted global action on climate change is due in large measure to the actions of large transnational corporations, especially those in the 'old energy' sectors such as coal mining (Lynch, Burns & Stretesky 2010; Brisman 2012). Given that the top private corporations are economically more powerful than many nation-states, and given that they own and control great expanses of the world's land, water and food resources, these corporations are individually and collectively a formidable force. On occasion, as well, business competitors may combine to use their collective muscle to influence world opinion or global efforts to curtail their activities. For example, analysis of how big business has responded to global warming reveals a multi-pronged strategy to slow things down, including challenging the science behind climate change through to influencing climate change negotiations through direct lobbying (Bulkeley & Newell 2010).

The issue of state/corporate collusion can also be examined through the lens of the politics of denial, involving various techniques of neutralisation (see Sykes & Matza 1957; Cohen 2001). This refers to the ways in which business and state leaders attempt to prevent action being taken on climate change while actively supporting specific sectoral interests. Typically, such techniques involve:

- denial of responsibility (against anthropocentric or human causes as the source of the problem)
- denial of injury ('natural' disasters are 'normal')
- denial of the victim (failure to acknowledge differential victimisation, especially among the poor and residents of the Global South)
- condemnation of the condemners (attacks on climate scientists)
- appeal to higher loyalties (American/Australian/Chinese economic interests ought to predominate over ecological concerns).

The net result is no action or inaction in addressing the key factors contributing to climate change, such as carbon emissions.

These types of denial should not be conflated with scepticism as such, but rather as a form of **contrarianism**. As Brisman (2012: 43) notes: '... while scepticism can be both a healthy part of the scientific process and an excuse to present political or value-laden perspectives (that are masked behind a scientific façade), contrarianism suggests an ideological, rather than scientific, impetus for disagreement'. Contrarianism involves a series of common tactics executed through a well-known sequence, which includes:

> ... denying the problem, down-playing its severity, predicting economic ruin, and relying on human adaptive capacity and ingenuity. All along the way, the proponents of these views exploit scientific uncertainties, use selective decontextualized scientific findings, call on flawed pseudoscientific studies, and bank on the ignorance of the general public to support their views, while peppering their public statements with derogatory name-calling and portrayals of scientists and politicians (Moser & Dilling 2004: 38).

In this way, particular economic and social interests are fostered over and above those of the common good.

As we have already established, the hard reality of much news journalism is that it is intertwined with big business. Where this is not directly the case (as with national public broadcasters such as the Australian Broadcasting Corporation, the British Broadcasting Corporation, Canadian Broadcasting Corporation, the US Public Broadcasting Service and so on), there is often political pressure to be 'even handed' and uncritical of certain people, policies and principles. Appeals to the 'national interest' are also used to shut out alternative voices and to deny the more critical perspectives on environmental matters (e.g. getting the Olympic bid requires silence about what to do about the toxic waste on the Olympic site).

What also affects media treatments of stories is the notion of *journalistic neutrality*. This notion is based upon three interrelated concepts (Beder 1997: 202–6):

> *Balance*—more radical opinions generally left out; both sides get equal coverage, regardless of numbers of people in demonstration or counter-demonstration; scientists with suspect credentials given equal weight to others.
>
> *Depersonalisation*—in order to downplay personal views, there is encouragement of uncritical reporting of official statements and those of authority figures; 'In this way, the individual biases of individual journalists are avoided but institutional biases are reinforced'.
>
> *Sphere of objectivity*—a story that supports the status quo is generally considered to be neutral (i.e. no perceived need for balance), while one that challenges the status quo tends to be perceived as having a 'point of view' and therefore biased; the former are 'facts', the latter 'opinions'.

The idea of being unbiased frequently translates into letting environmental sceptics have much more media time than they deserve. But this seems to work in only one direction. That is, the occasional scientist who has stood against the vast tide of scientific opinion to express doubt about climate change, and who thereby finds favour in conservative political circles, is more than likely to be given a voice in media 'debates' over the state of the environment. Meanwhile, scientists and environmental activists who for years have been trying to get their message across about specific threats (melting of the Arctic polar ice cap) or general trends (global warming) have been received less favourably. Research has shown that 'the journalistic norm of balance can compete with the journalistic value of accuracy, leading to biased depictions of knowledge on global climate change in the US prestige press—an unwarranted weight of those that deny its anthropogenic origins or that the problem is even scientifically provable' (Brisman 2012: 60). One social consequence of this type of reportage is that it tends towards inaction on climate change issues at precisely the time when action is what is needed (Brisman 2012).

MEDIA THAT IS CRITICAL OF THE POWERFUL

Even the more conventional or conservative media are forced into acknowledgment of environmental harms and corporate crimes when some events, trends or situations become too big to ignore, downplay or dismiss. As we have seen, this was certainly the case with the Enron scandal, once journalists, like Bethany McLean, shone a light on the corrupt business practices of the company's officials. The issues then become how to explain these crimes, and what is to be done about them. Some stories have to be told, and there will always be someone there to tell them.

Indeed, it is important to acknowledge that not all journalists are always complicit in turning a blind eye to corporate misdemeanours and wrongdoings; environmental activists, for example, can and do have allies in mainstream media. While there are structural parameters to media practices (relating to everything from content-format issues through to editorial control), claims-making only makes sense as an active process if there is some opportunity to make the claim stick. If there were not possibilities to exploit the chinks in the walls of access to the mainstream mediascape, then the present discussion would be about totalitarianism rather than social construction. There are, then, pressures and limits that define the process, but what occurs is nonetheless a process.

The ideals of journalism are such that journalists are expected to be independent and neutral recorders of history. This belies the many ways in which specific stories can be edited or pulled, depending upon content and the potential to disrupt the interests of media owners, advertisers or other powerful elites. It also ignores the ways in which so-called 'dissident' journalists, like John Pilger, are frequently derided and complained about for their perceived biases. But 'dissident' does not necessarily mean radical or 'underground'; it can include independent media such as *New Matilda* in Australia or *Mother Jones* in the United States, as well as more investigative forms of media, such as documentaries like *Enron: The Smartest Guys in the Room*, which can and do find the space and scope to tell deeper and more nuanced stories about corporate wrongdoing. The media can also be used as a vital source for understanding the dynamics and nature of specific instances of corporate and state-based criminality.

The Catholic Church has been among those in the front line of media coverage in recent years for its response to child sexual abuse. Here, the qualities of tenacity and fearlessness have featured in journalistic exposures of wrongdoing by priests. This is highlighted in the 2015 film *Spotlight*, which details the real-life efforts of *The Boston Globe*'s investigative journalist unit to uncover and reveal what was happening in that city. The work of the 'Spotlight' team earned them the 2003 Pulitzer Prize for Public Service for their 'courageous, comprehensive coverage of sexual abuse by priests, an effort that pierced secrecy, stirred local, national and international reaction and produced changes in the Roman Catholic Church'.

Similar tributes have been paid in an Australian context to the winner of the 2013 Gold Walkley award, journalist Joanne McCarthy of the *Newcastle Herald*, for her 'Shine The Light' series. McCarthy spent seven years writing over 350 articles about the sexual abuse of children, primarily by Catholic clergy in the Newcastle and Hunter Valley regions of New South Wales. Engaging in this type of 'crusade journalism' required much intestinal fortitude and gumption on McCarthy's part, especially when church authorities responded to complaints with obfuscation and threats of legal action. An 'ugly campaign of whispers' also emerged that accused McCarthy of being mad and obsessed. However, the success of the 'Shine The Light' campaign is best summed up by McCarthy herself: 'I am a regional person and I think only a regional paper could have done this. The truth is the truth. It doesn't matter where it appears. You just have to keep banging away' (The Walkley Foundation 2013). In the end, the effort paid off: McCarthy's investigation in part led to one of Australia's biggest Royal Commissions—the Royal Commission into Institutional Responses to Child Sexual Abuse.

Apart from the courage and tenacity of media practitioners, crimes of the powerful can also become newsworthy partly because of the global scope of the coverage, and partly because of the timing of the release of information. For example, the 'Panama Papers' refers to the leaking of secret documents from a law firm in Panama, and the provision of information on the illegal tax havens used by the world's rich and famous. Published by the International Consortium of Investigative Journalists <www.icij.org>, the papers identify more than 300 000 companies, trusts, foundations and funds that are incorporated in 21 tax havens, from Hong Kong to Nevada. For an Australian audience, the newsworthy features of this story include elements such as relevant political *juxtapositions* (unions as corrupt versus companies/politicians as corrupt); *timing* (a federal election was looming, and tax is an issue in terms of both raising taxes and reducing spending); and *celebrity* (in that then Prime Minister of Britain David Cameron and the President of Russia Vladimir Putin were implicated in the papers, while the Prime Minister of Iceland, Sigurdur Ingi Jóhannsson, was forced to resign).

However, when it comes to the powerful, there is always a 'but'. In this case, a number of wealthy Australians named in the Panama Papers, which revealed how the world's richest and most powerful people use offshore companies to hide their wealth, will not have their historical tax affairs investigated after striking secret deals with the Australian Tax Office (ATO). This is because, two years previously, the ATO's 'Project DO IT' offered a deal: come forward and disclose undeclared foreign income and gains on a confidential basis—and you will only be assessed for the previous four years, only be liable for a maximum shortfall penalty of 10 per cent, and will not be referred for criminal investigation. Those named in the Panama Papers who did this were thus afforded significant legal protection (Kitney 2016).

ISSUES FOR CONSIDERATION

The mobilisation of opinion is crucial to the determination of what is or is not considered a 'crime' (or 'harm'), and how the state will in the end respond to the phenomenon in question. This is well known to writers examining the nature of state crime, since state crime is typically denied by the perpetrator—the state itself. In these circumstances, it is frequently human rights definitions combined with world opinion that make certain harms *into* state crimes (see Green & Ward 2000; 2004). All media contribute to and are fundamental to this happening.

In a very similar vein, the actions of states on environmental matters sometimes elude consideration as a criminological matter because of the policy and political context within which the harm occurs. This is especially the case in respect to environmental harms associated with the processes and techniques of war. For example, there are major problems with the use of depleted uranium (DU) in weapons and armour in war situations such as Iraq, the Balkans and Kosovo (see White 2008). Thus, the damage caused by uranium weapons 'cannot be contained to "legal" fields of battle; they continue to act after the conclusion of hostilities; they are inhumane because they place the health of non-combatants, including children and future generations, at risk; and they cannot be used without unduly damaging the natural environment' (Medical Association for Prevention of War Australia 2003). Yet information about the full effects of DU is held tightly by precisely those most likely to bear the brunt of the criticism—governments such as the United States and the United Kingdom, which insist upon its continued use.

Crimes committed by corporations and by the state are 'protected' by the corporate veil and appeals to the national interest. They are also deflected through clever diversionary tactics that predispose the general public to think of crimes of the powerful in particular ways. For example, the US television series *White Collar* has a focus that is deliberately narrow and apolitical, showing typical occupational crimes such as employee theft and credit card fraud, but ignoring corporate abuses of power and harms. The first two seasons were produced by GE, a company whose 'frequent and prolific corporate offending includes environmental pollution, bribery, price fixing, defence contract fraud, safety concerns about their nuclear power reactor, and fraud in the sale of mortgage-backed securities' (Buist & Leighton 2015: 74). Not surprisingly, the types of transgressions characteristic of GE did not feature prominently, if at all, in *White Collar*. This is perhaps another example of what has been described as 'culturally constructed ignorance' whereby special interests obscure the truth (Buist & Leighton 2015).

On the other hand, there exist a number of 'watchdog' type organisations, agencies and individuals whose brief, at least in part, is to expose both the crimes of the powerful and those who are supposed to be exposing these crimes within news media. Examples of this include the ABC's *Fact Check* and *Media Watch* (the former was relaunched in 2017 in partnership with RMIT University); 'Corporate Watch' as an activist organisation; citizen journalists exposing evidence of corporate wrongdoing and environmental harm (often through blogs and social media); Al Jazeera and other international media providing alternative critical narratives that might otherwise not be heard; 'Google' tracking of stories and companies; and reader connections with and input to mainstream media websites and news stories. Even the powerful can find it hard to hide their transgressions in a world that is interconnected in so many different ways.

CONCLUSION

Corporate and state crimes are not rare nor are they infrequent. They also intertwine with each other in sophisticated and complicated ways (Tombs & Whyte 2015; Rothe & Kauzlarich 2016) and, ultimately, are distinct but inseparable. While fundamentally the most damaging and destructive of crimes, the crimes of the powerful are also those least likely to feature in mediated discourses about crime and crime control. Indeed, the silences pertaining to crimes of the powerful are well protected through a range of legal and extra-legal measures, as well as by the control exercised by media and telecommunication corporations themselves.

Simultaneously, the virtues and existential necessity of corporations are embedded at a commonsense level through continuous propaganda and policy decisions that naturalise their importance to the economic and social order. Accordingly, it is the grassroots activist, including the whistleblower, who is best placed to resist the imposition of top-down power and hegemonic ideas. Ironically, however, it may well be that the occasional counter-narrative to this overall picture serves, in its own peculiar way, to highlight the (apparently) overwhelming power of the mainstream, thereby propping up the concentrated wealth and power of the ruling classes of contemporary society. This, too, is part of the paradox of power and resistance in the twenty-first century.

DISCUSSION QUESTIONS

1. Examine local and national media sources, and provide examples of news stories that reflect 'crimes of the powerful' across its many definitions (e.g. state crime, corporate crime, environmental harms, etc.). How many can you find from a one-week reporting period?

2. What role do journalists play, directly and indirectly, in 'greenwashing' and/or 'whitewashing' the crimes of the powerful?

3. What are the social and ideological functions of a 'scapegoat'?

4. 'Who pays the piper chooses the tune.' Discuss this statement in relation to media portrayals of corporate crime.

5. State crime is generally presented as virtuous, as a necessary evil in defence of the national interest. Provide examples of this in action, and explain what the pitfalls of this portrayal might be.

WORKSHOP ACTIVITY 1: WHO IS WHO?

Crimes of the powerful involve powerful people. Therefore, an initial starting point is to identify which are the most powerful individuals and companies in Australia.

- What sources can be drawn on to identify the 'rich and powerful' (e.g. *Who's Who*, *Business Review Weekly*)?

- What does 'follow the money trail' actually mean and what kinds of skills are needed to do this?

- What local and global trends are worth bearing in mind in considering the likelihood of criminal activity among the powerful?

- Which independent experts might be drawn upon for help in investigating crimes of the powerful, especially corporate crime and state crime?

WORKSHOP ACTIVITY 2: THE ATTRIBUTION OF RESPONSIBILITY

In the fallout from the Enron scandal, the question of who was to blame for the culture of corruption within the company became a recurrent frame within news media coverage. This is what is called the 'attribution of responsibility' frame. Take a look at some of the news reports from around the time of the scandal; media outlets like *CBS News*, *The Guardian* and *The New York Times* should be useful sources for this, as should business publications, like *Fortune* and *Businessweek* magazines. Do your own framing analysis on a selection of these media texts, taking into consideration the following issues: How often does the 'attribution of responsibility' frame appear? What other frames (e.g. morality) are evident? Pay close attention to language choice: are there particular words, like 'wrongdoing', 'blame', 'failed', which repeatedly appear? How do they support the overall framing of the story?

If you can, locate a copy of the documentary *Enron: the Smartest Guys in the Room*, and compare the framing. What do you notice about its scope to explore the intricacies of the story, compared to the other media texts?

FURTHER READING

Beder, S. (1997). *Global Spin: The Corporate Assault on Environmentalism*. Melbourne: Scribe Publications.

Cohen, S. (2001). *States of Denial: Knowing About Atrocities and Suffering*. Cambridge: Polity.

Hannigan, J. (2006). *Environmental Sociology: A Social Constructionist Perspective*. London: Routledge.

Rothe, D. & Kauzlarich, D. (2016). *Crimes of the Powerful: An Introduction*. London: Routledge.

Tombs, S. & Whyte, D. (2015). *The Corporate Criminal: Why Corporations Must Be Abolished*. London: Routledge.

Walters, B. (2003). *Slapping on the Writs: Defamation, Developers and Community Activism*. Sydney: UNSW Press.

PART
IV

AUDIENCES, INDUSTRIES AND TECHNOLOGIES

10

CRIME AS ENTERTAINMENT—THE CSI EFFECT

CHAPTER HIGHLIGHTS

Introduction

CSI: A new team of crime fighters

Reel justice vs real justice

The plausibility of the CSI effect

Measuring effects: A matter of method or perception?

Conclusion

INTRODUCTION

Real-life crimes and images of violence have long been a staple of entertainment media in all its forms. As far back as the nineteenth century, writers and their readers had an appetite for crime stories. Street peddlers frequently sold broadsides to the lower classes for their reading pleasure. Printed single-sided on cheap paper, these publications detailed the gory details of recent murders and riots. Like modern-day programs at sporting events, they were often sold to audiences who had gathered to witness public executions. Broadsides typically featured a graphic account of the crime, arrest and trial; an illustration of the criminal, the crime scene or execution (obviously a fabrication since the body was still swinging in the gallows); and a ballad or rhyme (sometimes moral in nature, but more frequently lewd or comical) about the criminal (Flanders 2011). Like the tales of horror and highway robbery found in popular 'penny dreadfuls'—the sensationalist literature of mid-Victorian Britain, which cost a penny to buy—broadsides had a serial quality about them. They were often published in instalments as the narrative of the crime unfolded (Turnbull 2014).

By the twentieth century, it was true-crime magazines and scandal sheets (the equivalent of our modern-day tabloids) that splashed sensational headlines across their covers to captivate audiences. Headlines like those from the October 1961 issue of *True Detective* were common fare: 'The Riddle of Oregon's Dismembered Brunette: A Cold-Blooded Killer Hacked up His Victim and Strewed Body Parts all over the County'. Or try this one from the January 1962 cover: 'Killer with an Itch: Two Tennessee GIs had a Perfect Crime Going for Them—Till One Stopped to Scratch'. By this time, writers Dashiell Hammett and Raymond Chandler had also brought the mean streets of the United States to life through their typifications of the 'hard-boiled' private detective and the invention of now-classic literary characters like Sam Spade and Philip Marlowe. Such figures would go on to have a lasting influence on the development of contemporary television crime dramas—just as the evolution of the professionalised and paid police force of the early twentieth century would in terms of the development of police procedurals and other stories of crime investigation on the small screen.

Even with these real-life developments and the emerging popularity of crime genres through other more contemporary entertainment media, including podcasts and true-crime documentaries, preoccupations with the gruesome and sensationalised nature of mediated representations of crime have persisted. As media studies scholar Sue Turnbull (2014: 23) notes in her reflections on the pulp crime fiction of the nineteenth century: '... public moralists voiced what would become an ongoing concern about the imagined effects of such salacious material on the popular imagination, an anxiety that has hardly abated in relation to more recent depictions of crime on the screen'. While it was once mostly the sensationalist nature of these depictions that garnered public scrutiny and concern, now anxieties about the effects of the dramatisation of crime have as much to do with the corruption of mind and morals as they do with potential impacts on the administration of justice.

In recent years, these debates have played out most obviously in relation to the success of overnight sensations like *Serial, The Jinx* and *Making a Murderer* (see Chapter 4)—all of which have raised questions about the ethics of true-crime-as-entertainment, and the rules of procedure to which these productions are bound. But even before this, concerns proliferated about the realism of media portrayals of criminal justice, and the extent to which crime dramas, as seen on TV, could influence and potentially mislead viewers' perceptions of the work involved in the criminal investigation process. Among the supposed culprits, one television series in particular has stood apart as the subject of numerous scholarly critiques and measures of media effects—*CSI: Crime Scene Investigation. CSI* and other shows of its calibre sought to break from the 'cops on the box' formula previously adopted by many popular television crime dramas. Rather than focusing on police on the beat or the trials and tribulations of the legal fraternity, both within and outside the courtroom, *CSI* resolutely put forensic scientists in a starring role as the 'new law enforcement crime fighting hero' (Surette 2011: 95). Like its golden age literary predecessors of the twentieth century (and even harking back to the days of Sherlock Holmes in the nineteenth century), *CSI* took a scientific approach to detection (Moore 2014). In this chapter, we explore these stylistic conventions and revisit the controversy that *CSI* continues to court as a television crime series in terms of its representations of forensic science and the possible impacts of its blurring of fact and fiction.

CSI: A NEW TEAM OF CRIME FIGHTERS

The first series of the popular television franchise, *CSI: Crime Scene Investigation*, premiered in the United States on the CBS network in 2000, and quickly became one of the highest-rating dramas on American television. Its popularity proved that, just as murders can help sell newspapers, so too they can boost television ratings (Robbers 2008). Even in its sixth season, *CSI* continued to deliver more than 30 million viewers each week (Collins 2015). It won the most-watched television program in the world category several times over at the prestigious International Audience Awards, and was exported as a series to over 170 countries. *CSI*'s popularity spawned several spin-offs, including *CSI: Miami* (2002–12), *CSI: NY* (2004–13) and *CSI: Cyber* (2015–16), and influenced a number of other police dramas, where forensic science similarly became the key to solving crimes. The original *CSI* series concluded in 2015 in its 16th season with a two-hour finale, 'Immortality', which attracted a television audience of over 12 million viewers (Sims 2015).

Part of the appeal of the series lies in its ability 'to simplify the messy uncertainties of real-world crime' and restore the moral balance after law breaking (Tyler 2006: 1065)—not that the show's protagonists were ever short of opportunities to do so, given that '*CSI* is set in a city mired by criminality' (Moore 2014: 254). The convenience afforded by this endless torrent of vice and violence is inherent to prime-time forensics, where things are always a lot simpler and prettier than they are in reality. As Kluger and colleagues (2002) explain: watch an episode of CSI and you could be forgiven for thinking that all forensic investigators dress in pristine white lab coats and walk around underlit glass offices that are tastefully appointed with artfully positioned autopsy tables. The reality is that the competition most forensic labs are subject to in terms of funding leaves little room for such luxuries. This includes the high-tech gadgetry of mass spectrometers and the like, which frequently features as part of the CSI franchise, but is nowhere near as flashy in real life (Kluger et al. 2002).

Set in Las Vegas, *CSI*'s plot revolves around a team of forensic investigators, who are trained to solve serious crimes, usually murders and rapes. Despite some cast changes throughout the series, the show's main characters include supervisor and group leader, Gil Grissom, his second-in-command, blood spatter expert Catherine Willows, and specialist investigators Sara Sidle, Warrick Brown and Nick Stokes. The series is perhaps most distinctive for its opening credits, which appear to the familiar strains of The Who's hit song 'Who Are You?', and feature depictions of each of the characters interspersed with a montage of images, which includes X-rays of various body parts, blood spatter and the contents of a petri dish as seen through a microscope (Moore 2014). This framing serves to set up and reinforce the *CSI* narrative that 'science' is central to the pursuit of justice. Many of the show's episodes open at the scene of a crime or its aftermath—a narrative device not unfamiliar to its genre of the crime drama or whodunit. But what really sets *CSI* apart from its predecessors is its relentless focus on the 'science' of criminal investigation, rather than policing, detective work or court proceedings (Kruse 2010).

While the protagonists within the show testify as expert witnesses in court cases, this is rarely depicted in the episodes themselves. Grissom and his team are more often shown collecting '**trace evidence**' from crime scenes, analysing the evidence on-site or in their laboratories, and interrogating witnesses and suspects (Kruse 2010). Their work occurs independently of the functions of police and the courts. Some might even say that, in *CSI*, Grissom and his team *are* the law, carrying guns (albeit rarely used) and arresting suspects—something real-life forensic scientists are not permitted to do.

By contrast, to provide just one indication of what real forensic practice might entail, consider the employment positions that *actually* exist in the Las Vegas Metropolitan Police Department (LVMPD) (see Genge 2004):

- Evidence custodian:
    - Performs a variety of technical duties to ensure that *evidence* is properly processed, stored, protected and delivered, or to release and dispose of cleared property.
- Crime scene analyst I/II:
    - Responds to crime scenes, performing a wide variety of *investigative tasks* to document the crime including on-scene photography, recovery of physical evidence and processing latent fingerprints.
- Criminalist I/II:
    - Performs various scientific analyses in a *laboratory setting* on physical evidence to deliver scientific consultation; to interpret and form conclusions from test results; to document such interpretations and conclusions in a variety of reports; and to testify as an expert at court proceedings.
- Document examiner:
    - Examines *documents* and document-related evidence within the environment of the scientific laboratory; interprets results; forms conclusions; testifies at court as an expert witness.
- Firearms/tool-mark examiner:
    - Performs scientific and laboratory analyses on *firearms and tool-mark evidence*; interprets test results and forms conclusions; prepares reports; and testifies in court as an expert witness.
- Forensic laboratory technician:
    - Provides technical support in a *forensic laboratory* and maintains evidence control; provides responsible staff assistance to professional laboratory staff; completes a variety of laboratory tasks and procedures as assigned by the laboratory director.
- Latent print examiner:
    - Conducts *fingerprint* comparisons of latent prints and finger and palm print exemplar files; performs various tasks relative to assigned areas of responsibility.
- Photo technician:
    - Provides *photographic support* to LVMPD and neighbouring police agencies; operates and maintains complex photographic equipment; performs a variety of tasks relative to assigned areas of photography.

This list highlights the highly specialised nature of forensic science and the particular roles played by those engaged in forensic analysis. There is normally a separation between police work (although this does, however, include crime scene investigation) and forensic science work (which includes, but is not exclusive to, laboratory-based work), and each is guided by very different professional norms and practices (see Julian, Kelty & Robertson 2012). The more serious the crime, the more likely there will be more personnel involved, and the more likely they will be multidisciplinary (law enforcement, medicine, law, forensic science) and multi-organisational (health, justice, private legal/medical, police) (Kelty, Julian & Ross 2012). A large part of forensics activity, therefore, involves negotiating with many different professionals and agencies in order to secure appropriate and just outcomes. Crime scene investigation and the collection and processing of forensic evidence are far more complex than many lay people imagine, especially if public perceptions are primarily based on television depictions.

Stretching the bounds of reality has long been one of the hallmarks of debates about *CSI*'s depictions of the criminal investigation process. Concerns about the show's potential to mislead television audiences even resulted in calls for CBS to include a disclaimer at the start of each episode to clarify that *CSI* was indeed a work of fiction (see Cole & Dioso-Villa 2011; Harriss 2011)—an appeal that was never acted on. Over the years, these concerns have been associated with not only the depictions of forensic scientists themselves, but also what it is that they do—that is, their agency in the criminal investigation process. Evidence plays a vital role in this, since the *CSI* team are often portrayed as secondary authorities in relation to it; satisfied to 'follow the evidence' and let it 'speak' to them as forensic scientists. 'If there is an active agent in discovering the evidence's "voice"', writes Kruse (2010: 84), 'it is technology'. But even this is more sleight of hand than anything else, since much of the forensic analysis on *CSI* occurs off-screen, except when we see samples being inserted into high-tech laboratory equipment and mobile testing machines (see Box 10.1). The results are then more often reported in a laboratory setting than they are in a police station or courtroom (Kruse 2010). As a result, the need for a motive is rare; the key revelatory moments instead come from the results of scientific testing (Moore 2014).

BOX 10.1

FORENSICS *CSI*-STYLE

In Season 14, Episode 7 ('Under a Cloud') of *CSI: Crime Scene Investigation*, a nearly dead John Doe is pulled from a flood channel during torrential rains, and forensic scientist Sara Sidle (played by Jorja Fox) is sent in to investigate. Much to her surprise, she discovers a bomb inside the man's satchel, which is subsequently defused. After learning that he was planting a second bomb at the Mediterranean Casino when he slipped and fell into the flood channel, Sara takes Anthony Hurst (Jason Gerhardt), a bomb disposal expert, to examine the scene. Their walkthrough pieces together the incident for viewers using character dialogue interspersed with flashbacks, which reconstruct the event-as-it-happened. This is a common storytelling device within many television crime dramas, and resonates with what philosopher Tzvetan Todorov (1977) once identified as the dual narrative of classic detective fiction—the idea that crime stories contain not one, but two stories; the story of the crime itself ('what really happened') and the story of the investigation ('how the audience has come to know about what happened'). In *CSI*, the narrative device also serves to interpolate the viewer in the investigatory process by allowing them to share the position of the forensic scientist (Kruse 2010).

Back on scene, Sara and Anthony discover 'a little calling card' from the perpetrator—a smear of blood on the wire fence, which had been cut to access the flood channel. Producing a cotton bud, Sara takes a swab of the blood, telling Anthony it is the 'perfect time for my new DNA instrument'. Surprised, he asks, 'You have a mobile lab?' to which she responds: 'In the back of my car. No extractions, quick results. Want to see it?'. The episode cuts to Sara inserting the cotton bud into a machine to run a test on the sample. Within a matter of seconds, the screen flashes with the result that there are no DNA matches in the database.

In reality, forensic scientists say, these kinds of '*CSI* moments' are rare (Porter 2008). A comprehensive DNA analysis of the kind portrayed in 'Under a Cloud' would normally take days to complete and, like most real-life DNA analysis, would require some form of human intervention and interpretation. It would therefore also be subject to the potential for human error, although *CSI* and other television crime shows like it more commonly present forensic analysis as an automated or machine-driven process and physical evidence as flawless and indisputable; the evidence never lies. This is typical of what Kruse (2010: 85) describes as the 'unproblematic treatment of technology'—and physical evidence—in shows of this type. So too, it reflects the way in which technology is often framed as emblematic of the ideals of scientific objectivity, precisely because machines are not subject to the foibles of human behaviour and subjective decision-making.

The guilt of the perpetrator(s) in *CSI* is therefore established not by classic methods of detection and surveillance carried out by the show's crime fighters, but by the team's reliance on scientific analysis of the physical evidence, which is itself considered superior to other forms of evidence, such as eyewitness testimony. As Grissom declares in Season 1, Episode 3 of *CSI*: 'I tend not to believe people. People lie. But the evidence doesn't lie'. Later, in a two-part episode, 'A Bullet Runs through It', from the show's sixth season, he repeats the mantra, saying: 'Physical evidence cannot be wrong. It doesn't lie. It's not influenced by emotion or prejudice ... it's not confused by the excitement of the moment' (Grissom cited in Harriss 2011: 4). More than this, writes Kruse (2010: 81), the evidence in *CSI* is depicted 'as an agent in and of itself, as something that talks, testifies, proves, and raises questions'. But this way of talking about evidence is inconsistent with the realities of criminal investigation—a point raised in much of the research that has emerged in the years since *CSI*'s rise to fame, as well as the criticisms about the ways in which the show presents the public with 'a distorted view of what forensic science can and cannot do' (Dioso-Villa 2014: 23).

Trace evidence, for example, is not always detected at a crime scene. Even if it *is* apparent, it is not always recoverable (Dioso-Villa 2014). Police may collect evidence as part of their investigations, but not submit it for forensic analysis. So too, constraints on resources, equipment and expertise can mean that the tests required as part of an investigation are not always conducted. When they are, it is several crime labs, not one, which process the evidence from any given case, but the results are 'far from immediate given the backlog of cases most laboratories experience' (Dioso-Villa 2014: 23).

Despite *CSI*'s depictions to the contrary, forensic examination *does* require human intervention and interpretation. Evidence, after all, only becomes 'evidence' once it has been defined as such—by forensic scientists or by the courts, where its **probative value** is assessed and open to dispute and counter-claim. This can result in the evidence being deemed inadmissible in legal proceedings. In the United States, the 'Daubert test' is frequently used to decide whether or not a piece of evidence can be submitted to the court and to provide some measure by which to establish a reliability threshold. It considers four factors: whether the technique can be and has been tested; whether it has been subjected to peer review/ publication; what the known or potential error rate is; and whether the evidence has widespread acceptance in the scientific community (White 2016). According to Shelton (2011), the Daubert test changed the basic question of admissibility from simply 'general acceptance' to a requirement that the proponent of the evidence must establish the scientific validity of the evidence being offered, by demonstrating that its foundations are empirically sound and that its application to the particular case is appropriate.

There have been robust and long-standing discussions and critiques of how expert evidence is mobilised in court, particularly in respect to forensic evidence in criminal cases. The problem is not simply one of inaccuracy or skewed knowledge. Within the context of an adversarial system of criminal law, the difficulties revolve around the question of experts and bias (White 2016). According to the New South Wales Law Reform Commission (2005), there are three varieties of 'adversarial bias':

- *Deliberate partisanship*—an expert deliberately tailors evidence to support their client.
- *Unconscious partisanship*—the expert does not intentionally mislead the court, but is influenced by the situation to give evidence in a way that supports the client.
- *Selection bias*—litigants choose as their expert witnesses persons whose views are known to support their case.

In order to counter such biases and ensure greater reliability on the part of experts, a range of measures have been suggested to control expert evidence, including formalising processes for instructing experts and presenting experts' reports, requiring disclosure of fee arrangements, and imposing sanctions on experts for misconduct (see Parliamentary Office of Science and Technology 2005; Victorian Law Reform Commission 2008; Edmond 2012). The growth in the use of forensic evidence in Australian courts over the past three decades has heightened concerns that sufficient safeguards need to be put in place to guarantee as far as possible accurate outcomes based upon robust expert opinion. Close scrutiny of the use of forensic evidence has uncovered numerous problems and difficulties (Edmond & San Roque 2012). Among these, according to Julian and Kelty (2015), are six risks in the collection and use of forensic evidence from crime scene to courtroom: 1) low level of forensic awareness among first responders; 2) crime scene examiners (CSEs) as technicians rather than professionals; 3) inefficient and/or ineffective laboratory processes; 4) limited forensic literacy among key actors in the criminal justice system; 5) poor communication between key actors in the criminal justice system; and 6) financial resources not directed at the front end of the forensic process. Looking to the future, there are calls for institutionalisation of and commitment to excellence, first-class science, accuracy and transparency when it comes to forensic evidence (Kirby 2010).

The results of forensic testing are therefore sometimes inconclusive, and often contestable—even between forensic science experts (Goodman-Delahunty & Wakabayashi 2012). Highlighting this and the potential for systemic deficiencies in criminal investigation, the Innocence Project, a not-for-profit organisation based in the United States, has helped to exonerate over 300 wrongfully convicted individuals through DNA testing and re-testing, including 20 people who served time on death row. But this picture does not necessarily fit with that presented by *CSI*, where there are few, if any, contested narratives or miscarriages of justice—unless it is a miscarriage of justice that the *CSI* team has been recruited to resolve in the first place. Real-life forensics therefore works on the basis of probabilities and likelihood ratios. In television forensics, certainty reigns. For the *CSI* team, science equates to justice and a resolution to the crime is guaranteed by the end of each episode—as a direct consequence of the faultlessness of the forensic evidence and its reliability in 'speaking' absolute truth. Judgments are made in clear opposition to the principle that people should be presumed innocent until proven guilty—in a court of law.

REEL JUSTICE VS REAL JUSTICE

Concerns about the ways in which these fictional representations may be mistaken as fact have manifested into the phenomenon now commonly known as the 'CSI effect'. The term first entered the popular lexicon after it was mentioned in the *TIME* magazine cover story, 'How Science Solves Crimes', where Kluger and colleagues (2002) noted that forensic scientists had started to 'speak of something they call the CSI effect, a growing public expectation that police labs can do everything TV labs can'. Within three years, the phenomenon had infiltrated the media psyche, with mentions of the CSI effect identified in 56 newspaper and magazine articles published in 2005, and in another 78 articles the following year (Cole &

Dioso-Villa 2011). The phenomenon is an example of media effects in that it presupposes that media exposure directly translates into media influence.

Parallels have been drawn between the CSI effect and the ways in which pre-trial publicity (or lack thereof) can shape trial verdicts (see Tyler 2006). Broadly speaking, the CSI effect assumes that the often-misguided perceptions people have about forensic science and the process of criminal investigation are a direct result of their viewing habits; namely, the depictions that they see in popular television crime series like *CSI*, *NCIS*, *Criminal Minds*, *Crossing Jordan* and *Bones* to name a few. This is despite the efforts of the legal system to limit such influence through careful scrutiny and selection of potential jurors (through what is called the *voir dire*), and the admonishment of jurors not to take account of these influences during their decision-making processes (Tyler 2006).

It is also in spite of the fact that the producers of these *CSI*-type television series and the networks on which they are broadcast make few claims as to the accuracy of their portrayals or their correlation to the real-life workings of crime labs (Durnal 2010). Quite the opposite, in fact: Anthony Zuiker, the creator and executive producer of the *CSI* franchise, has previously said that making amends for television is part of his job. Speaking about the show's influence in the United States, he says:

> Our job really is to make great television, first and foremost. And so, we have to, quote 'sex it up'. I think Americans know that DNA doesn't come back in 20 minutes. I think Americans know that there's not some magical computer that you press and the guy's face pops up and where he lives. You think America knows that the time sheets when you're doing one hour of television have to be fudged a bit. Americans know that (Zuiker cited in Rath 2011).

Still, much has been written about the ways in which *CSI*-type television shows can create myths about forensic science and exaggerate the significance of certain types of evidence in the criminal investigation process (see Box 10.2).

BOX 10.2

COMMON *CSI* MYTHS

According to American researcher Evan W. Durnal (2010: 4–5), there are several primary areas in which the depictions in television shows like *CSI: Crime Scene Investigation* can create myths about forensic science and the criminal investigation process. These include:

- *The roles and responsibilities of the members of an investigative team*: In reality, there are no independent 'forensic investigators'; what is portrayed on television in *CSI*-type shows is, in fact, the work of several personnel and a combination of specialisations. The crime scene investigators depicted on television therefore represent an amalgamation of police, detective and forensic scientist. The latter of these do not collect evidence from the crime scene; they process it. Except in rare cases, Durnal says, most forensic scientists will never visit a crime scene at all. While shows like *CSI* portray characters, which are well versed in any and all forensic techniques, real-world forensic scientists are specialists in one specific genre of forensics, such as DNA or firearms, illegal and controlled substances, etc.

- *The amount of evidence normally found at a crime scene*: *CSI*-type television shows give the impression that there is an ample amount of evidence left at every crime scene—it is simply up to the forensic scientist to find it. But as criminals become more and more educated about the criminal investigation process (a CSI effect in itself—see Table 10.1), they leave less and less evidence, making the job of the evidence technician increasingly challenging.

- *The capabilities of a given test or analytical method*: Television crime dramas like *CSI* often suggest that there is an omniscient database that can search any kind of product ranging from tyres, cars and tools to make-up, coffee and soil samples. While there are databases that forensic scientists can access, such as DNA indexes and fingerprint identification systems, these are not without their shortcomings— they are only as good as the information that is recorded and stored in them by people like law enforcement officers. *CSI*'s depictions of the criminal investigation process also suggest that, when trace evidence is detected at the scene of a crime, it can be inserted immediately into some complex piece of technology for forensic analysis. In truth, a great deal of sample pre-treatment and clean-up is required before forensic analysis can be conducted. This is despite the fact that advances in science and technology have enhanced the capacity to identify unknown perpetrators.

- *The timeframe in which various techniques and tests can occur*: Even though most people readily recognise that real-world crimes are not solved within 45 minutes (the standard run time of a *CSI* episode), the perception persists that a DNA screen takes a matter of minutes and a search of a database can be done in a few seconds. As Durnal points out, good science takes a lot more time than this, and can be extremely tedious but necessary to ensure the correct conclusion is reached.

This has—at least anecdotally—created supposed burdens for real-world policing, the legal fraternity and the criminal justice system. For this reason, the CSI effect has been described as a 'conglomerate of several conceivable effects' (Kruse 2010: 87). A typology of these is summarised in Table 10.1. On the positive end of the 'effects' spectrum are claims that *CSI*-type television programs have created an appetite for increased knowledge of science among the viewing public (this is known as the *producer's effect*). There have also been unintended consequences from *CSI*'s arrival onto the small screen, such as the upsurge of interest in forensic science university courses and those of cognate disciplines, like criminology. This is referred to as the *educator's effect*. Less favourable claims, such as the *police chief's effect*, suggest that *CSI* and its iterations have educated criminals on how to avoid detection, with **criminalists** reporting greater use of bleach at crime scenes to clean up blood; the use of plastic gloves; criminals not licking envelopes (to reduce traces of DNA evidence); and the removal of cigarette butts from crime scenes (Cole & Dioso-Villa 2007).

TABLE 10.1   A typology of CSI effects

CSI effect	Effect on	Outcome
Strong prosecutor's effect	Jurors	Acquit in cases where they would have convicted had *CSI* not existed
Weak prosecutor's effect	Prosecutors	Compensate for absence or weakness of forensic evidence by altering their behaviours at trial or adopting remedial measures
Defendant's effect	Jurors	Attribute greater credibility to forensic scientists who testify as expert witnesses
Producer's effect	Jurors	Greater awareness and knowledge about forensic science
Educator's effect	Students	Attraction to careers in forensic science
Police chief's effect	Criminals	Adopt countermeasures to avoid detection through forensic analysis
Victim's effect	Crime victims	Expect forensic testing for all crimes
Tech effect	Jurors	Increased expectations towards forensic evidence and testing as a result of awareness of actual scientific and technological advances

Sources: Adapted from Cole & Dioso-Villa 2011, p. 22; and Dioso-Villa 2014, p. 27.

One of the most contentious 'effects', however, relates to the ways in which jurors now seem to hold 'unrealistic expectations of forensic evidence and investigation techniques' (Robbers 2008: 86). This 'effect'—known as the *strong prosecutor's effect*—is based on the premise that, when jurors watch television programs like *CSI*, they take what they see with them into the courtroom; convicting or acquitting defendants on the basis of their understandings and expectations of forensic science as it is portrayed on television. Research shows that jurors rely on evidence to justify their convictions, which means that this may be made more difficult in cases that do not involve scientific evidence (Tyler 2006). Of course, this privileges forensic evidence (and its probative value) over other forms of trial evidence in terms of possible ways to legitimate juror decision-making. This supports the way in which legal actors describe the CSI effect as they perceive it in operation within the courtroom. According to half of the American trial counsel and judges who participated in a survey by Robbers (2008), the CSI effect is most vividly demonstrated by the way in which juries will often discount the testimonies of victims and other eyewitnesses in favour of forensic evidence. The exception is expert forensic witnesses, to whom jurors may attribute greater credibility over other witnesses as a consequence of *CSI*'s heroic portrayals of Grissom and his team—thus advantaging the prosecution in what has become known as the *defendant's effect* (Cole & Dioso-Villa 2007; 2011).

The concern is that the combination of these factors has the potential to raise the burden of proof for criminal cases, 'because of jury expectations that forensic evidence should always be discussed at trial, and the belief forensic evidence is never wrong' (Robbers 2008: 86). Among other things (see Box 10.3), this can result in irrelevant forensic evidence being presented at trial as well as requests for forensic analysis beyond what is reasonable or required—if only to ensure 'completeness' (Julian & Kelty 2012). Without this, juries may view the absence of forensic testing as 'sloppy police work', regardless of whether scientific analysis is essential to the case (Robbers 2008: 93). As retired judge Donald Shelton (2008) recounts: 'I once heard a juror complain that the prosecution had not done a thorough job because "they didn't even dust the lawn for fingerprints"'. Claims such as these reinforce the notion that forensic evidence is incorruptible, incontrovertible and essential to the proper administration of justice. They also suggest that jurors are now holding the prosecution in criminal cases to a standard of proof that is *higher* than the traditional standard of 'beyond a reasonable doubt'. Many judges therefore believe that *CSI* has made it more difficult to convict defendants (Cole & Dioso-Villa 2011). If this is true, this presents certain concerns and implications for the criminal justice system.

BOX 10.3

CONSEQUENCES OF THE CSI EFFECT IN THE COURTROOM

- Juries discount eyewitness testimony in favour of scientific evidence.
- Even if it is not essential to the case, jurors can see a lack of forensic testing as 'sloppy police work'.
- Irrelevant forensic evidence may be introduced at trial to satisfy juror expectations.
- Negative evidence witnesses are increasingly called to testify as to why forensic evidence was not needed, or why forensic testing was not conducted.
- Judges spend greater amounts of time clarifying forensic evidence for jurors.
- Additional time is spent during the *voir dire* (i.e. the preliminary examination of prospective jurors to determine their qualifications and suitability to serve on a jury) to ascertain the extent of the CSI effect.
- Legal actors, like judges, prosecutors and defence lawyers, spend greater amounts of time trying to familiarise themselves with forensic tests and procedures, so that they are properly prepared for trial.
- Jurors expect more forensic evidence than they have historically, often incorrectly assuming that police have limitless resources and crime labs have small caseloads.

Source: Adapted from Robbers 2008.

THE PLAUSIBILITY OF THE CSI EFFECT

The idea that heavy television viewing can impact on individuals—more so than those who watch little television—causing them to perceive the world in ways that reflect the depictions shown on television is not a novel concept. **Cultivation theory** is based on precisely this hypothesis (see Box 10.4). So too, similar claims about the impact of media depictions of the law on jurors' judgments in real-life cases were levelled at television legal series like *The People's Court* in the 1980s (Tyler 2006).

The claim that jurors have been unduly influenced in their decision-making by their television viewing habits assumes that media audiences are unable to tell the difference between the real and the dramatic—which, as we know, is an outdated mode of thought in view of some of the early advances in media research, mentioned in Chapter 2, related to *active audience theory* (see Hall 1980) and the *uses and gratifications approach* (see Katz, Blumler & Gurevitch 1974). As Turnbull (cited in Stephens 2015) rightfully claims: 'Watching or reading crime always invites you to keep going in a process of speculation; you are trying to work it out. The activity of reading or watching has always been active, a process of interpretation'. If we are to believe that the CSI effect is a valid and individualised phenomenon then, as Harriss (2011: 11) argues, 'we must also believe that viewers are not watching the program with a critical eye. This is a problem we can solve'.

In spite of the many studies which have sought to validate the CSI effect, the results remain equivocal as to its existence, let alone its potential to compromise jury verdicts. As Baskin and Sommers (2010: 98) observe: 'The answer to the question of whether juror decisions regarding verdicts in criminal cases arise out of or in spite of the CSI Effect, or whether they bear any relationship to crime show viewing, remains elusive'. For this reason, the CSI effect remains a contested concept; some researchers argue it is simply a myth or a mediated phenomenon, while others continue to claim that the CSI effect is evident in the predisposition of jurors towards conviction or acquittal in criminal trials (see Baskin & Sommers 2010).

BOX 10.4

CULTIVATION THEORY

Cultivation theory, also known as the 'cultivation hypothesis' or 'cultivation analysis', is a theory of media effects developed by Professor George Gerbner in the mid-1960s. It is one of the most-cited theories within communications research; as of 2010, over 500 studies had been published directly relating to cultivation theory (Morgan & Shanahan 2010). The theory was originally conceived as part of the Cultural Indicators project, which sought to identify trends in television content as well as television's contribution to viewer conceptions of social reality. Results from this long-running media research showed that 'generally the more people watch television the more likely they are to understand certain aspects of reality in terms presented on television' (Gerbner et al. 1996: 3). So, if a viewer saw a lot of 'x' on television, they would have a tendency to believe that 'x' is common in the real world. While television was recognised as only one of many factors that influence individuals, it was considered 'the single most common and pervasive source of certain conceptions and actions' (Gerbner et al. 1996: 3).

One of the main concerns for Gerbner and his colleagues was the exposure of television viewers to representations of violence, with estimates that the average American child will have watched 8000 murders on television by the end of elementary school (i.e. about 12 years of age). Early research demonstrated that heavier television viewers were more likely to see the world as a mean and dangerous place, and to experience an increased fear of crime and victimisation, as well as perceptions of mistrust (Gerbner & Gross 1976; Morgan & Shanahan 2010). They viewed the world as more dangerous than it actually is—leading Gerbner and colleagues to term the phenomenon '**mean world syndrome**'. Later studies, such as those by Nabi and Sullivan (2001), found that the amount of television viewing not only influenced prevalence estimates of violence in society, but also the intentions of viewers to adopt measures to protect themselves against crime. So, a television viewer who perceives society as violent may be less inclined to walk home alone at night, and more inclined to invest in a home alarm system or to support initiatives to increase police presence on the streets.

Of course, cultivation theory is not without its critics, particularly within the contemporary media environment. The work of Gerbner and his colleagues has come under fire for what critics perceive as its insufficient emphasis on *context*, and the ways in which it divides the world into 'heavy' and 'light' television viewers without recognising that the contemporary media environment 'differs significantly from that which inspired cultivation theory' (Podlas 2006: 448). In distinguishing between 'heavy' and 'light' television viewing, cultivation theory also fails to measure the perceived realism of representations among television audiences: does everyone who watches portrayals of violence on television necessarily see these as a reflection of reality? How might we distinguish between perceptions of and responses to these representations on broadcast news vis-à-vis television crime dramas?

Similar criticisms have been directed towards some CSI effect studies and their failure to acknowledge the difference between television viewing habits and the extent to which individuals who regularly watch *CSI*-type television shows perceive their depictions of forensic science and criminal investigation as *realistic*. Few CSI effect studies have critically reflected on the role of media literacy in measuring potential media effects and the fact that, '[r]egardless of any *intended* communicative function of a given story, we must consider how it is understood. *CSI* is no different' (Podlas 2006: 452). This is where framing analysis can be useful to us as media criminologists. In terms of cultivation theory, questions have also been raised about its persistence and relevance in view of the popularity of social media and online networking sites like

Twitter, Facebook and YouTube. So too, the conceptualisation of 'fear' within cultivation analyses has attracted scrutiny, with some studies seeking to measure people's perceptions of the prevalence of societal violence and others exploring perceptions of personal risk or individuals' fear of crime and victimisation (Morgan & Shanahan 2010).

Part of the problem in proving or disproving the CSI effect lies in the methodological challenges inherent to studies that seek to validate its existence, including their different sampling techniques. As Cole and Dioso-Villa (2007: 455) point out, there are 'a number of ways in which the various CSI Effects could be empirically measured'—including interviews with the legal community, surveys, and analysis of acquittal rates after the airing of *CSI*—but measuring these effects in relation to the *strong prosecutor's effect* and the *defendant's effect* is challenging. What ultimately needs to be determined is whether juries acquitted defendants in cases in which they would have otherwise convicted them had *CSI* not existed. This is difficult to assess, because studying juries is 'notoriously difficult' because 'their deliberations are considered confidential, and only rarely have courts permitted researchers access to actual jury deliberations' (Cole & Dioso-Villa 2007: 456). Researchers have also noted that 'even if media *influences* jurors, that by no means necessarily translates into changed *verdicts*', with little evidence that there have been increases in reported jury acquittals (Cole & Dioso-Villa 2011: 21). For Cole (cited in Herzog 2016): 'Everything we know about juries seems to suggest that, while being on a jury is often unpleasant, they [jurors] take it very seriously and are making serious decisions about whether to find someone guilty or not guilty in a criminal case'. Although, as we have already explored in Chapter 4, for some jurors the enormity of this responsibility can be altogether too much, resulting in incredulous acts, such as jurors seeking guidance on a verdict from their Facebook friends and followers.

Other researchers have suggested that the impact on juror deliberations as a consequence of watching *CSI* may be unconscious—jurors themselves may not even recognise it. Alternatively, a person may regularly watch *CSI*, but not be significantly influenced by this in their decision-making as a juror. Some research even shows that jurors who are frequent viewers of television crime dramas like *CSI* may be more sceptical of forensic evidence when it is presented at trial than those who are non-*CSI* watchers—a potential measure of the perceived realism of *CSI*-type television shows (see Schweitzer & Saks 2007; Goodman-Delahunty, Rossner & Tait 2010). Other studies contest this. A survey of 3611 Australian jury-eligible individuals, for instance, showed that frequent *CSI* viewers placed more trust in forensic science and DNA evidence and were more motivated to serve as jurors than infrequent *CSI* television viewers (Goodman-Delahunty & Hewson 2010).

MEASURING EFFECTS: A MATTER OF METHOD OR PERCEPTION?

One way in which researchers have sought to untangle and test some of these contradictions is through the performance of jury simulations. One of the first researchers to adopt this method was Kimberlianne Podlas (2006), who surveyed undergraduate and graduate students at a large university in the northeast of the United States about their viewing habits, including whether they watched legal dramas, reality courtroom television shows and *CSI*. This line of questioning was based on the premise that 'because most viewers have no actual knowledge of this field to displace what they see on TV, the messages of *CSI* may exert an enhanced impact' on their assessment of evidence at trial (Podlas 2006: 451). In short, Podlas's study sought to test the validity of the CSI effect.

After surveying the students about their television viewing habits, Podlas asked the respondents to act as jurors in a mock trial, based on a hypothetical rape case, where no forensic evidence was provided; the scenario presented only issues of witness credibility and the question of whether or not the intercourse had been consensual. According to the victim in the scenario, she had been forced to have sex without consent, while the defendant claimed the sex had been wholly consensual. Participants in the study were asked to reach a verdict in the case; 41 respondents (14 per cent) arrived at a 'guilty' verdict, while the remaining 250 students (86 per cent) reached a 'not guilty' verdict. Because the scenario relied on witness testimony, rather than forensic evidence, Podlas (2006) contended that the only 'legally correct' verdict respondents should have rendered was 'not guilty', since it was not possible to see or hear the respective witnesses to assess their credibility. She explains: 'Therefore, it was not possible—if relying solely on the words of the scenario—for guilt to be proven beyond a reasonable doubt' (Podlas 2006: 458). This suggested that those who reached a 'guilty' verdict might have been influenced by contextual variables, such as the lived experience of sexual assault. Presumably, students in the study, who had self-identified as frequent viewers of *CSI*—if they were operating under a CSI effect—would have relied on *CSI* factors in reaching their verdicts when compared to infrequent viewers, who would not. What Podlas found among the students who had reached a 'not guilty' verdict was that frequent viewers of *CSI* constituted 75 per cent of the group; the remaining 25 per cent were non-frequent viewers. Of the frequent viewers of *CSI*, 79 per cent (n = 148) also frequently watched television programs such as *Law and Order* and the reality courtroom drama *Judge Judy*. The data therefore showed that, in rendering a 'not guilty' verdict, frequent viewers of *CSI* were no more influenced by *CSI* factors than non-frequent viewers. For Podlas, this exposed the CSI effect as a myth.

Attempting to move a step closer to understanding the motivations of real-life jurors, in 2006 then-American trial judge Donald Shelton teamed up with criminology professors Young S. Kim and Greg Barak to survey 1027 summoned jurors in Washtenaw County, Michigan, prior to their participation in trial processes. This was followed by another study involving 1257 jurors from a different jurisdiction in Michigan—Wayne County—a couple of years later. In each case, the prospective jurors were questioned about their television viewing habits as well as their expectations of and demands for scientific evidence. The goal was to ascertain whether jurors believed this evidence was a necessary 'condition for conviction' (Shelton 2008: 2). Participants in the study were also asked about their likely verdicts in particular types of cases, based on the availability of forensic evidence. While expectations for this evidence varied according to the type of crime involved, overall it remained high, with a significant number of the prospective jurors (42.1 per cent) in the Wayne County study reporting that they expected to see DNA evidence in every case. These figures were almost double the numbers from the Washtenaw County study previously conducted (Shelton, Barak & Kim 2011).

Unsurprisingly, the expectations for scientific evidence among the prospective Wayne County jurors were highest in the case of serious crimes, like murder, attempted murder and rape. But, even for lesser crimes like break-and-enter cases, participants in the study reported a strong demand for scientific evidence. Across the two studies, Shelton, Barak and Kim (2011: 16) drew similar conclusions to those of Podlas—namely, that 'the CSI effect is a myth'. Despite the high expectations and demands towards scientific evidence, they found no significant correlation between these and the television viewing habits of the participating jurors. Shelton, Barak and Kim (2011: 9) conceded that their findings did not necessarily mean that 'watching a plethora of forensic science television shows does not play a role in the juror behaviour we have documented'. But, they reasoned, the heightened expectations and demands of jurors were more likely attributable to contextual variables other than regular viewing of *CSI*-type shows.

ISSUES FOR CONSIDERATION

As media criminologists, it would be remiss of us if we did not acknowledge that *CSI* reflects but one genre of the broader category of 'crime as entertainment', and not all television crime dramas within this category follow the same structure or perform the same functions for their audiences (Turnbull 2014). So too, we must recognise the cultural specificity of debates about the CSI effect. For those in countries where the *CSI* franchise is not as pervasive or popular as it is, say, in Australia or the United States, the potential effects of frequent *CSI* viewing on people's expectations of scientific evidence and their behaviours in the courtroom are irrelevant. Where these same expectations and behavioural changes exist, they clearly do so for reasons other than a person's television viewing habits; presenting a potential control group for pre-existing CSI effect studies. In those jurisdictions where the CSI effect continues to be a hot button issue, researchers appear to at least agree that there is a heightened set of expectations among contemporary jurors as to what forensic science can do and what it can contribute to the assessment of guilt or innocence. But many have ruled out a CSI effect as the cause of these heightened expectations. If this is the case, the question remains as to what the potential catalyst(s) are for such effects, if *CSI* and other television shows of its calibre are not responsible.

One explanation, according to Shelton, Barak and Kim (2011: 8), is that the increased demands and expectations of jurors are symptomatic of a generalised *tech effect* (see Table 10.1), or rather the broader changes in popular culture 'regarding the use of modern science and technology, buttressed by media portrayals of those scientific advances', which extend far beyond the *CSI* genre. Put simply, because jurors are now accustomed to modern technologies and are more sophisticated in their use of them, they have come to expect that police and forensic scientists will demonstrate the same proclivities. This supports the idea that jurors tend to overestimate the probative value of forensic evidence, *regardless* or *in spite of* the popularity of *CSI*-type television programs—that is, they are 'already motivated to find ways to legitimate or justify their desire to convict' (Tyler 2006: 1071). This means that, where the need arises, jurors may invest similar levels of belief in the plausibility, strength and quality of other forms of trial evidence, like eyewitness testimony, as a way to validate and make them more comfortable with their legal decisions. Writes Tyler (2006: 1070): 'It follows that when people are more highly motivated to resolve a crime and provide justice for the victim, they will also be more highly motivated to overestimate the probative value of the evidence', regardless of whether it is of a forensic or testimonial nature.

However, not everyone agrees that the CSI effect is a phenomenon still worth chasing. For Harvey and Derksen (2009: 8), the CSI effect is potentially a 'generational effect', which bore its strongest relevance for jurors from Generations X and Y, who grew up in front of the television and in the computer age, respectively. This may explain some of the responses that our students received when they conducted their own 'straw poll' among their peers about the extent to which they thought *CSI* had influenced people's perceptions of forensic science. Many respondents—mostly from Generation Z (also known as the iGeneration); the generation that has grown up with the internet and social media—said they had never watched *CSI*, despite its frequent screening on free-to-air television, because it is too old-fashioned compared to other crime media, which has more successfully grabbed their attention. It is perhaps unsurprising that, among these productions, those we mentioned at the top of the chapter—the podcast *Serial* and Netflix's web television series, *Making a Murderer*— featured prominently. By the time this book is published, even these web-based sensations may seem passé, such is the lightning pace at which technology and digital storytelling are evolving. But, as we write this, online articles have started to emerge likening the potential effects and 'disruptive force' of these true crime docu-series on juror decision-making and courtroom behaviours to those associated with the CSI effect (Banks-Anderson 2016; see also Barden 2016; Herzog 2016). There is also reason to question whether the popularity of web-based series like *Making a Murderer* have engendered a new form of media effects, reigniting public and police interest in 'cold cases', and leading to the reopening of investigations into unsolved crimes and news media's interest in either calling for or reporting on such developments.

CONCLUSION

Whether or not the CSI effect is real remains a matter of conjecture, highlighting the difficulties associated with trying to *prove* media effects. This does not mean that media effects are not possible. But, in the case of the CSI effect, the absence of empirical evidence supporting its existence has led some scholars to question whether it is, in fact, nothing more than a media phenomenon spurred on by anecdotal reports of jury behaviours (Cole & Dioso-Villa 2007). Some lawyers, for instance, have said they suspect the CSI effect they have experienced in the courtroom has more to do with the public's response to press reports *about* the CSI effect than anything specifically to do with the television program itself (Harvey & Derksen 2009).

Yet, modifications to court procedures, such as the capacity for judge-only criminal trials, have been introduced as a counter to concerns about pre-trial publicity, the weight that juries may attribute to forensic analysis, and the ability of jurors to fully understand the legal significance of technical or scientific evidence (Nedim 2015). Lesser examined has been the prospect that legal actors, like lawyers and judges, have started to change their professional practices and courtroom behaviours on the basis of an unsubstantiated belief—that is, their own *perceptions* that a CSI effect exists. As Podlas (cited in Herzog 2016) explains:

> I think there's an effect of believing in the effect. If judges, prosecutors, and law enforcement think there is some kind of effect going on—whether they're correct or not—then that will necessarily influence their behaviors in the courtroom, in choosing cases, in deciding when they're going to have splashy conferences, what kind of experts they might choose.

If this is the case, any behavioural changes or modifications to court procedures as a consequence of the *perception* that a CSI effect exists (if only anecdotally or as a mediated phenomenon) could constitute a form of media effects. In which case, we might sensibly assume that such changes would result in **role strain** (see Hardy & Hardy 1988) for these individuals, because of increased workloads and the stress related to having one's professional expertise called into question. But even this is not necessarily the case. Many of the Canadian police detectives and forensic personnel interviewed by Huey (2010), for example, agreed that they thought *CSI* had impacted on their interactions with the public. However, the majority saw this as 'a routine element of the job' associated with the service component of their roles; only nine out of the 31 participants in the study expressed a sense of frustration, anxiety, irritability or distress as a consequence of a perceived CSI effect on their professional practices (Huey 2010: 65).

Where does this leave us in terms of a critical discussion about the CSI effect? Some may say no further advanced than when we started. If we consulted Grissom, he would tell us to follow the evidence. In which case, we would have to conclude that, despite the hype, the CSI effect is at best an oversimplified explanation for a more complex array of factors, which have led to real phenomena, such as the heightened expectations of jurors towards forensic science and the behavioural modifications of legal actors, like judges and lawyers, towards the presentation of evidence at trial. At worst, the CSI effect is simply a myth or a mediated phenomenon; something that has been *perceived* as real, because of the attention afforded to it by mainstream media. We'll leave the verdict to you.

DISCUSSION QUESTIONS

1. Is the CSI effect real, a myth or a mediated phenomenon?
2. Do television crime dramas like *CSI* do more to educate publics about forensic science or do they do more to undermine the complexities of criminal investigation?
3. How have media representations of the 'crime fighting hero' changed across time?
4. In what ways could 'cultivation theory' and the idea of 'mean world syndrome' be applied in the contemporary media environment?
5. The CSI effect is based on the assumption that media audiences see the show's representations of forensic science and criminal investigation as reflections of reality. To what extent do you think this is really the case?

WORKSHOP ACTIVITY: MEASURING ATTITUDES TOWARDS *CSI* AND COURTROOM EVIDENCE

The literature on the CSI effect makes some interesting observations about the difficulties of trying to validate the phenomenon and measure its potential impacts. It also offers some questionable assumptions (from a media criminology perspective) about how real the viewers of *CSI*-type television shows perceive their representations of forensic science and criminal investigation to be. Test out these observations by conducting your own 'straw poll' of your peers. Break into pairs, or small groups of three to four, and 'vox pop' other students on campus. Introduce yourselves and the purpose of the activity, and ask whether they would like to answer your questions. Be respectful if people choose not to participate. If they do, ask them:

- Do you watch *CSI*-type television crime dramas? If yes, how often? If no, why not?
- If you were a juror, would you have more confidence in eyewitness testimony or forensic evidence (e.g. DNA analysis)? Which would be more persuasive and why?
- Do you think television crime dramas like *CSI* are an accurate reflection of the realities of forensic science and the criminal investigation process?

Make some general observations about the demographic profile of the students you 'vox pop'. Obviously, if you were conducting a CSI effect study for research purposes, you would need to be more rigorous about the rationale behind the selection of your participant group, how you would recruit them, and how you would capture and reflect their profile. These are important points to discuss as a group on your return to the classroom. Collate the findings and discuss any trends that emerge or points of conflict.

What other information did your participants offer as a qualification to their responses? What conclusions might you make from your 'straw poll' about the CSI effect, the popularity of television crime dramas, about the status attributed to scientific objectivity, and about the challenges inherent to measuring media effects?

FURTHER READING

Cole, S. A. & Dioso-Villa, R. (2007). *CSI* and Its Effects: Media, Juries, and the Burden of Proof. *New England Law Review*, 41(3), 435–70.

Kruse, C. (2010). Producing Absolute Truth: *CSI* Science as Wishful Thinking. *American Anthropologist*, 112(1), 79–91.

Podlas, K. (2006). 'The CSI Effect': Exposing the Media Myth. *Fordham Intellectual Property, Media and Entertainment Law Journal*, 16(2), 429–65.

Robbers, M. L. P. (2008). Blinded by Science: The Social Construction of Reality in Forensic Television Shows and Its Effect on Criminal Jury Trials. *Criminal Justice Policy Review*, 19(1), 84–102.

Turnbull, S. (2014). *The TV Crime Drama*. Edinburgh: Edinburgh University Press.

11

SURVEILLANCE, CYBERSPACE AND CIVIL SOCIETY

CHAPTER HIGHLIGHTS

Introduction

The intersections between cyberspace and criminality

The emergence of the surveillance society

Rethinking the relationship between crime and digital technologies

Conclusion

INTRODUCTION

Depending on when you were born, it may be difficult to fully appreciate the profound changes that digital technologies, like the internet and social media, have brought about in contemporary society. For some readers, the digital age will be all they have ever known. Those who are a little older will have a different understanding (and lived experience) of how much these technologies 'have dramatically enhanced the capacities of ordinary citizens' (Grabosky 2016: 1)—albeit not always in productive or palatable ways.

While there is considerable scope for the positive use of cyberspace for the promotion of new learning and new personal and civic engagements, there is—at the same time—significant potential for its use to cause harms (White & Wyn 2017). As Grabosky (2016: 1) explains, our growing dependence on digital technologies means that 'many of the systems we depend on for communications, finance, health, transport, energy, and entertainment are vulnerable to disruption for fun or profit'. At the more bizarre and sensational end of the spectrum are cases like those of Armin Meiwes, a self-confessed German cannibal, who used the internet to advertise for victims willing to be slaughtered and consumed. More commonly, however, when we consider the intersections between crime and digital technologies, we think of those offences that have attracted the lion's share of media attention—that is, **cybercrimes** like online scams, hacking, identity and data theft, online child sexual abuse materials, cyberterrorism and cyberbullying. Either way, the point is that advances in technology, while often devised to deliver enjoyment, engagement and efficiencies, also embody the potential for crime and harms—some old, some new, but all with an increasingly pervasive and intricate nature.

The threat is not only criminals in the conventional sense; it also now includes terrorists, trolls and teenagers. Keeping track of these identities, let alone preventing them from doing harm, is both a significant challenge and complex undertaking. For these reasons, it goes without saying that there is only so much we can adequately address within the scope of a single chapter when it comes to a topic as broad and multifaceted as 'surveillance, cyberspace and civil society'. Given that the study of offences like cybercrimes has already been well covered in the field elsewhere (see, for example, Wall 2007; Grabosky 2016), we have therefore elected to focus more on general themes of relevance—such as the intersections between cyberspace and criminality, and the emergence of the 'surveillance society'—rather than dwell on particular sorts of crime in detail (see, instead, White & Perrone 2015).

THE INTERSECTIONS BETWEEN CYBERSPACE AND CRIMINALITY

Over the last three decades in the developed world, there has been exponential growth (almost a seven-fold increase) in the number of people who are online, with over 80 per cent of individuals now accessing the internet (International Telecommunication Union 2015). The **digital divide** that was once pronounced has continued to shrink as cheap internet-enabled smartphones abound in poor and rich communities alike, and telecommunications infrastructure reaches into the more remote parts of the planet. In Australia alone, there are now more than 12 million internet subscribers and a further 17.3 million mobile handset subscribers, while over 11 million Australians have a Facebook account (Australian Government 2013). By 2017, it is anticipated that 90 per cent of Australians will be online and that, by 2019, the average Australian household will have 24 internet-connected devices (Commonwealth of Australia 2016).

The changes that the internet and other digital technologies have introduced to our lives are manifold. Among them is the fact that cyberspace has overcome the traditional constraints of geographic boundaries. This has opened up opportunities for **digital citizenship** and the more active participation of individuals in society—to the point where our involvement in the virtual world has, in many cases, become a natural and meaningful extension of our terrestrial lives (i.e. our offline or 'real-world' existence). The evidence, as Wall and Williams (2007) point out, is all around us, with people participating in online communities of interest; more frequently working from home; developing emotional relationships online before meeting in person; and commonly sharing information online, including with governments and other social institutions. 'It therefore follows', they write, 'that if online behaviour has become a complex matter, then so has its governance' (Wall & Williams 2007: 410). In this regard, we know less about how to maintain law and order within these virtual communities—especially with their ability to function across jurisdictions—than we do mediated instances of transgression and criminality. Among the foremost and best known of the latter is cybercrime (see Box 11.1).

BOX 11.1

DEFINING CYBERCRIME

Broadly speaking, the term 'cybercrime' is used to describe:

- *Computer-assisted crimes:* Those offences, which while pre-dating the internet and existing independently of it find a 'new lease of life online' (Jewkes 2015: 256).
  - Examples include certain types of fraud; unauthorised sharing of copyrighted content; harassment, stalking, bullying behaviours, such as those associated with internet 'trolls'; and forms of defamation and hate speech.
- *Computer-oriented crimes:* Offences that take as their target 'the electronic infrastructure (both hardware and software) that comprises the "fabric" of the Internet itself' (Jewkes 2015: 257).
  - Examples include various forms of malicious software that corrupt files and hard drives; denial of service attacks; and the defacement, manipulation or deletion of web content without authorisation.
  - This interference, according to White and Perrone (2015: 323), can be conducted through a number of means, including:
    - o *Hackers*: People with sufficient technical ability to gain access to another person's computer or to a network through the use of stolen passwords or interference technology, which provides access to networks and individual computers.
    - o *Worms*: Self-replicating computer programs that can delete files or send email documents.
    - o *Viruses*: Pieces of program code that self-replicate and attach to a 'host' computer's operating system. They can be destructive, altering files or erasing information from disks. A virus can also allow third parties to gain access to a person's computer without authorisation.
    - o *Trojans*: Stand-alone programs that must be transferred intentionally, such as through email. When opened, they might alter or delete files on the machine or access the user's email.

A simple reading of history tells us that the 'relationship between crime and technology is by no means new and that the potential for creating harm never seems far away from any apparently beneficial technological development' (Wall 2007: 2). What has changed, though, is that the timeframe during which harmful behaviours can occur and substantively change has dramatically shortened within the context of the contemporary networked society (Wall 2007). The advent of the 'dark web'—that is, the collection of websites that are publicly visible, but for whom the internet provider (IP) addresses of the servers that run them are hidden—has also further complicated law enforcement efforts, with the emergence of illegal online marketplaces, such as 'Silk Road', and the regular sale of weapons, counterfeit documents and child pornography (Greenberg 2014). This has intensified concerns about how to regulate online spaces at the same time as it has highlighted the potential for elusive web spaces to become sites of social mobilisation; remembering that one of the first dark websites was WikiLeaks (see Box 11.2) and that mainstream media outlets like *The Guardian* and *The New Yorker* host their own dark web drop sites for anonymously leaked tips and documents.

BOX 11.2

WITH SECRETS TO SHARE

WikiLeaks, the not-for-profit organisation fronted by Australian-born founder and former professional computer hacker Julian Assange, accepts anonymous submissions of previously secret material for publication on its website. It is best known for its previously unprecedented collaborations with mainstream media organisations, including *The Guardian*, *The New York Times* and *Der Spiegel* newspapers; partnerships which, in 2010, brought 'global attention to a cache of confidential documents—embarrassing when not disturbing—about American military and diplomatic activity around the world' (Ellison 2011). In an interview with *TIME* magazine in the same year, Assange was asked whether WikiLeaks's publishing of the leaks constituted civil disobedience. 'Not at all,' he responded. 'This organization practices civil obedience, that is, we are an organization that tries to make the world more civil and act against abusive organizations that are pushing it in the opposite direction ... It's very important to remember the law is not what, not simply what, powerful people would want others to believe it is' (Assange cited in Chua-Eoan 2010). WikiLeaks's mission, therefore, is anti-censorship.

One of the key dilemmas that it and other 'digital dissidents' of its ilk present, however, is that what is in the 'national interest' may not always coincide with 'human rights' or 'citizen interests', let alone the ideals of civil liberties and freedom of expression. In this way, the meanings attached to hacktivist cultures and organisations like WikiLeaks and others, such as Anonymous—well known for its publicity stunts and denial-of-service attacks on government, religious and corporate websites—remain highly contested and polarising; they challenge our assumptions about what is simply 'different' as compared to deviant or criminal, who says so and why. Take, for example, the ways in which some people lauded Assange as a 'hero' and 'freedom fighter' after the leak of military documents and diplomatic cables, while at the same time others denounced him as a 'traitor', 'information anarchist' and 'hi-tech terrorist'.

Similar debates have been waged about Anonymous and whether the collective should be referred to as 'hackers' or 'hacktivists' (see 'Hacktivism' 2011). Here, the subtle distinctions between *socially mediated* and *legal* definitions or frames of criminality are identifiable in the connotations that each term embodies. 'Hacktivism' is typically seen as fusing digital technologies with political purpose (Jordan & Taylor 2004; Lindgren & Lundstrom 2011) to bring the world's attention to issues of freedom, open democracy, campaigns for social change, human rights violations, crimes of the powerful and the need to protect the responsible global flow of information (Fitri 2011). By comparison, 'hacking' more readily connotes sabotage, destruction, malicious intent for self-interest, the evasion of authority and disrespect for the rule of law, dangerousness and deviance—hence, the comparison of hackers to middle-class street gangs (Morris & Blackburn 2009). In either instance, however, hacking can be deemed an unlawful act where it involves 'black hat' (i.e. computer criminal) tactics to exploit the weaknesses in a computer system or computer network. This is in contrast to the practices of 'white hats' or ethical computer hackers, who specialise in and are often hired (and therefore authorised) to perform vulnerability testing and other forms of evaluation to ensure the security and integrity of an organisation's information systems.

Like crimes committed in the terrestrial world, the statistics purporting to measure the rates of victimisation from cybercrime must equally be read with some caution, given the likelihood of underestimates. Even in cyberspace offences go unreported, because crime victims regard the offence as 'too trivial, or because they believe the police will not be able to do anything about it' (Grabosky 2016: 61). Some victims may be inclined to 'seek a quick remedy, rather than mobilize the law'—contacting an internet service provider instead, for example—while others may be too embarrassed to report the offence or fearful of reprisal from the offender (Grabosky 2016: 62). As Brenner (2011: 16) also points out: 'Cybercrime is unbounded crime; the victim and perpetrator can be in different cities, in different states or in different countries'. Unlike many 'real-world' crimes, cybercrime does not even necessarily involve one-to-one victimisation; it can be automated (Brenner 2011).

Estimates put the cost of cybercrime in countries such as Australia as high as A\$2 billion annually, although there are some costs that cannot be quantified, such as the harm caused to victims 'by the distribution of child exploitation material or the compromise of personal information, or the emotional hardship of being left financially destitute' (Australian Government 2013: 4). So too, businesses can be hit by both the direct and indirect costs of cybercrime. Data suggest that among the 33 per cent of businesses in Australia that have experienced a cybercrime, the average time required to resolve the cyber intrusion was 23 days (Australian Government 2015). The average cost to an Australian business that experiences cybercrime is A\$276 323 plus the indirect costs of business disruption, productivity and information loss, and potential damage to infrastructure. Perhaps most shockingly, around 60 per cent of Australian businesses that have experienced a cybercrime will go out of business within six months of the attack (Australian Government 2015).

Cybersecurity therefore is often framed as a matter of keeping up with the rapid evolution of online attacks (Wolff 2016) and providing adequate defences against malicious cyber activities, including the improved education of end-users (see Commonwealth of Australia 2016). Although existing laws have been used to prosecute cybercriminals (see Box 11.3), on the whole, technological advances often outstrip policy-making, legislative amendments and attempts to protect interests online. Most countries, for example, are still trying to devise a legal approach to the management of **cyberbullying**—often in response to youth suicides—but many continue to find the endeavour difficult and complex (Katz et al. 2014). This is particularly the case where proposed laws serve to 'criminalise vulnerable young people who act impulsively or unthinkingly, and who do not have the capacity to process the consequences and impact of their behaviours' (Katz et al. 2014: 14).

So too, the nature of the online attacks and business models adopted by cybercriminals continue to rapidly evolve, as demonstrated by offences like **ransomware**. Where once it was profitable to steal stored data and sell it to fraudsters, cybercriminals have increasingly targeted a new cohort of potential buyers: the victims themselves. As Wolff (2016) explains:

> So, historically, the riskiest stages of cybercrimes have been the ones that come after the perpetrator has already successfully stolen data from a protected computer. Finding a way into a computer system to steal data is relatively easy, but finding a way to monetize that data—making sure that credit-card companies don't cancel stolen card numbers before they're sold, identifying buyers willing to pay a good price, and hiding those profits from the police—can be much harder. But the calculus changes if victims can be persuaded to buy back their own data, in some cases because of a ransomware attack, which encrypts their computers until they pay a ransom.

Of course, the catch is that, in almost every case, the payment of a 'ransom' only buys the silence of those who have committed the offence—'the criminals still have the data', says Joffe (cited in Wolff 2016). Like any ransom situation, there is also the possibility that the criminals will 'up the ante' by asking the victim for more money, once the initial ransom payment has been made. Alternatively, they may decide not to provide the decryption key required to unblock the victim's access to their data, even when the ransom has been paid.

BOX 11.3

THE PROSECUTION OF INTERNET TROLLS

The mainstream media have arguably shown a keen interest in reporting on how the perceived anonymity of the internet can make some users behave in ways that they would not if they were engaged in real-life face-to-face interactions. As a consequence, offences such as cyberbullying and '**trolling**' frequently lead news stories about the potential risks and harms of cyberspace—as do, increasingly, stories of revenge porn (see Salter 2017). Although the terms are often used synonymously, 'cyberbullying' and 'trolling' are, in fact, different things: while cyberbullies target someone and repeatedly attack or harass them, internet trolls set out to upset and provoke a response from anyone they possibly can—often for fun. Their interest is in watching people's reactions. One of the most common forms of trolling is the posting of offensive comments in response to another's online post or article.

Despite research having shown that there are significant overlaps in the patterns of victimisation and offending between cyberbullying and traditional face-to-face bullying (Katz et al. 2014), on the whole, news stories continue to depict the internet as an exceptional space of engagement; a 'Wild West' frontier where bad behaviour is allowed to flourish unremittingly and without consequence. What analysis of trolling has demonstrated, at least in the Australian context, is that the assumption of the 'lawless internet' is a myth—laws do in fact exist to regulate and penalise offensive online behaviours. For example, the first conviction of an internet troll in Australia occurred in March 2011, when Bradley Paul Hampson was found guilty of Facebook vandalism in the District Court of Queensland after he defaced the 'RIP tribute' pages for two murdered schoolchildren, whose deaths had received national news coverage. According to the Commonwealth Director of Public Prosecutions, Hampson had posted offensive and sexualised comments about the victims on the tribute pages. He had also morphed publicly available images of the children's faces into sexualised and/or offensive contexts. In total, police found 96 images on Hampson's personal computer depicting children in sexual acts and another 106 sadistic images of children; the majority of which were manipulated images of missing or murdered children, including Madeleine McCann and James Bulger. A judge sentenced Hampson to three years in prison for offences under the Commonwealth Criminal Code, but ordered he be released after 12 months on the condition of good behaviour for three years. Hampson appealed the decision and was freed in June 2011 after a Court of Appeal agreed that the sentence was 'manifestly excessive' and reduced Hampson's prison time from 12 months to six with immediate release for time already served with a two-year probation period (*R v Hampson* [2011] QCA 132).

From here, it is not difficult to see how discussions of cybersecurity, and the limitations of existing responses to cybercriminals, can quickly move to debates about the merits of surveillance more generally. If crime is ubiquitous, then perhaps the answer is to step up online surveillance of all activities and all users. In the same way that 'law and order' politics justifies enhanced street policing, so too 'security' politics rationalises the expanded use of different kinds of surveillance systems and techniques, in both online and offline realms.

THE EMERGENCE OF THE SURVEILLANCE SOCIETY

Digital technologies have massively increased 'the *speed* of crime, the *distance* over which it can be committed and also its *volume*' (Wall 2005/15: 3), as well as the potential points of exposure to such harms. These same technologies have also highlighted the extent to which surveillance practices have evolved as a mechanism for crime prevention and social control. But what do we mean by 'surveillance' in its contemporary contexts? Some would argue that, while technologies and tactics may have evolved with time, the principles of surveillance remain largely the same. It is, as Barnard-Wills (2012: 2) suggests, 'a fundamental social and political activity' and one that is almost as old as civilisation itself—we have, after all, historically invested considerable time and energy in spying on others, even if those 'others' have mostly been our enemies. But as Barnard-Wills (2012: 2) rightfully points out:

> Far from just being an activity associated with policing or intelligence agencies, any social process which functions through the gathering and processing of information can be understood to have a surveillant dimension. Surveillance is therefore linked to processes of the production and use of knowledge. It is also strongly linked to social sorting and discrimination, processes which use information about people to sort them into categories for differential treatment. Whilst this can be useful, it is also prone to being used in exclusionary politics with damaging and unjust impacts upon the lives of people and groups.

We might say therefore that surveillance is ultimately about power and, as a consequence, remains a 'contested social practice' (Barnard-Wills 2012: 2). The divergent perspectives on surveillance, as reflected in news discourses and the field of surveillance studies, attest to this. Analyses of closed-circuit television (CCTV), for example, have traditionally sought to determine whether this form of video surveillance has effectively reduced crime or merely displaced it to surrounding areas, with contradictory findings (Jewkes 2015). Emphasis has also been placed on gauging the degree to which CCTV systems have assuaged public concerns about personal safety. All in all, the research suggests that the effectiveness of CCTV as a crime prevention measure remains 'modest at best' with 'limited evidence of its impact on fear of crime and feelings of safety for users of the space under surveillance' (Anderson & McAtamney 2011: 1). Nonetheless, media-driven narratives count for a lot in the perceptions stakes. For example, in the wake of the widespread broadcast of shopping centre security footage showing two-year-old James Bulger being led away by his teenage killers, the British press shifted from questioning whether surveillance was a good thing to asking why CCTV cameras were not installed everywhere (Surette 2011).

The United Kingdom now leads the world in the use of surveillance cameras in public spaces, with the average Londoner recorded at least 300 times a day and the ratio of cameras to residents at one to 14 with further increases expected (Freund 2015). So too, there has been considerable growth in the use of video surveillance as a crime prevention measure in Australia, with studies finding that police are increasingly reliant on local government CCTV (Carr 2014; Hulme, Morgan & Browne 2015). Even though there remains little evidence to support the proposition that street cameras reduce crime, politicians continue to promote and heavily invest in the technology as part of their crime prevention strategies. In 2014, for example, the Australian Government committed $50 million towards the development of its *Safer Streets* program to assist local councils in funding the installation of CCTV systems and other safety infrastructure in what were considered crime 'hot spots' (Attorney-General's Department 2014). Sold as a means of making communities safer, the scheme's main effect was shown to be no more than the 'unchecked proliferation of highly profitable commercial arrangements between governments and private firms' (Carr 2016).

One point on which there does seem to be general agreement is that, compared to its earlier configurations, contemporary surveillance is more routinised, generalised, automated and potentially undetectable; it is no longer restricted to only those who fall into the category of 'suspected persons' (Marx 2002). As Haggerty and Ericson (2006: 22) explain, surveillance is now ubiquitous and pervasive, but it is also 'diverse, multi-faceted, and employed in such a panoply of projects that it is almost impossible to speak coherently about "surveillance" more generally'. Suffice to say, being watched is broadly accepted as an inevitable part of life today, although people's feelings towards being surveilled may vary. As Gans and Mann (2015) point out: 'Permission plays an important role in our attitudes about being watched. We don't mind being watched if we have given our consent to do so. But many public surveillance cameras are being used without our consent'. So too, our use of the internet and mobile phones are frequently (and often unknowingly) captured as part of bulk data collection programs conducted in the interests of national security and law enforcement (see Box 11.4).

In June 2013, former US intelligence analyst Edward Snowden revealed the extent to which this occurs when he copied and leaked classified information—initially published by *The Guardian* and *The Washington Post* newspapers—pointing to numerous mass surveillance programs conducted in cooperation with global telecommunications companies and governments. A media frenzy erupted over the leaks and the exposure of these surveillance measures, reigniting public debate about digital privacy and civil rights in the context of security, as well as the obligations and constraints on journalists in reporting on state-based monitoring activities. Opinion polls conducted in the United Kingdom shortly after the Snowden revelations showed that the balance between what citizens considered acceptable and unacceptable in terms of state powers and mass surveillance was fairly evenly split—although broad concerns persisted about potential infringements to personal online privacy across a range of contexts (Cable 2015).

BOX 11.4

SURVEILLANCE PRACTICES AND THE STATE

Digital technologies offer the promise of greater access to information for ordinary citizens. But they also open the door to the systematic collection of greater information *on* individuals; something which is undertaken by a range of state, governmental and commercial bodies for a variety of purposes. This type of information collection has been described as 'data mining' or '**dataveillance**' (Clarke 1988), and has attracted considerable media attention in the wake of the public disclosures by WikiLeaks and individuals such as former National Security Agency (NSA) contractor Edward Snowden, who revealed that 'millions of everyday communications and data transfers worldwide are actively, routinely and systematically monitored by the United States government' (White & Wyn 2013: 335). Of course, such practices are not limited to American state power alone; they also occur in other jurisdictions, including Australia.

Some forms of covert surveillance are seen to be legitimate, while others are not, and state-based activities can stretch the limits of legality in their own right. For example, public police services (including international and regional networks such as Interpol and Europol) regularly conduct monitoring and enforcement activities in relation to crimes such as online grooming and the threat of paedophiles, child pornography, fraudsters and terrorist groups. 'In some instances', write White and Wyn (2013: 335), 'police services will engage in their own version of identity "fraud" as part of law enforcement efforts'. Covert police surveillance can include the 'basics of scrutiny'—simply following, watching and listening to people without their awareness—through to telephone tapping, email monitoring, the use of civilian informants, and the infiltration of particular communities (Loftus & Goold 2011: 277). In the United Kingdom, this has controversially included the disruption of political collectives and the infiltration of activist groups by undercover police officers (see, for example, Lewis, Taylor & Syal 2011; Evans 2014; Misstear 2015). Federal law enforcement agents in the United States have augmented such surveillance practices by using social networking sites—including Facebook, LinkedIn, MySpace and Twitter—to search for evidence and witnesses in criminal cases, and to also track suspects (Nasaw 2010). This has involved FBI agents creating fake personalities to befriend suspects and lure them into revealing clues or confessing, and to access private information and map social networks. Similar tactics have also been applied in the context of internet chat rooms to identify and apprehend child sex offenders, while media reports claim that spy agencies in both the United States and United Kingdom have deployed real-life agents as avatars into video games (e.g. *World of Warcraft*) for the explicit purposes of identifying, approaching and monitoring potential terrorists, and recruiting informants (Ball 2013).

Similar tensions have also been noted in relation to the adoption of police body-worn cameras, which enable police to record their encounters with citizens on private property, including inside a person's home, without explicit consent. Concerns have been raised about the potential this introduces for the identification of victims and offenders without an indication of how long the video will be stored for or whether it may be released to the public or media. The use of video surveillance by law enforcement is not a new phenomenon (Freund 2015). But, unlike their precursors (e.g. CCTV systems in public spaces), body-worn cameras have the capacity to be even more invasive and their presence is less predictable. What this suggests is a double standard of sorts: surveillance, on the one hand, is considered appropriate where it relates to crime control, counterterrorism and national security (indeed, the terrorist attacks of September 11, 2001 remain a watershed in terms of contemporary surveillance practices). On the other hand, it is more frequently framed as inappropriate in the context of discourses about civil liberties and potential intrusions to personal privacy (Barnard-Wills 2011).

WAYS OF THINKING AND TALKING ABOUT SURVEILLANCE

Several theories and models have, over time, emerged as prominent ways of conceptualising 'surveillance', with one often building on another in parallel with evolutions in surveillance technologies and tactics. For example, in George Orwell's novel *Nineteen Eighty-Four*, the representative of a dictatorial government, 'Big Brother', is represented as towering over the citizens of Oceania, a society in which everyone is under the constant surveillance of the authorities—hence, the maxim 'Big Brother is Watching You'. The term 'Big Brother' has since entered the popular lexicon as a synonym for the abuse of government power with respect to civil liberties and the privacy of citizens, often in relation to mass surveillance. It has also been used to describe (some similarly titled) television programs in which participants are never out of the sight of strategically placed cameras.

It is almost impossible, however, to discuss the historical and cultural dimensions of surveillance without drawing reference to its most dominant metaphor—the **panopticon**— which was developed by eighteenth-century reformer Jeremy Bentham, and has subsequently been used in the architecture of asylums and prisons. A circular structure, the panopticon featured individual cells organised around a central watchtower from which prisoners could be observed; a case of *the few watching the many*. Lighting, which illuminated the cells but kept the watchtower in darkness, meant that although prisoners knew they were being watched, they never knew when. Those in the watchtower were effectively invisible. As a consequence, the inmates were inclined to behave as though they were *always* being surveilled, which ensured their complicity and passivity without the need for visible deterrents or overt force (Jewkes 2015). As Michel Foucault (1975/1991: 200) describes it in his classic work, *Discipline and Punish: The Birth of the Prison*, the invisibility of those in the watchtower resulted in 'a guarantee of order' among the inmates—precisely because of the latter's *pronounced visibility*. For Foucault, the panopticon was therefore the consummate disciplinary power in view of his belief that the most effective forms of social control were those that were self-imposed—that is, where individuals 'police' themselves and regulate their own behaviours for fear of punishment.

In this respect, the panopticon offers a precursor to contemporary CCTV systems with their 'purposely visible machines with human eyes hidden from view' (McMullan 2015).

Such claims are heightened in the context of 'dummy cameras', which—while fake—for all intents and purposes look as though they are real; thereby simulating the experience of being watched and serving to act as a potential deterrence mechanism. Like the panoptic thesis, the theory has it that, because people do not know the cameras are fake, they will self-regulate their behaviours on the basis that they *perceive* and *presume* they are real and their actions are being surveilled. While the principle may hold weight in some controlled environments, one can question its veracity in other contexts, such as urban streetscapes, where the ubiquity of surveillance systems means that, while people are constantly under surveillance, they rarely consciously think about this being the case.

This realisation has played out in class activities with our own students, who are continually amazed (and sometimes affronted) by the extent of their *visibility*—and, inversely, the increasing *invisibility* of modern monitoring—when we ask them to stop and think about their everyday encounters with surveillance technologies and practices. Most are able to easily identify the use of CCTV systems in the places where they work, shop and study, as well as on the streets where they live. Fewer students readily consider, however, the ways in which their images, identities and personal data are captured through numerous other encounters—for example, while they withdraw cash from an ATM or ride in a taxi; on speed cameras; via their own or others' dashcams and webcams; as they proceed through security screening at an airport; as a result of the covert surveillance of their activities online and through their use of other digital technologies, like smartphones; or as part of consumer profiling and the 'mining' of their online and offline purchase data for marketing purposes. Bauman and Lyon (2013) refer to this ceaseless monitoring of citizens through the use of digital technologies as '**liquid surveillance**', pointing out that people too voluntarily contribute to their own monitoring—for example, through the uploading of personal information to social media or the use of wearable devices like fitness trackers. If we start to add these things together, we very quickly come to the conclusion that perhaps 'Big Brother' *is* everywhere.

However, as Haggerty and Ericson (2006) explain, there is in fact no single Orwellian 'Big Brother' that oversees these monitory efforts. The power of contemporary surveillance, for the most part, lies in 'the ability of actors to integrate, combine, and coordinate various systems and components' and the 'proliferation of social visibility means that more people from more walks of life are now monitored' (Haggerty & Ericson 2006: 4–5). This has been compounded by the shift away from the confined and controlled environments and apparatuses of **governmentality** that dominated the panoptic thesis (e.g. prisons) to the convergence of what were once discrete and disconnected surveillance systems—in short, the coming together of technologies (e.g. CCTV systems, computer databases) and institutions (e.g. police, private security companies) with diverse capabilities and purposes into a larger surveillance whole. Haggerty and Ericson (2000) refer to this as the '**surveillant assemblage**'—a concept that captures many of the dynamics of contemporary surveillance technologies overlooked by the panopticon, but which nonetheless embraces similar ideas about hierarchies of observation.

SURVEILLANCE, CORPOREALITY AND SUBJECTIVITY

Compared to the panoptic thesis, the relationship between surveillance and the human body has been reconceptualised in view of the surveillant assemblage with less of a focus on the physical body and more on the trails of digital data, which are then aggregated to form an image of a person. According to Haggerty and Ericson (2006: 14), the surveillant assemblage reduces the body to a series of discrete informational flows, which are stabilised, captured and reassembled according to pre-established classificatory criteria to become our 'data double', which can then be 'scrutinized and targeted for intervention ... such that groups which were previously exempt from routine surveillance are now increasingly being monitored'. Although surveillance is now directed at all social groups, 'not everyone is monitored in the same way or for the same purposes' (Haggerty & Ericson 2006: 14). A study by Norris and Armstrong (1997), for example, found that CCTV operators often selectively target those social groups they believe are most likely to be deviant, singling out young black males for surveillance as much for their posture and dress as for their behaviour (see also Fiske 1998; Williams & Johnstone 2000). For Haggerty and Ericson (2006: 15) these examples of '**social sorting**' reflect a form of 'categorical suspicion that connects the operational requirements of surveillance systems with historical legacies of racism'. For Browne (2015: 16), such processes are an example of 'racialising surveillance' or a 'technology of social control' where surveillance practices, policies and performances serve to produce norms pertaining to race and exercise the power to define what is in or out of place.

If we reflect on the surveillant assemblage in the context of crime prevention, we cannot ignore the ways in which non-criminal justice organisations have now also been recruited to augment the surveillance capabilities of law enforcement agencies—for example, by requiring financial institutions to monitor and report suspicious transactions as part of the fight against money laundering and the funding of terrorism. The surveillant assemblage therefore marks what Haggerty and Ericson (2000: 619) describe as the progressive 'disappearance of the disappearance'—a process whereby 'it is increasingly difficult for individuals to maintain their anonymity', or to escape the surveillant gaze and the monitoring of social institutions. Writes Armstrong (2014): 'Even cyber-criminals are finding it impossible to maintain their privacy online, so what hope is there for the rest of us?'. For McMullan (2015), this condition has intensified with the advent of digital surveillance and dataveillance:

> In the private space of my personal browsing I do not feel exposed—I do not feel that my body of data is under surveillance because I do not know where that body begins or ends. We live so much of our lives online, share so much data, but feel nowhere near as much attachment for our data as we do for our bodies. My data, however, is under surveillance, not only by my government but also by corporations that make enormous amounts of money capitalising on it. Not only that, but the amount of data on offer to governments and corporations is about to go through the roof, and as it does the panopticon may emerge as a model once more. Why? Because our bodies are about to be brought back into the mix. The looming interconnectivity between

> objects in our homes, cars and cities, generally referred to as the internet of things, will change digital surveillance substantially … everything from washing machines to sex toys will soon be able to communicate, creating a vast amount of data about our lives. And this deluge of data won't only be passed back and forth between objects but will most likely wind its way towards corporate and government reservoirs.

To this grouping, we might add criminal lawyers, some of whom have already admitted that doing a social media check is an early automatic step in their firm's defence processes, given that the information individuals associated with a case may post to their social media accounts can provide crucial evidence at trial (Ford 2012).

So too, journalists frequently use social media as a source—not always favourably—in their construction of crime news; often to supplement the information they already have on 'ideal victims' and offenders. As mentioned in Chapter 3, a notable example is the case of American student, Amanda Knox, who was suspected of killing her British flatmate, Meredith Kercher, in Perugia, Italy, in 2007. Following Knox's arrest for the murder, the British and Italian news media characterised her as the femme fatale, 'Foxy Knoxy'— a nickname that had been lifted from Knox's own MySpace profile, but related to her childhood football skills, rather than her seduction technique. The press also used several photographs from Knox's MySpace account (including one showing her fooling around with an antique Gatling gun, while on holidays) to further solidify their portrayal of Knox as a duplicitous seductress and cold-blooded killer. In February 2014, two weeks after an Italian appeals court reinstated the guilty verdicts for Kercher's murder against her and former boyfriend Raffaele Sollecito Knox posted a black and white 'selfie' to Twitter with the declaration, 'SIAMO INNOCENTI' (We Are Innocent) handwritten on a placard held in front of her (Knox 2014a). She appeared bare-faced and solemn in the image; a direct contrast to the celebritised criminal identity, 'Foxy Knoxy', previously constructed for her within legal and news discourses. Regardless of your position on the guilt or innocence of Knox, the 'SIAMO INNOCENTI' tweet undeniably reflected an attempt by Knox to use social media to reclaim control of her public image through the symbolic act of self-representation—an act of 'speaking back' (Clifford 2016). In this way, it also invites us to reflect on the ways in which cyberspace and 'surveillance can itself give rise to distinctive forms of subjectivity' by encouraging 'new forms of self-identification' and resistance (Haggerty & Ericson 2006: 15).

THE DEMOCRATISATION OF SURVEILLANCE TECHNOLOGIES AND TACTICS

One of the main criticisms levelled at the panoptic thesis (and arguably, to some extent, the surveillant assemblage) in critical discussions of surveillance culture is 'that it overstates the power of systems, institutions and processes and underplays the importance of the individual actor' (Jewkes 2015). This may be symptomatic of the broader tendency to conceive of visibility as a concept that derives from 'a hierarchy that imposes a dominating and observing gaze as a mechanism of social control' (Welch 2011: 310). It may also reflect the persistent view of surveillance as being directed downwards towards the disenfranchised, and rarely upwards towards the powerful (Coleman & Sim 2000). These modes of thought have been challenged, however, by what Lee and McGovern (2014: 183) describe as the 'democratisation of surveillance', which has been reflected in the emergence of surveillance tactics, such as **sousveillance** and **counterveillance**.

Loosely translated as 'to watch from below', sousveillance operates as a form of 'inverse surveillance' where those conventionally perceived to be 'the watchers' have become 'the watched'. While *sur*veillance often involves the monitoring of individuals by bureaucratic organisations (e.g. police)—'the eye in the sky'—by contrast, *sous*veillance describes a situation where ordinary citizens are able to turn the camera back on institutional power to allow 'the surveillee to surveil the surveiller' (Mann, Nolan & Wellman 2003: 333). This is often facilitated through the use of small wearable devices or portable personal technologies, such as smartphones. Arguably, one of the earlier and most-cited examples of sousveillance— albeit serendipitous and fortuitous—is George Holliday's videotaping of the 1991 assault on Rodney King by Los Angeles Police Department officers after he was stopped for a traffic violation (see Chapter 6). Since then, technologies have advanced and more deliberate or planned acts of sousveillance have become routine, with it now increasingly common for bystanders to hold police accountable for their actions by recording their street encounters with citizens on mobile phones—in some cases, achieving justice where it may not have otherwise been possible (see Box 11.5). Smartphone apps, like the American Civil Liberties Union's 'Mobile Justice' app and 'Hands Up 4 Justice', have made it even easier for citizens to monitor and document evidence of misconduct during their encounters with frontline police.

BOX 11.5

WHEN THE WATCHERS BECOME THE WATCHED

Ian Tomlinson, a newspaper vendor, was struck from behind by a police baton and pushed to the ground by the same officer during the 2009 G20 summit protests in London, after he became caught up in a 'controlled dispersal' of protestors, while trying to return home (IPCC 2012). Images of the assault spread virally on the internet as a consequence of *The Guardian*'s publication of amateur footage of the altercation a week after the critical incident. The video, captured by an American businessman, showed no provocation on the part of Tomlinson, who managed to walk away from the incident, only to collapse and die a short time later. A subsequent coronial inquest found that Tomlinson had been unlawfully killed. PC Simon Harwood, the officer responsible for the assault on Tomlinson, was found not guilty of manslaughter charges in Southwark Crown Court in July 2012, but was found guilty of gross misconduct by a Metropolitan Police Service (MPS) panel in September of the same year, and discharged from service with immediate effect. In August 2013, the MPS apologised 'unreservedly' to Tomlinson's family for the use of 'excessive and unlawful force' and agreed to an out-of-court compensation settlement (Taylor 2013). Tomlinson's death sparked significant debate about the relationship between police and publics in the United Kingdom, and the role of citizens in monitoring policing practices and potential misconduct (Lyall 2009).

Similar debates emerged in the United States about race relations and law enforcement following the death of unarmed black teenager Michael Brown, who was fatally shot by a police officer in August 2014, in Ferguson, Missouri. The incident sparked the Twitter hashtag campaign #IfTheyGunnedMeDown, which sought to challenge media stereotypes of African Americans by encouraging social media users—mostly minorities—to post two images of themselves, which side-by-side could be interpreted as contrastingly positive and negative (Jackson 2016). In one photo, for example, the individual might be seen in military uniform reading to children in a classroom, while the accompanying photograph might depict the same individual in a gold neck chain, alcoholic beverage in hand, flashing a 'gang sign' for the camera. The images were often captioned with the question: 'If the police gunned me down, what picture would the media use to represent me?'. Michael Brown's death was followed by a spate of high-profile incidents involving police brutality towards African American men. Citizen mobile phone and police dashcam footage of many of the incidents and their aftermath (including, most notably, the deaths of Freddie Gray, Walter Scott, Eric Garner, Tamir Rice, Charly Leundeu Keunang, Kajieme Powell and Laquan McDonald) proliferated on social media and online news sites and, in several cases, resulted in murder charges being brought against the police officers involved—a rare occurrence. Without this user-generated content, the news framing and public understandings of many of these incidents may have been very different. Indeed, the high-profile nature of the incidents inspired the development of 'The Counted', a project by *The Guardian* newspaper combining traditional news reporting with verified crowdsourced information from the public to better track the number of people killed by police in the United States; see <www.theguardian.com/thecounted>.

Surveillance technologies adopted by police organisations to enhance their crime-fighting capabilities, police-community relations and officer safety have also been turned back upon police themselves in a form of counter-surveillance or 'counterveillance' (Welch 2011). As Lee and McGovern (2014: 184) explain, the surveillance practices of contemporary police leave 'an indelible digital trace of police activity, allowing for the increased oversight surveillance and panoptic self-government of police activity'. One of the first instances of this in Australia, for example, involved video coverage of a sequence of events leading up to an officer breaking the jaw of a 17-year-old in the Fremantle Police Station in May 1992. Although the videotape did not show the actual punch, which broke the young man's jaw, it did pick up the sound of the blow and the moans of the youth. The officer involved, Sergeant Desmond Smith, was subsequently fined A$5000 for the assault and was sacked by the Police Commissioner; only to be reinstated after successfully appealing to the Western Australian Industrial Relations Commission for unfair dismissal (White 1993). Today, dashcams, Tasercams, body-worn cameras and CCTV cameras in police charge rooms, station lobbies and custody suites may aim to 'protect police officers from frivolous charges of abuse and misconduct', but they also have the potential to provide a record of 'actual abuse and misconduct by officers' (Surette 2011: 174). This has raised suspicion within police ranks, given the ways in which such technologies serve to assist with law enforcement while doubling as a form of surveillance over police actions, exposing what are typically private, 'backstage' behaviours and professional practices. Like sousveillance, the tactic of counterveillance therefore has the potential to alter police behaviours (sometimes producing acts of resistance) as a consequence of the experience of being watched (Lee & McGovern 2014).

A study by Goold (2003), for example, analysed the impacts of CCTV on a large English police force and found that the presence of surveillance cameras had an effect on the professional attitudes and behaviours of individual police officers. Conscious of being monitored by CCTV and the ways in which this might be used against them in the future, a number of the police officers interviewed said they were more circumspect when using force or making arrests in view of the surveillance cameras; that it made it essential for them to 'go by the book' or to at least create the appearance of doing so (Goold 2003: 194). Similar findings emerged from a survey of 231 Canadian police officers, where 74 per cent of the respondents reported behavioural changes 'because of the capacity of citizens to videorecord their actions' (Brown 2016: 303). But studies of police body-worn cameras have shown that, regardless of the reasons for their implementation, the technology continues to only be as effective as its wearer. There have been reports, for example, of some police officers choosing not to turn on their camera as well as complaints that wearing the camera feels like having a supervisor watching over them all day, looking for minor misconduct (Brennan Center for Justice 2016). As Marx (1995: 107) explains: 'Surveillance technology is not simply applied, it is also *experienced* by users, subjects, and audiences'. But the performance and regulation of behaviours that accompanies the experience of being watched is not restricted to police alone.

RETHINKING THE RELATIONSHIP BETWEEN CRIME AND DIGITAL TECHNOLOGIES

At the start of this book, we elaborated on the fact that the contemporary mediascape has been marked by profound change, including a collapse in the traditional boundaries between *media producers* and *media consumers*. This is perhaps nowhere more apparent than in the context of digital and surveillance technologies, which have enabled 'the people formerly known as the audience' (Rosen 2006) to become 'media actors', who not only dictate their points of engagement with media, but also actively contribute to the production of media content (commonly referred to as user-generated content). This has significantly impacted on the practices of professional journalists and the ways in which news is constructed. But it has also impacted on other professional practices, such as law enforcement, and traditional assumptions about policing and social regulation. As we have detailed, now more than ever, the watchers (the police) have become the watched. This is, in part, thanks to their increased visibility to and the scrutiny of their actions by ordinary citizens, which have been afforded by the generalised adoption of digital and surveillance technologies—what was once primarily used to the advantage of these bureaucratic organisations is now available to all. This democratic turn in surveillance culture (and media practices more broadly) has also encouraged something of a cultural imperative towards mediated self-representation, or rather the idea that 'to be' in contemporary society is 'to be seen'—that 'one exists as a socially recognisable (and noteworthy) subject insofar as one is available and visible to others through mediated representation' (Yar 2012: 250). The '**selfie**' is perhaps one of the more explicit manifestations of this. While the act of self-mediation has become the focus of many contemporary analyses of media, the practice bears criminological significance too. This is especially the case where the 'will-to-representation' intersects with the enactment of offending behaviours (Yar 2012).

HAPPY SLAPPING AND THE POLITICS OF CRIMINAL PLEASURES

If, in surveillance culture, there is a drive to look, there is also in the twenty-first century, claims Jewkes (2015: 239), a drive to be looked at: a development which 'suggests that CCTV, video and webcam footage is as much about *entertainment* as it is *control*' (emphasis added). How often have we seen the 'spectacle' of these types of surveillance images exploited in the production of crime news or as part of the voyeuristic imperative that drives our television viewing of the contestants inside the *Big Brother* house? For Mathiesen (1997), these enhanced features of surveillance have been facilitated by the rise of the 'mass media' (a now-outdated term for what we call 'mainstream media') and the 'viewer society', which have helped to foster a culture of celebrity, where fame and notoriety—the ability to see and *be seen*—have become valuable commodities in their own right.

Mathiesen's turn towards the 'mass media' (specifically television) has often been regarded as a corrective to Foucault's earlier writings on the panopticon, which failed to acknowledge any relationship between surveillance, visibility and media. In particular, it has been claimed that Mathiesen sought to augment the panoptic gaze (where the few 'observe' the many) by constructing a reciprocal framework; recognising that visibility could also involve **synopticism** or rather the capacity for *the many* to observe *the few*. In a contemporary setting, this has arguably been reflected in the increasing numbers of individuals who are willing and enabled to 'expose intimate details of their private lives' online (Haggerty & Ericson 2006: 5; see also Niedzviecki 2009). The popularity of social networking sites like Facebook, Instagram, Snapchat, LinkedIn, YouTube and Twitter are a testament to this (Jewkes 2015). In engaging with such sites as these, users manufacture a virtual self to produce media content, often as a form of entertainment, for an imagined audience (Burnett & Marshall 2003; Van Dijck 2008; McQuire 2012). This can include the use of cyberspace to 'radically reconfigure' social behaviours to engage in 'pernicious, aggressive and often malicious' behaviours (Kenway, Kraack & Hickey-Moody 2006). What the synopticon therefore introduces in the context of this chapter is the potential for digital technologies to function as not only a *target* and *enabler* of crime itself, but also as a means for the self-representation of criminality (as an act of thrill-seeking for 'synoptic' pleasure). This is as opposed to surveillance simply being a *mechanism of social control*. To illustrate this point, we might consider the dynamics of the cultural phenomenon known as 'happy slapping'.

Broadly speaking, the phenomenon of happy slapping involves the unprovoked attack or assault of an unsuspecting individual, often in a public place, which is captured on a camera phone or other recording device for upload to the internet via video-hosting or file-sharing sites and social networks. For Yar (2012), these technologies and the user-generated representational practices that have become symptomatic of their use, are crucial motivators for the offending behaviour itself. 'In other words', he explains, 'the desire for social recognition through self-representation has a criminogenic dimension, one whose potentiality is more fully released once the means for such mediated self-presentation is widely available' (Yar 2012: 252). Cultural criminologist Keith Hayward (2012: 24–5) takes this another step further, arguing that happy slapping is emblematic of 'media technology's seepage into the practice of everyday life to the extent that, for some, if it is not performed on camera, it is not real'. He explains: 'Today, within contemporary youth culture, "real-life" crime, violence and brutality are cheap commodities, emptied of their embodied consequences, and sold as seductive digital spectacle' (Hayward 2012: 25). But unlike some of the user-generated content discussed earlier in the chapter where citizens may fortuitously capture incidents on their mobile phones as they unfold in their proximity, happy slapping is deliberately engineered and enacted for the explicit purpose of recording the assault and disseminating it via online communications platforms and social networking sites. In short, 'people offend in order to be seen doing so by others' and 'action and representation are part of an intertwined social practice in which mediation is an integral element' (Yar 2012: 253).

A mostly British phenomenon, happy slapping first appeared in newspaper reports in 2005, and included teachers' accounts of the craze in London schools. Since then, the phenomenon has spread to other countries including France, Germany, Italy and Australia. In Spain, variations on the phenomenon have been identified, the most notable being 'happy crashing', where perpetrators voluntarily jump out in front of oncoming traffic in an attempt to cause a car accident, which can then be filmed by friends nearby and uploaded online (Tremlett 2006). Despite its many permutations, happy slapping has often been associated in news media with a distinct range of alleged 'causes' and moral panics, including concerns about juvenile delinquency and youth gangs; the imitation of television shows like *Jackass*, which indulge in ritual humiliation and daredevil exploits; and the more generalised anxieties that persist around the use of mobile phones to capture videos of violence, especially in the context of school and gang fights, and more recently, girl fights—what Goggin (2010: 125) rightfully acknowledges as 'an enduring moral terrain of deviance and youth'. The challenging aspect of these over other forms of criminality and deviance, however, is that the term happy slapping conveys 'an element of fun and light-heartedness' (Chan et al. 2012: 44).

For its often-youthful perpetrators, the process of abuse thus can be enjoyable; it may be seen 'as a form of entertainment, similar to the rationale given by those who engage in joyriding and street racing' (Chan et al. 2012: 45; see also Palasinski 2013). This posits crime and the thrill-seeking often associated with offending behaviours like happy slapping as experiences that embody an element of *pleasure* (see Ferrell 1995; Ferrell, Milovanovic & Lyng 2001; Lyng 2004). Seeing the attack as entertainment has also been cited by cyberbullies (with which happy slapping has been considered synonymous) as a reason for their aggressive online behaviours (Smith et al. 2008). The social rewards of gaining popularity and status among peers—a kind of 'celebrated criminality' (Penfold-Mounce 2009)—have also been noted as a motivating factor (Chan et al. 2012). But the pleasure and status that may be derived from happy slapping does not excuse or expunge the real harms—emotional and physical—to its victims. These have, in their more extreme forms, included serious injury and death (see Box 11.6).

BOX 11.6

THE DEADLY CONSEQUENCES OF HAPPY SLAPPING

Ekram Haque, a retired care worker, was killed in a happy slapping attack by two teenagers in Tooting, South London, in August 2009. His attackers, 15-year-old Leon Elcock and 14-year-old Hamza Lyzai, ambushed the 67-year-old pensioner outside the mosque where he had been worshipping, recording the assault on a mobile phone. Haque died in hospital a week later having suffered serious brain damage after hitting his head on the pavement as he collapsed from being punched. Grainy footage of the incident, captured by nearby street surveillance cameras and made public at the family's request, showed the full extent of the tragedy, including the fact that Haque's three-year-old granddaughter had witnessed the incident. In the footage, which later featured in the BBC's four-part documentary series *Our Crime*, Mariam Haque can be seen sobbing in distress as she attempts to wake her unconscious grandfather. The assault on Haque was not the first perpetrated by Elcock and Lyzai; the youths had previously carried out several happy slapping attacks, recording each one and publishing the videos online under the name 'Lane Gang Productions' (Wright 2010). The mobile phone footage, some of which featured in the *Our Crime* episode, showed the youths laughing and running off after each of the attacks on their victims. At the time of the violent encounter outside the mosque, Leon Elcock was, in fact, on bail for another happy slapping attack on an elderly woman four days earlier. In a vivid account recorded for the *Our Crime* episode, one of Elcock's neighbours described how, after the attack, she had witnessed Elcock and his friend 'just sitting on the trampoline' at Elcock's house: 'no remorse, no guilt on their face, [they] carried on laughing and chatting like they'd just gone to the shop to pick up sweets or something, while this old woman's across the road injured' (Nicole cited in 'Attacked' 2012). Disturbingly, CCTV footage also showed the perpetrators laughing and dancing with others in the corridors of the casualty department at St George's Hospital in Tooting, where Ekram Haque lay fighting for his life in a nearby ward. The teenagers had ended up at the hospital because of an injury Lyzai had sustained to his finger while climbing over a fence as he fled from the scene of the crime ('Attacked' 2012). Both Elcock and Lyzai, once arrested, pleaded guilty to the manslaughter of Ekram Haque and to their involvement in the other happy slapping attacks, which they admitted they had carried out 'for fun' (Sinclair 2010). Elcock was sentenced to four-and-a-half years in prison, and Lyzai to three-and-a-half years, although both only served around two years of their sentences before being released from custody.

One of the more horrific happy slapping cases to emerge in an Australian context involved the recording of physical and sexual violence against a 17-year-old girl 'mildly delayed in her intellectual development' by a group of teenage boys in the outer-western Melbourne suburb of Werribee in Victoria (*R v P and others* [2007] VChC 3, para. 7). The footage, which showed the girl being urinated on and her hair set alight, was converted into DVD format and allegedly sold for five Australian dollars a copy in schools across the region (Miletic 2006; Petrie 2006). Parts of the DVD were also uploaded to YouTube. The story broke when the current affairs program *Today Tonight* screened excerpts from the DVD on one of its nightly broadcasts in October 2006; at which point, the police became involved. Eleven teenagers in total—part of a group, which called themselves 'the teenage kings of Werribee'—were charged over the incident and placed on youth supervision orders or probation, and made to attend counselling for young sex offenders (*R v P and others* [2007] VChC 3; *R v M and others* [2008] VChC 4). Eight had convictions recorded against them. One of the sentencing judges described the 'sustained attack' on the 'vulnerable young woman' as 'cowardly, brutal and above all else, a serious breach of the criminal law' (*R v P and others* [2007] VChC 3, para. 13). Three years later, one of the main offenders posted a rap music video online in which he boasted about his infamy as a consequence of the assault, and claimed that the victim had enjoyed herself throughout the ordeal (Dowsley & Healey 2009). As Heller-Nicholas (2014) writes, the search for answers as to the catalysts for the crime was widespread: 'Fingers were pointed at the ubiquity of digital technology; the influence of US hip hop culture; Australia's "Wild Colonial Boy" ethos; political correctness; political conservatism; the absence of corporal punishment; and the rise of violence in the broader mediasphere'.

ISSUES FOR CONSIDERATION

As Ferrell and Sanders (1995: 314) suggest: 'Paying attention to the various pleasures of crime—however distasteful—can begin to define not only its phenomenological foreground but its complex political underpinnings as well'. But, in the case of happy slapping, the distribution of responsibility between (and penalties for) those who commit and film the offences, distribute the footage, and provide the technology for its distribution have not always been entirely clear-cut, even in legislation. This has resulted in unexpected outcomes. In 2010, for example, an Italian court found three Google employees responsible for a happy slapping video, posted on Google Videos by school bullies in September 2006, because the video had been allowed to stay online for two months until Google was notified of its existence and had it removed (Chan et al. 2012). Each of the three defendants was given a six-month suspended sentence for failing to comply with the Italian privacy code, prompting Google to post a statement on its official blog, which in part read:

> To be clear, none of the four Googlers charged had anything to do with this video. They did not appear in it, film it, upload it or review it ... In essence this ruling means that employees of hosting platforms like Google Video are criminally responsible for content that users upload ... It attacks the very principles of freedom on which the Internet is built (Sucherman 2010).

The three Google employees—all senior executives—were subsequently exonerated of the charges in the Milan Court of Appeals in December 2012, after the judiciary drew a distinction between 'the processing of the video itself and the processing of the personal data depicted or contained in the uploaded video' (Berliri & Colonna 2013). The Court stipulated that 'data protection and e-commerce regulations are part of the same complete and coherent legal framework that, when read together, do not impose on the hosting provider a duty to monitor and assess the lawfulness of content uploaded by third parties' (Berliri & Colonna 2013). Nonetheless, the original ruling against the Google executives had demonstrated the potential to set what many saw as a dangerous legal precedent in relation to the innovations and freedoms afforded by the internet, and the responsibility and liability for 'gatekeeping' those individuals online who choose to behave inappropriately—and criminally—in response to such liberties.

Similar concerns were raised about governmentality and corporate **responsibilisation** in relation to the 2011 England riots, when it was revealed that Prime Minister David Cameron had considered shutting down access to social networking sites during the height of the disturbances and banning individuals suspected of inciting violence online from using internet services (see Halliday & Garside 2011; Williams 2011). Questions about the responsibility (as well as motivations) for criminal acts broadcast using digital technologies re-emerged in 2016 when an Ohio woman was accused of live streaming the rape of her 17-year-old friend on the Twitter-owned video app, Periscope. Several months later, part of an attack on two French police officials—murdered in their own home in an Islamic State group-inspired stabbing—was live streamed by the killer on Facebook. A statement subsequently issued by the company said that Facebook was working closely with the French authorities investigating the crime, and that it recognised the challenges of live streaming being used for malicious purposes: 'It's a serious responsibility, and we work hard to strike the right balance between enabling expression while providing a safe and respectful experience' (cited in Timms 2016).

The public and news discourses that emerged after each of the above cases closely correlated to those identifiable within broader debates over regulation and the governance of cyberspace. These discourses, as Wall and Williams (2007: 410) argue, have typically produced conflicting messages, particularly within media narratives, 'where the "cybercrime" problem is perceived either as a problem of weak law or poor technological control'. The social determinants of cybercrime and other acts of digitally-enabled deviance are consequently rarely explored, and the question of responsibility is often directed towards governments, legislators, law enforcement officials or technology service providers. In the midst of this, however, it is important to note that online communities also perform their own 'policing' practices to maintain order and safety in the virtual environment. This can range from informal surveillance and voluntary ad hoc partnerships with law enforcement and the private sector through to 'digital pillory' or the 'naming and shaming' of cyber-offenders online. In some cases, the latter has evolved into public shaming, where mainstream media have become involved in the reporting of the case (see Huey, Nhan & Broll 2012; Hess & Waller 2014). Private citizens have, as part of these surveillance measures, also found themselves performing illegal acts to obtain the information required to prevent future cybercrimes, as illustrated by those internet users who have illegally accessed the computers of others to confirm their suspicions about suspected paedophilia and other online abuses (see Grabosky 2016). Then, there are the more extreme forms of digital activism and **cybervigilantism**—actions that are often associated with hacktivist collectives like Anonymous and their use of digital technologies and cyberspace to expose injustices and the potential cover-up of serious crimes in the terrestrial world, such as the Steubenville sexual assault case (see Kushner 2013; Woods 2014; Armstrong, Hull & Saunders 2016).

Like all forms of criminal evidence though, even that which is obtained through acts of surveillance is subject to contestation. This includes the seemingly irrefutable nature of CCTV footage. Video surveillance, as Dovey (2001: 136) explains, is often deemed to be a reflection of the real (or 'truth') because '[t]he CCTV image appears to simply calibrate visual perception; it is operated by a machine, and no human mediation is involved in its production of "pure" evidence'. But human intervention *is* required in determining what the CCTV images portray, since the very act of looking is an act of interpretation (Sontag 1979; Biber 2006). For instance, there are numerous examples where the same surveillance images have been used to support contrary adjudications of guilt and innocence or lawful use of force versus police misconduct. In January 2015, for example, police in Texas shot and killed a mentally ill teenager after she entered the Longview police station with a knife and 'I have a gun' allegedly written on her hand. The hacktivist collective, Anonymous, retaliated by temporarily taking down the City of Longview's website in a distributed denial of service (DDoS) attack, warning that more attacks were likely if the surveillance video of the shooting was not made publicly available (Ortigo 2015). Vision of the shooting of 17-year-old Kristiana Coignard, captured by the security cameras in the lobby of the police station, was subsequently released by the Longview Police Department, citing 'public interest' in the incident. The footage has since been viewed over a million times on YouTube. The officers involved in the incident were ultimately cleared by a grand jury after a review of the surveillance footage and testimony from the Texas Ranger who conducted the investigation into the shooting (Dart 2015). But the vision itself had heightened the visibility of the Longview Police Department, and therefore public scrutiny of the critical incident (reflecting an example of counterveillance). Not everyone agreed that the footage showed the lawful use of force by the police officers involved, as reflected by a two-day rally, which was held outside the Longview police station a little over two weeks after Coignard's death. The City of Longview settled a civil lawsuit filed by the Coignard family for US$15 000 in March 2016. Kristiana Coignard's parents had originally sought US$10 million in damages, saying: 'We hoped justice would be carried out without having to resort to this. We're not going to stop fighting just because of their report' (cited in Kirst 2016).

CONCLUSION

The merits of surveillance technologies and tactics have been debated repeatedly in the context of these 'big issues'—crime control, personal safety, national security, protecting the interests of the private sector, and ensuring the accountability of state apparatuses. Their value, to a lesser extent, has been acknowledged in relation to *crime-solving* (think James Bulger and Jill Meagher) and, certainly, the impact of emerging technologies like police body-worn cameras on the civil liberties of victims and offenders alike has room left to run as a discussion point. This is despite the fact that, as Jewkes (2015: 233) observes: 'There is little doubt that surveillance technologies have radically destabilized the public/private boundary, and no other issue has generated public disquiet about surveillance to the extent that fears about loss of privacy have'. But high-profile crimes and acts of terror, such as those witnessed on September 11, 2001 and more recently in London, Mumbai, Paris, Boston and Orlando, have altered people's tolerance to surveillance, especially the tracking of those suspected of potential acts of violence and indecency (i.e. 'Others'). This has not stifled concerns, however, about the license that governments can take as a consequence of such acts—often using them as a rationale—to more generally oversee and regulate the activities of their citizens (Jewkes 2015).

One thing is certain: the evolution of digital and surveillance technologies and the scope for our engagement in cyberspace—and therefore, many of the above debates—will not stand still. New technologies, unforeseeable today, will no doubt be introduced in our lifetimes. Some will expand our capacities and make life more efficient, enjoyable, empowered and exciting—not to mention safer. But many will also present new opportunities for criminal exploitation and uncivil behaviours. For example, radio frequency identification (RFID) microchips have become so broadly accepted that predictions have it that, in the future, we will all have one implanted under our skins, leaving us potentially vulnerable to having our own bodies hacked. As Grabosky (2016) points out, webcams, baby monitors and smart TVs have already fallen prey to hackers, and 3D printing has enabled the global production and distribution of firearms across borders without the need to negotiate traditional crime control 'gatekeepers', like customs officers and postal inspectors. So too, the use of drones as a criminal investigation tool by police has been documented at the same time as the technology has been co-opted by criminals to facilitate drug smuggling and burglaries, counteract law enforcement efforts and remove rival crime groups. Perhaps, the moral to the story is therefore quite simple: we need only look to the past to be able to predict the future. Despite the fact that new digital and surveillance technologies and tactics may emerge, they will continue to demonstrate the potential to enable and constrain, to facilitate care as well as enhance control (Lyon 2001), and the behaviours and cultures they serve to produce will continue to both embolden and challenge us.

DISCUSSION QUESTIONS

1. Are groups like WikiLeaks and Anonymous good for democracy? Does 'hacktivism' result in real change? What are the unintended consequences (i.e. risks and harms)?
2. Has the pervasiveness of digital technologies and surveillance practices marked the end of privacy in contemporary society?
3. In what ways have digital and surveillance technologies expanded opportunities for the construction and performance of transgressive identities and deviant behaviours?
4. What strategies might be deployed to improve civility and citizenship in cyberspace and reduce the incidence of online harms and cybercrimes?
5. What might the future look like in terms of criminal offending and crime control in the context of an enhanced surveillance society?

WORKSHOP ACTIVITY: MAPPING THE FLUIDITY OF CONTEMPORARY SURVEILLANCE TECHNOLOGIES AND PRACTICES

Reflect on the range of everyday encounters we may have with digital and surveillance technologies and practices (include your own and those of others). You will need to think broadly and in some detail for this. Note your observations down in a table format. Alongside your answers, in a separate column, write down some examples of the ways in which each of the technologies and tactics you have identified could be used for the purposes of *enabling* or *constraining* individuals, groups or organisations. What do you notice? Are there any examples that fall into the former category, which would more commonly be considered a criminal activity or form of deviance? How do your findings compare to those of your peers?

FURTHER READING

Barnard-Wills, D. (2012). *Surveillance and Identity: Discourse, Subjectivity and the State*. Surrey, UK and Burlington, VT: Ashgate.

Chan, S., Khader, M., Ang, J., et al. (2012). Understanding 'Happy Slapping'. *International Journal of Police Science & Management*, 14(1), 42–57.

Foucault, M. (1975/1991). *Discipline and Punish: The Birth of the Prison*. Trans. A. Sheridan. London: Penguin Books.

Grabosky, P. (2016). *Cybercrime*. New York and Oxford: Oxford University Press.

Haggerty, K. D. & Ericson, R. V. (eds) (2006). *The New Politics of Surveillance and Visibility*. Toronto, Canada: University of Toronto Press.

12

CONCLUSION

CHAPTER HIGHLIGHTS

The importance of nuance

When journalism and media studies meets criminology

As we have discussed throughout this book, 'media' is not monolithic. Nor does it simply equate to 'news' or 'journalism'. Rather, from an infrastructure perspective, it includes many technologies, platforms and institutional settings that stretch far beyond traditional newsrooms and radio and television studios. As a social practice, media engagement involves a wide range of 'actors' who may interact with mainstream media, but who also utilise their own means to transmit information and opinion—to 'speak back'—for example, via online sites such as Facebook, YouTube, Twitter and Instagram. These actors also use these communications tools for a wide variety of social purposes (such as shoring up police legitimacy through to exposing corporate wrongdoing). Even as we write this, news reports have emerged about the use of digital technologies by police to circulate virtual 'wanted posters' to the mobile phones of millions of New Yorkers in the hunt for a bombing suspect—an approach that is being heralded as 'the future' of law enforcement (Leswing 2016). While we have focused primarily on mainstream news media in many of the case studies cited throughout the book, we have nonetheless tried to convey the complexities of (and opportunities afforded by) this contemporary and changing mediascape.

The contributions of this book, as part of that enterprise, are therefore twofold. First, the intention has been to introduce readers to new ways of looking at the media–crime nexus beyond the commonplace and commonsense. This has involved identifying a number of relevant concepts, which have been utilised in order to help us better understand and explain how media does what it does when it comes to crime-related topics. We have tried to explore certain key concepts thematically throughout a number of chapters. For example, 'moral panic' is described and deployed in different ways in accordance to the evolution of media and the further sophistication of the concept itself. Likewise, media practices and framing effects take many diverse and specific forms, and this variability, too, has been expressed in a number of chapters in the book.

Second, our aim has been to provide a new synthesis between journalism and media studies expertise and criminological knowledge. Here the concern has been to acknowledge and marshal experience and expert input across two distinct fields of theory, practice, research and analysis. In this regard, we believe that the book both affirms and confirms the importance of the conceptual and analytical outcomes of such a synthesis. Certainly, as authors we have been challenged by the perspectives and specialist language-use of the other. It has been a learning experience for each of us as we have tried to understand and appreciate the, at times, subtle differences offered by slightly different disciplinary terms and concepts to describe particular mediated representations and narratives about crime, criminality and criminal justice. The outcome, we believe, is a coherent combination of insight from both fields that altogether provides for a more innovative and sophisticated interweaving of themes and analysis than otherwise may have been the case.

THE IMPORTANCE OF NUANCE

One of the more apparent consequences of this synthesis of disciplinary expertise is greater sensitivity to 'nuance' when it comes to interpreting the relationship between media and crime. Much criminological work, for example, seems to have the flavour of critique of 'the media', rather than providing critical studies of 'media' in its broadest definition. There is an important difference between the two.

The first veers towards the condemnatory and the making of sweeping generalisation— the news about crime is always 'bad news' and always 'distorted', or so it is implied. There is nonetheless a truth of sorts lurking here. The totality of crime news and in particular its mediated representation in and by mainstream media organisations does indeed tend to reinforce a negative framing of 'law and order' issues, events and subjectivities. Bad news sells, as does fear of crime, and so there are hard financial realities that drive the framing of such news in certain directions. Moral panics and 'crime waves' may be socially constructed, but they are done so in ways that reflect particular interests, including those of moral entrepreneurs. And, of course, those who own and control mainstream media have particular powers of persuasion and discretion in terms of 'house style' and therefore, to some extent, story selection and agenda-setting.

There is much to be critical of when it comes to mainstream media portrayals of crime, criminality and criminal justice. For critical criminologists and those wishing to foster progressive changes within the institutions of criminal justice, news media can be a major source of frustration and annoyance. This is especially so when good criminal justice policies, good policing practices and more than adequate criminal laws—that is, those supported by experience-based expertise and evidence-based research, as well as human rights values—are undermined by ill-informed political decisions that are a consequence of media-inspired moral panics. The result is bad policy, bad practice and bad laws. Years of hard work, community lobbying and careful planning can be wiped out by extravagant claims and knee-jerk politics.

Yet mediated representations of crime, while overall weighted in particular directions, are not totally 'bad news' oriented or distorting in content. The second approach mentioned above (one that is alert to nuance) acknowledges this and seeks to unpack the media–crime nexus in a more detailed, contextualised and less morally imbued manner. Criticisms are still made, but critique is primarily adopted as 'methodology' rather than outcome—some news about crime is 'bad' and 'distorted', some news is not. Explaining why this is the case requires a form of analysis that pulls apart the issues, exposes the framing techniques, highlights the social interests and power dynamics, and attempts to comprehend how positive portrayals of 'crime' and 'criminals' and 'criminal justice' are indeed possible. This view of the relationship between 'media and crime' is informed by a practitioner perspective that understands the world of journalism and media, its practices, stakeholders, values and ideals, as well as the production pressures, editorial battles and owner biases.

Implicitly, this too is acknowledged by criminologists who engage with media and crime. The fact is, criminologists are very often the 'experts' to whom media practitioners turn when wanting comment on criminal justice issues. Criminologists also write the occasional newspaper column, feature on television current affairs programs and produce their own blogs and podcasts. They, therefore, also help to construct the framing of crime issues in particular ways. So, while heavily critical of some stories and some sorts of media framing, even the most critical of criminologists still tend to want to 'use' media, as best they can, to convey counter-narratives to the 'bad news' paradigm. In doing so, they frequently encounter like-minded allies *within* the ranks of media. Professional journalists, social media activists and documentary filmmakers are among those who are well-placed to seek truth, carry out social justice campaigns and advocate for redress in the case of wrongdoings by the criminal justice system. Just as we might evaluate the media we have, so too, as Couldry (2012: 181) reminds us, we can 'imagine something different' when it comes to its relationship with crime, criminality and criminal justice.

As illustrated in each chapter of this book, media do not provide an exclusively one-sided picture of crime and criminality. Rather, there are frequently multiple dimensions to the media gaze—good news stories about prisoners coexist with frightening portrayals of offenders deemed to be evil monsters; journalistic exposés of those at the top end of town reveal greed, avarice and criminality among the rich and powerful while news media plays down or is silent on the systemic transgressions of corporations and states. Media are not always 'fair' and 'balanced'. News values and the tension between particular journalistic ideals (such as impartiality) often result in unintended biases and unanticipated versions of 'truth'. This is precisely why a critically informed analysis of media and crime is so important.

WHEN JOURNALISM AND MEDIA STUDIES MEETS CRIMINOLOGY

We have tried to approach the subject matter, then, as both criminologist and media practitioner. The subsequent analysis provided in this book has therefore traversed concepts that are central to each profession. Notions of desistance and hate crime have gone hand-in-hand with concepts like media framing and mediatisation. The book has provided a theoretically informed analysis of concrete issues and events, but this orientation has required each of us to incorporate key ideas from our respective professional domains.

The content of the book has centred on crime topics—ranging from media coverage of police work and portrayals of victims, through to the mediated images of forensic science and youth gangs—and this is true of most books on 'media and crime'. But what makes this exercise a form of 'media criminology' is not the topic per se. It is the synthesis of concepts and the broad conceptual approach adopted herein that value-adds to the analysis. Rather than simply telling readers what media, in its many forms and across its many technologies and uses, says about crime, criminality and criminal justice, we have provided tools and language that hopefully will assist the reader in interpreting the processes and consequences of media framing of crime.

Media criminology, at its simplest and as we understand it, involves *the systematic study of media and crime based upon the combined conceptual insights of journalism and media studies and criminology*. This involves actively drawing upon the theoretical models of these fields in explaining the particular phenomenon at hand (e.g. a criminological explanation of the changing nature of imprisonment, a media studies explanation for diverse discourses about youth crime). The blending and overlapping of these conceptual lenses both broadens and deepens the analysis and increases the number of angles from which any particular issue can be approached and understood.

This approach to the study of media and crime also means taking the world of the media practitioner and the criminologist seriously. That is, as professionals defined by their expertise, practical skills and abstract theoretical knowledge, we cannot ignore the opportunities and obstacles that shape how each attempt to intervene in the world around them—or, equally, what crime, criminality and criminal justice can offer to the practice of journalism itself. There is such a thing as 'good' law-and-order journalism (as exposure of institutional child abuse illustrates and journalism awards for such reporting further endorse), and sometimes criminologists do succeed in gaining positive media support for important initiatives (witness, for instance, the substantial growth of and mostly media praise for 'juvenile conferencing' as part of a wider shift in favour of restorative justice methods of conflict resolution since the early 1990s). More recently, the popularity of true-crime docudramas, such as *Making a Murderer* and *Serial*, has also inspired innovations in journalistic practice in the form of significant investments from mainstream media in the production of their own crime podcasts like the six-part series *Phoebe's Fall* (2016), created by Fairfax Media in Australia. The series investigates the life and death of 24-year-old Phoebe Hansjuk, who died under suspicious circumstances in Melbourne in 2010. For the journalist who produced it, the success of *Phoebe's Fall* and the public's unswerving interest in stories of crime and injustice present a lifeline of sorts for major media organisations willing to capitalise on the 'armchair detective' phenomenon—proving, in the process, that 'journalism is alive and well' in spite of popular conceptions that newspapers are dying (Bachelard cited in Ward 2016).

Doing media criminology, therefore, is not about unpacking and interrogating solely the complexities and emerging dynamics of *representation* (images, frames and discourses), but also *praxis* (reflecting on who is doing what, and why, and under what conditions or motivations, which are often shifting). So too, it involves reflection on fundamental questions, such as what constitutes 'justice', or specific injustices, and how we should discuss these in relation to media and the negotiation of individual voice, social recognition and institutional action (Couldry 2012). This means, as media criminologists, we must be prepared to not only challenge the assumptions of others in relation to the media–crime nexus, but to also confront our own disciplinary biases and potential blind spots (see Box 12.1).

BOX 12.1

UNTANGLING THE COMPLEXITIES (AND SILENCES) OF 'MEDIA JUSTICE'

Scholars within journalism and media studies have long been motivated by an implicit concern with 'media justice' and how marginalised individuals and groups 'fight to get heard from a position outside the media mainstream' by using resources to speak in their own voice or by having their problems and injustices represented by other individuals or institutions (Couldry 2012: 199). Each scenario calls to mind notions of 'voice' and 'access to important media infrastructures on an equal basis', along with the opportunity for marginalised individuals and groups to 'have some agency or control over one's own image or representation' (Gies 2016: 214; see also Couldry 2011).

But this has the potential to obscure the ways in which access to media can sometimes give voice to those who may explicitly seek to do harm and injustice to others (as is the case with some forms of citizen journalism and online vigilantism). Within criminology, this problem has been linked to criticisms of so-called 'postmodern perspectives'. Such perspectives typically argue that 'language structures thought' and, given this, 'grand narratives' that provide a normative basis for action ('justice', 'rights' and 'equality') should be rejected since these too are socially constructed (White, Haines & Asquith 2017). The key task of criminology from this point of view is to offer a voice to those who have been silenced by the dominant discourses of the law. But whose voices and which groups should be supported in this way?

If the key criterion is that of looking to those voices that have been 'silenced' by the dominant discourses of the law (and mainstream media), then it raises the prospect of not only enabling oppressed minorities (e.g. Indigenous people) to resist better, but also, likewise, supporting extreme right-wing nationalist or white supremacist groups (e.g. neo-Nazis groups) (see Lea 1998). Thus, there needs to be a values framework regarding what is deemed to be 'good' and 'right', otherwise 'free speech'—regardless of how hurtful and harmful it is—becomes privileged over and above 'social justice', as oppressing voices are given the same space as voices of the oppressed in public discourse. The point is not to actively restrict or coercively shut down hate speech. Rather, it is to assign greatest normative value to working with and assisting those who are most vulnerable in society, and to thereby devoting media resources to tackling issues of inequality, dispossession and oppression. As seen below, however, justice is not only about disadvantage or, equally, about the essentialising binaries of privilege and marginalisation or the silenced and silencers—it is also about fairness and balance.

The emphasis on the idea of 'giving voice' to the margins can in itself overestimate the potential for self-expression to provide full redress for media and other injustices (Couldry 2012)—something we must remain mindful of in our analyses as media criminologists. Being able to 'speak up' and 'speak back' may be useful and cathartic, and provide an opportunity to 'speak truth to power' (thereby also *empowering* those who speak). But the existing media narratives may be too overwhelming in scope (in terms of the sheer number of representations of a particular kind) and longevity (in terms of the length of time in which these narratives have been repeated) to allow for these counter-narratives to be adequately heard, recognised and responded to. On the other hand, there are also no benefits to the argument that 'everyone needs to listen to everyone'. As Dreher (2009: 452) explains: 'Such a position would be both practically impossible and politically inadequate'.

Nonetheless, it is tempting, within this context, to assume that marginalisation is synonymous with social or economic disadvantage, and to favour examples that characterise this dynamic within our own analyses. However, as we have attempted to show through the inclusion of several of the case studies within this book, this is not always the case—even people from middle-class backgrounds can be the subjects of social and criminal injustices, as well as the injustices brought about by media misrecognition and/or neglect. Individuals like Vanessa Robinson (see Chapter 5) offer a clear illustration of this as do others, such as Raffaele Sollecito—pointing to the 'complex interplay' between experiences of injustice and marginalisation and 'a host of other social variables', including gender and nationality (Gies 2016: 215).

In 2009, Sollecito was found guilty of the murder of British student, Meredith Kercher, two years earlier in Perugia, Italy. In 2011, he walked free from an Italian prison, four years into a 25-year sentence, after the verdict was reversed. But, as Greenslade (2011) points out, no American or British newspaper chose to tell the story that way (and, arguably, many scholars have since followed suit in their analyses of the crime and its mediated representations, with the exception of Gies and Bortoluzzi 2016). Instead, Sollecito was mentioned 'only in passing in stories which concentrated instead on the woman who had been convicted with him, his then girlfriend Amanda Knox' (Greenslade 2011). Knox, as we have pointed out in previous chapters, was consistently cast as the mastermind behind Kercher's murder; the inference being that she had seduced and manipulated Sollecito, and their co-accused, Rudy Guede, into participating in the killing (Clifford 2016). In short, Sollecito was 'eclipsed by his co-defendant to a point that his guilt was inferred from her culpability by both the media and the criminal justice system'

(Gies 2016: 227). This later prompted Knox to declare in a blog post that 'Raffaele is not a slave' (Knox 2014b). 'The only reason he has been dragged into this', she writes, 'is because he happens to be my alibi. He is collateral damage in the unreasonable, irresponsible, and unrelenting scapegoating of the prosecution's grotesque caricature that is "Foxy Knoxy"' (Knox 2014b). Despite his best attempts, including the release of his own memoir about the ordeal, Sollecito never managed to attract the same levels of media attention that Knox was able to command, leaving him to suffer 'the kind of casual neglect that comes with being seen as the less interesting party' (Gies 2016: 227). In this way—as his supporters would no doubt suggest—Sollecito became a victim of not only a potential miscarriage of justice, but also media injustice.

Finally, then, as should be apparent to the reader by now, there is no shortage of material (or angles from which to approach and analyse it) for those wishing to pursue media criminology as a *bona fide* area of study. This is because crime is intrinsically interesting and exciting. It reflects an area of social life that is 'the subject of heated conversation in the workplace and at the bus stop, a primary focus of cinema and television drama, the animated stuff of video games, the staple diet of the news media, and a central theme in a multitude of popular literary genres, from crime thriller to serial killer' (Ferrell, Haywood & Young 2008: 64). Such matters are highly emotive and cover the range of human passions, foibles and pretentions. Moreover, the globalisation of media and the evolving nature of the contemporary mediascape (and digital technologies) provide a ready stage for endless variations on the crime and morality theme.

Making sense out of all this is the essence of contemporary media criminology. For this, we need the right tools. In our view, examination of the content, context and consequences of the relationship between media and crime is an ongoing project; one that is best approached by application of the kinds of approaches and concepts utilised in this book. The challenge is to forge a media criminology suited to the times, and that will constructively contribute to both understanding this world and perhaps, in its own small way, changing it.

GLOSSARY

Accumulative criminality:
  refers to corporate or organisational crime—as a direct link and natural flow-on of the capital accumulation process (i.e. profit enhancement and cost minimisation).

Audience reception analysis:
  explicitly advocates for the idea of an 'active audience' and media texts as 'polysemic'—that is, open to more than one reading.

Augmentative criminality:
  refers to the closely connected but distinct personal wealth-enhancement component in the criminality process that flows from the access and advantage gained from an ownership and control position in the capital accumulation process.

Binary oppositions:
  the presentation of identities and actions through polarised constructions of difference, which are fixed and absolute (e.g. victim/villain; good/evil; guilty/innocent).

Broadsides:
  nineteenth-century publications, which were printed single-sided on cheap paper and featured the gory details and graphic illustrations of recent murders and riots. Often sold to audiences who had gathered to witness public executions.

Chequebook journalism:
  involves the payment of money to a source for the right to publish or broadcast information; often also referred to as 'cash for comment'.

Citizen journalism:
  the process whereby ordinary members of the public contribute to the gathering and reporting of news.

Contempt of court:
  any action that has the potential to interfere with or undermine the authority of the courts and the opportunity for a fair trial.

Contrarianism:
  an ideological, rather than scientific, impetus for disagreement.

Counterveillance:
  when surveillance technologies adopted by police organisations to enhance their crime-fighting capabilities, police-community relations and officer safety are turned back upon police themselves in a form of counter-surveillance.

Crime wave:
  the way in which increased reporting of particular types of crimes (especially street crimes like assault, rape or homicide) heightens public awareness of these crimes. There need not have been an actual increase in the rates of the crime; the increase exists only in public perception. The concept of a crime wave is closely linked to, but separate from, that of *moral panics*.

Criminalists:
  forensic professionals who apply scientific methods and techniques to examine and analyse evidentiary items and testify in court as to their findings.

Criminogenic:
  producing or tending to cause crime or criminality.

CSI effect:
  a '*media effects*' phenomenon that assumes the often-misguided perceptions people have about forensic science and the process of criminal investigation are a direct result of their viewing habits; namely,

the depictions that they see in popular television crime series like *CSI: Crime Scene Investigation*.

Cultivation theory:
a theory of '*media effects*' developed by Professor George Gerbner in the mid-1960s, which sought to identify trends in television content as well as television's contribution to viewer conceptions of social reality. One of the main concerns was the exposure of television viewers to representations of violence.

Cyberbullying:
refers to repeated and targeted harassment and bullying involving the use of digital technologies, such as the internet.

Cybercrimes:
broadly speaking, cybercrimes involve the use of digital technologies to conduct criminal activities, the destruction or altering of stored information, and the use of computers to store information about a crime.

Cybersecurity:
the measures taken to provide adequate defences against malicious cyber activities, including the improved education of end-users.

Cybervigilantism:
extreme forms of digital activism often associated with hacktivist collectives like Anonymous and their use of digital technologies and cyberspace to expose injustices and the potential cover-up of serious crimes in the terrestrial world.

Dangerousness:
the state or quality of being dangerous. Criminological understandings of the term refer to actual violent behaviour, while populist notions imply being a risk or threat to others or being a problem in some way to institutional authorities. The latter,

however, does not refer to formally defined serious and repeat violent offending.

Dataveillance:
the systematic collection of information on individuals undertaken by a range of state, governmental and commercial bodies for a variety of purposes. This type of information collection has attracted considerable media attention in the wake of the public disclosures by WikiLeaks and former National Security Agency contractor Edward Snowden, who revealed the systematic monitoring of everyday communications and data transfers by governments in cooperation with global telecommunications companies.

Defamation:
any intentional false communication, either written or spoken, that harms a person's reputation; decreases the respect, regard or confidence in which a person is held; or induces disparaging, hostile or disagreeable opinions or feelings against a person.

Desistance:
refers to the social process in which an offender de-escalates and ultimately ceases taking part in further criminal and antisocial behaviours.

Deviance:
behaviour that breaks a rule within a social group and is viewed with disapproval and negatively labelled by the group. Deviance implies deviation from a presumed norm, and the transgression marks the person as an outsider to the mainstream.

Deviancy amplification:
the public labelling attached to particular groups or activities (e.g. graffiti artists; *happy slapping*) that can actually generate further or increased deviant behaviour because of the public notoriety or fame associated with the group or activity.

Digital citizenship:

denotes the changing nature of citizenship in a digitally networked society and encompasses civic agency reified through the use of digital media.

Digital divide:

the gap between those who can access media technology (as a consequence of wealth, culture and/or geographical location) and those who cannot.

Fear of crime:

the anxiety or alarm brought on by the feeling of being at risk of criminal victimisation.

Folk devils:

refers to certain individuals and groups who are labelled as threats or risks to societal values and interests as a result of their behaviours, which are seen to fall outside the boundaries of social and moral conventions. They are often stereotyped and scapegoated so as to appear as *the* problem in society. Examples of contemporary folk devils include asylum seekers, particular religious and ethnic minorities, and motorcycle gangs.

Framing devices:

the representational, rhetorical and discursive techniques evident within media texts, which contribute to the overall *media framing* of a story. These include: headlines; subheads; photos; photo captions; story leads; source selection; quote selection; pull quotes; logos; statistics and charts; and concluding statements and paragraphs.

Freedom of information (FOI):

for media practitioners, the fundamental legal right to access important information held by public bodies and to communicate this to media audiences. Access is often sought through what is known as an FOI request; also referred to as a right to information request in some Australian states and territories.

Generativity:

involves a process of giving to others with the consequence of positive changes in the self-esteem and social attitudes of those doing the giving.

Governmentality:

a term coined by philosopher Michel Foucault in reference to the ways in which the state exercises control over, or governs, the bodies of its populace. The concept widens understandings of power; encouraging us to think of power as not only hierarchical and top-down state power, but also inclusive of other forms of social control in disciplinary contexts (e.g. schools, prisons, psychiatric institutions) and knowledge production.

Greenwashing:

a form of spin or *public relations* that is deceptively used to promote the perception that an organisation's aims, policies and/or products are environmentally friendly. More time and money is spent claiming to be 'green' through advertising and marketing than is expended on actually implementing business practices that minimise environmental impact.

Happy slapping:

a phenomenon that involves the unprovoked attack or assault of an unsuspecting individual, often in a public place, which is captured on a camera phone or other recording device for upload to the internet.

Hard news:

news stories that generally refer to up-to-the-minute issues and events, and which provide publics with the information required to participate as fully informed citizens in the democratic process. These

stories adopt a very factual approach—
who, what, when, where, why—in their
presentation and often cover topics like
politics, economics and crime. Hard news
is often distinguished from *soft news*.

Hate crime:
  violence that is directed at individuals
  or groups on the basis of their actual
  or perceived sexuality, disability or
  membership of a racial, ethnic or
  religious group.

Hierarchy of victimisation:
  a situation wherein the differential status
  arising from perceptions of particular types
  of crimes and crime victims creates what
  Greer (2007) refers to as 'a pecking order
  of sorts' where 'ideal victims' are positioned
  at the top and those perceived as less
  deserving of crime victim status (and as less
  vulnerable) sit at the bottom.

House style or style guide:
  a policy (often recorded in document
  form) that provides guidance on a media
  organisation's stylistic conventions specific
  to their construction of media texts. This
  includes rules of spelling, punctuation,
  pronunciation, capitalisation and visual
  composition.

Hyperincarceration:
  a concept based on the notion that there is
  a broad complex of law, policy and practice
  that frames the use of imprisonment, and
  that increases in imprisonment are not
  undifferentiated, but very selective.

Hypodermic syringe model:
  a model of communications that suggests
  audiences are passive recipients of (and
  therefore wholly accept) preferred media
  messages.

Ideal victim:
  a person or category of individuals who
  are most readily given the complete and

legitimate status of being a victim after an
experience of crime. These include people
who are perceived as vulnerable, innocent
or worthy of compassion—for example,
children and the elderly.

Infotainment:
  a blurring of *hard news* and *soft news*
  to produce stories that both entertain
  and inform. The label 'infotainment' is
  often applied in a derogatory sense and is
  emblematic of concerns and criticism that
  journalism has devolved from a practice
  that conveys serious information about
  issues in the public interest, into a form of
  entertainment that happens to add fresh
  'facts' into the mix.

Liquid surveillance:
  a term used to describe the ways in which
  surveillance technologies and practices
  have developed in response to globalisation
  and the fluid nature of modern life,
  seeping into areas where they once had
  only marginal sway. Liquid surveillance is
  characterised by data flows, the reduction
  of the body to data, and the monitoring
  and sorting of everyone.

Mastheads:
  a publishing term that refers to the titles of
  newspapers and magazines as they appear
  across the front-page of the publication
  (and, increasingly, as the banner on the
  homepage of the publication's website).

Mean world syndrome:
  a phenomenon identified by Gerbner and
  colleagues (1976; 1996) as part of their
  cultivation theory analysis wherein heavier
  television viewers were more likely to see
  the world as a mean and dangerous place,
  and to experience an increased fear of crime
  and victimisation, as well as perceptions
  of mistrust, than individuals who watched
  lesser amounts of television.

Media criminology:

the theoretically and experientially informed analysis of the constantly shifting intersections and relationship between crime, criminality and criminal justice, on the one hand, and mediated representation and media framing on the other.

Media effects:

a theory of (mostly negative) media influence which assumes that mediated representations can inspire certain perceptions and preoccupations among media audiences, thus leading public opinion and the emergence of certain behaviours.

Media framing:

how media practitioners (both of a professional or amateur orientation) 'package' information for interpretation and how that information is represented and portrayed. Media framing includes the selection and rejection of information in the construction of a media text by placing emphasis on a particular angle or aspect of the story.

Media literacy:

the development of an understanding of how media is organised; how meanings are produced and contested; the basic conventions of various media genres, texts and industries; an ability to be responsive to changes in the media environment; and to read, analyse, evaluate, create and communicate in and through media.

Media releases:

documents written by *public relations* practitioners in a journalistic style to provide a story intended for use by mainstream media.

Media templates:

serve as a 'rhetorical shorthand' for the narrativisation of similar future events in that they allow media audiences to 'call to mind' the familiar and sometimes iconic media frames of past events.

Mediascape:

constituted by all of the institutionalised forms of media that we use and create to communicate; the global cultural flows of information and images that connect us and shape our understandings of the world; and the virtual spaces or environments we inhabit. The mediascape encompasses everything from traditional newspapers and broadcast media to evolving forms of digital technologies and social media.

Mediated:

refers to the tension between the 'real' world and the world as it is perceived or understood via media—that is, *mediated experience* or *mediated visibility*. In this equation, media functions as a system, social process or 'lens' through which particular messages are communicated.

Mediated experience:

the comparative experience that an individual has when they experience an event via the media versus actually personally experiencing it.

Mediated visibility:

a concept that suggests a transformation in the relations between visibility and power, whereby the pervasiveness of media and digital technologies has increased the public's ability to 'see' and scrutinise the actions of elites (e.g. police).

Miscarriages of justice:

primarily defined by the conviction and punishment of a person for a crime they did not commit or by a wrongful conviction reached in an unfair or disputed trial.

Moral panics:

occur when moral outrage is created as a consequence of the mainstream media labelling certain groups (*folk devils*) or activities as deviant and a threat to the social and moral order. A sensationalised image of crime is constructed along with a protective view of police and policing practices—making unusual events usual events in people's lives.

Neoliberalism:
a political philosophy that supports the enhancement of the private sector in contemporary society through economic liberalist measures, including freeing up trade, opening markets, privatisation and deregulation.

News embargo:
a request by a news source that the information provided by them not be published or broadcast until a specific time and date or until certain conditions have been met. The information contained in *media releases* will often be subject to a news embargo.

News sources:
a person, publication or document that provides timely information to a journalist for a news story. Sources lend credibility and legitimacy to news journalism, since they provide the supporting evidence that serves as the basis of a news story as well as validates its factuality. News sources can include spokespeople or contacts within organisations, official records or even the witnesses to a crime.

News values:
the criteria of relevance in the routine practices of journalism that enable news media professionals to determine which stories are 'newsworthy' and which are not, as well as which stories are major 'lead' stories and which are relatively insignificant.

Newsbeats:
where journalists are charged with the responsibility of reporting exclusively and in-depth on specialised topics, like crime and courts, and rely heavily on their contacts to do so. Also commonly referred to as 'news rounds'.

Newsworthiness:
when an issue or event is interesting enough to the public to warrant its reporting or coverage by news media.

Open justice:
a principle that assumes an accountable, impartial and well-functioning judicial system should be transparent and open to public scrutiny (via media access to courtrooms and their reporting on trials), thereby engendering confidence in the courts.

'Other':
refers to individuals who are labelled as being outside of the self (i.e. they are the not-self; separate to the rest of 'us') as a consequence of learned differences and the norms against which others are perceived and judged. Otherness is frequently used to criminalise and demonise those who differ in background, appearance and/or religious belief.

Panopticon:
architectural design (primarily for a prison) conceived by English philosopher and social theorist Jeremy Bentham in the eighteenth century. Based on the concept that an observer (the few) is able to watch all prisoners (the many) without the prisoners being able to determine whether they are being watched. The effect is an inclination on the part of the inmates to act as though they are *always* being surveilled.

Particularism:

the drafting of offences where the particular wording of offences provides the definitional detail that exemplifies rather than delimits the wrongdoing. The result is that new specific offences are created (such as 'rock throwing') that could have been covered underneath a general overarching principal offence (such as 'assault'). Often arises out of *moral panics*.

Police media units:

also sometimes referred to as police public relations branches. Communications staff offer a media advisory service to police and journalists, responding to media inquiries and informing the public about crime-related incidents.

Police procedurals:

a crime subgenre (traditionally associated with detective fiction, but also including crime television dramas) which attempts to convincingly depict the everyday activities and investigatory procedures of police.

Primary definers:

individuals in powerful and privileged institutional positions who, because of their professional authority and their general willingness and availability to talk to media, are repeatedly consulted as preferred news sources by journalists (e.g. police).

Primary victims:

those who are subject to or feel the direct impacts of a crime.

Probative value:

when evidence is sufficiently useful to prove something important in a trial.

Procedural justice:

concerns the fairness and transparency of the processes by which decisions are made, particularly in the administration of justice and legal proceedings.

Pro-social modelling:

a therapeutic intervention technique and behaviour modification strategy used primarily in the criminal detention, probation and education fields. The purpose is to transform client behaviours by demonstrating and reinforcing positive social behaviours such as cooperating, sharing and helping others.

Public health model of reporting:

advocated by Coleman and Thorson (2002), this is an approach that sees the causes of death and injury as preventable rather than inevitable. By studying the interaction among victims, the agent and the environment, the public health approach seeks to define risk factors, then develop and evaluate methods to prevent problems that threaten public health.

Public interest:

in journalistic terms, the 'public interest' involves any matters that are capable of affecting the public so that they might be interested in or concerned about what is going on, or what might happen to them or to others.

Public relations (PR):

the deliberate, planned and sustained effort to establish and maintain communication, mutual understanding and relationships between individuals, groups or organisations and their key stakeholders, including media and publics.

Ransomware:

a type of malicious software used to block access to a computer system until a sum of money is paid. More advanced versions encrypt the victim's files, making them inaccessible, until a ransom payment is made to decrypt them.

Recidivism:

repeat offending, which can involve repeating the same offences (e.g. drug dealing), an escalation in the type of offence (say, from graffiti to robbery) and an increase in the number of offences.

Reflexivity:

the ability to critically reflect on one's position (including contextual influences and potential biases and shortcomings) in relation to the creation of one's work.

Responsibilisation:

the shift in the burden of responsibility for crime and safety matters from the state to individuals, families and communities.

Restorative justice:

An approach to dealing with offenders that emphasises repairing harm, and involving victims and communities as well as offenders in the reparation process. Restorative justice offers hope that opportunities will be enhanced for victims, offenders and their immediate communities.

Ride-along:

an arrangement for a civilian to spend a shift in the passenger seat of an emergency vehicle to observe the work day of a police officer, firefighter or paramedic.

Risk society:

the manner in which contemporary society organises itself in relation to risk; it is a society increasingly preoccupied with the future and with safety.

Role strain:

refers to the difficulties individuals feel when attempting to meet excessive obligations or multiple demands on time, energy or available resources within the one role.

Saliency of information:

in the context of media framing, this relates to the information that is considered most important and is subsequently foregrounded within media texts.

Secondary victims:

individuals other than *primary victims* who are witnesses to or impacted by crime. They can include first responders, family members, friends, bystanders, neighbours, whole communities and even media practitioners, who can suffer tangible losses and/or intangible harms, including trauma, as a result of a crime.

Selfie:

a photograph that one takes of oneself, typically with a digital camera or a camera-enabled smartphone, often for the purposes of sharing the image via social media.

Signal crimes:

crimes that impact on broader publics (beyond those individuals involved in the incident—for example, victims, witnesses, offenders, emergency responders and those known to them) as a result of their mediatisation, and can animate potentially positive social reactions to and debates about risk and vulnerability as well as other wider systemic issues that require a corrective response.

Social constructivist approach:

the recognition that media does not present reality, but a version of reality, and that law and order problems are bounded by what humans determine to be important or significant (i.e. they are socially constructed).

Social sorting:

a process that uses information about people to sort them into categories for differential treatment.

Soft news:

news that is generally concerned with background information and human interest stories. This type of news does not have a high priority in the news values scale and encompasses such fields as entertainment, sport, lifestyle, celebrity and the arts. Soft news stories tend to entertain or advise their media audiences. In this way, they are often distinguished from *hard news* stories.

Sousveillance:

describes a situation whereby ordinary citizens are able to turn the camera back on institutional power to allow those conventionally perceived to be 'the watchers' to become 'the watched'. Loosely translates as 'to watch from below'.

Stigmatisation:

the application of a negative label that becomes the 'master' (or dominant) definition of the person to whom it is applied. The negative label can colour the perceptions of people with whom the individual interacts and influence how the community in general treats that person.

Suite crime:

a crime committed by a person of respectability and high social status in the course of their occupation; also known as 'white collar crime'.

Super injunctions:

distinct from *suppression orders*, these relate to restrictions on not only the reporting of certain details from the trial, but also the existence of the injunction itself. A breach can result in financial penalties, charges of *contempt of court*, or even imprisonment.

Suppression orders:

restrictions on the publication of certain details, including the reporting of names, from civil and criminal trials. Suppression orders may relate to the more sensitive elements of a case or they can apply to the case as a whole.

Surveillant assemblage:

a concept that sees the body reduced to a series of discrete informational flows, which are stabilised, captured and reassembled according to pre-established classificatory criteria to become our 'data double', which can then be scrutinised and targeted for routine surveillance and intervention.

Synopticism:

describes a situation where the many observe the few (as opposed to the principles of the *panopticon* where the inverse is true). Facilitated by the enhanced features of surveillance, which have helped to foster a culture of celebrity, where fame and notoriety—the ability to see and be seen—have become valuable commodities in their own right.

Tabloidisation:

the transformation of news into a more popularised, lurid and easily absorbed form, often featuring photographs accompanied by sensational news delivered in an informal style.

Trace evidence:

created when objects make contact with one another. Fibres, hair, soil, wood, gunshot residue and pollen are only a few examples of trace evidence that may be transferred between people, objects or the environment during a crime.

Trial by media:

characterises crime cases in which a person is found guilty in the court of public opinion without any of the safeguards guaranteeing a fair hearing in a court of law.

Trolling:

the practice of deliberately setting out to upset and provoke a response from others online—often for fun. The interest for internet trolls is in watching people's reactions. One of the most common forms of trolling is the posting of offensive comments in response to another's online post or article.

Typification:

the process of defining situations in ways that allow for mutual communication, as well as defining what is 'normal' and 'abnormal'. How people typify one another (e.g. 'mentally ill'), and how people relate to one another on the basis of these typifications, have major social consequences.

User-generated content:

the results of when ordinary citizens actively contribute to the production of media content in any form. Commonly includes blogs, podcasts, photographs and other digital images, video and audio files, advertisements, posts, chats and tweets.

Uses and gratifications:

an approach to audience studies, which turned traditional ways of thinking about *media effects* on its head by asking not what media do to people, but what people do to and with media.

Victim rights:

provisions (sometimes enshrined in legislation) which require that victims of crime have certain information, protections and involvement in the criminal justice process.

Victimology:

a key area of concern within criminology that focuses on societal conceptualisations of the 'victim'; victimisation profiles and risk distribution for various categories of crime; the impacts and fears of victims over time; causative theories on victimisation; and the relationship between victims and offenders.

Vulnerability:

refers to offenders, victims and communities that suffer from some sort of harm, risk, disability or disadvantage that places them in jeopardy in terms of economic, social, cultural and political life.

Vulnerable people policing:

a distinct approach to managing diversity within law enforcement organisations that recognises the pervasive nature of *vulnerability* in the criminal justice system (both in terms of vulnerability-related incidents and vulnerable people), and normalises it within policing practices.

Will-to-representation:

the proliferation of acts of mediated self-representation and performance by ordinary citizens, brought about by innovations in digital technologies, for sharing with others via electronic means (e.g. over the internet). Examples include individuals staging criminal exploits for the camera, which are then uploaded and disseminated online (e.g. *happy slapping*).

REFERENCES

AAP. (2012). Thousands March to Honour Jill Meagher. *The Age*, 30 September. <www.theage.com.au/victoria/thousands-march-to-honour-jill-meagher-20120930-26t6v.html>. Accessed 20 January 2015.

ABC TV. (2008). Media Hunt a Monster. *Media Watch* [Transcript], 14 July. <www.abc.net.au/mediawatch/transcripts/s2303501.htm>. Accessed 19 May 2016.

ABC TV. (2009). Facing Dennis Ferguson. *Four Corners*, 2 November. <www.abc.net.au/4corners/special_eds/20091102/offender>. Accessed 19 May 2016.

ACMA. (2007). *Investigation Report No. 1485: Breakfast with Alan Jones*. Broadcast by 2GB on 5, 6, 7, 8 and 9 December 2005. <www.acma.gov.au/webwr/_assets/main/lib101068/2gb%20-%20report%201485.pdf>. Accessed 19 January 2015.

Akerman, P. (2012). Social Media Could Impact Jury Trial of Jill Meagher's Alleged Killer Adrian Ernest Bayley. *The Australian*, 1 October. <www.theaustralian.com.au/news/social-media-could-impact-jury-trial-of-jill-meaghers-alleged-killer-adrian-ernest-bayley/story-e6frg6n6-1226485743514>. Accessed 20 January 2015.

Albury, K. & Crawford, K. (2012). Sexting, Consent And Young People's Ethics: Beyond Megan's Story. *Continuum*, 26(3), 463–73.

Allard, T. (2016). Locked Up for Life. *The Sydney Morning Herald*. <www.smh.com.au/interactive/2016/locked-up-for-life>. Accessed 2 August 2016.

Altheide, D. L. (1997). *Creating Fear: News and the Construction of Crisis*. New York: Aldine De Gruyter.

Altheide, D. L. (2013). Media Logic, Social Control, and Fear. *Communication Theory*, 23(3), 223–38.

Altheide, D. & Coyle, M. (2006). Smart on Crime: The New Language for Prisoner Release. *Crime Media Culture*, 2(3), 286–303.

Andersen, B. (2009). Facebook's Arson Vigilantes Could Face Prosecution. *ABC Local*, 16 February. <www.abc.net.au/news/stories/2009/02/16/2492984.htm?site=victoria>. Accessed 24 February 2015.

Anderson, J. & McAtamney, A. (2011). Considering Local Context When Evaluating a Closed Circuit Television System in Public Spaces. *Trends & Issues in Crime and Criminal Justice (No. 430)*. Canberra, ACT: Australian Institute of Criminology.

APC. (2014). *Adjudication No. 1594: Nicole Lamb/news.com.au (March 2014)*. <www.presscouncil.org.au/document-search/adj-1594>. Accessed 19 May 2016.

Appadurai, A. (1990). Disjuncture and Difference in the Global Cultural Economy. *Public Culture*, 2(2), 1–24.

Armstrong, S. (2014). Make Surveillance Work for the People: Let Them Spy Back. *The Conversation*, 8 January. <https://theconversation.com/make-surveillance-work-for-the-people-let-them-spy-back-21634>. Accessed 8 June 2016.

Armstrong, C. L., Hull, K. & Saunders, L. (2016). Victimized on Plain Sites. *Digital Journalism*, 4(2), 247–65.

Ashtari, S. (2013). 11 Amazing Prison Stories from 2013. *The Huffington Post*, 31 December. <www.huffingtonpost.com/2013/12/31/prisons-2013_n_4505165.html>. Accessed 24 March 2014.

Asquith, N. (2008). Race Riots on the Beach: A Case for Criminalising Hate Speech? Papers from the British Criminology Conference, vol. 8: 50–64. British Society of Criminology.

Asquith, N. & Poynting, S. (2011). Anti-Cosmopolitanism and 'Ethnic Cleansing' at Cronulla. In K. Jacobs & J. Malpas (eds), *Ocean to Outback: Cosmopolitanism in Contemporary Australia*. Perth: UWA Publishing.

Athanasiou, T. (1996). *Divided Planet: The Ecology of Rich and Poor*. Boston: Little, Brown and Company.

'Attacked'. (2012). *Our Crime*. Episode 4. BBC3, 26 April.

Attorney-General's Department. (2014). *$50 million to Tackle Crime: Budget 2014–15*. [Media Release]. 13 May. <www.ag.gov.au/Publications/Budgets/Budget2014-15/Pages/50-million-to-tackle-crime.aspx>. Accessed 14 June 2016.

Australian Government. (2013). *National Plan to Combat Cybercrime*. Barton, ACT: Business and Information Law Branch, Attorney-General's Department. <www.ag.gov.au/CrimeAndCorruption/Cybercrime/Documents/national-plan-to-combat-cybercrime.pdf>. Accessed 2 June 2016.

Australian Government. (2015). *Stay Smart Online: Small Business Guide*. Canberra, ACT: Department of Communications and the Arts. <www.communications.gov.au/sites/g/files/net301/f/SSO%20Small%20Business%20Guide.pdf>. Accessed 2 June 2016.

Australian Human Rights Commission. (2015). *Deaths from Family and Domestic Violence*. <www.humanrights.gov.au/our-work/family-and-domestic-violence/projects/deaths-family-and-domestic-violence>. Accessed 27 January 2016.

Australian Institute of Criminology. (2015). *Homicide in Australia, 2010–11 and 2011–12: National Homicide Monitoring Report*. Canberra, ACT: Australian Institute of Criminology. <www.aic.gov.au/publications/current%20series/mr/21-40/mr23.html>. Accessed 30 January 2016.

Australian Institute of Health and Welfare (AIHW). (2012). *Children and Young People at Risk of Serial Exclusion: Links Between Homelessness, Child Protection and Juvenile Justice*. Data linkage series no. 13. Cat. no. CSI 13. Canberra: AIHW.

Australian Institute of Health and Welfare (AIHW). (2014a). *Youth Justice in Australia 2012–13*. AIHW Bulletin 120. Cat. no. AUS179. Canberra: AIHW.

Australian Institute of Health and Welfare (AIHW). (2014b). *Youth Justice Fact Sheet No. 27. Long-term Trends in Youth Justice Supervision: 2012–13*. Cat. no. JUV43. Canberra: AIHW.

Australian Institute of Health and Welfare (AIHW). (2014c). *Youth Justice Fact Sheet No. 32. Remoteness Area and Socioeconomic Status: 2012–13*. Cat. no. JUV48. Canberra: AIHW.

Bagli, C. V. & Yee, V. (2015). Robert Durst of HBO's 'The Jinx' Says He 'Killed Them All'. *The New York Times*, 15 March. <www.nytimes.com/2015/03/16/nyregion/robert-durst-subject-of-hbo-documentary-on-unsolved-killings-is-arrested.html?_r=0>. Accessed 14 January 2016.

Bakan, J. (2004). *The Corporation: The Pathological Pursuit of Profit and Power*. London: Constable.

Ball, J. (2013). Xbox Live among Game Services Targeted by US and UK Spy Agencies. *The Guardian*, 10 December. <www.theguardian.com/world/2013/dec/09/nsa-spies-online-games-world-warcraft-second-life>. Accessed 4 June 2016.

Balthaser, J. (2015). 'Hot Convict' Jeremy Meeks Plans His Modeling Future from Prison. *ABC News*, 27 February. <http://abcnews.go.com/US/hot-convict-jeremy-meeks-plans-modeling-future-prison/story?id=29270589>. Accessed 1 October 2015.

Banks, D. (2010). Tweeting in Court: Why Reporters Must Be Given Guidelines. *The Guardian*, 16 December. <www.theguardian.com/law/2010/dec/15/tweeting-court-reporters-julian-assange>. Accessed 20 December 2015.

Banks-Anderson, L. (2016). The 'Making a Murderer' Effect. *Pursuit*, 16 March. <https://pursuit.unimelb.edu.au/articles/editing-the-making-a-murderer-effect>. Accessed 10 May 2016.

Barak, G. (1988). Newsmaking Criminology: Reflections on the Media, Intellectuals, and Crime. *Justice Quarterly*, 5(4), 565–87.

Barak, G. (2007). Doing Newsmaking Criminology from within the Academy. *Theoretical Criminology*, 11(2), 191–207.

Barak, G. (2011). Media, Society, and Criminology. In G. Barak (ed.), *Media, Process, and the Social Construction of Crime: Studies in Newsmaking Criminology*. New York and London: Routledge, pp. 3–45.

Barber, S. R. (1985). Televised Trials: Weighing Advantages against Disadvantages. *The Justice System Journal*, 10(3), 279–91.

Barden, D. (2016). How Making a Murderer Will Change the Way We Think about Justice. *The Huffington Post*, 31 March. <www.huffingtonpost.com.au/2016/03/30/making-murderer-effect_n_9579150.html>. Accessed 10 May 2016.

Baresch, B., Hsu, S. H. & Reese, S. D. (2012). The Power of Framing: New Challenges for Researching the Structure of Meaning in News. In S. Allan (ed.), *The Routledge Companion to News and Journalism* (revised edition). London: Routledge, pp. 637–47.

Barnard-Wills, D. (2011). UK News Media Discourses of Surveillance. *The Sociological Quarterly*, 52(4), 548–67.

Barnard-Wills, D. (2012). *Surveillance and Identity: Discourse, Subjectivity and the State*. Surrey, UK and Burlington, VT: Ashgate.

Bartels, L. & Lee, J. (2013). Jurors Using Social Media in Our Courts: Challenges and Responses. *Journal of Judicial Administration*, 23(1), 35–57.

Bartkowiak-Théron, I. & Asquith, N. (eds) (2012). *Policing Vulnerability*. Annandale, NSW: Federation Press.

Baskin, D. R. & Sommers, I. B. (2010). Crime-Show-Viewing Habits and Public Attitudes toward Forensic Evidence: The 'CSI Effect' Revisited. *Justice System Journal*, 31(1), 97–113.

Batsas, M. (2010). Interview with Justice Betty King. *Young Lawyers Journal*, 44, 10–11.

Bauman, Z. & Lyon, D. (2013). *Liquid Surveillance: A Conversation*. Cambridge: Polity.

Beck, U. (1992). *Risk Society: Towards a New Modernity*. London: Sage.

Becker, H. S. (1963). *Outsiders: Studies in the Sociology of Deviance*. New York: The Free Press.

Becker, H. S. (1967). Whose Side Are We On? *Social Problems*, 14(3), 239–47.

Beder, S. (1997). *Global Spin: The Corporate Assault on Environmentalism*. Melbourne: Scribe Publications.

Beder, S. (2004). Moulding and Manipulating the News. In R. White (ed.), *Controversies in Environmental Sociology*. Melbourne: Cambridge University Press, pp. 204–20.

Berliri, M. & Colonna, M. (2013). Italy: Court of Milan Overturns 2010 Convictions of Google Executives Over Bullying Video. *Hogan Lovells Global Media and Communications Watch*, 13 March. <www.hlmediacomms.com/2013/03/13/italy-court-of-milan-overturns-2010-convictions-of-google-executives-over-bullying-video>. Accessed 2 June 2016.

Bernard, T. & Kurlychek, M. (2010). *The Cycle of Juvenile Justice* (2nd edition). New York: Oxford University Press.

Best, J. & Furedi, F. (2001). The Evolution of Road Rage in Britain and the United States. In J. Best (ed.), *How Claims Spread: Cross-National Diffusion of Social Problems*. New York: Aldine De Gruyter, pp. 107–27.

Biber, K. (2006). Photographs and Labels: Against a Criminology of Innocence. *Law Text Culture*, 10(1), 19–40.

Biber, K. (2014). Inside Jill Meagher's Handbag: Looking at Open Justice. *Alternative Law Journal*, 39(2), 73–7.

Black, S. (2009). The Media on Dennis Ferguson. *Crikey*, 18 September. <www.crikey.com.au/2009/09/18/and-the-wankley-goes-to-the-media-on-dennis-ferguson>. Accessed 18 May 2016.

Blacker, T. (2009). Reality TV Police Shows are Criminal. *The Independent*, 10 November. <www.independent.co.uk/voices/commentators/terence-blacker/terence-blacker-reality-tv-police-shows-are-criminal-1817749.html>. Accessed 4 January 2016.

Blood, W. & Holland, K. (2004). Risky News, Madness and Public Crisis: A Case Study of the Reporting and Portrayal of Mental Health and Illness in the Australian Press. *Journalism*, 5(3), 323–42.

Bloustien, G. & Israel, M. (2003). Real Crime and the Media. In A. Goldsmith, M. Israel & K. Daly (eds), *Crime and Justice: An Australian Textbook in Criminology*. Sydney: Law Book Co., pp. 39–60.

Bloustien, G. & Israel, M. (2006). Crime and the Media. In A. Goldsmith, M. Israel & K. Daly (eds), *Crime and Justice: A Guide to Criminology*. Sydney: Lawbook Co., pp. 45–63.

Bonn, S. (2010). *Mass Deception: Moral Panic and the U.S. War on Iraq*. New Brunswick: Rutgers University Press.

Box, S. (1983). *Power, Crime and Mystification*. London: Tavistock.

Brennan Center for Justice. (2016). *Police Body Camera Policies: Accountability*, 5 February. New York University School of Law. <www.brennancenter.org/analysis/police-body-camera-policies-accountability>. Accessed 14 June 2016.

Brenner, S. W. (2011). Cybercrime: Re-thinking Crime Control Strategies. In Y. Jewkes (ed.), *Crime Online*, London and New York: Routledge, pp. 12–28.

Brisman, A. (2012). The Cultural Silence of Climate Change Contrarianism. In R. White (ed.), *Climate Change from a Criminological Perspective*. New York: Springer, pp. 41–70.

Brisman, A. & South, N. (2014). *Green Cultural Criminology: Constructions of Environmental Harm, Consumerism, and Resistance to Ecocide*. London: Routledge.

British Broadcasting Corporation (BBC). (2016a). *Crime: Guidance in Full—Editorial Guidelines*. <www.bbc.co.uk/editorialguidelines/guidance/crime/guidance-full>. Accessed 11 November 2016.

British Broadcasting Corporation (BBC). (2016b). *Crime: Summary—Editorial Guidelines*. <www.bbc.co.uk/editorialguidelines/guidance/crime>. Accessed 11 November 2016.

Brody, R. (2005). The Road to Abu Ghraib: Torture and Impunity in U.S. Detention. In K. Roth, M. Worden & A. Bernstein (eds), *Torture: A Human Rights Perspective*. New York: Human Rights Watch, pp. 145–54.

Brown, G. R. (2016). The Blue Line on Thin Ice: Police Use of Force Modifications in the Era of Cameraphones and *YouTube*. *British Journal of Criminology*, 56(2), 293–312.

Browne, S. (2015). *Dark Matters: On the Surveillance of Blackness*. Durham, NC: Duke University Press.

Brunton, N. (1999). Environmental Regulation: The Challenge Ahead. *Alternative Law Journal*, 24(3), 137–43.

Buist, C. & Leighton, P. (2015). Corporate Criminals Constructing White-Collar crime: Or Why There Is No Corporate Crime on the USA Network's *White Collar* series. In G. Barak (ed.), *The Routledge International Handbook of the Crimes of the Powerful*. New York: Routledge, pp. 73–85.

Bulkeley, H. & Newell, P. (2010). *Governing Climate Change*. London: Routledge.

Burnett, R. & Marshall, P. D. (2003). *Web Theory: An Introduction*. London: Routledge.

Butler, J. (2009). *Frames of War: When is Life Grievable?* New York: Verso.

Cable, J. (2015). *UK Public Opinion Review Working Paper—An Overview of Public Opinion Polls since the Edward Snowden Revelations in June 2013*. Cardiff, UK: Cardiff University. <https://sites.cardiff.ac.uk/dcssproject/files/2015/08/UK-Public-Opinion-Review-180615.pdf>. Accessed 13 June 2016.

Carlson, M. & Franklin, B. (eds). (2011). *Journalists, Sources and Credibility: New Perspectives*. London and New York: Routledge.

Carlton, B. (2007). *Imprisoning Resistance: Life and Death in an Australian Supermax*. Sydney: Institute of Criminology, University of Sydney.

Carr, R. (2014). Surveillance Politics and Local Government: A National Survey of Federal Funding for CCTV in Australia. *Security Journal*, DOI:10.1057/sj.2014.12.

Carr, R. (2016). Safety—or Profit? The Booming Business of CCTV and Safer Streets. *The Conversation*, 7 June. <http://theconversation.com/safety-or-profit-the-booming-business-of-cctv-and-safer-streets-59393>. Accessed 8 June 2016.

Carrabine, E., Iganski, P., Lee, M., Plummer, K. & South, N. (2004). *Criminology: A Sociological Introduction*. London: Routledge.

Carrington, K. (2013). Girls and Violence: The Case for a Feminist Theory of Female Violence. *International Journal for Crime, Justice and Social Democracy*, 2(2), 63–79.

Chagnon, N. (2015). Reverberate, Resonate, Reproduce: A Reconsideration of Ideological Influence in Crime News Production. *Critical Criminology*, 23(1), 105–23.

Chakraborti, N. & Garland, J. (2012). Reconceptualizing Hate Crime Victimization through the Lens of Vulnerability and Difference. *Theoretical Criminology*, 16(4), 499–514.

Chan, J. (1995). Systematically Distorted Communication? Criminological Knowledge, Media Representation and Public Policy. *Australian and New Zealand Journal of Criminology*, 28(1 suppl.), 23–30.

Chan, S., Khader, M., Ang, J., et al. (2012). Understanding 'Happy Slapping'. *International Journal of Police Science & Management*, 14(1), 42–57.

Cheliotis, L. (2010). The Ambivalent Consequences of Visibility: Crime and Prisons in the Mass Media. *Crime Media Culture*, 6(2), 169–84.

Chermak, S. (1995). Crime in the News Media: A Refined Understanding of How Crimes Become News. In G. Barak (ed.), *Media, Process, and the Social Construction of Crime: Studies in Newsmaking Criminology*. New York and London: Routledge, pp. 95–129.

Cherry, M. & Sneirson, J. (2012). Chevron, Greenwashing, and the Myth of 'Green Oil Companies'. *Washington & Lee Journal of Energy, Climate & Environment*, 3, 133–53.

Chibnall, C. (2015). Broadchurch Writer Chris Chibnall: 'I Stand By the Drama's Court Scenes'. *The Guardian*, 4 March. <www.theguardian.com/tv-and-radio/2015/mar/04/broadchurch-writer-chris-chibnall-i-stand-by-the-dramas-court-scenes>. Accessed 24 November 2015.

Chibnall, S. (1977). *Law-and-Order News: An Analysis of Crime Reporting in the British Press*. London and New York: Routledge.

Christie, N. (1986). The Ideal Victim. In E. A. Fattah (ed.), *From Crime Policy to Victim Policy: Reorienting the Justice System*. London: Palgrave Macmillan, pp. 17–30.

Chua-Eoan, H. (2010). WikiLeaks Founder Julian Assange Tells TIME: Hillary Clinton 'Should Resign'. *TIME*, 30 November. <http://content.time.com/time/nation/article/0,8599,2033771,00.html>. Accessed 3 June 2016.

Clarke, R. A. (1988). Information Technology and Dataveillance. *Communications of the ACM*, 31(5), 498–512.

Clifford, K. (2012). The Vulnerable Thin Blue Line: Representations of Police Use of Force in the Media. In I. Bartkowiak-Théron & N. L. Asquith (eds), *Policing Vulnerability*. Leichhardt: The Federation Press, pp. 101–14.

Clifford, K. (2013). Mental Health Crisis Interventions and the Politics of Police Use of Deadly Force. In D. Chappell (ed.), *Policing and the Mentally Ill: International Perspectives*. Boca Raton, FL: CRC Press, pp. 171–95.

Clifford, K. (2014a). Media and Violence. In B. Griffen-Foley (ed.), *A Companion to the Australian Media*. North Melbourne: Australian Scholarly Publishing, pp. 257–8.

Clifford, K. (2014b). Crime Reporting. In B. Griffen-Foley (ed.), *A Companion to the Australian Media*. North Melbourne: Australian Scholarly Publishing, pp. 125–6.

Clifford, K. (2014c). Amanda Knox: A Picture of Innocence. *Celebrity Studies*, 5(4), 504–7.

Clifford, K. (2016). SIAMO INNOCENTI: Twitter and the Performative Practices of the 'Real' Amanda Knox. In L. Gies & M. Bortoluzzi (eds), *Transmedia Crime Stories: The Trial of Amanda Knox and Raffaele Sollecito in the Globalised Media Sphere*. London: Palgrave, pp. 89–109.

Cloud, J. (2011). How the Casey Anthony Murder Case Became the Social-Media Trial of the Century. *TIME*, 16 June. <http://content.time.com/time/nation/article/0,8599,2077969,00.html>. Accessed 4 February 2014.

Clough, J. & Mulhern, C. (2002). *The Prosecution of Corporations*. Melbourne: Oxford University Press.

Coffey, H. (2014). Are Jack the Ripper Tours Blighting London? *The Telegraph*, 26 September. <www.telegraph.co.uk/travel/destinations/europe/uk/london/11123209/Are-Jack-the-Ripper-tours-blighting-London.html>. Accessed 16 January 2015.

Cohen, S. (1972). *Folk Devils and Moral Panics: The Creation of the Mods and Rockers*. London: MacGibbon and Kee Ltd.

Cohen, S. (1985). *Visions of Social Control*. Cambridge: Polity Press.

Cohen, S. (1993). Human Rights and Crimes of the State: The Culture of Denial. *Australian and New Zealand Journal of Criminology*, 26(2), 97–115.

Cohen, S. (2001). *States of Denial: Knowing About Atrocities and Suffering*. Cambridge: Polity.

Cohen, S. & Young, J. (1981). *The Manufacture of News: Social Problems, Deviance and the Mass Media* (revised edition). London: Sage.

Cohn, V. & Cope, L. (2012). *News & Numbers: A Writer's Guide to Statistics* (3rd edition). Malden, MA: Wiley-Blackwell.

Cole, S. A. & Dioso-Villa, R. (2007). *CSI* and Its Effects: Media, Juries, and the Burden of Proof. *New England Law Review*, 41(3), 435–70.

Cole, S. A. & Dioso-Villa, R. (2011). Should Judges Worry About the 'CSI Effect'?. *Court Review: The Journal of the American Judges Association*, 47(1–2), 20–31.

Coleman, R. & Sim, J. (2000). You'll Never Walk Alone: CCTV Surveillance, Order and Neo-Liberal Rule in Liverpool City Centre. *British Journal of Sociology*, 51(4), 623–39.

Coleman, R. & Thorson, E. (2002). The Effects of News Stories that Put Crime and Violence into Context: Testing the Public Health Model of Reporting. *Journal of Health Communication*, 7(2), 401–25.

Collins, S. (2015). CSI's 'Immortality' Finale Draws Highest Ratings in Nearly 4 Years. *Los Angeles Times*, 28 September. <www.latimes.com/entertainment/tv/showtracker/la-et-st-csi-finale-immortality-ratings-nielsen-20150928-story.html>. Accessed 4 March 2016.

Collins, J., Noble, G., Poynting, S. & Tabar, P. (2000). *Kebabs, Kids, Cops and Crime: Youth, Ethnicity and Crime*. Sydney: Pluto Press.

Commonwealth of Australia. (2016). *Australia's Cyber Security Strategy*. Canberra, ACT: Department of the Prime Minister and Cabinet. <https://cybersecuritystrategy.dpmc.gov.au/assets/pdfs/dpmc-cyber-strategy.pdf>. Retrieved 8 June 2016.

Conboy, M. (2011). Glimpses of Potential amidst the Devilish Detail: Assessing Research in Journalism Studies in the UK. *Australian Journalism Review*, 33(1), 45–7.

Conley, D. & Lamble, S. (2006). *The Daily Miracle: An Introduction to Journalism* (3rd edition). South Melbourne: Oxford University Press.

Cottle, S. (2000). Rethinking News Access. *Journalism Studies*, 1(3), 427–48.

Couldry, N. (2010). New Online News Sources and Writer-Gatherers. In N. Fenton (ed.), *New Media, Old News*. Los Angeles: Sage, pp. 138–52.

Couldry, N. (2011). *Why Voice Matters: Culture and Politics After Neoliberalism*. London: Sage.

Couldry, N. (2012). *Media, Society, World: Social Theory and Digital Media Practice*. Cambridge: Polity Press.

Cowdery, N. (2013). Thomas Kelly: This Was Never a Case of Murder. *The Sydney Morning Herald*, 10 November. <www.smh.com.au/comment/thomas-kelly-this-was-never-a-case-of-murder-20131109-2x99g.html>. Accessed 14 October 2016.

Critcher, C. (2009). Widening the Focus: Moral Panics as Moral Regulation. *British Journal of Criminology*, 49(1), 17–34.

Crofts, T., Lee, M., McGovern, A. & Milivojevic, S. (2014). Sexting and Young People. *Legaldate*, 26(4), 2–4.

Cross, C. (2016). Why the Victim can also Become the Offender in Online Fraud. *The Conversation*, 13 April. <http://theconversation.com/why-the-victim-can-also-become-the-offender-in-online-fraud-57560>. Accessed 15 May 2016.

Cunneen, C., Baldry, E., Brown, D., Brown, M., Schwartz, M. & Steel, A. (2013). *Penal Culture and Hyperincarceration: The Revival of the Prison*. Farnham, UK: Ashgate.

Cunneen, C., Fraser, D. & Tomsen, S. (1997). Introduction: Defining the Issues. In C. Cunneen, D. Fraser & S. Tomsen (eds), *Faces of Hate: Hate Crime in Australia*. Sydney: Hawkins Press, pp. 1–14.

Cunneen, C., White, R. & Richards, K. (2015). *Juvenile Justice: Youth and Crime in Australia*. Melbourne: Oxford University Press.

D'Angelo, P. (2002). News Framing as a Multiparadigmatic Research Program: A Response to Entman. *Journal of Communication*, 52(4), 870–88.

Dale, A. (2013). New Pictures Show Smouldering Beauty of Lisa Harnum as Simon Gittany Admits He was a 'Jealous Partner'. *The Daily Telegraph*, 11 November. <www.dailytelegraph.com.au/news/nsw/new-pictures-show-smouldering-beauty-of-lisa-harnum-as-simon-gittany-admits-he-was-a-jealous-partner/story-fni0cx12-1226756912341>. Accessed 25 January 2016.

Dart, T. (2015). Family of 17-Year-Old Killed By Police at Station Is 'Not Going to Stop Fighting'. *The Guardian*, 8 July. <www.theguardian.com/us-news/2015/jul/07/kristiana-coignard-killed-texas-police-station>. Accessed 8 June 2016.

Dart Centre Asia Pacific. (2014). *'Getting It Right': Teaching Notes to Accompany the DVD*. <http://dartcenter.org/files/Getting%20It%20Right_Teaching%20Notes_0.pdf>. Accessed 24 March 2014.

Davies, P. (2011). *Gender, Crime and Victimisation*. London: Sage.

de Burgh, H. (2003). Skills Are Not Enough: The Case for Journalism as an Academic Discipline. *Journalism*, 4(1), 95–112.

de Vreese, C. H. (2005). News Framing: Theory and Typology. *Information Design Journal + Document Design*, 13(1), 51–62.

de Zwart, M., Lindsay, D., Henderson, M. & Phillips, M. (2011). Randoms vs Weirdos: Teen Use of Social Networking Sites and Perceptions of Legal Risk. *Alternative Law Journal*, 36(3), 153–7.

Decker, S., van Gemert, F. & Pyrooz, D. (2009). Gangs, Migration, and Crime: The Changing Landscape in Europe and the USA. *International Migration & Integration*, 10, 393–408.

Devine, M. (2012). Thomas Kelly Is Everyone's Son—Time to Reclaim Our Streets. *The Daily Telegraph*, 11 July. <www.dailytelegraph.com.au/blogs/miranda-devine/thomas-kelly-is-everyones-son--time-to-reclaim-our-streets/news-story/5da74218ae8c516903c19981abb4a09d>. Accessed 14 October 2016.

Dick, T. (2011). Reality TV the New Frontline for Police. *The Sydney Morning Herald*, 9 September. <www.smh.com.au/business/media-and-marketing/reality-tv-the-new-frontline-for-police-20110908-1jzm7.html>. Accessed 23 May 2012.

Dioso-Villa, R. (2014). Is There Evidence of a 'CSI Effect'? In K. J. Strom & M. J. Hickman (eds), *Forensic Science and the Administration of Justice: Critical Issues and Directions*. Thousand Oaks, California: SAGE Publications, pp. 21–41.

Dockterman, E. (2015). How *The Jinx* and *Serial* Strain the Blurry Ethical Lines of Crime Reporting. *TIME*, 20 March. <http://time.com/3746792/jinx-serial-ethics>. Accessed 18 January 2016.

Dover, H. (2015). One Dimensional Muslims: Why Irresponsible Reporting is Making a Bad Situation Worse. ABC Religion and Ethics, 9 December. <www.abc.net.au/religion/articles/2015/12/09/4368958.htm>. Accessed 14 October 2016.

Dovey, J. (2001). Big Brother. In G. Creeber (ed.), *The Television Genre Book*. London: BFI Publishing, pp. 136–7.

Dowler, K. & Zawilski, V. (2007). Public Perceptions of Police Misconduct and Discrimination: Examining the Impact of Media Consumption. *Journal of Criminal Justice*, 35(2), 193–203.

Dowsley, A. & Healey, K. (2009). Werribee Sex DVD Ringleader's Hate-filled Rap Song on Web. *Herald Sun*, 13 April. <www.heraldsun.com.au/news/werribee-bully-failed-by-system/story-e6frf7jo-1225697193516>. Accessed 28 May 2016.

Dreher, T. (2003). Speaking Up and Talking Back: News Media Interventions in Sydney's 'Othered' Communities. *Media International Australia*, 109, 121–37.

Dreher, T. (2009). Listening Across Difference: Media and Multiculturalism Beyond the Politics of Voice. *Continuum*, 23(4), 445–58.

Durnal, E. W. (2010). Crime Scene Investigation (as Seen on TV). *Forensic Science International*, 199, 1–5.

Edmond, G. (2012). Advice for the Courts? Sufficiently Reliable Assistance with Forensic Science and Medicine (Part 2). *International Journal of Evidence & Proof*, 16(3), 263–97.

Edmond, G. & San Roque, M. (2012). The Cool Crucible: Forensic Science and the Frailty of the Criminal Trial. *Current Issues in Criminal Justice*, 24(1), 51–68.

Ellison, S. (2011). The Man Who Spilled the Secrets. *Vanity Fair*, February. <www.vanityfair.com/news/2011/02/the-guardian-201102>. Accessed 15 June 2016.

Entman, R. M. (1993). Framing: Toward Clarification of a Fractured Paradigm. *Journal of Communication*, 43(4), 51–8.

Ericson, R. V., Baranek, P. M. & Chan, J. B. L. (1989). *Negotiating Control: A Study of News Sources*. Milton Keynes: Open University Press.

Ericson, R. V., Baranek, P. M. & Chan, J. B. L. (1991). *Representing Order: Crime, Law, and Justice in the News Media*. Toronto: University of Toronto Press.

Esbensen, F-A., Winfree, Jr, L., He, N. & Taylor, T. (2001). Youth Gangs and Definitional Issues: When is a Gang a Gang, and Why Does It Matter? *Crime & Delinquency*, 47, 105–30.

Evans, R. (2014). Police Demand Notes from Channel 4 on Lawrence Spying Whistleblower. *The Guardian*, 14 January. <www.theguardian.com/uk-news/2014/jan/13/police-channel-4-stephen-lawrence-undercover-spying>. Accessed 12 June 2016.

Faruqi, S. (2015). Social Media Leads to Murder Arrest. *TPSNews*, 10 December. Canada: Toronto Police Service. <http://tpsnews.ca/stories/2015/12/social-media-leads-murder-arrest>. Accessed 11 December 2015.

Faubel, C. L. (2013–14). Cameras in the Courtroom 2.0: How Technology is Changing the Way Journalists Cover the Courts. *Reynolds Courts & Media Law Journal*, 3(1), 3–32.

Feigenson, N. & Spiesel, C. (2009). *Law on Display: The Digital Transformation of Legal Persuasion and Judgment*. New York and London: New York University Press.

Fernandez, C. (2008). Mr Average Breaks the Law at Least Once a Day from Speeding or Illegal Downloading. *The Daily Mail*, 22 September. <www.dailymail.co.uk/news/article-1059071/Mr-Average-breaks-law-day-speeding-illegal-downloading.html>. Accessed 19 January 2015.

Ferrell, J. (1995). Style Matters: Criminal Identity and Social Control. In J. Ferrell & C. R. Sanders (eds), *Cultural Criminology*. Boston: Northeastern University Press, pp. 169–89.

Ferrell, J. (1999). Cultural Criminology. *Annual Review of Sociology*, 25, 395–418.

Ferrell, J., Haywood, K. & Young, J. (2008). *Cultural Criminology: An Invitation*. Los Angeles: Sage Publications.

Ferrell, J., Milovanovic, D. & Lyng, S. (2001). Edgework, Media Practices and the Elongation of Meaning. *Theoretical Criminology*, 5(2), 177–202.

Ferrell, J. & Sanders, C. R. (eds). (1995). *Cultural Criminology*. Boston: Northeastern University Press.

Fiske, J. (1998). Surveilling the City: Whiteness, the Black Man and Democratic Totalitarianism. *Theory, Culture & Society*, 15(2), 67–88.

Fitri, N. (2011). Democracy Discourses through the Internet Communication: Understanding the Hacktivism for the Global Changing. *Online Journal of Communication and Media Technologies*, 1(2), 1–24.

Flanders, J. (2011). *The Invention of Murder: How the Victorians Revelled in Death and Detection and Created Modern Crime*. New York: Thomas Dunne Books.

Flynn, A., Halsey, M. & Lee, M. (2016). Emblematic Violence and Aetiological Cul-De-Sacs: On the Discourse of 'One-Punch' (Non) Fatalities. *British Journal of Criminology*, 56(1), 179–95.

Foley, M. & Lennon, J. J. (1996). JFK and Dark Tourism: A Fascination with Assassination. *International Journal of Heritage Studies*, 2(4), 198–211.

Ford, C. (2012). Working the Net: Crime and Social Media. *Law Institute Journal*, 86(10). <www.liv.asn.au/practice-resources/law-institute-journal/archived-issues/lij-october-2012/working-the-net--crime-and-social-media>. Accessed 5 November 2016.

Foucault, M. (1975/1991). *Discipline and Punish: The Birth of the Prison*. Trans. A. Sheridan. London: Penguin Books.

Freund, K. (2015). When Cameras are Rolling: Privacy Implications of Body-Mounted Cameras on Police. *Columbia Journal of Law & Social Problems*, 49(1), 91–133.

Friedrichs, D. (1996). *Trusted Criminals: White Collar Crime in Contemporary Society*. Belmont: Wadsworth.

Furedi, F. (2002). *Culture of Fear* (revised edition). London and New York: Continuum.

Gabler, N. (2001). This Time, the Scene was Real. *The New York Times*, 16 September. <www.nytimes.com/2001/09/16/weekinreview/this-time-the-scene-was-real.html>. Accessed 7 November 2016.

Gagliardone, I., Gal, D., Pinto, T. & Sainz, G. (2015). *Countering Online Hate Speech. UNESCO Series on Internet Freedom*. Paris: United Nations Educational, Scientific and Cultural Organization.

Gale, F. (ed.) (2011). *Pulp Friction in Tasmania: A Review of the Environmental Assessment of Gunn's Proposed Pulp Mill*. Launceston: Pencil Pine Press.

Galtung, J. & Ruge, M. H. (1965). The Structure of Foreign News. *Journal of Peace Research*, 2(1), 64–91.

Gamson, W. A. & Modigliani, A. (1989). Media Discourse and Public Opinion on Nuclear Power: A Constructionist Approach. *American Journal of Sociology*, 95(1), 1–37.

Gans, H. J. (1979). *Deciding What's News: A Study of CBS Evening News, NBC Nightly News, Newsweek, and Time*. New York: Pantheon Books.

Gans, J. & Mann, S. (2015). When the Camera Lies: Our Surveillance Society Needs a Dose of Integrity to be Reliable. *The Conversation*, 12 January. <http://theconversation.com/when-the-camera-lies-our-surveillance-society-needs-a-dose-of-integrity-to-be-reliable-35933>. Accessed 8 June 2016.

Garland, D. (2001). *The Culture of Control: Crime and Social Order in Contemporary Society*. Chicago: University of Chicago Press.

Garland, D. (2008). On the Concept of Moral Panic. *Crime Media Culture*, 4(1), 9–30.

Garland, J. (2011). Difficulties in Defining Hate Crime Victimization. *International Journal of Victimology*, 18(1), 25–37.

Garner, H. (2014). Mother Courage: At Home with Rosie Batty. *The Monthly*, October. <www.themonthly.com.au/issue/2014/october/1412085600/helen-garner/mother-courage>. Accessed 21 May 2016.

Geis, G. & DiMento, J. F. C. (2012). Extraordinary Rendition. In Beare, M. (ed.), *Encylopedia of Transnational Crime & Justice*. Los Angeles: Sage, pp. 136–9.

Genge, N. (2004). *The Forensic Casebook: The Science of Crime Scene Investigation*. London: Ebury Press.

Gerbner, G. & Gross, L. (1976). Living with Television: The Violence Profile. *Journal of Communication*, 26(2), 172–94.

Gerbner, G., Morgan, M., Signorielli, N. & Ozyegin, N. (1996). *Cultural Indicators: A Research Project on Trends in Television Content and Viewer Conceptions of Social Reality*. <http://web.asc.upenn.edu/gerbner/Asset.aspx?assetID=110>. Accessed 11 March 2016.

Gerrard, N. (2014). Move Over, Morse: Female TV Detectives are on the Case Now. *The Guardian*, 5 October. <www.theguardian.com/tv-and-radio/2014/oct/05/female-tv-detectives-move-over-morse>. Accessed 24 November 2015.

Gest, T. (2015). Getting Criminology to the Public in Today's New Media Age. *The Criminologist: The Official Newsletter of The American Society of Criminology*, 40(1), 1–7.

Gies, L. (2011). Stars Behaving Badly: Inequality and Transgression in Celebrity Culture. *Feminist Media Studies*, 11(3), 347–61.

Gies, L. (2016). 'My Name Is Raffaele Sollecito and Not Amanda Marie Knox': Marginalisation and Media Justice. In L. Gies & M. Bortoluzzi (eds), *Transmedia Crime Stories: The Trial of Amanda Knox and Raffaele Sollecito in the Globalised Media Sphere*. London: Palgrave, pp. 211–30.

Gies, L. & Bortoluzzi, M. (eds) (2016). *Transmedia Crime Stories: The Trial of Amanda Knox and Raffaele Sollecito in the Globalised Media Sphere*. London: Palgrave.

Glasbeek, H. (2003). The Invisible Friend. *New Internationalist*, Issue 358, 1 July. <https://newint.org/features/2003/07/01/legal-fiction>. Accessed 5 September 2016.

Glasbeek, H. (2004). *Wealth by Stealth: Corporate Crime, Corporate Law, and the Perversion of Democracy*. Toronto: Between the Lines.

Goffman, I. (1963). *Stigma: Notes on the Management of Spoiled Identity*. Englewood Cliffs: Prentice Hall.

Goggin, G. (2010). Official and Unofficial Mobile Media in Australia: Youth, Panics, Innovation. In S. H. Donald, T. D. Anderson & D. Spry (eds), *Youth, Society and Mobile Media in Asia*. London and New York: Routledge, pp. 120–34.

Goldsmith, A. (2015). Disgracebook Policing: Social Media and the Rise of Police Indiscretion. *Policing & Society*, 25(3), 249–67.

Goldsmith, A. & Brewer, R. (2015). Digital Drift and the Criminal Interaction Order. *Theoretical Criminology*, 19(1), 112–30.

Goldson, B. (ed.) (2011). *Youth in Crisis? 'Gangs,' Territoriality and Violence*. London: Routledge.

Goldson, B. (2014). Youth Justice in a Changing Europe: Crisis Conditions and Alternative Visions. In Council of Europe and the European Commission (ed.), *Perspectives on Youth: 2020 What Do You See?*. Strasbourg: Council of Europe Publishing, pp. 39–52. <http://pjp-eu.coe.int/documents/1017981/7110731/PoY1-full.pdf/0da8d1d9-2886-4f13-a42b-ad5ad4ff6e69>. Accessed 14 October 2016.

Goode, E. & Ben-Yehuda, N. (1994). *Moral Panics: The Social Construction of Deviance*. Oxford: Blackwell.

Goodey, J. (2005). *Victims and Victimology: Research, Policy and Practice*. London: Pearson Longman.

Goodman, P. & Dawe, M. (2016). Prisoners, Cows and Abattoirs: The Closing of Canada's Prison Farms as a Political Penal Drama. *British Journal of Criminology*, 56(4), 793–812.

Goodman-Delahunty, J. & Hewson, L. (2010). *Enhancing Fairness in DNA Jury Trials*. Canberra, ACT: Australian Institute of Criminology. <www.aic.gov.au/media_library/publications/tandi_pdf/tandi392.pdf>. Accessed 20 April 2016.

Goodman-Delahunty, J., Rossner, M. & Tait, D. (2010). Simulation and Dissimulation in Jury Research: Credibility in a Live Mock Trial. In L. Bartels & K. Richards (eds), *Qualitative Criminology: Stories from the field*. Leichhardt, NSW: Hawkins Press, pp. 34–44.

Goodman-Delahunty, J. & Wakabayashi, K. (2012). Adversarial Forensic Science Experts: An Empirical Study of Jury Deliberation. *Current Issues in Criminal Justice*, 24(1), 85–103.

Goodyear, S. (2010). A Shopping Center Tries to Repel Teens with the Buzz of a Powerful Mosquito. *grist*, 11 September. <http://grist.org/article/2010-09-10-a-shopping-center-in-washington-d-c-tries-to-repel-teens-with-a>. Accessed 14 October 2016.

Goold, B. J. (2003). Public Area Surveillance and Police Work: The Impact of CCTV on Police Behaviour and Autonomy. *Surveillance & Society*, 1(2), 191–203.

Graber, D. (1980). *Crime News and the Public*. New York: Praeger.

Grabosky, P. (1989). *Wayward Governance: Illegality and Its Control in the Public Sector*. Canberra, ACT: Australian Institute of Criminology. <www.aic.gov.au/publications/previous%20series/lcj/1-20/wayward.html>. Accessed 5 September 2016.

Grabosky, P. (2016). *Cybercrime*. New York and Oxford: Oxford University Press.

Grabosky, P. & Wilson, P. (1989). *Journalism & Justice: How Crime is Reported.* Leichhardt: Pluto Press.

Graham, C. (2016). Cole Miller and Trevor Duroux: Some One-Punch Deaths are Good for Media Business, Some Not-So-Much. *The Insider—The Official New Matilda Blog,* 5 January. <https://newmatilda.com/2016/01/05/cole-miller-and-trevor-duroux-some-one-punch-deaths-are-good-for-media-business-some-not-so-much>. Accessed 14 October 2016.

Graham, H. & White, R. (2015). *Innovative Justice.* Abingdon: Routledge.

Graham, K. & Homel, R. (2008). *Raising the Bar: Preventing Aggression In and Around Bars, Pubs and Clubs.* Devon: Willan Publishing.

Grealy, L. (2014). Menacing Dennis: Representing 'Australia's Most Hated Man' and Popular Protests for Policy Change. *Crime Media Culture,* 10(1), 39–57.

Greek, C. E. (1995). Becoming a Media Criminologist: Is 'Newsmaking Criminology' Possible? In G. Barak (ed.), *Media, Process, and the Social Construction of Crime: Studies in Newsmaking Criminology.* New York and London: Routledge, pp. 265–85.

Green, D. A. (2008). *When Children Kill Children: Penal Populism and Political Culture.* Oxford: Oxford University Press.

Green, S. (2007). Crime, Victimisation and Vulnerability. In S. Walklate (ed.), *Handbook of Victims and Victimology.* Devon: Willan Publishing, pp. 91–117.

Green, P. J. & Ward, T. (2000). State Crime, Human Rights, and the Limits of Criminology. *Social Justice,* 27(1), 101–15.

Green, P. & Ward, T. (2004). *State Crime: Governments, Violence and Corruption.* London: Pluto Press.

Greenberg, A. (2014). Hacker Lexicon: What Is the Dark Web? *Wired,* 19 November. <www.wired.com/2014/11/hacker-lexicon-whats-dark-web>. Accessed 14 June 2016.

Greenslade, R. (2011). 'Foxy Knoxy', Murder and Double Standards. *Evening Standard,* 5 October. <www.standard.co.uk/business/media/foxy-knoxy-murder-and-double-standards-6450470.html>. Retrieved 30 September 2015.

Greer, C. (2007). News Media, Victims and Crime. In P. Davies, P. Francis & C. Greer (eds), *Victims, Crime and Society.* London: SAGE Publications, pp. 20–49.

Greer, C. (2010a). *Crime and Media: A Reader.* London and New York: Routledge.

Greer, C. (2010b). News Media Criminology. In E. McLaughlin & T. Newburn (eds), *The SAGE Handbook of Criminological Theory.* London: SAGE Publications, pp. 490–513.

Greer, C. & McLaughlin, E. (2012). Trial by Media: Riots, Looting, Gangs and Mediatised Police Chiefs. In T. Newburn & J. Peay (eds), *Policing: Politics, Culture and Control—Essays in Honour of Robert Reiner.* Oxford and Portland, Oregon: Hart Publishing, pp. 135–53.

Gregg, M. & Wilson, J. (2010). *Underbelly,* True Crime and the Cultural Economy of Infamy. *Continuum,* 24(3), 411–27.

'Hacktivism.' (2011). *Insight.* SBS Television, 27 September. <www.sbs.com.au/news/insight/tvepisode/hacktivism>. Retrieved 29 January 2014.

Hagedorn, J. (2008). *A World of Gangs: Armed Young Men and Gangsta Culture.* Minneapolis: University of Minneapolis.

Haggerty, K. D. & Ericson, R. V. (2000). The Surveillant Assemblage. *British Journal of Sociology*, 51(4), 605–22.

Haggerty, K. D. & Ericson, R. V. (eds) (2006). *The New Politics of Surveillance and Visibility*. Toronto, Canada: University of Toronto Press.

Hall, G. (1905). *Adolescence: Its Psychology and Its Relations to Physiology, Anthropology, Sociology, Sex, Crime, Religion and Education*. New York: Appleton.

Hall, S. (1973). *Encoding and Decoding in the Television Discourse*. Birmingham: Centre for Contemporary Cultural Studies, University of Birmingham.

Hall, S. (1980). Encoding/Decoding. In S. Hall, D. Hobson, A. Love & P. Willis (eds), *Culture, Media, Language*. London: Hutchison, pp. 128–38.

Hall, S. (1981). The Determination of News Photographs. In S. Cohen & J. Young (eds), *The Manufacture of News: Social Problems, Deviance and the Mass Media* (revised edition). London: Sage, pp. 226–43.

Hall, S., Critcher, C., Jefferson, T., Clarke, J. & Roberts, B. (1978/2013). *Policing the Crisis: Mugging, the State and Law and Order* (2nd edition). Basingstoke: Palgrave Macmillan.

Halliday, J. (2013). Woolwich Attack First UK Murder to be Transmitted 'Live' on Internet. *The Guardian*, 20 December. <www.theguardian.com/uk-news/2013/dec/19/woolwich-attack-first-uk-murder-transmitted-live-internet>. Accessed 21 December 2015.

Halliday, J. & Garside, J. (2011). Rioting Leads to Cameron Call for Social Media Clampdown. *The Guardian*, 12 August. <www.theguardian.com/uk/2011/aug/11/cameron-call-social-media-clampdown>. Accessed 10 June 2016.

Hallsworth, S. (2013). *The Gang and Beyond: Interpreting Violent Street Worlds*. Basingstoke: Palgrave Macmillan.

Hallsworth, S. & Brotherton, D. (2011). *Urban Disorder and Gangs: A Critique and a Warning*. London: Runnymede.

Hallsworth, S. & Young, T. (2008). Gang Talk and Gang Talkers: A Critique. *Crime Media Culture*, 4(2), 175–95.

Hannigan, J. (2006). *Environmental Sociology: A Social Constructionist Perspective*. London: Routledge.

Harcup, T. (2011). Research and Reflection: Supporting Journalism Educators in Becoming Scholars. *Journalism Practice*, 5(2), 161–76.

Harcup, T. & O'Neill, D. (2001). What Is News? Galtung and Ruge Revisited. *Journalism Studies*, 2(2), 261–80.

Harding, L. (2014). Footage Released of Guardian Editors Destroying Snowden Hard Drives. *The Guardian*, 31 January. <www.theguardian.com/uk-news/2014/jan/31/footage-released-guardian-editors-snowden-hard-drives-gchq>. Accessed 19 January 2015.

Hardy, M. & Hardy, C. (1988). Role Stress and Role Strain. In M. Hardy & M. Conway (eds), *Role Theory: Perspectives for Health Professionals* (2nd edition). Norwalk, CT: Appleton and Lange, pp. 159–240.

Harriss, C. (2011). The Evidence Doesn't Lie: Genre Literacy and the CSI Effect. *Journal of Popular Film and Television*, 39(1), 2–11.

Harvey, D. (1996). *Justice, Nature and the Geography of Difference*. Oxford: Blackwell.

Harvey, D. (2005). *A Brief History of Neoliberalism*. Oxford: Oxford University Press.

Harvey, E. & Derksen, L. (2009). Science Fiction or Social Fact?: An Exploratory Content Analysis of Popular Press Reports on the *CSI* Effect. In M. Byers & V. M. Johnson (eds), *The CSI Effect: Television, Crime, and Governance*. Lanham: Lexington Books, pp. 3–28.

Hasham, N. (2015). Sydney Siege Aftermath: Stop Paid Interviews from Going to Air, Says Former Coroner. *The Sydney Morning Herald*, 22 January. <www.smh.com.au/nsw/sydney-siege-aftermath-stop-paid-interviews-going-to-air-says-former-coroner-20150121-12u3qy.html>. Accessed 22 January 2015.

Hayward, K. (2012). A Response to Farrell. *Social Policy & Administration*, 46(1), 21–34.

Heath, L. & Gilbert, K. (1996). Mass Media and Fear of Crime. *American Behavioral Scientist*, 39(4), 378–92.

Heller-Nicholas, A. (2014). Teenage Kings and 'Heroic' Rapists. *Overland*, 21 February. <https://overland.org.au/2014/02/teenage-kings-and-heroic-rapists>. Accessed 28 May 2016.

Henderson, A. (2015). Indonesia Labels Former Prime Minister Tony Abbott's Critique of Islam 'Unhelpful' and 'Divisive'. *ABC News*, 10 December. <www.abc.net.au/news/2015-12-09/abbott's-critique-of-islam-unhelpful-and-divisive-says-indonesia/7015120>. Accessed 14 October 2016.

Henry, S. & Milovanovic, D. (2000). Constitutive Criminology. In J. Muncie & E. McLaughlin (eds), *The Sage Dictionary of Criminology*. London: Sage.

Herald View. (2011). Commission Is Long Overdue. *Herald Scotland*, 24 May. <www.heraldscotland.com/opinion/13030489.display>. Accessed 18 March 2014.

Herman, E. & Chomsky, N. (1994). *Manufacturing Consent: The Political Economy of the Mass Media*. London: Vintage.

Herrington, V., Clifford, K., Lawrence, P. F., Ryle, S. & Pope, R. (2009). *The Impact of the NSW Police Force Mental Health Intervention Team: Final Evaluation Report*. Sydney: Charles Sturt University Centre for Inland Health and Australian Graduate School of Policing. <www.police.nsw.gov.au/__data/assets/pdf_file/0006/174246/MHIT_Evaluation_Final_Report_241209.pdf>. Accessed 7 November 2016.

Herrnstein, R. & Murray, C. (1994). *The Bell Curve*. New York: Basic Books.

Herzog, K. (2016). From the *CSI* Effect to *Making a Murderer*: Will True-Crime Docuseries Change How Jurors Think? *Vulture*, 15 January. <www.vulture.com/2016/01/making-a-murderer-jurors-csi-effect.html#>. Accessed 11 March 2016.

Hess, K. & Waller, L. (2014). The Digital Pillory: Media Shaming of 'Ordinary' People for Minor Crimes. *Continuum: Journal of Media & Cultural Studies*, 28(1), 101–11.

High Court of Australia. (2013). *High Court of Australia: Press Release*. <www.hcourt.gov.au/assets/news/MR-audio-visual-recordings-Oct13.pdf>. Accessed 19 February 2015.

Hinerman, S. (1997). (Don't) Leave Me Alone: Tabloid Narrative and the Michael Jackson Child-Abuse Scandal. In J. Lull & S. Hinerman (eds), *Media Scandals: Morality and Desire in the Popular Culture Marketplace*. Cambridge: Polity, pp. 143–63.

Hogg, R. & Brown, D. (1998). *Rethinking Law and Order*. Sydney: Pluto Press.

Huey, L. (2010). 'I've Seen This on CSI': Criminal Investigators' Perceptions about the Management of Public Expectations in the Field. *Crime Media Culture*, 6(1), 49–68.

Huey, L. & Broll, R. (2012). 'All It Takes Is One TV Show to Ruin It': A Police Perspective on Police-Media Relations in the Era of Expanding Prime Time Crime Markets. *Policing and Society: An International Journal of Research and Policy*, 22(4), 384–96.

Huey, L., Nhan, J. & Broll, R. (2012). 'Uppity Civilians' and 'Cyber-Vigilantes': The Role of the General Public in Policing Cyber-Crime. *Criminology & Criminal Justice*, 13(1), 81–97.

Hulme, S., Morgan, A. & Browne, R. (2015). *CCTV Use By Local Government: Findings from a National Survey*. [Research in Practice Series, No. 40]. Canberra, ACT: Australian Institute of Criminology.

Human Rights & Equal Opportunity Commission. (1991). *Racist Violence: Report of the National Inquiry Into Racist Violence in Australia*. Canberra: AGPS.

Hurst, D. (2014). It's a 'Coward's Punch': Man Whose Son Died at Party Says 'King Hit' Hides Truth. *The Guardian*, 3 January. <www.theguardian.com/world/2014/jan/03/coward-punch-says-brisbane-father>. Accessed 20 January 2014.

Hussein, S. (2015). Not Eating the Muslim Other: Halal Certification, Scaremongering, and the Racialisation of Muslim Identity. *International Journal for Crime, Justice and Social Democracy*, 4(3), 86–96.

Hybels, S. & Weaver, R. L. (2004). *Communicating Effectively*. Boston: McGraw Hill.

Ichou, R. (ed.) (2015). *World Trends in Freedom of Expression and Media Development: Special Digital Focus 2015*. Paris: United Nations Educational, Scientific and Cultural Organization.

Idato, M. (2016). Gold Logie 2016 Winner Waleed Aly Stuns with Powerful Speech. *The Sydney Morning Herald*, 9 May. <www.smh.com.au/entertainment/tv-and-radio/logies/gold-logie-2016-winner-waleed-aly-stuns-with-powerful-speech-20160508-gopg7c.html>. Accessed 14 October 2016.

Innes, M. (2004). Crime as a Signal, Crime as a Memory. *Journal for Crime, Conflict and the Media*, 1(2), 15–22.

Innes, M. & Fielding, N. (2002). From Community to Communicative Policing: 'Signal Crimes' and the Problem of Public Reassurance. *Sociological Research Online*, 7(2). <www.socresonline.org.uk/7/2/innes.html>. Accessed 4 February 2014.

Innes, M. & Graef, R. (2012). 'The Anvil' in the Information Age: Police, Politics and Media. In T. Newburn & J. Peay (eds), *Policing: Politics, Culture and Control—Essays in Honour of Robert Reiner*. Oxford and Portland, Oregon: Hart Publishing, pp. 155–72.

Innes, M., Roberts, C. & Rogers, D. (2014). Critical Timing. *Police Professional*, 16 January, 17–18.

International Telecommunication Union. (2015). *ICT Facts & Figures: The World in 2015*. Geneva, Switzerland: ICT Data and Statistics Division, Telecommunication Development Bureau, International Telecommunication Union. <www.itu.int/en/ITU-D/Statistics/Documents/facts/ICTFactsFigures2015.pdf>. Accessed 2 June 2016.

IPCC. (2012). *Independent Investigation Into the Death of Ian Tomlinson on 1 April 2009*. Home Office: Independent Police Complaints Commission. <www.ipcc.gov.uk/sites/default/files/Documents/investigation_commissioner_reports/inv_rep_independent_investigation_into_the_death_of_ian_tomlinson_1.pdf>. Accessed 11 December 2015.

Iyengar, S. (1991). *Is Anyone Responsible? How Television Frames Political Issues*. Chicago, IL: University of Chicago Press.

Iyengar, S. & Hahn, K. (2009). Red Media, Blue Media: Evidence of Ideological Selectivity in Media Use. *Journal of Communication*, 59, 19–39.

Jackson, J. & Gray, E. (2010). Functional Fear and Public Insecurities about Crime. *British Journal of Criminology*, 50(1), 1–22.

Jackson, R. (2016). If They Gunned Me Down and Criming While White: An Examination of Twitter Campaigns through the Lens of Citizens' Media. *Cultural Studies Critical Methodologies*, Online First, 1–7.

Jaishankar, K. (2008). What Ails Victimology? *International Journal of Criminal Justice Sciences*, 3(1), 1–7.

Jakubowicz, A. (2006). Hobbits and Orcs: The Street Politics of Race and Masculinity. *Australian Options*, 44, 2–5.

Jakubowicz, A. & Goodhall, H. (1994). *Racism, Ethnicity and the Media*. St Leonards, NSW: Allen & Unwin.

Jarvis, B. (2007). Monsters Inc.: Serial Killers and Consumer Culture. *Crime Media Culture*, 3(3), 326–44.

Jenkins, P. (1992). *Intimate Enemies: Moral Panics in Contemporary Great Britain*. New York: Aldine De Gruyter.

Jerin, R. A. & Fields, C. B. (2009). Murder and Mayhem in the Media: Media Misrepresentation of Crime and Criminality. In R. Muraskin & A. R. Roberts (eds), *Visions for Change: Crime and Justice in the Twenty-First Century*. New Jersey: Pearson Prentice Hall, pp. 217–29.

Jewkes, Y. (2007). Prisons and the Media: The Shaping of Public Opinion and Penal Policy in a Mediated Society. In Y. Jewkes (ed.), *Handbook on Prisons*. Cullompton, Devon: Willan Publishing, pp. 447–66.

Jewkes, Y. (2008). Prisoners and the Press. *Criminal Justice Matters*, 59(1), 26–7.

Jewkes, Y. (2011). *Media & Crime* (2nd edition). London: Sage.

Jewkes, Y. (2012). Autoethnography and Emotion as Intellectual Resources: Doing Prison Research Differently. *Qualitative Inquiry*, 18(1), 63–75.

Jewkes, Y. (2015). *Media & Crime* (3rd edition). London: SAGE Publications.

Johnston, J. & Breit, R. (2010). Towards a Narratology of Court Reporting. *Media International Australia*, 137, 47–57.

Johnston, J., Keyzer, P., Holland, G., Pearson, M., Rodrick, S. & Wallace, A. (2013). *Juries and Social Media: A Report Prepared for the Victorian Department of Justice*. <www.lccsc.gov.au/agdbasev7wr/sclj/documents/pdf/juries%20and%20social%20media%20-%20final.pdf>. Accessed 26 February 2015.

Joint Committee on Privacy and Injunctions. (2012). *Privacy and Injunctions: Session 2010–12*. London: The Stationery Office by Order of the House of Lords and House of Commons. <www.publications.parliament.uk/pa/jt201012/jtselect/jtprivinj/273/273.pdf>. Accessed 21 December 2015.

Jordan, T. & Taylor, P. (2004). *Hacktivism and Cyberwars: Rebels With a Cause?* London and New York: Routledge.

Judge, The Rt Hon. Lord. (2010). *Jury Trials*. Judicial Studies Board Lecture, Belfast, Northern Ireland. 16 November. <http://webarchive.nationalarchives.gov.uk/20131202164909/http://

judiciary.gov.uk/media/speeches/2010/speech-by-lcj-jsb-lecture-jury-trials>.   Accessed   21 December 2015.

Julian, R. & Kelty, S. F. (2012). From 'Forensic This' to 'For Completeness': Changing Discourses on the Need for Forensic Evidence. Paper presented at the Australian and New Zealand Society of Criminology Conference, Auckland, New Zealand, November 2012.

Julian, R. & Kelty, S. F. (2015). Forensic Science as 'Risky Business': Identifying Key Risk Factors in the Forensic Process from Crime Scene to Court. *Journal of Criminological Research and Practice*, 1(4), 195–206.

Julian, R., Kelty, S. & Robertson, J. (2012). 'Get It Right the First Time': Critical Issues at the Crime Scene. Current Issues in Criminal Justice, 24(1), 25–37.

Karmen, A. (2010). *Crime Victims: An Introduction to Victimology* (8th edition). Belmont, CA: Wadsworth, Cengage Learning.

Katz, E., Blumler, J. G. & Gurevitch, M. (1974). Uses and Gratifications Research. *The Public Opinion Quarterly*, 37(4), 509–23.

Katz, I., Keeley, M., Spears, B. et al. (2014). *Research on Youth Exposure to, and Management of, Cyberbullying Incidents in Australia: Synthesis Report (SPRC Report 16/2014)*. Sydney: Social Policy Research Centre, University of New South Wales.

Katz, J. (1987). What Makes Crime 'News'? *Media, Culture & Society*, 9(1), 47–75.

Katz, J. (1988). *Seductions of Crime: Moral and Sensual Attractions in Doing Evil*. New York: Basic Books.

Kelty, S., Julian, R. & Ross, A. (2012). Dismantling the Justice Silos: Avoiding the Pitfalls and Reaping the Benefits of Information-Sharing Between Forensic Science, Medicine and Law. Forensic Science International, 10(230), 8–15.

Kenway, J., Kraack, A. & Hickey-Moody, A. (2006). *Masculinity Beyond the Metropolis*. Basingstoke: Palgrave Macmillan.

Khan, E. (2013). Youths Tell of Life Inside Port Phillip Prison in New Documentary 'Stories from the Inside'. *Herald Sun*, 16 October. <www.heraldsun.com.au/news/law-order/youths-tell-of-life-inside-port-phillip-prison-in-new-documentary-8216stories-from-the-inside8217/story-fniOffnk-1226741209009>. Accessed 24 March 2014.

Khan, U. (2008). Juror Dismissed from a Trial after Using Facebook to Help Make a Decision. *The Telegraph*, 24 November. <www.telegraph.co.uk/news/newstopics/lawreports/3510926/Juror-dismissed-from-a-trial-after-using-Facebook-to-help-make-a-decision.html>.   Accessed 26 February 2015.

Kirby, M., The Hon Justice. (2001). *Judicial Accountability in Australia*. Speech presented to the Commonwealth Legal Education Association, Brisbane, 6 October. <www.michaelkirby.com.au/images/stories/speeches/2000s/vol48/2001/1748-JUDICIAL_ACCOUNTABILITY.doc>. Accessed 12 June 2016.

Kirby, M. (2010). Forensic Evidence: Instrument of Truth or Potential for Miscarriage? *Journal of Law, Information and Science*, 20(1), 1–22.

Kirst, K. (2016). City of Longview, Coignard Family Reach Settlement in $10 Million Lawsuit. *CBS19*, 19 March. <www.cbs19.tv/story/31513684/city-of-longivew-coignard-family-reach-settlement-in-10-million-lawsuit>. Accessed 16 June 2016.

Kitik, Z. (2009). The Gang of 49: A Contemporary Example of the Social Construction of a Gang and the Accompanying Moral Panic. BA(Hons) Sociology Thesis, School of Communication, International Studies and Languages, University of South Australia, Adelaide.

Kitney, D. (2016). Secret Deals Protect Rich Taxpayers. *The Weekend Australian—Business Review*, 30 April–1 May, pp. 25–6.

Kitzinger, J. (2000). Media Templates: Patterns of Association and the (Re)construction of Meaning Over Time. *Media, Culture & Society*, 22(1), 61–84.

Kitzinger, J. (2004). *Framing Abuse: Media Influence and Public Understanding of Sexual Violence Against Children*. London and Ann Arbor, MI: Pluto Press.

Kitzinger, J. & Reilly, J. (1997). The Rise and Fall of Risk Reporting: Media Coverage of Human Genetics Research, 'False Memory Syndrome' and Mad Cow Disease. *European Journal of Communication*, 12(3), 319–50.

Klebold, S. (2016). *A Mother's Reckoning: Living in the Aftermath of the Columbine Tragedy*. London: WH Allen.

Kleinig, X., Walters, A. & Dale, A. (2009). Unit Renovated to Look Brand New for Paedophile Dennis Ferguson, Builder Says. *The Daily Telegraph*, 16 September. <www.dailytelegraph.com. au/unit-renovated-to-look-brand-new-for-paedophile-dennis-ferguson-builder-says/story-e6freuy9-1225774661803>. Accessed 18 May 2016.

Kluger, J., Cray, D., McDowell, J., et al. (2002). How Science Solves Crimes. *TIME*, 21 October, 41, 28.

Knottnerus, J., Ulsperger, J., Cummins, S. & Osteen, E. (2006). Exposing Enron: Media Representations of Ritualized Deviance in Corporate Culture. *Crime Media Culture*, 2(2), 177–95.

Knox, A. (2014a). @amamaknox. 11 February, 9:35. <https:twitter.com/amamaknox/ status/433293146617688064>. Accessed 10 April 2014.

Knox, A. (2014b). Raffaele Is Not a Slave. *Amanda Knox*, 11 February. <www.amandaknox. com/2014/02/11/raffaele-is-not-a-slave>. Accessed 10 April 2015.

Krawitz, M. (2012). *Guilty as Tweeted: Jurors Using Social Media Inappropriately During the Trial Process*. University of Western Australia—Faculty of Law Research Paper. No. 2012-02. <http://papers.ssrn.com/sol3/papers.cfm?abstract_id=2176634>. Accessed 26 February 2015.

Krinsky, C. (2013). Introduction: The Moral Panic Concept. In C. Krinsky (ed.), *The Ashgate Research Companion to Moral Panics*. Farnham, Surrey: Ashgate, pp. 1–16.

Kruse, C. (2010). Producing Absolute Truth: *CSI* Science as Wishful Thinking. *American Anthropologist*, 112(1), 79–91.

Kuehn, R. (2000). Denying Access to Legal Representation: The Attack on the Tulane Environmental Law Clinic. *Journal of Law & Policy*, 4(1), 33–147.

Kushner, D. (2013). Anonymous vs. Steubenville. *Rolling Stone*, 27 November. <www.rollingstone. com/culture/news/anonymous-vs-steubenville-20131127>. Accessed 29 January 2016.

Lane, A. (2001). This Is Not a Movie. *The New Yorker*, 17 September. <www.newyorker.com/ magazine/2001/09/24/this-is-not-a-movie>. Accessed 7 November 2016.

Larsson, S. (2008). *The Girl with the Dragon Tattoo*. New York: Knopf.

Lashmar P. (2013). The Journalist, Folk Devil. In C. Critcher, J. Hughes, J. Petley & A. Rohloff (eds), *Moral Panics in the Contemporary World*. New York and London: Bloomsbury, pp. 51–71.

Lattouf, A. (2016). Girl Fights: Are Aussie Women Becoming More Violent? *ABC News*, 18 March. <www.abc.net.au/news/2016-03-18/girl-fights-are-aussie-women-becoming-more-violent/7253378>. Accessed 14 October 2016.

Lawrence, R. G. (2000). *The Politics of Force: Media and the Construction of Police Brutality*. Berkeley & Los Angeles, California: University of California Press.

Lea, J. (1998). Criminology and Postmodernity. In P. Walton & J. Young (eds), *The New Criminology Revisited*. London: Macmillan, pp. 163–89.

Lea, J. & Young, J. (1984). *What Is to Be Done about Law and Order?* London: Penguin.

Lee, M. (2007). *Inventing Fear of Crime: Criminology and the Politics of Anxiety*. Cullompton, Devon: Willan Publishing.

Lee, M., Crofts, T., Salter, M., Milivojevic, S. & McGovern, A. (2013). 'Let's Get Sexting': Risk, Power, Sex and Criminalisation in the Moral Domain. *International Journal for Crime and Justice*, 2(1), 35–49.

Lee, M. & Farrall, S. (2008). *Fear of Crime: Critical Voices in an Age of Anxiety*. Abingdon: Routledge-Cavendish.

Lee, M. & McGovern, A. (2013). Force to Sell: Policing the Image and Manufacturing Public Confidence. *Policing & Society: An International Journal of Research and Policy*, 23(2), 103–24.

Lee, M. & McGovern, A. (2014). *Policing and Media: Public Relations, Simulations and Communications*. London and New York: Routledge.

Leishman, F. & Mason, P. (2011). *Policing and the Media: Facts, Fictions and Factions*. London and New York: Routledge.

Leswing, K. (2016). 'This Is the future': To Catch the Chelsea Bombing Suspect, the NYPD Sent a Virtual 'Wanted Poster' to Millions of Phones. *Business Insider*, 20 September. <www.businessinsider.com.au/nypd-pushes-emergency-alert-to-iphones-and-android-2016-9?r=US&IR=T>. Accessed 12 October 2016.

Leszkiewicz, A. (2016). From Serial to Making a Murderer: Can True Crime as Entertainment Ever Be Ethical? *New Statesman*, 15 January. <www.newstatesman.com/culture/tv-radio/2016/01/serial-making-murderer-can-true-crime-entertainment-ever-be-ethical>. Accessed 18 January 2016.

Leveson, B. H. (2012). *An Inquiry into the Culture, Practices and Ethics of the Press: Executive Summary and Recommendations, The Right Honourable Lord Justice Leveson*. 29 November. <www.gov.uk/government/uploads/system/uploads/attachment_data/file/229039/0779.pdf>. Accessed 20 January 2015.

Levi, M. (2008). White-Collar, Organised and Cyber Crimes in the Media: Some Contrasts and Similarities. *Crime, Law and Social Change*, 49(5), 365–77.

Levy, M. (2015). Robert Allenby Says Hawaii Kidnapping 'Felt Like the Film Taken'. *The Sydney Morning Herald*, 19 January. <www.smh.com.au/sport/golf/robert-allenby-says-hawaii-kidnapping-felt-like-the-film-taken-20150119-12t1vz.html>. Accessed 19 January 2015.

Lewis, C. S. (1953). The Humanitarian Theory of Punishment. *Res Judicatae*, 6, 224–30.

Lewis, P., Taylor, M. & Syal. R. (2011). Third Undercover Police Spy Unmasked as Scale of Network Emerges. *The Guardian*, 15 January. <www.theguardian.com/uk/2011/jan/14/third-undercover-police-spy-cardiff>. Accessed 12 June 2016.

Lindgren, S. & Lundstrom, R. (2011). Pirate Culture and Hacktivist Mobilization: The Cultural and Social Protocols of #Wikileaks on Twitter. *New Media & Society*, 13(6), 999–1018.

Linebaugh, P. (2003). *The London Hanged: Crime and Civil Society in the Eighteenth Century*. London: Verso.

Little, J. (2013). *Journalism Ethics and Law: Stories of Media Practice*. South Melbourne: Oxford University Press.

Loftus, B. & Goold, B. (2011). Covert Surveillance and the Invisibilities of Policing. *Criminology & Criminal Justice*, 12(3), 275–88.

Loughnan, A. (2010). Drink Spiking and Rock Throwing: The Creation and Construction of Criminal Offences in the Current Era. *Alternative Law Journal*, 35(1), 18–21.

Lowe, L. (2012). 'Trial by Social Media' Worry in Meagher Case. *The Sydney Morning Herald*, 28 September. <www.smh.com.au/technology/technology-news/trial-by-social-media-worry-in-meagher-case-20120928-26pe4.html>. Accessed 20 January 2015.

Lumby, C. (1999). *Gotcha: Life in a Tabloid World*. Sydney, NSW: Allen & Unwin.

Lumby, C. (2010). Between Heat and Light: The Opportunity in Moral Panics. Plenary presentation at the Moral Panics in the Contemporary World conference, Brunel University. 10–12 December. <www.youtube.com/watch?v=fe9IlJw9fZw>. Accessed 25 February 2014.

Lyall, S. (2009). Critics Assail British Police for Harsh Tactics During the G-20 Summit Meeting. *The New York Times*, 30 May. <www.nytimes.com/2009/05/31/world/europe/31police.html?pagewanted=all&_r=0>. Accessed 19 March 2015.

Lynch, M., Burns, R. & Stretesky, P. (2010). Global Warming and State-Corporate Crime: The Politicalization of Global Warming under the Bush Administration. *Crime, Law and Social Change*, 54, 213–39.

Lyng, S. (2004). Crime, Edgework and Corporeal Transaction. *Theoretical Criminology*, 8(3), 359–75.

Lyon, D. (2001). *Surveillance Society: Monitoring Everyday Life*. Buckingham and Philadelphia: Open University Press.

Maddox, G. (2015). Cronulla Race Riot Fuels Director Abe Forsythe's New Black Comedy. *The Sydney Morning Herald*, 9 March. <www.smh.com.au/entertainment/movies/cronulla-race-riot-fuels-director-abe-forsythes-new-black-comedy-20150308-13wzd4.html>. Accessed 14 October 2016.

Magnay, J. (2016). Families Who'll Now Never Walk Alone. *The Weekend Australian—Inquirer*, 30 April–1 May, p. 19.

Males, M. (1996). *The Scapegoat Generation: America's War on Adolescents*. Monroe ME: Common Courage Press.

Mangan, J. & Houston, C. (2012). The Long Arm of Modern Technology. *The Age*, 30 September. <www.theage.com.au/victoria/the-long-arm-of-modern-technology-20120929-26skq.html>. Accessed 20 January 2015.

Mann, S., Nolan, J. & Wellman, B. (2003). Sousveillance: Inventing and Using Wearable Computer Devices for Data Collection in Surveillance Environments. *Surveillance & Society*, 1(3), 331–55.

Marr, D. (2011). *Panic*. Collingwood, Victoria: Black Inc.

Marsh, H. L. (1991). A Comparative Analysis of Crime Coverage in Newspapers in the United States and Other Countries from 1960–1989: A Review of the Literature. *Journal of Criminal Justice*, 19(1), 67–79.

Marsh, I. & Melville, G. (2009). *Crime, Justice and the Media*. London and New York: Routledge.

Martin, L. (1996). Women Police in the Media—Fiction Versus Reality. Australian Institute of Criminology Conference. Sydney, 29–31 July. <www.aic.gov.au/media_library/conferences/policewomen/lmartin.pdf>. Accessed 4 January 2016.

Maruna, S. (2001). *Making Good: How Ex-Convicts Reform and Rebuild Their Lives*. Washington DC: American Psychological Association.

Maruna, S. (2006). Who Owns Resettlement? Towards Restorative Reintegration. *British Journal of Community Justice*, 4(2), 23–33.

Marx, G. T. (1995). Electric Eye in the Sky: Some Reflections on the New Surveillance and Popular Culture. In J. Ferrell & C. R. Sanders (eds), *Cultural Criminology*. Boston: Northeastern University Press, pp. 106–41.

Marx, G. T. (2002). What's New about the 'New Surveillance'? Classifying for Change and Continuity. *Surveillance & Society*, 1(1), 9–29.

Mason, G. (2011). Naming the 'R' Word in Racial Victimization: Violence against Indian Students in Australia. *International Review of Victimology*, 18(1), 39–56.

Mason, G. (2012). 'I Am Tomorrow': Violence against Indian Students in Australia and Political Denial. *Australian and New Zealand Journal of Criminology*, 45(1), 4–25.

Mason, P. (2003). *The Thin Blurred Line: Reality Television and Policing*. The British Criminology Conference: Selected Proceedings. Vol. 5. <www.britsoccrim.org/volume5/003.pdf>. Accessed 11 December 2015.

Mason, P. (ed.) (2005). *Captured by the Media: Prison Discourse in Media Culture*. Cullompton, Devon: Willan Publishing.

Mason, P. (2006). Lies, Distortion and What Doesn't Work: Monitoring Prison Stories in the British Media. *Crime Media Culture*, 2(3), 251–67.

Massina, M. & White, R. (eds) (2000). *Beyond Imprisonment: Conference Proceedings*. Hobart: Tasmania Council of Social Services & Criminology Research Unit, University of Tasmania.

Mathiesen, T. (1997). The Viewer Society: Michel Foucault's 'Panopticon' Revisited. *Theoretical Criminology*, 1(2), 215–34.

Mawby, R. C. (1999). Visibility, Transparency and Police–Media Relations. *Policing and Society: An International Journal of Research and Policy*, 9(3), 263–86.

Mawby, R. C. (2002). *Policing Images: Policing, Communication and Legitimacy*. Cullompton, Devon: Willan Publishing.

Mawby, R. C. (2014). The Presentation of Police in Everyday Life: Police–Press Relations, Impression Management and the Leveson Inquiry. *Crime Media Culture*, 10(3), 239–57.

Mazur, A. & Lee, J. (1993). Sounding the Global Alarm: Environmental Issues in the US National News. *Social Studies of Science*, 23(4), 681–720.

McEnery, T., McGlashan, M. & Love, R. (2015). Press and Social Media Reaction to Ideologically Inspired Murder: The Case of Lee Rigby. *Discourse & Communication*, 9(2), 237–59.

McGarry, R. & Walklate, S. (2015). *Victims: Trauma, Testimony and Justice*. London and New York: Routledge.

McGloin, J. (2005). Policy and Intervention Considerations of a Network Analysis of Street Gangs. *Criminology and Public Policy*, 4(3), 607–36.

McGovern, A. & Lee, M. (2010). 'Cop[ying] It Sweet': Police Media Units and the Making of News. *Australian and New Zealand Journal of Criminology*, 43(3), 444–64.

McMullan, T. (2015). What Does the Panopticon Mean in the Age of Digital Surveillance? *The Guardian*, 23 July. <www.theguardian.com/technology/2015/jul/23/panopticon-digital-surveillance-jeremy-bentham>. Accessed 22 May 2016.

McNair, B. (1994). *News and Journalism in the UK*. London: Routledge.

McNeill, F. (2012). Four Forms of 'Offender' Rehabilitation: Towards an Interdisciplinary Perspective. *Legal and Criminological Psychology*, 17(1), 18–36.

McQuire, S. (2012). Photography's Afterlife: Documentary Images and the Operational Archive. *Journal of Material Culture*, 18(3), 223–41.

Meadows, M. (2011). The Meaning of Life: Journalism Research and ERA 2010. *Australian Journalism Review*, 33(1), 9–15.

Medhora, S. (2016). Rosie Batty's Legacy: More Women Leaving Abusive Relationships. *The Guardian*, 24 January. <www.theguardian.com/society/2016/jan/24/rosie-battys-legacy-more-women-leaving-abusive-relationships>. Accessed 21 May 2016.

Media Entertainment & Arts Alliance. (2014). *Secrecy and Surveillance: The Report into the State of Press Freedom in Australia in 2014*. Redfern: Media Entertainment & Arts Alliance. <www.pressfreedom.org.au/administration/press-freedom-report-archives>. Accessed 19 January 2015.

Media, Entertainment & Arts Alliance. (2015). *Journalist Code of Ethics*. Strawberry Hills: Media, Entertainment & Arts Alliance. <www.meaa.org/resource-package/meaa-code-of-ethics>. Accessed 2 December 2015.

Medical Association for Prevention of War, Australia. (2003). *Policy Statement: Uranium Munitions—'Tolerable' Radiological Weapons?* November. <www.mapw.org.au/mapw-policy/03-11uranium.html>. Accessed 21 August 2006.

Meldrum-Hanna, C. & Worthington, E. (2016). Evidence of 'Torture' of Children Held in Don Dale Detention Centre Uncovered by Four Corners. *ABC News*, 26 July. <www.abc.net.au/news/2016-07-25/four-corners-evidence-of-kids-tear-gas-in-don-dale-prison/7656128>. Accessed 14 October 2016.

Meyer, A. (2007). *The Child at Risk: Paedophiles, Media Responses and Public Opinion*. Manchester: Manchester University Press.

Meyer, P. (2002). *Precision Journalism: A Reporter's Introduction to Social Science Methods* (4th edition). Lanham, MD: Rowman & Littlefield Publishers.

Miletic, D. (2006). Outcry over Teenage Girl's Assault Recorded on DVD. *The Age*, 25 October. <www.theage.com.au/articles/2006/10/24/1161455722271.html>. Accessed 20 April 2014.

Milivojevic, S. & McGovern, A. (2014). The Death of Jill Meagher: Crime and Punishment on Social Media. *International Journal for Crime, Justice and Social Democracy*, 3(3), 22–39.

Mindframe National Media Initiative. (2014a). *Mental Illness & Suicide in the Media: A Mindframe Resource for Police*. Canberra, ACT: Commonwealth of Australia.

Mindframe National Media Initiative. (2014b). *Mindframe for Courts*. Canberra, ACT: Commonwealth of Australia.

Mindframe National Media Initiative. (2014c). *Mindframe for Police*. Canberra, ACT: Commonwealth of Australia.

Minogue, C. (2011). Why Don't I Get the Joke? Prison Rape in the Public Discourse. *Alternative Law Journal*, 36(2), 116–18.

Misstear, R. (2015). Police Being Sued Over Alleged Sexual Abuse Committed by an Undercover Police Officer in Cardiff. *Wales Online*, 23 March. <www.walesonline.co.uk/news/wales-news/police-being-sued-over-alleged-8905129>. Accessed 12 June 2016.

Mitchell, A. (2012). Fatal Obsessions. *Overland*. Issue 208, Spring. <http://overland.org.au/previous-issues/issue-208/feature-alex-mitchell>. Accessed 25 July 2013.

Mitchell, B. (2002). OJ Simpson and the Backlash against Cameras in Court. *Poynter.org*, 25 August. <www.poynter.org/2002/oj-simpson-and-the-backlash-against-cameras-in-court/2097>. Accessed 4 January 2016.

Mnookin, S. & Qu, H. (2013). Organize the Noise: Tweeting Live from the Boston Manhunt. *Nieman Reports*, 67(1), 26–30. <http://niemanreports.org/issues/spring-2013>. Accessed 20 January 2015.

Moore, S. E. H. (2014). *Crime and the Media*. Basingstoke: Palgrave Macmillan.

Morgan, G. & Poynting, S. (eds) (2012). *Global Islamophobia: Muslims and Moral Panic in the West*. Farnham, UK: Ashgate.

Morgan, M. & Shanahan, J. (2010). The State of Cultivation. *Journal of Broadcasting & Electronic Media*, 54(2), 337–55.

Morley, D. (1980). *The 'Nationwide' Audience: Structure and Decoding*. London: B.F.I.

Morri, M. (2013). Sydney's State Rail to Trial High-Pitched Devices to Get Vandals to Buzz Off. *The Daily Telegraph*, 28 May. <http://www.dailytelegraph.com.au/news/buzz-beats-graffiti-vandals/news-story/0930d3cb95dd5b47f033435d5d61e615>. Accessed 17 January 2017.

Morris, N. (1994). Dangerousness and Incapacitation. In A. Duff & D. Garland (eds), *A Reader on Punishment*. Oxford: Oxford University Press, pp. 238–60.

Morris, N. & Miller, M. (1985). Predictions of Dangerousness. In M. Tonry & N. Morris (eds), *Crime and Justice: An Annual Review of Research*, vol. 6. Chicago: University of Chicago Press, pp. 1–50.

Morris, N. & Rothman, D. (1998). *The Oxford History of the Prison: The Practice of Punishment in Western Society*. New York: Oxford University Press.

Morris, R. & Blackburn, A. (2009). Cracking the Code: An Empirical Exploration of Social Learning Theory and Computer Crime. *Journal of Crime & Justice*, 32(1), 1–34.

Morrissey, B. (2003). *When Women Kill: Questions of Agency and Subjectivity*. London and New York: Routledge.

Moser, S. & Dilling, L. (2004). Making Climate Hot: Communicating the Urgency and Challenge of Global Climate Change. *Environment*, 46(10), 32–46.

Murray, C. (1990). *The Emerging British Underclass*. London: Institute for Economic Affairs.

Myhill, A. & Beak, K. (2008). *Public Confidence in Police*. London: National Policing Improvement Agency.

Nabi, R. L. & Sullivan, J. L. (2001). Does Television Viewing Relate to Engagement in Protective Action Against Crime? A Cultivation Analysis from a Theory of Reasoned Action Perspective. *Communication Research*, 28(6), 802–25.

Nasaw, D. (2010). FBI Using Facebook in Fight against Crime. *The Guardian*, 16 March. <www.theguardian.com/world/2010/mar/16/fbi-facebook-crime-study>. Accessed 5 September 2016.

Nash, C. (2013). Journalism as a Research Discipline. *Pacific Journalism Review*, 19(2), 123–35.

National Australia Day Council. (2015). Australian of the Year 2015: Rosie Batty. *Australian of the Year Awards Honour Roll*. <www.australianoftheyear.org.au/honour-roll/?view=fullView&recipientID=1179>. Accessed 21 May 2016.

Nedim, U. (2015). Judge-Alone Trials: Minimising the Risk of Unfair Prejudice? *NSW Courts*, 27 January, Sydney, NSW: Sydney Criminal Lawyers. <http://nswcourts.com.au/articles/judge-alone-trials-minimising-the-risk-of-unfair-prejudice>. Accessed 25 April 2016.

Needham, K. & Smith, A. (2014). Daniel Christie Dies Following King-Hit Punch. *The Sydney Morning Herald*, 12 January. <www.smh.com.au/nsw/daniel-christie-dies-following-kinghit-punch-20140111-30ndv.html>. Accessed 14 October 2016.

Nelson, F. (2015). Lawyers Shouldn't 'Assume' Judges Know How Social Media Works. *Lawyers Weekly*, 2 September. <www.lawyersweekly.com.au/news/17076-don-t-assume-judges-know-how-social-media-works>. Accessed 4 January 2016.

New South Wales Bureau of Crime Statistics and Research (BOCSAR). (2014). Media Release: Trends in Assault in Kings Cross. BOCSAR, Sydney, 15 January 2014.

New South Wales Law Reform Commission. (2005). *Expert Witnesses*. Report no. 109. Sydney: NSWLRC.

Newbold, G., Ross, J., Jones, R., Richards, S. & Lenza, M. (2014). Prison Research from the Inside: The Role of Convict Autoethnography. *Qualitative Inquiry*, 20(4), 454–63.

news.com.au. (2013a). Could You Spot a Paedophile? Here Are the Warning Signs. 19 September. <www.news.com.au/national/could-you-spot-a-paedophile-here-are-the-warning-signs/story-fncynjr2-1226722713261>. Accessed 26 February 2016.

news.com.au. (2013b). Child Abuse Survivors' Group Responds to Paedophile Story. 20 September. <www.news.com.au/national/child-abuse-survivors8217-group-responds-to-paedophile-story/story-fncynjr2-1226723692226>. Accessed 26 February 2016.

Niblock, S. (2005). Practice and Theory: What Is News? In R. Keeble (ed.), *Print Journalism: A Critical Introduction*. London and New York: Routledge, pp. 74–81.

Nicholls, S. (2012). Paedophile Ferguson Fought to the End. *The Sydney Morning Herald*, 31 December. <www.smh.com.au/nsw/paedophile-ferguson-fought-to-the-end-20121231-2c2f0.html>. Accessed 18 May 2016.

Niedzviecki, H. (2009). *The Peep Diaries: How We're Learning to Love Watching Ourselves and Our Neighbors*. San Francisco: City Lights Books.

Noble, G. (ed.) (2009). *Lines in the Sand: The Cronulla Riots, Multiculturalism and National Belonging.* Sydney Institute of Criminology Series No. 28. Sydney: Sydney Institute of Criminology.

Nobles, R. & Schiff, D. (2004). A Story of Miscarriage: Law in the Media. *Journal of Law and Society,* 31(2), 221–44.

Nomani, A. & Arafa, H. (2015). As Muslim Women, We Actually Ask You Not to Wear the Hijab in the Name of Interfaith Solidarity. *The Washington Post,* 21 December. <www.washingtonpost.com/news/acts-of-faith/wp/2015/12/21/as-muslim-women-we-actually-ask-you-not-to-wear-the-hijab-in-the-name-of-interfaith-solidarity>. Accessed 14 October 2016.

Norris, C. & Armstrong, G. J. (1997). *The Unforgiving Eye: CCTV Surveillance in Public Space.* Hull, UK: Centre for Criminology and Criminal Justice, University of Hull.

Novak, B. (2013). *Tim Pool: The Journalism Revolution.* New York: Melcher Media and Brett Novak Films. <www.youtube.com/watch?v=SEVNA8EnTeA>. Accessed 14 May 2014.

Novak, K. J. (2009). Reasonable Officers, Public Perceptions, and Policy Challenges. *Criminology and Public Policy,* 8(1), 153–61.

Oaten, J. (2016). Don Dale: Royal Commission into Youth Detention Underway in Darwin. *ABC News,* 6 September. <www.abc.net.au/news/2016-09-06/royal-commission-underway-in-darwin/7818476>. Accessed 14 October 2016.

O'Brien, S. (2010). Seeking Help Crucial for Parents. *Herald Sun,* 1 June. <www.heraldsun.com.au/news/opinion/seeking-help-crucial-for-parents/story-e6frfhqf-1225873724531>. Retrieved 13 May 2016.

Ofcom. (2014). Not in Breach: Broadcast News Coverage of the Woolwich Incident on 22 May 2013. *Ofcom Broadcast Bulletin,* 6 January. Issue 245. <http://stakeholders.ofcom.org.uk/binaries/enforcement/broadcast-bulletins/245/obb245.pdf>. Accessed 19 March 2015.

Ogle, G. (2005). *Gunning for Change: The Need for Public Participation Law Reform.* Hobart: Wilderness Society.

Ogle, G. (2007). Beating a SLAPP Suit. *Alternative Law Journal,* 32(2), 71–4.

Ortigo, B. (2015). Longview Warned about More Cyberattacks. *Longview News-Journal,* 27 January. <www.news-journal.com/news/2015/jan/27/longview-warned-about-more-cyberattacks>. Accessed 8 June 2016.

O'Shaughnessy, M. & Stadler, J. (2006). *Media and Society: An Introduction.* South Melbourne: Oxford University Press.

Ott, B. & Aoki, E. (2002). The Politics of Negotiating Public Tragedy: Media Framing of the Matthew Shepard Murder. *Rhetoric & Public Affairs,* 5(3), 483–505.

Pakes, F. (2012). A Panicky Debate: The State of Moroccan Youth in the Netherlands. In G. Morgan & S. Poynting (eds), *Global Islamophobia: Muslims and Moral Panic in the West.* Surrey: Ashgate, pp. 35–46.

Palasinski, M. (2013). Turning Assault into a 'Harmless Prank'—Teenage Perspectives on Happy Slapping. *Journal of Interpersonal Violence,* 28(9), 1909–23.

Papadakis, M. (2013). Courts Struggle to Find Solution to Social Media Misuse. *Australian Financial Review,* 19 November. <www.afr.com/p/technology/courts_struggle_to_find_solution_SDOyRpnllXjk0rjLwwO4XI>. Accessed 12 February 2014.

Parliament of Victoria Law Reform Committee. (2013). *Inquiry into Sexting: Report of the Law Reform Committee for the Inquiry into Sexting*. Parliamentary Paper No. 230. Melbourne: Parliament of Victoria.

Parliamentary Office of Science and Technology. (2005). Science in Court. Postnote no. 248. London: POST.

Pearson, G. (1983). *Hooligan: A History of Respectable Fears*. London: Macmillan.

Pearson, M. & Polden, M. (2015). *The Journalist's Guide to Media Law: A Handbook for Communicators in a Digital World* (5th edition). Crows Nest: Allen & Unwin.

Penfold-Mounce, R. (2009). *Celebrity Culture and Crime: The Joy of Transgression*. London: Palgrave Macmillan.

Perry, B. (2009). The Sociology of Hate: Theoretical Approaches. In B. Levin (ed.), *Hate Crimes Volume 1: Understanding and Defining Hate Crime*. Westport: Praeger Publishers, pp. 55–76.

Petrie, A. (2006). Parents Tell of Horror at DVD Attack. *The Age*, 27 October. <www.theage.com.au/news/national/parents-tell-of-horror-at-dvd-attack/2006/10/26/1161749253955.html>. Accessed 20 April 2014.

Pirkis, J., Blood, R. W., Dare, A. & Holland, K. et al. (2008). *The Media Monitoring Project—Changes in Media Reporting of Suicide and Mental Health and Illness in Australia: 2000/01–2006/07*. Canberra, ACT: Commonwealth of Australia.

Pirkis, J., Blood., R. W., Francis, C., et al. (2002). *The Media Monitoring Project: A Baseline Description of How the Australian Media Report and Portray Suicide and Mental Health and Illness*. Canberra, ACT: Commonwealth Department of Health and Aged Care.

Podlas, K. (2006). 'The CSI Effect': Exposing the Media Myth. *Fordham Intellectual Property, Media and Entertainment Law Journal*, 16(2), 429–65.

Poniewozik, J. (2011). Casey Anthony Is Acquitted; the Media Trial Is Just Beginning. *TIME*, 5 July. <http://entertainment.time.com/2011/07/05/casey-anthony-is-acquitted-the-media-trial-is-just-beginning>. Accessed 4 January 2016.

Porter, L. (2008). Academic Sleuths on Trail of CSI Evidence. *The Sydney Morning Herald*, 1 June. <www.smh.com.au/national/academic-sleuths-on-trail-of-csi-evidence-20080531-2k92.html>. Accessed 8 April 2016.

Posetti, J. (2014). Is Social Media to Blame for the Increasingly Graphic Images in Our Newspapers? *World News Publishing Focus*, 29 July. <http://blog.wan-ifra.org/2014/07/29/is-social-media-to-blame-for-the-increasingly-graphic-images-in-our-newspapers>. Accessed 7 September 2014.

Poynting, S. & Morgan, G. (eds) (2007). *Outrageous! Moral Panics in Australia*. Hobart: Australian Clearinghouse for Youth Studies.

Poynting, S., Noble, G., Tabar, P. & Collins, J. (2004). *Bin Laden in the Suburbs: Criminalising the Arab Other*. Sydney Institute of Criminology Series No. 18. Sydney: Sydney Institute of Criminology.

Press Association. (2014). Hundreds of Police Staff Investigated over Use of Facebook and Twitter. *The Guardian*, 19 August. <www.theguardian.com/uk-news/2014/aug/19/police-facebook>. Accessed 17 December 2015.

Pring, G. & Canan, P. (1996). *SLAPPs: Getting Sued for Speaking Out*. Philadelphia: Temple University Press.

Purtill, J. (2015). Meet the Man Who Wants to Celebrate the Cronulla Riots. *ABC Triple J Hack*, 10 December. <www.abc.net.au/triplej/programs/hack/meet-the-nick-folkes-who-wants-to-celebrate-the-cronulla-riots/7014848>. Accessed 14 October 2016.

Queally, J. (2015). Jeremy Meeks, Whose Handsome Mugshot Went Viral, Sentenced to Prison. *Los Angeles Times*, 6 February. <www.latimes.com/local/lanow/la-me-ln-jeremy-meeks-sentenced-20150206-story.html>. Accessed 1 October 2015.

Quilter, J. (2014). One-Punch Laws, Mandatory Minimums and 'Alcohol-Fuelled' as an Aggravating Factor: Implications for NSW Criminal Law. *International Journal for Crime, Justice and Social Democracy*, 3(1), 81–106.

Rabe-Hemp, C. E. (2011). Female Forces: Beauty, Brains, and a Badge. *Feminist Criminology*, 6(2), 132–55.

Rane, H., Ewart, J. & Martinkus, J. (2014). *Media Framing of the Muslim World: Conflicts, Crises and Contexts*. Basingstoke, Hampshire: Palgrave Macmillan.

Raptopoulos, L. (2014). The OJ Simpson Case 20 Years Later: Making 'Trials into Television'. *The Guardian*, 18 June. <www.theguardian.com/world/2014/jun/17/oj-simpson-trial-cameras-court-justice-culture>. Accessed 4 January 2016.

Rath, A. (2011). Is the 'CSI Effect' Influencing Courtrooms? *National Public Radio*, 5 February. <www.npr.org/2011/02/06/133497696/is-the-csi-effect-influencing-courtrooms>. Accessed 11 March 2016.

Reese, S. (2001). Prologue—Framing Public Life: A Bridging Model for Media Research. In S. D. Reese, O. H. Gandy & A. E. Grant (eds), *Framing Public Life: Perspectives on Media and Our Understanding of the Social World*. Mahwah, New Jersey: Lawrence Erlbaum Associates, pp. 7–31.

Reiner, R. (2002). Media Made Criminality: The Representation of Crime in the Mass Media. In M. Maguire, R. Morgan & R. Reiner (eds), *The Oxford Handbook of Criminology*. Oxford: Oxford University Press, pp. 376–416.

Reinfrank, A. (2015). Canberra Jail Inmates' Cell Selfie on Facebook Draws Fire from ACT Liberals. *ABC News*, 11 May. <www.abc.net.au/news/2015-05-11/canberra-jail-inmates-cell-selfie-on-facebook-draws-fire/6459976>. Accessed 14 October 2016.

Rentschler, C. A. (2011). *Second Wounds: Victims' Rights and the Media in the U.S.* Durham and London: Duke University Press.

Republic of the Philippines. (2010). *First Report of the Incident Investigation and Review Committee on the August 23, 2010, Rizal Park Hostage Taking Incident*. Manila: Department of Justice and Department of the Interior and Local Government. 17 September. <www.gov.ph/2010/09/17/first-report-of-the-iirc-on-the-rizal-park-hostage-taking-incident>. Accessed 22 January 2015.

Reynolds, E. (2016). What the Real Piper from Orange is the New Black Has to Say about Australia. *news.com.au*, 8 March. <www.news.com.au/lifestyle/real-life/true-stories/what-the-real-piper-from-orange-is-the-new-black-has-to-say-about-australia/news-story/a5eb33012fe5a1c5da6ec2c8c7a51c14>. Accessed 10 June 2016.

Robbers, M. L. P. (2008). Blinded by Science: The Social Construction of Reality in Forensic Television Shows and Its Effect on Criminal Jury Trials. *Criminal Justice Policy Review*, 19(1), 84–102.

Roberts, A. (2014). The 'Serial' Podcast: By the Numbers. *CNN International*, 23 December. <http://edition.cnn.com/2014/12/18/showbiz/feat-serial-podcast-btn>. Accessed 19 January 2015.

Roberts, C., Innes, M., Preece, A. & Spasic, I. (2015). Soft Facts and Spontaneous Community Mobilisation: The Role of Rumour After Major Crime Events. In P. Baeck (ed.), *Data for Good: How Big and Open Data Can Be Used for the Common Good*. London: Nesta, pp. 37–43.

Roberts, L. D. & Indermaur, D. (2005). Social Issues as Media Constructions: The Case of 'Road Rage'. *Crime Media Culture*, 1(3), 301–21.

Rodrick, S. (2014). Achieving the Aims of Open Justice? The Relationship between the Courts, the Media and the Public. *Deakin Law Review*, 19(3), 123–62.

Rojek, C. (2001). *Celebrity*. London: Reaktion Books.

Rollason, A. (2012). Use of Audio Device to Deter Young People Raises Alarm. *ABC The World Today*, 24 May. <www.abc.net.au/worldtoday/content/2012/s3509990.htm>. Accessed 14 October 2016.

Rosen, J. (2006). The People Formerly Known as the Audience. *PressThink* [blog], 27 June. <http://archive.pressthink.org/2006/06/27/ppl_frmr.html>. Accessed 12 May 2016.

Roshier, B. (1981). The Selection of Crime News By the Press. In S. Cohen & J. Young (eds), *The Manufacture of News: Social Problems, Deviance and the Mass Media* (revised edition). London: Sage, pp. 40–51.

Rosoff, S., Pontell, H. & Tillman, R. (1998). *Profit Without Honor: White-Collar Crime and the Looting of America*. Upper Saddle River: Prentice Hall.

Roth, K. (2005). Justifying Torture. In Roth, K., Worden, M. & Bernstein, A. (eds), *Torture: A Human Rights Perspective*. New York: Human Rights Watch, pp.184–201.

Rothe, D. & Kauzlarich, D. (2016). *Crimes of the Powerful: An Introduction*. London: Routledge.

Ruddock, A. (2013). *Youth and the Media*. London: Sage.

Ruigrok, N., van Atteveldt, W., Gagestein, S. & Jacobi, C. (2016). Media and Juvenile Delinquency: A Study into the Relationship Between Journalists, Politics, and Public. *Journalism*, 1–19: DOI: 10.1177/1464884916636143.

Rule, A. & Richardson, N. (2013). Crime Writing. In S. Tanner & N. Richardson (eds), *Journalism Research and Investigation in a Digital World*. South Melbourne: Oxford University Press, pp. 208–16.

Salter, M. (2017). *Crime, Justice and Social Media*. Abingdon, Oxford: Routledge.

Sasson, T. (1995). *Crime Talk: How Citizens Construct a Social Problem*. New York: Aldine De Gruyter.

Saunders, B. & Goddard, C. (2002). *The Role of the Mass Media in Facilitating Community Education and Child Abuse Prevention Strategies*. No. 16. Melbourne: Australian Institute of Family Studies and National Child Protection Clearing House.

Scheufele, D. (1999). Framing as a Theory of Media Effects. *Journal of Communication*, 49(1), 103–22.

Schissel, B. (1997). *Blaming Children: Youth Crime, Moral Panics and the Politics of Hate*. Halifax: Fernwood Publishing.

Schlesinger, P. & Tumber, H. (1994). *Reporting Crime: The Media Politics of Criminal Justice*. Oxford: Clarendon Press.

Schmid, D. (2005). *Natural Born Celebrities: Serial Killers in American Culture*. Chicago: University of Chicago Press.

Schudson, M. (2003). *The Sociology of News*. New York and London: W. W. Norton & Company.

Schulz, P. D. H. (2010). *Courts and Judges on Trial: Analysing and Managing the Discourses of Disapproval*. Berlin: LIT Verlag.

Schweitzer, N. & Saks, M. (2007). The CSI Effect: Popular Fiction about Forensic Science Affects Public Expectations about Real Forensic Science. *Jurimetrics*, 47(3), 357–64.

Scraton, P. & Chadwick, K. (1987). 'Speaking Ill of the Dead': Institutionalized Responses to Deaths in Custody. In P. Scraton (ed.), *Law, Order and the Authoritarian State*. Milton Keynes: Open University Press, pp. 212–36.

Semetko, H. A. & Valkenburg, P. M. (2000). Framing European Politics: A Content Analysis of Press and Television News. *Journal of Communication*, 50(2), 93–109.

Sercombe, H. (1995). The Face of the Criminal Is Aboriginal. In J. Bessant, K. Carrington & S. Cook (eds), *Cultures of Crime and Violence: The Australian Experience*. Bundoora, Vic.: La Trobe University Press, pp. 76–94.

Sexton, M. (2003). Snowtown trial reveals 'degenerate sub-culture.' *The 7.30 Report*, 9 November. <www.abc.net.au/7.30/content/2003/s942499.htm>.

Sharkey, N. & Knuckey, S. (2011). Occupy Wall Street's 'Occucopter'—Who's Watching Whom? *The Guardian*, 21 December. <www.theguardian.com/commentisfree/cifamerica/2011/dec/21/occupy-wall-street-occucopter-tim-pool>. Accessed 15 February 2014.

Shelton, D. (2008). The 'CSI Effect': Does It Really Exist? *National Institute of Justice Journal*, 259 (March). <www.nij.gov/journals/259/pages/csi-effect.aspx>. Accessed 11 March 2016.

Shelton, D. (2011). *Forensic Science in Court: Challenges in the Twenty-First Century*. New York: Rowman & Littlefield Publishers.

Shelton, D. E., Barak, G. & Kim, Y. S. (2011). Studying Juror Expectations for Scientific Evidence: A New Model for Looking at the CSI Myth. *Court Review: The Journal of the American Judges Association*, 47(1–2), 8–17. <http://digitalcommons.unl.edu/ajacourtreview/354>. Accessed 11 March 2016.

Shoemaker, P. J. & Reese, S. D. (2014). *Mediating the Message in the 21st Century: A Media Sociology Perspective* (3rd edition). New York and London: Routledge.

Shover, N. & Wright, J. (2001). *Crimes of Privilege: Readings in White-Collar Crime*. New York: Oxford University Press.

Sims, D. (2015). The Long, Slow End for *CSI*. *The Atlantic*, 28 September. <www.theatlantic.com/entertainment/archive/2015/09/how-csi-didnt-burn-out-but-faded-away/407770>. Accessed 8 April 2016.

Sinclair, L. (2010). Teens Jailed for Killing Grandfather Ekram Haque in Filmed Attack. *The Daily Telegraph*, 26 July. <www.dailytelegraph.com.au/teens-jailed-for-killing-grandfather-ekram-haque-in-filmed-attack/story-e6freuyi-1225897216909>. Accessed 10 June 2016.

Sky News. (2014). *Oscar Pistorius: A Case for Cameras in Court*. 12 September. <http://news.sky.com/story/1333994/oscar-pistorius-a-case-for-cameras-in-court>. Accessed 4 January 2016.

Smart, C. (1976). *Women, Crime and Criminology: A Feminist Critique*. London: Routledge and Kegan Paul.

Smith, P. K., Mahdavi, J., Carvalho, M., et al. (2008). Cyberbullying: Its Nature and Impact in Secondary School Pupils. *Journal of Child Psychology and Psychiatry*, 49(4), 376–85.

Snell, K. & Tombs, S. (2011). 'How Do You Get Your Voice Heard When No-One Will Let You?' Victimization at Work. *Criminology & Criminal Justice*, 11(3), 207–23.

Society of Professional Journalists. (2008). *A Uniform Act Limiting Strategic Litigation against Public Participation: Getting It Passed.* <www.spj.org/antislapp.asp>. Accessed 7 November 2016.

Sontag, S. (1979). *On Photography.* London: Penguin Books.

Spalek, B. (2006). *Crime Victims: Theory, Policy and Practice.* London: Palgrave.

Speers, J. (2015). Domestic Violence: Jodie Speers Asks Why She Hasn't Heard about Two Thirds of Victims. *news.com.au*, 27 April. <www.news.com.au/lifestyle/relationships/marriage/domestic-violence-jodie-speers-asks-why-she-hasnt-heard-about-two-thirds-of-victims/news-story/b32421e876b9711d246cb3109121aed5?pg=1>. Accessed 25 January 2016.

Spierenburg, P. (1995). The Body and the State: Early Modern Europe. In N. Morris & D. J. Rothman (eds), *The Oxford History of the Prison: The Practice of Punishment in Western Society.* New York: Oxford University Press, pp. 49–77.

Standing Council on Law and Justice. (2013). *National Framework for Rights and Services for Victims of Crime 2013–2016.* Barton, ACT: Australian Government. <www.victimsupport.org.au/UserFiles/File/SCLJ_Framework-2013-16.pdf>. Accessed 12 November 2016.

Stephens, A. (2015). Partners in Crime: Why Do We Sit Spellbound as Humans Do Their Worst? *The Sydney Morning Herald*, 20 November. <www.smh.com.au/entertainment/partners-in-crime-why-do-we-sit-spellbound-as-humans-do-their-worst-20151115-gky3hr.html>. Accessed 7 May 2016.

Stewart, C. (2012). How I Was Drawn into Toxic Police Politics. *The Australian*, 15 December. <www.abc.net.au/mediawatch/transcripts/stewart_151212.pdf>. Accessed 1 December 2015.

Sucherman, M. (2010). Serious Threat to the Web in Italy. *Google Official Blog*, 24 February. <https://googleblog.blogspot.com.au/2010_02_01_archive.html>. Accessed 2 June 2016.

Surette, R. (2011). *Media, Crime and Criminal Justice: Images, Realities, and Policies* (4th edition). Belmont, CA: Wadsworth Cengage Learning.

Sutherland, E. (1949). *White Collar Crime: The Uncut Version.* London: Yale University Press.

Sutton, A., Cherney, A. & White, R. (2014). *Crime Prevention: Principles, Perspectives and Practices.* Melbourne: Cambridge University Press.

Sykes, G. & Matza, D. (1957). Techniques of Neutralization: A Theory of Delinquency. *American Sociological Review*, 22(6), 664–70.

Tankard, J. W., Jnr. (2001). The Empirical Approach to the Study of Media Framing. In S. D. Reese, O. H. Gandy & A. E. Grant (eds), *Framing Public Life: Perspectives on Media and Our Understanding of the Social World.* Mahwah, New Jersey: Lawrence Erlbaum Associates, pp. 95–105.

Taylor, M. (2013). Ian Tomlinson's Family Win Apology from Met Police over Death in 2009. *The Guardian*, 6 August. <www.theguardian.com/uk-news/2013/aug/05/ian-tomlinson-apology-met-police>. Accessed 10 December 2015.

The Age. (2008). UK in Tune with Aussie Muzak Attack. 14 February. <www.theage.com.au/news/music/uk-in-tune-with-aussie-muzak-attack/2008/02/14/1202760437175.html>. Accessed 17 May 2016.

'The Blackout Part 1: Tragedy Porn.' (2012). Television Program. *The Newsroom*. HBO Cable Network. United States. 12 August.

The Walkley Foundation. (2013). *Walkley Award Winners: Joanne McCarthy.* <www.walkleys.com/walkleys-winners/2013_gold_walkley_joanne_mccarthy>. Accessed 10 October 2016.

Third, A., Richardson, I., Collin, P., Rahilly, K. & Bolzan, N. (2011). *Intergenerational Attitudes Towards Social Networking and Cybersafety: A Living Lab.* [Research Report]. Melbourne: Cooperative Research Centre for Young People, Technology and Wellbeing.

Thompson, J. B. (2005). The New Visibility. *Theory, Culture & Society*, 22(6), 31–51.

Timms, P. (2016). French Police Killer Live Streamed Part of Attack Prompting Questions over Social Media Responsibility. *ABC News*, 15 June. <www.abc.net.au/news/2016-06-15/role-of-social-media-questioned-after-attack-live-streamed/7514330>. Accessed 17 June 2016.

Todorov, T. (1977). The Typology of Detective Fiction. In *The Poetics of Prose*. Trans. Richard Howard. Ithaca, NY: Cornell University Press, pp. 42–52.

Tombs, S. & Whyte, D. (2015). *The Corporate Criminal: Why Corporations Must Be Abolished.* London: Routledge.

Tomsen, S. (1997). Youth Violence and the Limits of Moral Panic. *Youth Studies Australia*, 16(1), 25–30.

Tomsen, S. (2009). *Violence, Prejudice and Sexuality*. New York: Routledge.

Tonry, M. (ed.) (2004). *The Future of Imprisonment*. Oxford: Oxford University Press.

Toronto Police Service. (2015). *Homicide #2/2012, Mike Pimentel, 24, Update, Shawn Poirier, 30, Arrested, Charged With Second-Degree Murder.* <http://torontopolice.on.ca/newsreleases/33534>. Accessed 12 December 2015.

Tremlett, G. (2006). Frenchmen Arrested for Bringing 'Happy Crashing' to Spanish Roads. *The Guardian*, 10 August. <www.theguardian.com/world/2006/aug/10/spain.gilestremlett>. Accessed 20 April 2014.

Trigger, D. (1995). 'Everyone's Agreed, the West is All You Need': Ideology, Media and Aboriginality in Western Australia. *Media Information Australia*, 75, 102–22.

Tuchman, G. (1972). Objectivity as Strategic Ritual: An Examination of Newsmen's Notions of Objectivity. *American Journal of Sociology*, 77(4), 660–79.

Tuchman, G. (1973). Making News By Doing Work: Routinizing the Unexpected. *American Journal of Sociology*, 79(1), 110–31.

Turnbull, S. (2014). *The TV Crime Drama*. Edinburgh: Edinburgh University Press.

Turvill, W. (2015). UK Police Forces Spend More than £36m a Year on PR and Communications. *PressGazette*, 1 May. <www.pressgazette.co.uk/uk-police-forces-spend-more-than-36m-a-year-on-pr-and-communications>. Accessed 5 May 2016.

Tyler, T. R. (2006). Viewing *CSI* and the Threshold of Guilt: Managing Truth and Justice in Reality and Fiction. *The Yale Law Journal*, 115(5), 1050–85.

United States Senate Select Committee on Intelligence. (2014). *Committee Study of the Central Intelligence Agency's Detention and Interrogation Program: Executive Summary.* Washington, DC: US Senate.

Van Dijck, J. (2008). *The World of Crime: Breaking the Silence on Problems of Security, Justice, and Development Across the World.* Los Angeles: Sage.

van Gemert, F., Peterson, D. & Lien, I-L. (eds) (2008). *Youth Gangs, Migration, and Ethnicity.* Devon: Willan Publishing.

van Gulijk, C. (2014). Oil Spills: A Persistent Problem. In T. Spapens, R. White & M. Kluin (eds), *Environmental Crime and Its Victims: Perspectives Within Green Criminology*. Surrey: Ashgate, pp. 133–48.

Victims Services. (2014). *A Guide to the Media for Victims of Crime*. Parramatta, Australia: NSW Department of Justice.

Victoria Police. (2010). *Police Investigate Deaths of Two Boys in Mooroopna*. 30 May. <www.abc.net. au/mediawatch/transcripts/1018_vicpolice.pdf>. Accessed 19 January 2015.

Victorian Law Reform Commission. (2008). *Changing the Role of Experts*. Civil Justice Review: Report. Melbourne: VLRC.

Wacquant, L. (2008). *Urban Outcasts: A Comparative Sociology of Advanced Marginality*. Cambridge: Polity Press.

Wacquant, L. (2009). *Prisons of Poverty*. Minneapolis: University of Minnesota Press.

Wadds, P. (2013). Policing Nightlife: The Representation and Transformation of Security in Sydney's Night-Time Economy. PhD Thesis, University of Western Sydney, Sydney.

Wadds, P. (2015). Crime, Policing and (In)Security: Press Depictions of Sydney's Night-time Economy. *Current Issues in Criminal Justice*, 27(2), 95–112.

Wahl-Jorgensen, K. & Franklin, B. (2008). Journalism Research in the UK: From Isolated Efforts to an Established Discipline. In M. Loffelholz & D. Weaver (eds), *Global Journalism Research: Theories, Methods, Findings, Future*. Oxford: Blackwell, pp. 172–84.

Walklate, S. (2007). *Imagining the Victim of Crime*. Berkshire, UK: Open University Press.

Walklate, S. (2009). Are We All Victims Now? Crime, Suffering and Justice. *British Journal of Community Justice*, 7(2), 5–16.

Walklate, S. (2012). Courting Compassion: Victims, Policy, and the Question of Justice. *The Howard Journal of Crime and Justice*, 51(2), 109–21.

Walklate, S. (2013). Victims, Trauma, Testimony. *Nottingham Law Journal*, 22, 77–89.

Wall, D. S. (2005/15). The Internet as a Conduit for Criminal Activity. In A. Pattavina (ed.), *Information Technology and the Criminal Justice System*. Thousand Oaks, CA: SAGE Publications, pp. 77–98. <http://papers.ssrn.com/sol3/papers.cfm?abstract_id=740626>. Accessed 8 June 2016.

Wall, D. S. (2007). *Cybercrime: The Transformation of Crime in the Information Age*. Cambridge, UK: Polity Press.

Wall, D. S. & Williams, M. (2007). Policing Diversity in the Digital Age: Maintaining Order in Virtual Communities. *Criminology & Criminal Justice*, 7(4), 391–415.

Wallace, A. & Johnston, J. (2015). Tweeting from Court: New Guidelines for Modern Media. *Media Arts Law Review*, 20(1), 15–32.

Walsh, C. (2008). The Mosquito: A Repellent Response. *Youth Justice*, 8(2), 122–33.

Walters, B. (2003). *Slapping on the Writs: Defamation, Developers and Community Activism*. Sydney: UNSW Press.

Walters, B. (2005). Let the People Speak. *Current Issues in Criminal Justice*, 16(3), 340–50.

Walters, G. (2014). It's Case Closed for Jack the Ripper—Alas. *The Age*, 10 September. <www.theage. com.au/comment/it8217s-case-closed-for-the-jack-the-ripper--alas-20140910-10et93.html>. Accessed 16 January 2015.

Walters, R. (2013). Air Crimes and Atmospheric Justice. In N. South & A. Brisman (eds), *Routledge Handbook of Green Criminology*. London: Routledge, pp. 134–49.

Ward, M. (2016). Fairfax's First Investigative Podcast Series Proof that 'Journalism Is Alive and Well'. *Mumbrella*, 24 September. <https://mumbrella.com.au/fairfaxs-first-investigative-podcast-series-proof-journalism-alive-well-397565>. Accessed 11 October 2016.

Weaver, B. & McNeill, F. (2010). Travelling Hopefully: Desistance Theory and Probation Practice. In J. Brayford, F. Cowe & J. Deering. (eds), *What Else Works? Creative Work with Offenders*. Willan Publishing: Cullompton, pp. 36–60.

Weinman, S. (2016). True-Crime Stories: A Centuries-Old Craze from Ben Franklin to Making a Murderer. *The Guardian*, 8 January. <www.theguardian.com/culture/2016/jan/07/making-a-murderer-serial-true-crime-genre>. Accessed 4 October 2016.

Welch, M. (2011). Counterveillance: How Foucault and the Groupe d'Information sur les Prisons Reversed the Optics. *Theoretical Criminology*, 15(3), 301–13.

White, R. (1990). *No Place of Their Own: Young People and Social Control in Australia*. Melbourne: Cambridge University Press.

White, R. (1993). Police Vidiots. *Alternative Law Journal*, 18(3), 109–12.

White, R. (2008). Class Analysis and the Crime Problem. In T. Anthony & C. Cunneen (eds), *The Critical Criminology Companion*. Sydney: Hawkins Press, pp. 30–42.

White, R. (2013). *Youth Gangs, Violence and Social Respect: Exploring the Nature of Provocations and Punch-Ups*. Basingstoke: Palgrave Macmillan.

White, R. (2015). Global Youth Culture and Dynamic Social Contexts. In S. Baker, B. Robards & B. Buttigieg (eds), *Youth Culture and Subcultures: Australian Perspectives*. London: Ashgate, pp. 31–41.

White, R. (2016). Experts and Expertise in the Land and Environment Court. *Australian Journal of Forensic Sciences*. DOI 10.1080/00450618.2016.1218544.

White, R. & Cunneen, C. (2015). Social Class, Youth Crime and Justice. In B. Goldson & J. Muncie (eds), *Youth Crime and Justice: Critical Issues* (2nd edition). London: Sage, pp. 17–29.

White, R. & Graham, H. (2010). *Working with Offenders: A guide to Concepts and Practices*. Abingdon, UK: Willan Publishing.

White, R., Haines, F. & Asquith, N. (2017). *Crime and Criminology* (6th edition). Melbourne: Oxford University Press.

White, R. & Perrone, S. (2015). *Crime, Criminality and Criminal Justice* (2nd edition). South Melbourne, Vic.: Oxford University Press.

White, R., Perrone, S., Guerra, C. & Lampugnani, R. (1999). *Ethnic Youth Gangs in Australia: Do They Exist? [7 Reports—Vietnamese, Latin American, Turkish, Somalian, Pacific Islander, Anglo-Australian, Summary]*. Melbourne: Australian Multicultural Foundation.

White, R. & van der Velden, J. (1995). Class and Criminality. *Social Justice*, 22(1), 51–74.

White, R. & Wyn, J. (2013). *Youth and Society* (3rd edition). South Melbourne: Oxford University Press.

White, R., Wyn, J. & Robards, B. (2017). *Youth and Society* (4th edition). South Melbourne: Oxford University Press.

Williams, C. (2011). Cameron Told Not to Shut Down Internet. *The Telegraph*, 1 November. <www.telegraph.co.uk/technology/news/8862335/Cameron-told-not-to-shut-down-internet.html>. Accessed 10 June 2016.

Williams, K. & Johnstone, C. (2000). The Politics of the Selective Gaze: Closed Circuit Television and the Policing of Public Space. *Crime, Law and Social Change*, 34(2), 183–210.

Wilson, J. (2001). Watching from a Distance: September 11 as Spectacle. *Sense of Cinema*, November. <www.sensesofcinema.com/contents/01/17/symposium/wilson.html>. Accessed 12 December 2002.

Wilson, L. & Stewart, C. (2009). Melbourne Terror Attack 'Could Have Claimed Many Lives'. *The Australian*, 4 August. <www.theaustralian.com.au/news/melbourne-terror-attack-could-have-claimed-many-lives/story-e6frg6n6-1225757754932>. Accessed 1 December 2015.

Wolff, J. (2016). The New Economics of Cybercrime. *The Atlantic*, 7 June. <www.theatlantic.com/business/archive/2016/06/ransomware-new-economics-cybercrime/485888>. Accessed 9 June 2016.

Wood, M. A. (2016). Antisocial Media and Algorithmic Deviancy Amplification: Analysing the Id of Facebook's Technological Unconscious. *Theoretical Criminology*, 17 April. DOI: 10.1177/1362480616643382.

Woods, H. S. (2014). Anonymous, Steubenville, and the Politics of Visibility: Questions of Virality and Exposure in the Case of #OPRollRedRoll and #OccupySteubenville. *Feminist Media Studies*, 14(6), 1096–8.

Wright, S. (2010). Teenage 'Happy Slappers' Who Killed Grandfather Outside Mosque Sent Down for a Total Eight Years... But Could Walk Free in Months. *The Daily Mail*, 27 July. <www.dailymail.co.uk/news/article-1297742/Happy-slapper-grandfather-killers-sent-total-8-years.html>. Accessed 5 June 2016.

Wright, S. (2015). Moral Panics as Enacted Melodramas. *British Journal of Criminology*, 55(6), 1226–44.

Wykes, M. (2001). *News, Crime and Culture*. London and Sterling, VA: Pluto Press.

Yar, M. (2012). Crime, Media and the Will-To-Representation: Reconsidering Relationships in the New Media Age. *Crime Media Culture*, 8(3), 245–60.

Young, A. (1997). *Imagining Crime*. London: Sage.

Young, J. (1971). The Role of the Police as Amplifiers of Deviancy, Negotiators of Reality and Translators of Fantasy: Some Consequences of Our Present System of Drug Control as Seen in Notting Hill. In S. Cohen (ed.), *Images of Deviance*. Harmondsworth: Penguin, pp. 27–61.

Young, J. (2004). Voodoo Criminology and the Numbers Game. In J. Farrell, K. Hayward, W. Morrison & M. Presdee (eds), *Cultural Criminology Unleashed*. London: The Glasshouse Press, pp. 13–27.

Zelizer, B. (2004). *Taking Journalism Seriously: News and the Academy*. London: Sage.

LEGISLATION AND COURT CASES

Crimes Act 1900 (NSW).

R v Bunting and Others (No. 3) (2003) SASC 251.

R v Hampson [2011] QCA 132.

R v M and others [2008] VChC 4.

R v Murray [2015] NSWSC 1034.

R v P and others [2007] VChC 3.

INDEX